Daughters & Dads

Daughters & Dads

BUILDING A LASTING RELATIONSHIP

Chap & Dee Clark

NAVPRESS

BRINGING TRUTH TO LIFE
NavPress Publishing Group
P.O. Box 35001, Colorado Springs, Colorado 80935

The Navigators is an international Christian organization. Our mission is to reach, disciple, and equip people to know Christ and to make Him known through successive generations. We envision multitudes of diverse people in the United States and every other nation who have a passionate love for Christ, live a lifestyle of sharing Christ's love, and multiply spiritual laborers among those without Christ.

NavPress is the publishing ministry of The Navigators. NavPress publications help believers learn biblical truth and apply what they learn to their lives and ministries. Our mission is to stimulate spiritual formation among our readers.

Photograph by Art Montes de Oca

Some of the anecdotal illustrations in this book are true to life and are included with the permission of the persons involved. All other illustrations are composites of real situations, and any resemblance to people living or dead is coincidental.

Unless otherwise identified, all Scripture quotations in this publication are taken from the *HOLY BIBLE: NEW INTERNATIONAL VERSION* ® (NIV®). Copyright © 1973, 1978, 1984 by International Bible Society. Used by permission of Zondervan Publishing House. All rights reserved.

Clark, Chap, 1954–
    Daughters and dads : building a lasting relationship / Chap and Dee Clark.
        p.   cm.
    ISBN 1-57683-048-9
    1. Fathers and daughters—United States.   2. Parent and teenager—United States—Religious aspects—Christianity.
    I. Clark, Dee.   II. Title.
    HQ755.85.C57   1998
    306.874'2—dc21   97-44063
                                                                         CIP

Printed in the United States of America

1 2 3 4 5 6 7 8 9 10 11 12 13 14 15 / 99 98

FOR A FREE CATALOG OF
NAVPRESS BOOKS & BIBLE STUDIES,
CALL 1-800-366-7788 (USA)
OR 1-416-499-4615 (CANADA)

Published in association with the literary agency of
Wolgemuth & Hyatt, Inc., Brentwood, Tennessee

Contents

Foreword

Being good fathers to our sons is something that comes somewhat naturally to dads. We teach them to play football, how to change the oil, and model what it means to be men of God.

But in the midst of it all, we often lose sight of fathering our daughters. Feeling lost in the world of makeup, developing bodies, and bad hair days, we step back. We lose the emotional ties we had when they were little girls. They no longer climb up in our laps to share their secrets and we're unsure how to relate.

Fathers, this must change.

Our daughters desperately need us. They need our love, our attention, our hugs, and our friendship. In this truthful and poignant book, Chap and Dee Clark examine the relationship between father and daughter, shedding light on our fears and questions about our girls.

For fathers of young daughters, this book is a road map of what's ahead, showing detours around potential problems and disasters. For fathers of teenage daughters, this book is a wake up call to the important role we play in their lives. And for fathers of grown daughters, this book is a path toward healing as we make amends for past failures. My daughter, Kristy, is grown and has her own home and family. Yet, I have many opportunities to restore what was lost in previous years.

I pray that God will use this book to draw you and your daughter closer together and build a lasting relationship.

Bill McCartney

Preface

Over the last two decades we have been involved in the lives of hundreds—perhaps many hundreds—of teenage girls. Through our work in local churches and with Young Life, a Christian organization that relationally seeks to introduce Jesus Christ to adolescents on their own turf, we've had the chance to hear and even experience firsthand how deeply daughters want to be close to their fathers. Several times we've wanted to help fathers see and understand just how powerful a force they are in their daughters' lives and what these young women want and need from the man they call Daddy. We trust that this book will be a helpful resource for the father who loves his daughter enough to provide her the leadership, friendship, and love she needs to prepare for healthy adulthood.

In a way, this book is born of five "parents": Our years spent in ministry with adolescent girls; our education and research (Dee holds an M.A. in counseling and is a therapist, and Chap has a Ph.D. in father-adolescent communication and is on the faculty of Fuller Seminary); Dee's history of growing up without the benefit of a father; and a daughter of our own who is just beginning the process of going through adolescence. The strongest fibers of the book, however, and where we got the idea in the first place, are the hundreds of letters we've received from adolescent girls across America during the last year and a half. After reading a few random letters that dealt with the relationships girls have (or would like to have) with their fathers, we began to see that many young people are more likely to write a letter to a stranger about their dads than they are to communicate directly with their fathers. This prompted us to begin soliciting letters wherever we went to speak, inviting girls to write a letter to their dads that they would not necessarily give to them. We received more than two hundred letters in a short time, and a few letters have been trickling in ever since. We have included many of these letters, changing only the names and specific cities while leaving the basic area of the country and the age of the writer.

Most of the letters were heartbreaking (we cried *a lot!*), and some were downright nasty. But many letters came from daughters who wanted to give their fathers the benefit of the doubt and yet honestly tell them something they needed to hear. The more letters we received, the more convinced we were of being on the right track. Indeed, fathers in America—even *churchgoing* fathers—need to hear what these young women have to say.

Nearly everything we assert in this book was either spawned or supported by one or more letters. The latest research on adolescent girls' developmental needs matched up completely with the letters we read (and many of these insights and results of years of study have yet to make it into even college textbooks on development).

Dee's experiences of growing up from the time she was five years old without much of a relationship with her father are reflected within each chapter in a sidebar called "From Dee: Memories of an Adult Daughter." These remembrances focus on Dee's reflections on how it felt not to have her father's support in relation to the issues presented in each chapter. Our intent is to sober fathers with a picture of just how serious and necessary their role is in their daughters' lives.

Society in general, and even some Christian leaders, may not believe that daughters need their dads, but social science—and, we believe, the Scriptures—clearly call fathers to love and stand with their kids, especially through the minefield of adolescence.

One last note: This book is overtly designed for fathers who are currently the parents of an adolescent girl. But everything stated herein is valuable for the father who has a younger daughter or whose daughter is no longer living at home. For the former, this book will help you get ready for the relational ride of your life! For the latter, it's never too late to reconnect with your daughter. Use the principles and letters in this book to reflect on how you are doing now as a father. Perhaps you could even use them as a springboard for a new round of talks. In short, every father of a daughter, this book is for you.

This book offers fathers an opportunity to hear from a few daughters out there who have stories to tell their own fathers but have a hard time, for one reason or another, being honest with them. For the dad who is reading this book, this is a chance to slow down and consider the gift God has given you in your daughter. She is a blessing, a joy, and a treasure. Be a steward of this treasure by asking God to help you get a firm grasp of the power of your role in her life. She will never let you forget it!

Chap and Dee Clark
Englewood, Colorado

Acknowledgments

As we were finishing this book, we were presented with an offer to move from Denver to southern California. We have lived in Colorado for eleven years. We've raised our children here, built deep, lifelong friendships, and lived out of a rich and satisfying network of relationships. We love Denver, our friendships, and the life we have here; but somehow all five of us sensed that God was directing us to move. Because of this decision, we wish to dedicate this book to our Colorado friends and colleagues.

To our friends in and around the Downing House, Greenwood Community Church, and Young Life: Thank you for eleven years of friendship, fun, and adventure. We've loved the time we've spent with you and will cherish each opportunity we have to be together in the future.

To our couples group (known affectionately as "Bubbles"): When we first got together we never imagined we would go so deep or connect so intimately. Thank you all for the honesty, vulnerability, compassion, and commitment each of you has shown to us. To be known and loved by such a gifted and diverse group of people has helped us to grow up. We can't stop now, just because we're moving!

Acknowledgments

To the Denver Seminary community: Thank you for the six-plus years of serving together. We've learned a great deal and been encouraged to be ourselves and boldly use our gifts. We will miss you.

CHAPTER ONE

My Princess Is Growing Up

A few years ago, as I winged across the country on a commercial flight, I was blindsided by the reminder that my
daughter and I are intimately and powerfully linked together.

Accompanying the airline's chicken salad croissant was a
showing of the film, *Father of the Bride*. I'd seen it in a theater,
and like most of the men I know who have daughters, I was
moved as I watched that little girl become a woman in less than
two hours. But on the airplane, one glance at the screen was all
it took before I was hit with a roundhouse of emotion like none
I'd ever felt. I had just kissed my daughter Katie goodbye, and
I was perhaps only slightly aware of those mixed feelings I carried of longing and guilt for leaving her behind. There before my
eyes was the cinematic evolution of child to adult, of princess
to queen. The director took no prisoners. He knew his trade and
milked the moment. As I watched the scene where the father
(Steve Martin) remembers his daughter as a small child, then a
preteen, an early adolescent, a high school beauty, and finally a
woman, I saw my daughter. And I cried. No—I wept!

I was embarrassed and confused. I am not a man who cries

From Dee
Memories of an Adult Daughter

—

I remember my teen years like they were yesterday. Some days I felt like a little girl who wanted to stay home where I would feel safe and warm. Other days I resisted those walls and fought for independence and freedom. At times I just longed to be hugged; but sometimes I also felt awkward and resentful around everyone, feeling as if I was being treated like a child. Even now I can see myself pushing to make decisions for myself, claiming I was confident in my choices, but inside not being so sure. I carefully studied the words, dress, and lifestyle of my older sister and her friends, hoping to gain some tips on how to navigate my independence. It was so hard to grow up!

Horrified by one full year of being called "gorilla legs," I took the big plunge into womanhood by getting intimately acquainted with my new Lady Remington razor.

(continued)

a lot—those guys whom I verbally admire but often secretly disdain. Yet that day I had a hard time controlling myself. I'd been doing exactly what my culture told me to do—"provide for and protect" my family, the life task of the father—and yet I felt an emptiness and a deep sense of loss as I considered my little girl growing up. *She's leaving me,* I thought, *and I can't stop it!* My little "Angel Eyes," the special name we gave her when she was three years old, was growing up and leaving me behind.

I know that most fathers care, at least a little. But something happens to those men who love to be called "Daddy," whose hearts miss a beat with every hug, and whose eyes tear up when she says her prayers. A price must be paid for that kind of caring. As our daughters grow up, the wonder of innocence and the freshness of spirit are like a narcotic we want to harness, bottle, and keep handy for when we need a dose of goodness and a taste of heaven. Of course, mothers feel this way, too. But it's different for dads, because what we feel goes beyond pride to something it seems we're barely allowed to feel in our world—affection, tenderness, and intimacy. Our daughters represent a kind of intimate, innocent connection that gives us hope in an often lonely, hectic world.

What is your pet name for your daughter? The 1950s sitcom *Father Knows Best* made popular the name "Kitten", but

16

"Princess," "Angel," and "Pumpkin" all describe that same feeling a father has for his daughter: "You're something small, simple, and helpless. You are cute and warm and bring me great pleasure. You are my own treasure, to guard and protect, to cherish and hold, to watch over and defend."

This sense of fatherly protection/affection is fine when your daughter is three years old, or maybe even six. But soon she'll begin to want to break out of this "box" of love you've built and become more than a beautiful pet or a painting to be admired. She wants—and needs—to become a woman.

> *Dear Daddy,*
> *I know you love me, and that I can always count on your love. But I feel so small around you, like I'm your toy or something. I'm not a child—I'm fifteen—but to you I am your "little girlfriend." I'm not your little girlfriend! I want you to hold me and tell me you love me, but you have got to realize that you need to let me go!*
> *Please don't hate me for telling you this, but I would rather have you leave me alone than treat me like a child.*
>
> —Susan, age 15, Arkansas

Susan's letter reflects a conflict of powerful emotion for both a daughter and her

My body was starting to take on new shapes and perform functions that, quite honestly, grossed me out! I worried that my clothes weren't just right, my hair was too curly, and that a pimple might rear its ugly head right in the middle of my face. These were some of the darkest days of my life. I didn't necessarily want to talk about these things, I just needed to know someone was there for me.

Even the boys I grew up with suddenly seemed different. Without me even noticing, life began to change, and it seemed to happen out of nowhere. We all seemed different, traveling now in "packs"—girls with girls and boys with boys, sending conflicting messages back and forth. These were the same boys I had played soccer with for years. But now when they were around, my stomach got tight and I couldn't control my giggling. Everything around me was changing. I was terrified and ecstatic at the same time.

During those turbulent years, I felt strangely disconnected from Mom, and I wished Dad was around

(continued)

17

(continued from previous page)

more. I always wanted to have the kind of relationship with him in which we could talk about some of these feelings, but he seemed so nervous and distant around me. Even now I wonder if he might have helped me understand those strange new feelings. But that didn't happen. My dad wasn't there for me when I needed him.

———

father—an emotion neither one is prepared for. The move from child to woman is a confusing process at best, yet every family with a daughter goes through it. For most of these families it hurts a little, for some it hurts a lot. A few families pretend it makes no difference. But it always makes a difference for the daughter!

As his daughter grows up, these years make their mark on a father's heart in three ways: (1) the realization of lost innocence, (2) the stark reality that nothing stays the same, and (3) the confusion of conflicting emotions and relational roles as his precious little girl is becoming a woman.

The Realization of Lost Innocence

Dee and I have spent our adult lives working with and caring for young people. Although I should be used to it, there remains for me an emotional struggle as I watch girls enter sixth grade as (usually) wide-eyed children with sweet, innocent faces, and leave eighth grade as savvy veterans of growing up in America.

By the time today's children have reached high school, no dark corner of humanity's shadows remains that they have not heard and learned about, if not seen and experienced firsthand. The innocence of childhood is being lost in today's uncensored society. Author and speaker Mike Yaconelli tells the story of two five-year-olds talking. One says to the other, "I found a condom on the patio," to which the other replied, "Neat! Uh, what's a patio?"

Consider for a moment what your daughter was like at age seven. Do you remember conversations with her about the complex world into which she was entering? Did a television show or commercial cause her to ask a question about sex, divorce, racism, hatred, or human cruelty? Perhaps she hardly ever asked, but you knew that she wanted you to help her understand how life can sometimes be so ugly, dark, and random. You are not alone if those conversations were rare or even nonexistent because most men in our culture are uncomfortable when it comes to these types of discussions. But can you remember having the *feeling* that you really wanted to say *something?* Can you recall a time when you first woke up to the fact that the little girl whose diapers you studiously avoided changing was suddenly and forcefully being "thrown to the wolves" of contemporary culture? Were you scared? Sad? Or, as with so many fathers, did you attempt to turn off the internal switch of despair, hoping your fear would just go away?

Jennifer is sixteen going on twelve. Her parents have always been afraid of what the culture might do to their daughter if it wrapped its ugly tentacles around her soul. From the time she was a little girl, Jennifer was told about the dark, hostile world that awaited her innocent and tender spirit. Her pastor was aware of this parental fear, and the youth minister at their church felt the pressure to help protect Jen from anything that might damage her God-given innocence. To date, Jennifer has not been allowed to watch television without her parents, to go on a date (or even to consider a romantic relationship), to attend youth group meetings without prior parental consent regarding content, or to have any friends whom her parents deem unacceptable (defined as those whose families do not conform to their family's standards). She was allowed to go to a conference this past summer, but her parents came with her, "to make sure she was not exposed to anything that might harm her."

Jennifer came up to me following a message I had delivered. She wasn't crying, but she displayed a chilling sense of despair. In explaining her family to me, she first wanted me to know that her parents loved her. Her dad, however, had such a fear of the "world" that she felt smothered, overly sheltered, and ill-prepared for life. She was speaking to me because I had referred to those who have received Christ as "bread to a starving world." She said that she didn't know many nonbelievers, and those she did know she had been taught to avoid. She went on to explain that she wanted to go to college in two years, but her parents were afraid for her. The more she talked, the more desperate she became. As she walked away, I felt sad—for her and for her family. Fear had surrounded them like a blanket. Life was not a "grand adventure" as I had proclaimed during my talk; it was a defensive struggle for survival against a powerfully hostile world.

Perhaps Jennifer's story sounds extreme to you. Maybe you identify more with Meagan. She talked to me at the same conference.

Meagan says that her parents so completely trust her that she hasn't had a curfew or any parental restrictions since junior high school. With the skin around her nose ring slightly infected and her sagging pants indicating what has come to be known as an "alternative" lifestyle, Meagan was still a warm, sweet fifteen-year-old who carried a sheen of toughness as a consequence of her life choices. Meagan had a gentle heart underneath the makeup and, not unlike Jennifer, her story also made me sad.

Meagan told me that she knew her father loved her but he "wasn't very good at expressing it—he's a guy, you know?" When she was in seventh grade, her first boyfriend wanted her to drink alcohol, smoke cigarettes, and have sex with him. She felt uncomfortable with the situation and a bit confused and out of control, but she liked him. She thought about talking to her dad and even tried a few times, but he was obviously nervous about such matters and told her that whatever was bothering her, he had confidence she would do the right thing. However, Meagan wanted and needed more.

She decided to take one day at a time and do the best she could. This began for her a journey that included experimentation with alcohol and some drugs ("nothing real bad"), unhealthy friendships and social alliances ("I guess my friends haven't been the best"), and several sexual encounters ("It's hard to go back once you've been there"). Meagan lost her innocence at thirteen. Now a junior in high school, and all grown up, Meagan lived with the emotional and relational calluses of growing up too fast and too soon.

Two girls, two parental responses to a daughter's adolescent journey: Jennifer, sheltered to the point of being socially inept; Meagan, left to fend for herself without boundaries or guidelines. Two girls who are gently bitter, each believing they were let down by parents who love them.

Earl Palmer, pastor at University Presbyterian Church in Seattle, recently stated in an address to youth workers and parents: "We cannot nor should we try to prepare the road for the child. It is our job to prepare the child for the road." This is the task of parenting in a world where innocence is quickly lost. We must help our daughters know and understand how deeply they are loved and give them the foundational security to slowly take off the glasses of innocence in order to see the world as it is. We must be there with them and for them, as they slowly learn the difference between the ideal of God's desire in creation and the stark reality of humanity's selfishness and consequent brokenness.

Our role as parents is neither to throw a protective cover over our children's eyes and minds, as with Jennifer's family, nor to leave them to figure life out on their own, as with Meagan's parents. Rather, our role as fathers — and mothers — is to maintain a family environment where love, mercy, and kindness are the rule without closing our eyes to the plight of the world. When we love our "little girls," our role is hard to acknowledge and even more difficult to balance. But as our daughters grow up, we must be there to help them deal with the complex and confusing transition from the warmth of parental protection to the exposure of grown-up life.

Nothing Stays the Same

There is no better demonstration of the word *cute* than a young girl all dressed up. When my daughter started dance lessons, I would find myself choking back tears every time the biannual recitals rolled around. Not tears of sadness, really. The word *melancholy* better describes it. Those precious, tender, sweet five-year-old darlings in makeup and lace were a stark reminder of what happens in every family. Those events were a wake-up call for me to life's ultimate reality: nothing you cherish stays the same (except, of course, for the consistent love and character of Christ; and as I change, even my understanding of that changes!).

This principle of change presents one of the most difficult aspects of being a daddy: The little girl who fell asleep on my lap, the precious angel who loved to finger paint personalized Picasso-like originals, the innocent cherub who couldn't wait for the kiss *and* the present when I came in from out of town now has a miniskirt in the closet, a boyfriend with an earring, and a nearly psychotic fear of being seen with me in public! My baby is changing right before my eyes!

In 1991, pollster George Barna offhandedly remarked on a syndicated radio program, "The next decade will be the most important decade in the history of humanity." He went on to assert that the rapid changes in information distribution, financial complexity, and societal structure would cause a fundamental shift in how every person orders his or her life. "Change is inevitable," he claimed, "and we must be ready for the changes that come."

For fathers, this obvious truth meets emotional, if not intellectual, resistance. Everyone knows that life is about change and movement and growth. But when you love something, when you cherish what is happening right now, it's hard to accept and honor change. Like the video collage in *Father of the Bride*, we all want to grab hold and not let go of the process of our daughters growing from little girls into women. Although each stage of life has its own set of unique joys and lasting memories, in the midst of one of these stages—especially with girls—many fathers will want to wrap the memory, store it away in a safe place, and preserve it. We want to render it untouchable by time and life experience.

Inevitably, little girls become big girls, then young women, and, eventually, fully grown women. The father who understands this and has the resolve and emotional energy to accept life's changes and prepare for them will be able to build a deeper, more powerful set of memories of life with his daughter. And he will send her off into the world of adulthood a healthy, capable woman.

Change is inevitable. A daughter will become a woman. As she begins to think for herself, to assert herself, a father's role changes. He can be a friend, an ally, and a trusted confidant if he recognizes that change will come. The stakes are high. The woman God has given you needs to know that you believe in her, trust her, and care enough to help her to experience the fullness of God's dream for her.

A Father's Confusion

The third area where a father feels his daughter's move from child to woman is in the sheer confusion this life transition creates for him. Every dad knows how to hold, cuddle, and play with his baby girl. As she gets older, this relationship obviously changes. No one would argue that some father-daughter activities and behaviors are appropriate with a child but not with a teenager. For instance, a six-year-old sleeping on her father's lap presents a beautiful picture of nurture and love. That picture with a sixteen-year-old would raise some eyebrows. There's no mystical cutoff date for any given activity, but over time a father and his daughter will relate to one another in a different way from before. Often this change goes unnoticed and unspoken. But it's there.

Several studies have demonstrated that today's fathers want

to be better at the role than their own fathers. Historically, social scientists ignored a father's role and influence. But starting in the late 1980s, family researchers began to take a deeper look. Even as early as 1986, psychologist Stanley Cath discovered that most men felt that their own fathers had let them down, and many were determined they wouldn't do the same with their children. His findings have been affirmed consistently in subsequent studies.[1]

It is also true that many men are frustrated with this "new role" or at least their perception of it. Research has also shown that while men may desire to be better fathers than their own fathers, their behavior has not caught up with this desire. Many men haven't yet figured out how to be the father they say they want to be. A man may desire to relate to and nurture his own children better than his own father nurtured him, but he's also likely to be unaware of how he will accomplish his goal. If he's not aware of how his children—especially daughters—perceive him, as well as what they are going through and need from him, he will be unable to fulfill his desires as a father.

Several deeply buried but everpresent questions haunt the modern father: "What does it mean to be the dad of an adolescent girl?" and "What does a father need to be and do differently as his daughter grows up?"

While popular theories abound regarding the role of fathers, few men understand where they can go to become more equipped. Most fathers want to be supportive, involved, and have a nurturing influence on their children. But exactly what daughters need is often a mystery to them. It's one thing to raise a son—after all, nearly every father was at one time a son himself! But raise a daughter? This is a different ballgame altogether. Dr. Bruce Narramore pointedly synthesizes the issues facing today's fathers:

> Our society requires seventeen years of education before certifying a person to teach in public school. Medical

doctors and psychologists must have twenty years of schooling before they practice on your children. And many states require teenagers to take a course in driver's education before they can be licensed to drive a car. But to rear children from the cradle to their twenties, our society doesn't require one hour of formal training.[2]

Some men, then, simply plow ahead, presuming there is really no difference between raising a son and raising a daughter. However . . .

Kristy's dad wanted to be close to her. He had raised two sons and he felt he'd done a pretty good job. He was still close with both boys. They had basically stayed out of trouble and they were doing well in college. Now that they were gone, his attention turned to Kristy. But for her, it was too little too late.

Kristy's letter reflects pain and disappointment as she seeks to help her father understand what she wants and needs from him:

Dear Dad,

I'm tired of trying to compete with my brothers for you. Now that they are gone, you want me to be just like them. But I'm not just like them! A long time ago I wanted you to talk to me, and to listen to me. But you were too busy with Jeff and Tim—going to games, coaching their sports, and playing golf. Now that they're gone, it's my turn. But I don't really want to do things, I just want you to know me. I love you, Dad, and I know you are trying (sometimes too hard!). But you need to stop, Daddy, stop and listen to me.

—Stacy, 14, Orlando, FL

Stacy's letter is a cry to be noticed, to be taken seriously. Her father may be confused over his role, but she's ready to forgive him and move on. Her love for him is stronger than her disappointment and frustration.

Without exception, the letters we've received from daughters have expressed a desire for reconciliation and a fresh start with their dads. Every daughter we've heard from wanted to connect with her father, regardless of circumstances or history.

Face it. If you are a dad, change is inevitable. Your daughter's innocence will eventually give way to knowledge, and you may not know exactly what to do as her father. But don't let that stop you! Your little princess is growing up and she needs her daddy!

Chapter Two

"I Need You, Daddy!"

Dear Daddy,

I guess you don't need me to tell you, but I'm growing up. I used to love to sit on your lap and listen to you tell me stories, but now I just don't. I want you to realize that I am a young woman, and that I know what I am doing. When I cry, I don't need you or Mom to "fix it." I may just want to cry! You were such a good dad when I was little—you used to be fun and funny and I liked to listen to you tell your dumb stories. But now I'm getting older and don't really need anybody to tell me stories. I just want you to know this stuff.

—Phylis, 12, Nashville, TN

Not long ago, the people of Boulder, Colorado, were rocked by the news that a young girl was brutally raped and murdered in her own home. The striking thing about her was the extraordinary life this little girl had lived. She was a rising star in the world of child beauty pageants. Photographs of her enraptured and enraged a nation—a six-year-old dressed up in a

(continued)

sequined gown, a hairstyle more fitting for the senior prom than the playground, and enough properly applied makeup to physically attract the most hardened or even virtuous of men. In short, the videos and pictures of this angel-seductress only added to the intrigue of this cruel and tragic event.

We watched the news, waiting for an arrest and ultimate conviction, but the lingering memory of the beauty-child remains fixed. She had grown up way too fast. The dads of girls I know all felt the same as they watched the spectacle: *It won't be long until my little girl is wearing makeup and walks out the door dressed like a grown woman going out on the town.*

For dads, little girls are the epitome of innocence and beauty. Every father knows the feeling of having his little princess run across a room to jump into his arms and kiss him on the cheek. There are very few sounds that can rival a daughter's delighted squeal—"Dadddddyyyyyyy!"—when he comes home from a long day of fighting the battles of the world. The warmth of her embrace, the touch of her cheek against his—these are what every father loves and holds dear in his heart.

When she is young, a daughter is something soft and gentle, small and frail, innocent and precious. She's like a figurine on the mantel to be aggressively guarded, as well as tenderly cherished.

The intuitive father also knows that

From Dee
Memories of an Adult Daughter

—

So many times as a teenager I felt as though no one understood me. I'm not sure I understood *myself*. At times I felt like a woman trapped in a kid's skin, and at other times I wanted to run to the safety of my room and stuffed animals. Day by day, minute by minute, I was acting like different people. I recall the incredible pressure to act mature and adult on the outside, yet on the inside I felt so small and helpless, lost and confused.

I longed for a safe place to talk about these feelings, but my dad was too far away, and my mom and I just seemed to butt heads during those years, *especially* when I was feeling lost and confused. I couldn't seem to let her in when I was struggling—she was *my mom!* I loved her and trusted her (in many ways she was all I had, she and my sister), but somewhere inside I knew that I needed someone to cherish me, to comfort me,

(continued)

this gentle beauty he holds is far more excited about the idea of closeness with him than she is about the reality. When she falls off her bike or kids make fun of her in school, she runs to her mom. Dad may personify for her the idea of safety and warmth, but the stronger bond still remains with Mom. Sure, she loves her dad, often with passion and abandon. But her heart still belongs to her mother.

During the childhood years, this mother-daughter bond is unique. It is a secret world where a man, even Dad, is not invited. Every father senses it, and most fathers appreciate it, but the relationship is undeniably closed. From shopping, dressing up, and "doing her hair," to endless conversations about boys and friends and fears and rivals, mothers have an "in" that serves to keep fathers away. But something begins to happen around age ten or eleven to this mother/child bond. In some cases this may manifest itself in a daughter seeing her mother shift from friend to rival, confidant to opponent.

When daughters begin the adolescent journey, everything starts to change. And it's the rare family that is prepared for the coming relational storm.

Dee and I are involved as volunteers in a junior high outreach ministry called, appropriately enough, Wild Life. For the past four years we've watched a remarkable and seemingly overnight change occur as sixth-grade girls enter our lives only to leave as sophisticated, budding young women. As we watch this metamorphosis, one thing invariably stands out: The adult exterior is but a thin veneer covering a fragile person who still feels and even often acts like a little girl. The physical changes her body experiences are deceiving to her and the world around her, for her mind, heart, and spirit have yet

> and to encourage me.
> I know now that God created in me a longing to be close to my dad, but I didn't know it then. He was too disconnected and too involved in his own world to be my rock or comfort. I often wondered, *Who can I trust to help me find my way through these changes?* I felt so alone.

to catch up with the new woman who is emerging.

Along with the physical changes, she is also beginning to feel a developmental difference inside. She begins to realize that she's no longer a little girl, yet she doesn't understand what the new world of womanhood will be like. The newness of this process, and the convoluted mixture of fear and excitement it brings, causes emerging young women to question just about everything. Like the newborn butterfly that pushes out of the warmth and safety of a cocoon, your daughter often feels as if she's seeing and experiencing life for the first time. Believe it or not, Dad, she longs to grab you by the hand as she takes her first steps as a woman.

> Dear Daddy,
> You have always been my hiding place. I remember when I was a little girl, scared or lonely, and I would crawl up into your lap, just to be reassured that you were there. But now it's different. You still want me to crawl in your lap. But I don't want to sit in your lap. I'm growing up, and you can't even see it! Why can't you just talk to me, listen to me, or just treat me like a person instead of your stupid "little princess"? Come on, Dad. Get a clue!
> —Julie, 15, Chicago, IL

Julie's letter presents a common dilemma that adolescent girls feel during this time of transition. Julie *loved* the times she shared with her dad, the cuddling and being close, the tickling and the quiet talks. But something is changing, and she's scared. More important, her frustration shows that she understands it little more than her father does. She's mad at him because he treats her with tenderness and affection! He's probably reeling as he wonders, *What have I done? Why is she running from me? Why doesn't she know that I love her and want to do the best I can to comfort her?*

This response helps neither Julie nor her dad. She wants more from him, not less! She needs him to treat her differently now that she has embarked on this new emotional adventure called adolescence. As a little girl, she needed her dad only for physical comfort and assurance. Now she wants him to take her seriously, to show her he cares about what she thinks as well as how she feels, to allow her to grow beyond the little girl he has always protected, just by being her dad.

As your daughter enters adolescence, she starts to drop little hints everywhere she goes. Telltale signs include outbursts of unexplained anger or depression, radical mood swings, and sometimes a noticeable chip on her shoulder. It seems as if she's just daring you to take her on. But just as quickly as you identify a sign of her emerging womanhood, she just as quickly reverts to being a cuddly little "princess" again, wanting to be held and hugged and led. Parents who are unaware of the reason for these frequent changes are often frustrated with such a seemingly schizophrenic child. Sometimes parents overreact to the point of actually hindering the growth process. The parents who know that a daughter's behavior is simply a marker of a major life transition will be able to help her make the most of this exciting yet frightening time.

The Story of Scott and Jill

Scott's daughter Jill was twelve years old going on twenty when it hit them. Jill came downstairs on a Saturday afternoon visibly frustrated. Scott, who was watching a football game, noticed she was bothered but he didn't think twice about it. More out of courtesy than compassion, he casually commented, "Can I do anything for you, honey?" Jill, who perhaps should have known that her dad didn't actually mean for her to sit down and talk about her confused array of feelings (at age twelve she was only learning), came into the room and started to tell him everything she was feeling. Scott was caught completely off guard. He'd looked forward to this game for weeks and didn't really want to be interrupted. After all, everything she was saying seemed to be fairly petty and relatively unimportant. So he pretended to listen and continued to watch the game.

Jill, being a young woman, took about thirty seconds to realize that her dad's concern rang hollow. He had no intention of listening to her story. Scott hadn't lied. He had just implied a willingness to be there for her although he really wasn't all that interested. When she slowed her monologue and hesitated in the recounting of her day, Scott did what many men are so good at. Without looking up from the game, he offered her a terse, fifteen-second, quick-fix piece of advice: "Just call her and tell her you'll go with someone else to the party!"

At first Jill just sat there, stunned. Then she meekly walked out of the room, mumbling, "You never listen to me . . . you don't even care . . . all you care about is your stupid game."

Scott barely heard her and felt quite good that he had been a compassionate and available dad. And he hadn't missed much of the game to boot!

Of course you can see what's coming. But when you're in the thick of life, not actively prepared to be a father to your daughter, would you have responded any differently?

A father must provide his daughter three important elements as she begins this journey. First, he must take her seriously. Second, he must care about what she thinks. Third, he must be committed to walking with her through the journey of adolescence.

Taking Your Daughter Seriously

When a child enters adolescence, the key word for her is *independence*. This is the essence of the adolescent quest—to be treated as and to feel like an individual who matters (often, of course, while blending into the crowd and not being noticed!). Fathers are among the greatest offenders at the outset of this process. Although you may mean well, Dad, it's truly amazing what you will say when you don't recognize just how fragile and needy your daughter is.

Like Scott, we fathers tend to forget that our daughters honestly need us to care about them. That means caring about the things they care about. Our daughters need to know that they are not just interruptions, they are one of the highest priorities in our lives. This is especially true for daughters in those most formative early teen years.

At this point your daughter doesn't really know what she needs or even wants. She's caught between two worlds. She feels a sense of comfort in the world of childhood; it's the world she knows and understands. But the new world of imminent adulthood is frightening and overwhelming, even as she intuitively knows it is right and exciting to enter it. Because of this tension, your daughter may subconsciously revert to the safety and protection of childhood, even as she is compelled to press on. This will cause her to constantly contradict herself. She'll be happy at five o'clock and depressed at six. She'll kiss you then turn around and yell at you. As she pushes you away and then tugs at your heartstrings, remember one thing: She loves you and needs you to take her seriously!

Daddy,
When I was little you called me "Daddy's little girl." We walked hand-in-hand through the mall, your big hand holding mine. All my dreams and fears were expressed to you. When I was with you I felt as if nothing could harm me. When I started to get older I pushed you away. You usually would have put your arm around me, but you soon stopped trying. I couldn't express my feelings to you anymore and my emotions seemed to be crazier than ever. Daddy, I still wanted you to hold me and call me Daddy's little girl. But I was so confused inside. I wanted to hold your hand and tell you everything. I saw your face when I

went through that time in my life and I just wanted to apologize. Daddy, I know you just don't know what to say so I'll say it. I love you and I need to be your little girl.

—Brittany, 17, Oklahoma City, OK

Caring About What She Thinks

The second way you can begin to be the kind of father your daughter needs is to let her know that her opinions and ideas are important to you. For some fathers—perhaps most fathers—this can be a difficult task, especially in early adolescence, as she continually vacillates between being the logical, rational, and clear-thinking girl you knew so well just a few short years ago, and the incoherent, emotional, distracted "Dr. Jekyll and Mr. Hyde" with whom you now live! Most dads have very little patience with this and mistakenly mention it to their wives and even their daughters.

A friend recently clued me in on a television cartoon show that is popular with younger kids (and many of their parents): "Animaniacs." One of the minor characters is Katie Ka-Boom, a teenager who has an amazing character trait. When her parents don't seem to understand her, or they frustrate her, she turns into a monster and explodes. When the dust clears, she's standing in the midst of the rubble with her mom, dad, and little brother cautiously looking on. Then she says, "Nothing's wrong!"

The explosion of adolescence can cause a family to feel like they've been blown apart. Does this scenario sound familiar? Your thirteen-year-old daughter gets off the phone after talking with a friend and now has to decide whether or not she "likes" a boy who "likes" her. (In our community it's called "going out," and these relationships often last as long as two weeks!) She comes downstairs and tells you about the conversation. She speaks calmly and clearly, and she's able to sift out what is important and what she values. She seems to be on a track of making a wise, albeit juvenile, decision regarding this snot-nosed kid who has never said "boo" to her. You hear her out and tell her it sounds like she's doing a good job of thinking through the issues. As she happily goes upstairs to bed, you think to yourself, *Ah, my little girl is growing up. She's learning how to make good decisions.* When you kiss her goodnight and say a prayer with her, you go to bed confident that she's becoming all you ever dreamed her to be.

The next night she is quiet at dinner. You, being the nurturing father of the new millennium, ask how it's going with her new love interest. She stares down at her untouched food, her chin begins to quiver, and she suddenly erupts with what is to you an hysterical, irrational outburst of anger toward you (although later she says that she simply "got a little emotional"). She storms up the stairs, reminding the family in no uncertain terms (and in particular you, Dad) that nobody understands her and it's just fine if she'll never be able to get a boyfriend, and she probably won't ever get married (and you, Dad, are the reason) and she'll probably end up as a nun! (Door slams.)

Stunned, the family looks at you, wondering, some aloud, "What did you say to her?" Or worse, "What did you do to her!" You sit there, completely baffled. You've changed from Ann Landers to Attila the Hun in less than twenty-four hours.

Now is the moment that marks the kind of father your daughter wants and so desperately needs. Now is not the time to take her words personally or to get angry or to tell her, "Grow up!" Obviously, something has happened to hurt her, and she needs a place where she can express her pain, fear, and insecurity. For some completely irrational reason, she's chosen you as the focal point for all of her anxiety and frustration (and if you make yourself a willing mark by caring, you can be sure that when she needs a target, you may get hit).

Right now, what she needs is to know that you care about what she thinks, even if it's contradictory, confusing, or illogical.

Her desire is that you will take the time to listen and try to understand what she's thinking and feeling. She doesn't want answers, advice, or platitudes. She wants you to care about what she thinks.

The caring dad in this scenario would wait a few minutes and then go to her room. He would gently knock and ask permission to enter her private world. Even though she may not seem to want to talk, in most cases she will. (When she doesn't, it may have more to do with the timing than the desire to open up and connect.) Now is the time to simply say something like, "Honey, I sure haven't intended to upset you. If my question hurt you, I'm sorry." This could be followed up by, "Do you want to talk?" The important thing is that she knows she matters to you and that you're not trying to pry your way into her life. She just needs to know that you care and that you're willing to enter her world of hopes and fears, dreams and disappointments. This is the most precious gift you could ever give your daughter as she grows up.

Walking with Her Through the Journey of Adolescence
As your daughter enters adolescence, a subtle shift takes place: She inherently needs and usually desires a unique relationship with her father.

Although her mother remains a significant figure in her life, it is at this stage that she longs for her daddy to treat her differently, to relate to her in a more grown-up way, and to trust and encourage her as she navigates the minefield of adolescence. Her need for him to treat her as a young woman instead of his "little princess" (though she hopes his adoration for her will never wane) is at the core of this budding stage of development. She needs to feel like she's more than a cute little doll. She wants her father to see her as an emerging young woman who has gifts and talents and the strength to make her mark on the world.

Although there's some truth in the idea that this is a private journey, no life quest is truly a private affair. We walk where others have walked. There are other travelers alongside us, before and behind us. A daughter's journey through the twisting, exhilarating, and sometimes painful wilderness of adolescence can be a living abyss when she feels she's undertaking it alone. Yet the sad fact is that many young women feel alone much of the time. For most there is always Mom. But an integral part of an adolescent girl's process is to identify herself as distinct from her mother. Even friends find it hard to travel this journey together, for each individual is required to follow her own path toward womanhood.

Who can provide her comfort and hope in the journey? We believe that God has designed the father to take on that crucial role as his daughter moves through adolescence. She needs a teacher more than a judge, a guide more than a boss, and a friend more than a protector. For this to happen, she needs a dad who is willing to walk beside her during these years. Unfortunately, as Terry Apter points out, for most girls this is rare:

> Fathers are often less involved with their daughters during their teenage years than they have been up to that point. Studies show that while fathers tend to be extremely attached and involved with their [young] daughters, closeness diminishes as girls reach puberty and adolescence. Girls talk to their fathers less, tell them less about their lives, spend less time with them, and in return receive less support and encouragement from them.[1]

You can be a different kind of father. If you choose to do so, you can look beyond the incongruity of her behavior and see past her tendency to push you out of her life. Remind yourself how difficult this time is for her, and remember that she loves you and needs you. Many times she doesn't want to tell you or she won't be able to find the words to express her need for you. But she desperately wants you to care, and she longs for your approval and your friendship.

Daddy:

I don't know where to start . . . there is so much I want to tell you about the real me, but you only see me as your "little girl." In fact, we've even joked about it before.

I remember when we first moved to Kansas. I was growing out of the back rub stage, but I guess the move made me need you even more. You wrote me a letter when I was eight, commenting on this, but I still needed those back rubs. You sent me the letter nine years later and I read it for the first time a week ago. I sobbed when I read it. I realized that every once in a while I still need a daddy to take me in his arms and protect me from this awful world and keep me out of harm's way. Yet I need a father, too. Someone who will prepare me for the real world. Daddy, will you be my father, too?

—Sally, 17, Lawrence, KS

CHAPTER THREE

Trust: The Glue That Holds Relationships Together

Dear Daddy,
When I was little, you always told me that the most
important thing for me was to tell you the truth and
that you wanted to know you could trust me. Because you
lied to me about [my brother], I don't know if I can trust
you! Because of what you have done, I'm not sure I can
trust you with anything anymore. And you need to know
that it hurts really bad!

—Marie, 16, Colorado Springs, CO

Trust is a precious but fragile gift. It takes years to earn, yet it can be destroyed in seconds. When Marie handed me that letter, it was obvious that she had been weeping. She *wanted* to trust her father with sensitive information, but somehow his response had produced a serious violation of one of Marie's most deeply cherished values, a value that her father had worked so hard to instill in the first place!

Webster's dictionary defines *trust* as "confident expectation." For a daughter to allow herself to draw close to her father and open herself up to his influence in her life, she must have an unshakable confidence that he will take her seriously, treat her tenderly, and be unconditionally committed to her throughout these years. She must be convinced that when she lets him into the morass of thoughts and feelings that adolescence brings, he will be very careful. Most fathers would be shocked to realize how little their daughters trust them. Marie was not alone.

> Dear Dad,
> I'll never understand where I stood in your life. Every time I tried to talk to you, you wouldn't look up from your paper, or you turned away. I do remember a few meals together— sitting at the dinner table with a broken shoulder and being told to "sit still" because it was "my own stupid fault!" I do remember getting mostly straight A's in school but you only asking, "Why did you get a B in (fill in the blank)?" I never felt that you knew anything about me. I wanted to tell you about me, get your advice, but I just didn't know what you would say or think about me. . . .

—Elisabeth, 19, Atlanta, GA

From this letter it's impossible to tell what kind of father this man is. Were these

---

From Dee
Memories of an Adult Daughter

Sometimes when I was a teen, it was just easier not to have any expectations of Dad. Then I wasn't disappointed when he let me down. (Even as I write these words, I know deep in my heart that what I'm saying is a lie; he *did* let me down, and it *did* hurt.) My relationship with Dad was distant and impersonal. I rarely saw him, and when I did he didn't seem to take me very seriously. Instead, I remember feeling like a child around him.

Many times I *wanted* to talk to him and get to know him. But as I look back I could sense that, as much as he told me he loved me, he never seemed willing to open up to me to talk about anything real or personal. I guess it was easier and safer for both of us to keep conversations on the surface. By not talking about real issues and feelings, he was never stuck with not knowing how

(continued)

40

normative events that simply serve as examples of a broad-stroke pattern, or were they isolated incidents that happen to have been crystallized in Elisabeth's memory? If the former is the case, the issue in their relationship is not so much a matter of trust as it is a general disregard and lack of care for his daughter. But perhaps this dad is actually a good, conscientious father. Maybe he cared about her but had a few bad moments. Every father slips up once in a while and fails in his relationship with his daughter, and he will occasionally hurt her. But when she is hurt and trust is broken, he must take proactive steps to repair the relationship.

The issue of trust is not always related to a specific incident or event. It may represent a growing internal sense of betrayal based on years of a daughter's careful observation of her father.

Dear Dad,
Sometimes I feel that you love me but
you don't respect what I say because
I'm a girl. At least that's what I get
from how you always listen to and
respect my brother but not me.

—Kristen, 15, New Jersey

to answer my questions. He didn't have to be accountable for any of his own mistakes . . . like leaving me, my mom, and my sister.

Sitting in my room at his house after another weekend of superficial conversation and meaningless activity, I wondered if things were ever going to change between us. I wanted a relationship with him, but I couldn't tell if he wanted one with me. Did he even realize I was growing up? Did he ever sense my desire to know him and to be known by him? Could I ever be honest with him about my life and my anger at him for what he had done? I now know it would have been so easy to forgive him and to be close to him if only he had *tried* to get to know me. I wanted so badly to tell him of my plans, to hear his advice, to receive his approval.

Instead, I was left with a void—a hole in my heart that still causes pain.

Girls who grow up with a brother near the same age frequently struggle with what they see their brother getting from Dad and what they *perceive* they are not getting from Dad by comparison.

When we conducted a comprehensive research study on the differences between the way adolescent brothers and sisters perceive their individual relationships to their fathers, we found that more than 99 percent of the time boys reported a closer relationship to their dads than did their sisters. This was true regardless of what their respective ages were and who was older (as long as they were between twelve and nineteen and still living at home with their biological fathers). In terms of trust, daughters overwhelmingly reported they had less trust of their father than did the brothers (98 percent).

Our research team had some hints that there might be small differences between how boys and girls view their relationship to their fathers, but no one had yet studied brothers and sisters in the same family with the same father. The huge difference in reported closeness (or attachment) took the research team off guard. However, one message was loud and clear: Fathers somehow relate differently to sons than to daughters during the adolescent years. Their daughters sense this and it seems to cause them to back off from trusting their dads.

One more letter presents another issue that affects trust. This from an unnamed twelve-year-old girl whose parents were fighting to the point of separation.

Dear Daddy,
Both of you get angry with me for doing stuff you don't like with my "bad" friends. Maybe they are bad; probably they are. But what reason have you given me to think you care? And they have problems, too; why shouldn't I hang out with kids like me? They accept me as I am. They don't criticize.
The thing is, kids should love their fathers. And I don't know if I love you. Maybe if you died I would cry, and realize how much I did love you. But right now, when my mind is clouded only by sadness and grief, I find I

don't. I don't even like you very much. I can barely tolerate you in the same room with me.

—No name given, 12, Dallas, TX

Although the letters are written from different angles, all of them point to an eroded trust in fathers.

Trust is a funny concept. We all so desperately desire that those closest to us trust us, yet our trust in them is often fragile and easily shattered.

Most dads would probably not even consider that their daughters might not trust them. At least that's the case with the fathers we've spoken to. Perhaps you're thinking that you've loved your little girl since she was born. You cuddled her, changed her diapers, took her on walks, played with her on your knee. As she grew, you told her she was beautiful, watched her dance or play soccer, and helped her with her math homework. But once she hit adolescence, it may have become harder to show your love for her.

Maybe she doesn't want to sit on your lap anymore or tell you about her life. Could it be that your little girl has needed something from you that goes deeper than "watching" her during activities and helping her out with the mundane tasks of life? For her to experience the best life has to offer her, she needs to know that she can trust her father.

A Two-Way Street

Every relationship begins with trust. Your daughter needs and powerfully desires to trust you. But here is the real dichotomy: Your daughter not only wants to trust you, she also desires *you* to trust *her*! The issue of trust is a two-way street, but it is the rare parent and child who recognize this.

Whether or not you know it, your daughter wants your stamp of approval, your unconditional acknowledgment that you believe in her. As Doug Webster points out in *Dear Dad:*

What Kids Want Their Fathers to Know, kids (both boys and girls) want two things from their fathers: "Trust me" and "Leave me alone." As Webster presents what adolescents want to say to their fathers, he goes on to say that kids want "a dad who trusts his kids to grow up on their own."[1]

In this definition, trust is equated with giving a child the room to make decisions on her own. But I think this definition misses the core of trust, which is less about control and more about relationship. Your daughter wants to know that you trust *in* her far more than you intrinsically trust her *behavior.*

All children are looking for parents who will care more about character and heart than choices and lifestyle. Social scientists affirm that behavior and lifestyle are symptomatic of something going on inside. In other words, there is a reason for everything we do. But when your daughter says that she wants you to trust her, she's saying that she needs to know you believe in and trust *her,* even when you can't (or shouldn't) trust her *behavior* (and might even have to discipline her).

Now, as much as she wants you to trust her, your daughter is also longing to trust you. This idea of mutual trust is so important for kids that much of their self-esteem and healthy sense of personal power is directly associated with the perception of the trust they have in their dads.

This is how it works: If a twelve-year-old girl trusts her father to tell the truth, to be honest, to show respect, and to be gentle even in the midst of failure and mistakes, and if her dad seeks to understand what she is going through, it is far more likely that she will let him into her life. If this father proactively works to assure the reinforcement of this perception as she moves through adolescence, her confidence in him as a leader and guide will allow her the emotional freedom to open up to him, even when life gets messy and painful.

If, on the other hand, a girl approaches the teen years with a perception of her father as a distant, controlling, and argumentative dictator, she will not trust him with her emotions, decisions, and failures. As she grows up, she will look for someone to replace the male assurance she wants from her dad. Although she deeply wants Dad's guidance, counsel, and approval, if she doesn't trust him to care for her with gentleness and respect, she will look elsewhere.

Today's daughter needs a father who takes the time to stop, listen, and respond with great mercy and warmth. That's what trust is. The father who has built into his daughter the ability to trust *him* will not need to question whether or not he can trust *her!*

The Three Dimensions of Trust

Adolescent behavior is, by nature, haphazard and erratic. That's why it's called *adolescent* behavior (as opposed to *adult* behavior)! During these years of transition, your daughter will make poor choices; she will fail and disappoint both you and herself. You must regularly address the behavioral trust that gets eroded during down times or strengthened during victorious times, especially as it relates to privilege and responsibility. But the greater understanding of trust must be built on the deeper foundation of *relational* and *character* trust. *Respect, acceptance,* and *understanding* are three essential elements of such a trust relationship.

Respect

After a presentation, one father approached me with scowling face and said, "My father taught me that respect is something to be earned, not granted!" This dad was obviously taking issue with my encouragement to respect his daughter simply because she needed and deserved it.

As we talked, he became even more irate. In essence, he was having a hard time getting his fifteen-year-old daughter to perform on a level that warranted his idea of "earned respect." I asked him if we could see what the Scriptures taught, and he (reluctantly) agreed. We looked at these two passages:

> Show proper respect to everyone: Love the brotherhood of believers, fear God, honor the king. (1 Peter 2:17)
> Give everyone what you owe him: If you owe taxes, pay taxes; if revenue, then revenue; if respect, then respect; if honor, then honor. (Romans 13:7)

As we talked, he admitted that he wanted to freely offer his daughter the gift of respect, but he carried what he described as "an inner block" to such an idea. The longer we talked, the more he softened, and it became clear that he loved his daughter so much that the way he showed his love to her was how he had received love from his own father: You must perform, be good, live "holy," and then you will be worthy of my respect.

Once this father realized he was passing on his own father's philosophy of parenting, a style that had been so deeply destructive to himself, he was able to see how he had been treating his daughter and denying her what she truly needed. Once he realized this, he was able to take his eyes off himself and his own ingrained need to perform. Then he was able to rethink how he could show his daughter the respect she deserved. This father came to realize that love is hollow if respect is an elusive goal that must be earned by performance.

Acceptance

Dear Daddy,
I know that I have been a disappointment to you, especially lately. When you cried and told me that you could no longer trust me, and that you couldn't believe what I had done, I was so sorry. But when you went from

there and got mad, yelling, "How could you do this to me?" I kind of shut you out. I am sorry for what I did, and I will try not to do it again. But I'm also afraid now to tell you what's going on in my life because I'm not sure how you will take it. You always told me you want me to be honest, but can I really be honest with you? Can you handle it without taking it so personally?

—Christine, 16, Madisonville, KY

Most people think that to accept means to condone. This is a battle the church has fought for centuries, and we will not solve it here. But there are two unmistakable factors that come into play with the whole idea of "acceptance."

The first is that our Lord modeled an acceptance of those who were considered "outside" of the religious and ethical boundary lines of the day:

The Son of Man came eating and drinking, and they say, "Here is a glutton and a drunkard, a friend of tax collectors and 'sinners.'" (Matthew 11:19)

He is also said to have "welcomed" such people—the "sinners" and "tax collectors"—who lived in apparent disrespect for morality and the law:

While Jesus was having dinner at Levi's house, many tax collectors and "sinners" were eating with him and his disciples, for there were many who followed him. When the teachers of the law who were Pharisees saw him eating with the "sinners" and tax collectors, they asked his disciples: "Why does he eat with tax collectors and 'sinners'?" On hearing this, Jesus said to them, "It is not the healthy who need a doctor, but the sick. I have not come to call the righteous, but sinners." (Mark 2:15-17)

In Luke 15, Jesus reveals to us the heart of God for those who have wandered away—those who are "lost" and those whose behavior has hurt others and been squandered on sinful living. If Jesus' understanding of those who fail and who are "lost" is that God loves and pursues them anyway, certainly our call as fathers is to pursue and welcome our daughters, even in light of disappointment, failure, and heartache.

The second factor that comes into play in understanding acceptance is our own deep need for the unconditional acceptance of our Father in heaven when we have failed Him. Each of us needs regularly to return to the cross and resurrection of Jesus to heal us of our own sin and lostness. If we were as sensitive to welcome and "eat" with our daughters, especially in their times of need and struggle, as God is with us when we fail or are broken, we would begin to get at the character of acceptance.

"Hate the sin, love the sinner." What a wonderful, neat, clean religious platitude. But what a difficult calling! If you want to build your daughter's sense of trust in you, then do whatever you can to communicate that you will *always* welcome her with open arms as her devoted father—even in the midst of failure or painful circumstances. This does not imply that her behavior will have no consequences. There may be times when you're forced to allow her to go her own way. But like the Prodigal's father, who kept his eyes on the road, waiting for his child's return (Luke 15:20-32), you must convince your daughter that you will always, unequivocally, accept her as your own when she needs to rest in your embrace.

Understanding
Trust is withheld when there is fear of being misunderstood. Who hasn't had the experience of being misunderstood or misjudged? We've all been hurt by others who haven't taken the time to understand us or show gentleness and mercy when

we're down. In order to trust someone, we must believe they know us well and what they don't know will make an effort to find out.

As with respect and acceptance, your daughter needs to know that you have some sense of who she is and what she feels. To trust you, she must have confidence that even if you don't understand something she does or says, you are willing to listen to her and to find out *her* perspective before you jump to give advice or draw conclusions.

Dad,

Why do you insist on telling me what I'm thinking all the time? When you say that, it makes me want to run away from you. You think you know me and understand me, but you don't! Why don't you ask me questions before going off on one of your little speeches?

You don't like most of my friends, but at least they understand me. They listen, and they don't judge me. They just love me. You say you love me every day, but if you really did you would try to understand me.

—Jennifer, 15, Denver, CO

There's no way around it. Understanding your daughter takes work. First, it means respecting her to the point of listening really hard! Second, it means that you have to gather all the facts, both objective and emotional, before you attempt interaction. And it means honestly trying to "walk in her shoes."

Of course, the problem with walking in her shoes is that you're still using your feet! You can say you understand and think you actually do understand her, but she may not be convinced. It's your job as a father to bend over backward to communicate that you truly want to know your daughter and understand her. This takes a great deal of energy, a willingness to hang in there when you feel like walking away, and a commitment to love your daughter enough to wade through layers of issues, feelings, and thoughts.

Sometimes this works itself out in the most mundane of circumstances, yet the little things add up to a lifetime of trust. Take, for instance, the following letter. This daughter shared the first thing that popped into her head when asked to write a letter to her dad:

> Dad,
> I want to thank you for not embarrassing me too much when I go on dates or bring someone over, even when you "accidentally" catch me kissing him. That's kind of embarrassing, but you don't say anything about it, until the next day when you tease me, for about five hours!
>
> —Meagan, 16, Columbus, OH

When your daughter thanks you for something as ordinary as how you treat her around her peers, it shows that she knows you not only care about her but you understand what she needs in those situations. As simple as that sounds, it has powerful implications for other areas of your relationship with her. Meagan obviously trusts her dad because she knows he understands her—at least a little bit.

When your daughter comes to the conclusion that she can trust you to work at knowing and understanding her, the groundwork for a lifetime of intimate and warm connection is created. This is the dream of every dad and the immense need of every daughter.

> Dear Dad,
> You have always made sure that I knew you loved me. And guess what? You are my number one hero. I talk about you all the time to my friends. I am so proud of you.
>
> —Mandy, 17, Tulsa, OK

When a daughter believes in her father and trusts him, her confidence is lifted, her sense of self is clear, and she learns how to trust herself. When she trusts herself, she can more freely trust others. Most important, she can more fully trust God. This is the ultimate goal of any father who truly loves his children—to create an atmosphere in which they will be able to trust in the One who created them.

CHAPTER FOUR

Closeness: The Adolescent Safety Net

Dear Daddy,
I haven't been able to tell you this, but I've been scared
lately. School was harder this year, and my friends don't
seem the same. But I guess what scares me most is that
I'm changing and I don't know what to do. I've always
told you I would tell you everything, but we don't talk any
more. I know it's mostly me, and I don't act like I want to
talk, but I still need you, you know?

The speaker tonight talked about a poem a girl wrote
called "Don't Be Fooled by Me." Don't be fooled by me,
Dad. Please! I need to know that you are right beside me,
even when I don't seem to care.

—Cherie, 15, Boca Raton, FL

Being "close" to someone is hard to describe and harder still to define, but we all want it with those we love. Closeness, although tied to expectations and attention, is defined more by a feeling than by something objective, measurable, or tangible. It's like a garden that must be looked after even though the gardener

From Dee
Memories of an
Adult Daughter

—

Few girls in my town dated older guys, but I did. Now I have a pretty good understanding of what drove me to them. Once they paid attention to me, I was hooked!

I sometimes worried about dating an older guy. Our relationship was deep nd very serious, almost pm the beginning. So ich of my world focused him. Often, I made the ice to be with him at the ense of family and ds. I remember telling lf that I didn't have of a choice, that love ly. But I did feel about letting go of e and everything w should be to me—all for guy.

"love" became In my head I my relation- excessive, her ips in

(continued)

realizes that growth is far beyond his control. The garden must be constantly tended through energy and focus. It doesn't matter to the wise gardener that the blossoms may not be realized until a future season. He recognizes that the fruit of his labor will eventually bring him the joy and beauty he seeks.

Throughout the early years of adolescence, every daughter is almost desperate to have a warm, close relationship with her father, but the struggle, the fighting, and the misunderstanding often cause her to deny what she craves. As the years progress, if her father is not responsive to what she wants and needs, she will look to other people—especially to other men—to fill the gap. For the father who realizes his daughter really does want a close relationship with him, the road to intimacy and depth is well marked.

The father who carefully plants, lovingly waters, and mercifully prunes—and who places his ultimate trust in his heavenly Father—will someday be close to his daughter. The roots of connection will be deeply embedded in the soil of the trust and intimacy he has built with her. Dad, your daughter wants to know you and love you. It is your task to allow her in.

Father-daughter closeness is a strange thing. In our research it was expressed by daughters in an either-or, black-or-white way. Either a daughter felt a closeness to her father and was grateful for it, or she felt distant from him, and along with it sadness and sometimes bitterness. These two letters are examples of the contrast we experienced.

Dear father,
I'm tired of trying so hard only to be hurt. I'm not the perfect daughter. So what if my clothes are different? I just wish you would accept me as me. You have hurt me in so many ways yet I still try to love you. Can't you do the same?

—Brenda, 15, Charlotte, NC

Dear Dad,
It may not seem like it sometimes, but I am so glad that God gave me you as my father. All my friends know what good friends we are, and I can tell they envy me! You are my biggest hero, you listen to me, you care about me, and I know I don't tell you often enough how much that means to me. I love you so much, and I am so glad that you are my dad!

—Cindy, 17, Baton Rouge, LA

These two letters flow from the same desire—a daughter's longing to be connected to her dad. The letter from Cindy doesn't mention specifically how close she my life suffered. But emotionally I was consumed by him. I felt so right with him: He was there for me, he loved me, and I needed him. If I didn't see him for even one day I felt empty inside and longed to connect with passion and intimacy. I was barely sixteen.

Yet, even in the midst of adolescent passion, I sometimes wondered if the whole thing—the love, the depth, the longing—was right. Whenever I would get nervous, or scared, or even stop to think about my life, I would always come back to the single fact that this man loved me, and he proved it continually for three years. I needed his love, and without him I knew I would be lost. I had no one else. I felt like I needed a man in my life—a man who was kind, who listened, and who made sure I knew that I was valuable.

Dad, where were you when I needed you? What would you have said to me when I fell in love? Would I have fallen so hard had you blessed me, held me, loved me?

——

feels, but the tone of her letter describes a warmth and comfort that she experiences with her father. Brenda's letter, however, seems a desperate plea for acceptance. What she's really expressing is a desire to be close.

From the letters we've received, our experience with kids, and the latest social science research, it appears that, for most families, it's up to the father to determine the strength of the connection in his relationship with his daughter. If this is true, every father must ask himself (and perhaps even ask his daughter) one question: How close are we?

The Role Fathers Play

During the past several decades of studies on the role of parents in the family, only a small handful of studies have focused specifically on fathers. Of those, the overwhelming majority were devoted exclusively to incestuous and abusive relationships. The father-child relationship is by far the most understudied of all human relationships, and fatherhood in general is the most understudied of all human roles. One research team reported that "a father was once popularly viewed as a distant, uninvolved role—a biological necessity, but a social accident, according to one famous definition."[1]

Perhaps this historically negative view of fatherhood has caused too little interest in the role a father plays. Yet all of us know that, for good or bad, our own fathers played a very important role in our lives. Only during the last few years have researchers started to take a serious look at the impact dads have on their kids. In seeking to understand how a father affects his children, researchers J. S. Turner and D. B. Helms summarized their findings this way:

> Until recently the role and impact of the father in child care has been overlooked. While the importance of the father in the household is generally recognized, part of

the problem is that American society has been "mother-centered" in its philosophy of child care. . . . [But current] research has clearly indicated that the father has strong influences on the child's overall emotional, social, and intellectual development. His presence and the attention that he directs toward his children has short- and long-term benefits. The absence of his care also seems to affect the development of the child.[2]

While the results are not yet conclusive, strong evidence suggests that a father's impact on his daughter during adolescence is far-reaching. A daughter's sense of self, for example, is usually connected to how she thinks her father sees her. If she feels that he thinks she is smart, she's far more likely to believe it herself. If she thinks he sees her as stupid or slow, the odds are strong that she will go through life believing it. While this is not universal, the majority of authentically confident women were raised by parents, and usually fathers, who constantly told them they were sharp and gifted leaders. A woman may achieve a sense of wholeness and health apart from the assurances of a committed, loving father, but she has a far better chance with one who cared about her as a young adolescent woman.

The Nature of Father-Adolescent Daughter "Closeness"

The term associated with relational closeness in the family system is *attachment*. Attachment is defined as a feeling of closeness and intimacy with another person. Generally, attachment theory has focused on infants and their primary caretakers—usually mothers. But adolescent attachment is now understood as an important way to describe how close a young person feels to his or her parents (and peers). The strategic relational concept of adolescent attachment is gaining strength as one of the most important factors in an adolescent's development.

What is important for fathers to know is that attachment

seems to matter more than any other developmental character-istic in the father-adolescent relationship. When trying to under-stand how close or attached a father-adolescent relationship is, social scientists measure the adolescent's *perception* of how close he or she feels to the father. Why not measure the father's per-ception of the attachment in the relationship? Researchers have discovered that it doesn't make any measurable difference what a father may believe, or even what an independent observer believes, about the relationship. The only thing that matters in the long run for the child's development is how *the adolescent feels* about the relationship. If she feels close to her father, the relationship is considered close or highly attached. If she feels distant from her father, the relationship is seen to be distant or detached.

Attachment is different for adolescents than for infants. Obviously, there's no way to measure the sense of attachment in infants until they are old enough to talk about feelings and per-ceptions. In infant attachment research, a set of inferences is derived by trained observers of the relationship. It is an inexact method of research at best. For adolescents, the idea of attach-ment comes from how an adolescent *feels* about a given rela-tionship, regardless of what others see or experience. For adolescents, it is not the actual attachment that is being mea-sured but rather their *perception* of the feelings around attach-ment. Adolescent attachment is a far more accurate and helpful notion for understanding a young person's view of life and how he or she will live. If, for example, a father thinks he is fairly close to his daughter, but the daughter feels that they are actu-ally very distant, the daughter will live her life as disconnected from her dad. This in turn could cause her great pain as she moves through adolescence. Conversely, Dad may feel like he's failing miserably with his daughter. Yet, if *she* believes they are close, she will experience life as one set free by the perceived security of a close attachment relationship with her dad.

Adolescent attachment is not some lofty theory without any grounding in reality. Many researchers are concluding that the most important factor in how a child will respond to life's circumstances is the perception she carries of her attachment to her parents, and more specifically, to her father. Even those developmentalists who have virtually ignored adolescent attachment are beginning to recognize this growing body of evidence. As leading developmental author and educator John Santrock notes:

> Adolescents who were securely attached to parents also were securely attached to peers; those who were insecurely attached to parents were more likely to be insecurely attached to peers. And in another investigation, college students who were securely attached to their parents as children were more likely to have securely attached relationships with friends, dates, and spouses than their insecurely attached counterparts.[3]

Daddy,

I was just writing you 'cause I was thinking about you. I have been doing it a lot lately. I have so many things to ask and say. I always wonder why you don't love me or want to be around me. What could I have done in my sixteen years to make you hate me? It really hurts me deep inside and always will. It affects me every day of my life and will for the rest of it. I pray that one day we could be like all of the other girls and dads I see. I feel so left out.

P.S. I'll always love you, no matter what.

—Lisa, 16, Orlando, FL

For daughters, the feeling of closeness or attachment to their fathers is extremely important to their growth as women. These maturing women want and need to make a clear break from the bonds and roles of childhood. Every daughter must be set free to grow up, to experience life on her own, and to develop a personal sense of autonomy and identity.

For a daughter to break free from seeing herself as a child, she deeply desires and intuitively knows that she needs a close, warm, and intimate relationship with both her mother and her father. As she grows into adolescence, she no longer experiences her mother as a primary nurturer and caretaker; she desires to relate to her as a friend. This process takes several years and is not without struggle until they are both able to first recognize and then handle this switch in roles.

This is the time when a daughter's father plays such an important role in her life. He is the one she needs to form an attachment with while she begins to shift roles with her mother. She knows she must separate from Mom, for to become a woman she needs to see herself as a woman distinct from her mother. But she also knows that she cannot venture too far out there on her own as she takes those baby steps into adulthood. Adolescence is a time of *transition,* and a daughter needs her dad to catch her when she falls and to encourage her to keep moving ahead on this perilous yet exhilarating journey.

Because the power of father–adolescent daughter attachment is a relatively new concept, it is rarely addressed in books and articles. A few child development experts, however, have observed the process of shifting attachment needs from the mother to the father. Carol Gilligan, for example, who specializes in young women's development, describes this process:

> For women, the developmental markers of separation
> (from mother) and attachment (to father), allocated
> sequentially to adolescence and adulthood, seem in
> some sense to be fused . . . [but this is] currently
> obscured in psychological texts.[4]

Of course, both adolescent boys and girls need and desire to break off from the dependent relationship they had with their moms and develop more mature strong attachment relationships with their fathers. Boys have the same need of father attachment as do girls, but how they express and describe their need, how they see their fathers fulfilling their desires, and how they ultimately experience this attachment is very different from girls, at least in North American culture.

Researchers have observed two general differences between a boy's understanding of his father-attachment needs and a girl's understanding of the same. First, a girl is more in tune with what she wants from the relationship. Second, a girl is more aware of what is actually going on in the relationship.

An in-depth analysis into adolescent girls' needs is found in the book *Meeting at the Crossroads: The Landmark Book About the Turning Points in Girls' and Women's Lives.* This study discovered that a widespread trait of adolescent girls is the ability to intuitively perceive complex relational dynamics and alter their behavior accordingly: "Girls talk about the importance of paying close attention, of observing carefully, in determining the existence or extent of another person's pain."[5]

In our culture, girls talk more than boys do about relationships. They allow themselves to feel more in relationships than do boys, and they thoughtfully consider their own relational needs more than their male counterparts do. A son may want to be closer to his dad, but when he and his dad throw a ball around, he is generally somewhat satisfied. For a boy, in most cases, time spent together is usually all that matters.

For a girl, relational activities are a means to an end. She wants the emotional intimacy that comes with closeness and attachment, and so she will gladly participate in activities that she hopes will serve to deepen her relationship with her father. But she will not be satisfied until an intimate connection is established and growing.

Studies are just now being done to continue the quest to probe the depths of these understudied, mysterious, and highly complex relationships. But the early indications on the father–adolescent daughter relationship are overwhelming: This relationship is powerful, important, and has long-lasting impact on developing adolescents.

Do fathers desire a warm, intimate relationship with their daughters? Undoubtedly. Do daughters desire the same? Absolutely! What, then, must a father do to prove to his daughter that he, too, desires to connect with her? First, we'll look at obstacles to a close relationship and then explore four ways to make it happen.

Obstacles to Father–Adolescent Daughter Attachment

Your Own History

Few fathers in today's culture have seen models of what it means to attach to a daughter. The fathers who were raised from the 1950s until the 1970s experienced a cultural understanding of fatherhood in which men were seen as benevolent advice-givers who basically left the parenting role to the mothers. Naturally, exceptions abound. But in our society, few men have been taught what it means to parent a daughter. Even today, men's organizations are calling fathers to the importance of being nurturing parents, but the focus remains on being a good father to *sons*. Virtually no one is talking about how a father can (and must) invest in his daughter.

The important thing for you and your daughter to consider is the impact of your own history on the way you see the father role. What kind of models have you seen? Did you grow up with a warm, relational, and nurturing father who enjoyed close relationships with his children? Or was your father distant, unconnected, and removed from the family's daily affairs? The odds are great that you will relate to your kids in the same way your father related to you. You can work to break the trend, but the older you get, the more you will hear your dad's voice coming out of you as you interact with your own family.

Specifically, when it comes to being a dad to your daughter, how your own father treated your sisters and/or how he honored, respected, and valued your mother has planted seeds of behavior deep inside you that cannot help but come out as you deal with your own daughter. Many fathers want to be different from their dads, yet they are held back by powerful unseen forces that cause them to maintain multigenerational patterns of neglect and distance. The best antidote to a poor model of father-attachment is to take a close look at your family history and commit to working through the patterns and voices that keep you from caring for your daughter in the way she needs and deserves.

In other words, does your history and experience keep you from developing a close and attached relationship with your daughter? She's growing up and she needs you, Dad.

Leaving It Up to Her

"If or when she needs me, she knows I'll always be there for her. All she's got to do is ask." This can be called the "parenting by default" method of raising daughters. But it's clear that unless a father proactively decides that he's going to cultivate an intimate relationship with his adolescent daughter and reaches out to her, it will not happen.

Dear Jerk (remember when you called me that?),
Remember when you said it was up to us (kids) if we
wanted to have a relationship with you? Well, let me tell
you now that is the biggest bunch of bull I've ever heard!
—May, 15, Dallas, TX

Being Unavailable

The demands of our hectic world are overwhelming. It's almost a cliché to say that. But it's so true that it's often hard for fathers to remember just what is important as they go through each day.

The years with your daughter are few and precious. She needs you to be around and to keep her on the "front burner" of your schedule. It's easy to forget how deeply our children long to connect with us and even easier to forget how much they *need* to connect with us. But we must be diligent and disciplined, or we will miss the opportunity to love our daughters into adulthood.

> Dear Dad,
> Some nights I would stay up crying until 3:00 A.M. when you were gone on a trip, wishing you would come and comfort me and say it was all right. You never did.
> P.S. I can't wait until you are home for good!
>
> —Virginia, 11, Kansas City

Fear

There's no question that the biggest obstacle fathers face in attaching to their daughters is summed up in one word: fear. What do I *say*? How do I *act*? What happens when we argue and fight? How do I know the balance between tough love and discipline, between compassion and forgiveness?

In addition to the nuts-and-bolts, everyday issues fathers face, there lurks the broader and more complex dynamic of what happens when your daughter's body changes from Shirley Temple to Cheryl Ladd. As the inevitability of physiological change begins to affect how a daughter looks, moves, and dresses, most fathers are caught off guard, and many are uncomfortable. No longer does it "feel right" to give your daughter that bear hug or bounce her on your knee. She seems more like a woman and less like a little girl, and this can change how you feel and think about her. It also can change how you treat her. Yet it's vital for you to remember that even with a seventeen-year-old body, she is still your twelve-year-old daughter! And as she changes, she needs you more than ever. Letting these changes sneak up on you is forgivable. But letting these changes drive you away from her is relational suicide, for both you and her.

Making It Happen

Your daughter wants you to attach to her, but she will probably wait for you to take the initiative. As an adolescent girl, it's likely that she's quite intuitive relationally, and she needs to know that you truly want to be close to her. She also needs to know that you are willing to do what it takes to be close to her before she will open up to a highly attached relationship. This is a process that can take many months or even years to achieve, depending on how close your relationship has been during her growing up years. But every father can make it happen. It's possible to develop a deeply attached relationship with your adolescent daughter.

Unfortunately, father-daughter attachment does not occur through a specific set of techniques or follow-the-manual methodology. Building a close relationship with your daughter takes a new way of thinking. Let's look at four principles that will help create the framework for a father and his adolescent daughter to build a lifelong attachment bond.

Knowing That It's Your Job
If your daughter knows you care enough about her to gently and carefully pursue her, even when she acts as though she doesn't want to be pursued, she will intuitively begin to trust you. And that is one of the key issues in healthy attachment. It's not a

"constantly on her back" kind of pursuing, but rather the tender, subtle, and consistent way you show her that she matters to you.

> *Dear Daddy,*
>
> *I sometimes find it hard to say thank you, and I wonder if you know how much I love you and appreciate all you do for me. Thank you for all your words of wisdom and all of your guidance in my walk with the Lord. Thank you for listening to me cry about things that are so small but that hurt so much! Something that I never thanked you for—my knee surgery and making me call you when I get where I'm going. Thank you for loving Christ and praying for me every day. I admire you—you are the best daddy in the whole world.*
>
> —Pooh Bear, 14, Glendale, CA

Don't leave it up to your daughter to come to you. Just like the parable of the Good Shepherd in Luke 15, let her know that you will always be out there seeking to care for her and connect with her, even when she runs away.

She does need space to develop a healthy sense of self apart from the family, as well as the room to begin to make her own choices and decisions. Knowing that it's your job to attach to her means that, as you allow her freedom to grow up and find her way, you are there—praying, listening, and caring every step of the way.

Knowing What She Needs

Without considering her developmental processes and individual needs, a father could actually do more harm than good if he simply tries to "attach" to his daughter in his own way and in his own time. Remember, the idea of father-adolescent attachment matters *only from the perspective of the adolescent*. You,

Dad, are not the one who needs to obtain and experience the depth of relationship and attachment. Watch out for those signs and signals that tell you how she's feeling and what she's going through. Your task then, as we will discuss later, is to be a guide more than a boss, a friend more than a protector, and a teacher more than a judge.

Using the Calendar

If you're like most American men, unless a priority gets put on your schedule, it won't get attention. The Stephen Covey revolution (*The 7 Habits of Highly Effective People*) was so simple in concept yet profound in impact. Essentially, this management and lifestyle guru has told millions of people about the value of ordering life around what is important. He's made a lot of money by cleverly stating the obvious in a way that sounds new and profound. How did this happen? Covey and other you-can-make-it-happen types touched a nerve inside people with the message: You know what's important and you want to live healthy, whole lives. Now, do it!

Most fathers who think about it know that they need and want to spend significant time with their adolescent daughters. But many don't know what they need to do with that time. That's why we've written this book—not as a superficial "how-to" manual, but as a catalyst for the desire that God has placed inside every caring parent's heart. As a dad, you were *created for intimate relationships* (despite what pop-psychologists say to the contrary). Your daughter is "flesh of your flesh" and she longs to connect with you as she enters the minefield of adolescence.

Now, take that inner desire and make the decision to change the way you live by opening up time to take walks with her, go to breakfast, write a note, watch a rainstorm, or talk on the phone. Learn how to "waste" time efficiently. Learn the art of listening to the silence of intimate relationship. Slow down, relax, and breathe in the joy of an attached relationship with your daughter.

Trusting God's Call

God knows exactly what He's doing when He gives us children. A child is God's way of saying to us as parents, "Here's how precious you are to me. Your joy is but a meager taste of the pleasure I receive from loving you." The term *father* is a gift to allow us into the heart of God by pointing to the intimate and personal nature of the relationship He offers to each one of His children. And as He loves you, He also loves your daughter, far more than you do!

To parent in today's dark and lonely world is a frightening thought. Danger and evil seem to lurk in the shadows, waiting to devour anyone who ventures too far from the light. It's amazingly easy for even the heartiest of parents to be paralyzed with fear over the "What if . . ." questions when it comes to their kids. We must learn how to relax, let go, and trust in God's power, love, and sovereignty.

He allowed us the honor of loving this precious soul for a few short years. Our role as parents is not to make sure the road is clear and that our child will never stumble, fail, make a mistake, or disappoint us. Though we are His flawed and human children, God desires for us be the kind of father He is with us, trusting that He's firmly in command of the universe, which includes our daughters.

May God grant you the faith to trust Him and to love as He loves. Attach to your daughter, but never stand in the way of her attachment to the One who is her first and true love.

Dear Dad,

I don't think there is anyone on this earth who God could have picked to be a better father for me. I know He couldn't have. I just want you to know that no matter what, I love you. I will always love you, and I will never lose you, because I'll be up there in God's kingdom with you for eternity. You can count on it.

—Sally Jo, 19, Nashville, TN

CHAPTER FIVE

Communication: The Heart of Father-Daughter Intimacy

Dear Dad,

I love you very much but we don't spend a lot of time together. We are two totally different people. I wish we had more things in common. I love to play soccer and you love to hunt. I love to talk on the phone and you love to watch sports. I think that is why we fight so much. I would love to spend more time with you. I would love to be able to talk about my problems to you. I love you very much.

—Brigette, 13, Grand Rapids, MI

Communication can be defined as "the art of being understood." Most children think their parents never listen to them; most parents think their children never talk! Parents often think they've communicated with their child when they have verbally (and, in their view, clearly) expressed their thoughts, wishes, or demands. To these parents, communication is the art of speaking logically, rationally, forcefully. But to a child, especially an adolescent, communication occurs when a parent is more concerned with seeing the child's point

From Dee
Memories of an Adult Daughter

———

It took years of adult life—faith, marriage, and children—for me to be able to hold a conversation with my dad. All the years I was growing up I never really knew how to talk to him, and he really didn't know how to talk to me! We were like two strangers walking side by side on a crowded street. When I was with him, nothing was there!

Talking for me came easy, especially with those I loved—both men and women, guys and girls. As a teenager, I could spend hours talking to a friend on the phone or hanging out with some guys I knew (especially my boyfriend). But when it came to my dad, it felt like he just wanted the basic facts in three minutes or less. I found myself feeling like an item in his appointment book instead of someone he wanted to invest his time in.

We used to spend more time together when I was

(continued)

of view than with any sort of dialogue.

To most kids, the biggest problem with parent-child communication is that parents are so busy talking that they never listen. To most parents, the biggest problem with parent-child communication is that kids never seem to *want* to open up to them.

Perhaps this is among the most basic of all family problems and issues—a failure on both sides to realize that expressing one's view is only one component of the communication process. Other essential elements of the communication process involve tone of voice, timing of the discussion, eye contact, meaning of words and terms, body language, and the way the receiver experiences (or feels) the message. In short, parents and adolescents often misunderstand each other, and both usually blame the other for the ensuing conflict.

Dear Dad,

I don't know why you don't want to talk to me. I've tried so many times, but when you are ready to talk, you only lecture. I want you to know what I think for once. You've told me my whole life what you think, and now it's my turn. Come on, Dad, I know you can talk to me without lecturing . . . you do it with [my brother]. Is it because I'm a girl that you don't want to talk to me?

—MaryAnne, 17, San Diego, CA

John Gray, author of *Men Are from Mars, Women Are from Venus*, has made a fortune telling Americans that the difference between men and women is simple: They're from different planets! On Venus, according to this popular prophet, women love to talk. This is his explanation for the way women interact and why they seem to relate better with each other than with men.

On Mars, men live in caves, where they fight and struggle with each other, are aggressive and domineering, do not talk much, and flee relational depth. Men, therefore, are nearly incapable of being emotionally and relationally intimate. This philosophy states that because men do not like to talk, and because it is not natural for them, they have a hard time experiencing depth in relationships *simply because they are from another planet!* The result of this overly simplistic descriptive formula is that men are encouraged—indeed, given permission—to deny any need to emotionally and verbally connect with others in a meaningful way.

In our culture, the majority of men do seem to live out this celestial description. But according to the Bible, both men and women are created in the image of God. Of course there are differences between men and women. And it's true that men as a group tend to be less verbal than women. But to first trivialize and then ultimately glorify a man's difficulty in intimate conversation is to rob him of the joy of experiencing relationships the way God intended.

As God's image bearers, both men and women possess a powerful and beautiful gift—communication—that gives them the unique ability to allow another person into the deepest part

little. But as a young woman we became virtual strangers. I remember wishing that we could go back to the way things were when I was a child. I wished we could be a family again and that I could know what it was like to have a dad who was there for me.

I would wonder: *Does he ever think about me? Does he miss me as much as I miss him?* So many times, especially late at night, I wondered what it would be like to be friends with my dad—to talk and to listen. It's what I wanted all along. It's all I ever wanted from him.

———

of themselves. Contrary to popular wisdom, sex is not the most intimate of human activities. The most sacred and vulnerable thing any of us can do is to share the intimacy of our thoughts with another person. Communication is what defines us as divine image bearers, and the willingness to participate meaningfully in an intimate verbal and nonverbal exchange is the greatest gift God has given to us in relationships.

We are most human when we are listening and talking, and men are endowed by God to be every bit as verbal as women. It is our cultural training, popular mythology, and socially reinforced stereotyping that holds men back from being fully themselves. As a father, the greatest gift you can offer the daughter you love is to connect with her at the deepest level through the hard work of intimate communication.

> *Dear Dad,*
> *I love you, but we don't talk like we should. I know you let me do stuff that Mom doesn't let me do, but we have to talk at least once a week. We love each other, so can we talk, please?*
> *I love you like crazy,*
>
> —Stephanie, 12, Lexington, KY

A father must learn how to communicate with his daughter if he's going to develop the kind of relationship that will launch her into healthy adulthood. He must learn to recognize which modes of communication best convey information and which cause her to rebel.

Your daughter knows this intuitively, for women in our society are much more in tune with this truth. What she doesn't yet know, however, is that you have been socialized to hide emotions, to avoid verbal intimacy, and to give a nod to any deep interaction with a kind of rhetorical "head fake." She's heard you proclaim your love for her, but when she hits adolescence she's waiting for you to show your love by spending time and energy in the fascinating world of verbal give-and-take. This is where she truly lives, and her desire is to share this place with you. But it's the rare father who has even approached his daughter in the sanctuary of her soul. Most dads don't even know it exists.[1]

What does it take to enter this holy place of intimate communication with your daughter? Here are six hints to help you leave Mars and enter the land of Venus:

- take time to talk
- become a world-class listener
- develop the art of asking questions
- tell her about what you feel as well as what you think
- constantly bless her
- remember that communication is more than mere words

These tips will enable even the coldest and most distant dad to break down the communication barrier that seeks to destroy his relationship with his adolescent daughter.

Take Time to Talk

You cannot escape this axiom of relating to your daughter: It takes time to build your relationship with her.

Maybe you feel that you do spend a lot of time with your daughter. Perhaps you do things to support her, like going to her dance recital or watching her play a sport. While she may appreciate this attention, most likely she wants more from you. She wants you to invest in your relationship with her, to "waste" time with her.

Men in our culture have been trained to order and structure their lives in such a way that life is more a problem to be solved than a life to be lived. But your daughter knows better, and so do you. What is most important in life is relationship, especially with the people we love the most.

Dear Dad,
I have become a young woman now, and i'd like to talk to you about some of the difficult times and the good times. What i really want to say is that in the future, i hope we can spend more time together.

—LouAnn, 13, Madisonville, KY

LouAnn knows what she wants from her dad. The tragedy is that she may not have felt comfortable telling him what she wrote to us.

Your daughter wants to take time to be with you. Do you really want to take time to be with her? Once you decide that you really do care, and you determine that she is, indeed, one of the highest priorities in your life, you're well on the way to truly connecting with her. Communication can only happen when you want to be there. You pave the way for the chance to talk and to listen.

Become a World-Class Listener

Dad,
i want to give you this [letter], but i don't think it's my place to tell you [these things]. And i'm not sure if you would listen. You've been a great encouragement to me, always admiring and giving me advice on how to go for my goals. But at the same time, you never seem to listen. You like to interrupt or tell me i'm wrong. Sometimes i feel that you love me but that you don't respect what i say because i'm a girl. When you always listen and respect my brother but not me, that's just how i feel.

—A. J., 16, St. Louis, MO

In all likelihood, A. J.'s father would be hurt if he were to read this letter (remember, the names and cities have been changed). He might think he's doing a great job of caring for his daughter. He must be aware that he's a "great encouragement" to her, and he may be feeling fairly confident in his abilities as a dad. But the troubling truth is that the older A. J. gets, the more she needs him to change his style. She needs him to talk less and listen more. In chapter three we talked about respect. The most important way to communicate respect is to learn how to listen.

Here's a little test to see from a daughter's perspective what kind of listener you are. Give yourself a 1 (terrible) to 5 (terrific) score for how your daughter would grade you on each question:

_____ 1. I like to get my father's point of view on things I'm concerned about.
_____ 2. I tell my father about my problems and troubles.
_____ 3. Talking over my problems with my father makes me feel good and safe.
_____ 4. When we discuss things, my father cares about my point of view.
_____ 5. If my father knows something is bothering me, he asks me about it.
_____ 6. My father can tell when I'm upset about something.
_____ 7. My father helps me to talk about my difficulties.
_____ 8. My father has his own problems, but I still don't mind telling him about mine.

This instrument records your perception of how well you communicate with your daughter. Add up the numbers you recorded and compare your final score with this table:

08 - 13 Get a clue, Dad!
14 - 20 You've got some work ahead of you.
21 - 27 Not bad, but she still needs you to show you're willing to work at it.
28 - 34 Pretty good! But don't rest on your laurels; she

needs your focused attention.

35 - 40   Way to go, Dad! You're there for her.

Remember, this is a test of *your perception* of how your daughter sees your communication. If you *really* want to know, ask her to take the same test. She may not feel free to be completely honest with you, but if you've worked hard to prove that you really want to know how you're doing, she'll give you some idea of what she thinks. Communication with your daughter is not so much how you feel, rather it is how she perceives your ability and willingness to listen to her.

Develop the Art of Asking Questions

Good discussions rarely just happen with any teenager. The busyness of their lives; the constant demands placed on them; the shifting expectations of parents, teachers, and friends; and the ever present nagging thoughts about self-worth and identity all keep the mind and lifestyle of an adolescent preoccupied. It's a wonder our kids survive at all! Add to this the confusion of transitioning from childhood to adulthood, and you have a person dealing with incredible stress, living on the edge of a breakdown.

Some people think this description is a gross overstatement, and it may be for some kids who are temperamentally better suited to cope with life's demands. But for the majority of kids, we believe that life is a never-ending drag race — powerful engines at full bore, no time to stop and regroup — as they live on the edge of frenzied and dangerous exhilaration, never really knowing if they are winning or losing the race. It's not easy to get those who are feeling this way to sit down and focus long enough for a meaningful conversation. Fathers (and mothers) are the ones who must help their children slow down and experience an intimate, trusting connection with them.

We hate to be blunt, but it's a fact that most parents are terrible at drawing out their kids' thoughts. The questions parents ask are usually so obvious and directive that a child doesn't have to stop and think to answer them; or they're so obscure that they make little sense in the world of an adolescent. A question like, "Did you have a good time?" or "Did you have a good day at school?" may sound to an adult like a leading question. But it's all too easy to say "Yes," "No," or even to grunt a sophomoric noise in response.

A question like, "What's one thing at school that made you feel good today?" is more likely to help your daughter reflect on something positive and then express it to you. Even better is a question like, "What's the worst thing about the worst teacher at school?" If she believes you really want to know, and you won't criticize her response, she'll easily become engaged in the conversation.

It's not just the *wording* of the question that makes a difference, it's the *timing* as well. A question asked over a Coke or while taking a walk—a question that drew little response the night before—could initiate a conversation that lasts through the dinner hour.

As you attempt to become a world-class listener, remember that your daughter may be carrying all kinds of burdens that even she may not understand. Sometimes the best way to listen is simply to ask to sit with her for a few minutes and talk about your day—not the "work" part but the "heart" part. If she seems interested, and you sense her readiness to respond, then turn the conversation around so that she feels safe and comfortable enough to open up.

Tell Her What You Feel, Not Just What You Think

Most contemporary men think in terms of problems and solutions. At work this mindset is even more pronounced. But this isn't what your daughter wants or even needs to hear from you. She's far more interested in how you *feel* about any given situation or circumstance. This may be the toughest part of the father-daughter relationship—that your daughter is probably not the slightest bit interested in the mechanical or corporate struggles you have at work. She will at best feign interest whenever you drift to the business aspect of your day. But watch her perk up when you tell her how it felt when your boss criticized you for poor performance, or how hard it's been to watch the people in your company who have been laid off.

If you're honest, you know that you process these types of feelings every day. The trick is to have the courage to admit to your daughter the fear, loneliness, and insecurity you experience, even if you're tempted to think she won't understand or she won't be interested. She's far more interested in these things than in the business side of life or even her own activities and interests. She wants to know *you,* and she is intuitively capable of recognizing that you may try to hide behind the technical aspects of life. If she senses a defensiveness in you, or an unwillingness to allow her into your heart on this level, she will shut you out of hers.

> Dad,
> You've been an excellent dad, as much as you could. You have been through so much and learned so much wisdom but you just won't share it with me. You're always saying that your dad told you not to share your problems with your kids, but it's time to share your thoughts and beliefs. I'm really interested in what you've experienced and learned and believed. Tell me about you, Daddy. I really want to know you!
>
> —Samantha, 15, Charlotte, NC

Constantly Bless Her

When Gary Smalley and John Trent wrote *The Blessing,* they reminded readers of an invaluable philosophy of parenting that many cultures have experienced for years. They describe the power that parents, and especially fathers, have in the lives and psyches of their kids by regularly offering the simple gift of a verbal affirmation. To bless our children is to hand them a lifelong gift of emotional, relational, familial, and spiritual rootedness. When we express to our kids how we believe in them as people, we help create an environment where their minds and hearts are shaped according to that blessing.

Henri Nouwen says that "to bless is *benedicere,* which means literally: saying good things."[2] The blessing you give your daughter is the gift of a "good word" that you proclaim to and for her. As these "good words" pile up and form layers of blessings within her soul, she will find herself surrounded by messages that will be a reminder of her unique beauty, her high standing before her family and God, and her ability to make an impact as she lives out who God has created her to be.

The letters we receive from daughters seem to fall neatly into one of two categories: those that reflect lives shaped by loving fathers who have spent years blessing their daughters, and those that reflect lives in which the blessing has been withheld. Indeed, the difference between a healthy father–daughter relationship and one in crisis is relative, constantly changing, and runs somewhere along a continuum between these two polarities. Those girls who tend to feel better about themselves seemed to express that their fathers had intentionally passed on scores of blessings through the years.

Communication Is More Than Words

I am a very focused person. In fact, when I read, it takes a focused, all-out assault to interrupt me. It doesn't matter whether I'm reading the newspaper, a cheesy novel, or Calvin's *Institutes.* When I read, my mind goes into a trancelike state of concentration.

Enter my daughter, whom I love, as I read how the Colorado Rockies are the team to beat in the National League pennant race. She has been run over (literally) by one of her brothers (who happens to also be my son, but that's another book), and is in need of a sympathetic paternal ear and a focused fatherly heart. She comes into the kitchen and stands a few feet from where I sit, reading my paper, and doesn't make a sound (not counting, of course, the subtle yet discernible occasional whimpers of pain made more intense by the frustration of knowing I'm clueless). Of course I don't hear or notice her. Finally she speaks, "Dad! I've been standing here for five minutes!" I, being the fathering expert, momentarily glance up and say, "Oh, hi honey" and return to my morning's first love.

At this stage of our lives, my daughter still feels that I, while exasperatingly ignorant, am within some range of hope. Thus, she approaches the paper. "Dad, I need to talk to you!"

"Okay, honey, I'm almost done," I say, not looking up.

"DAD! I NEED TO TALK TO YOU—NOW!"

I finally get the message. And I am truly sorry, for I love my daughter and really want her to know that she's far more important to me than the sports section. (Now, for those fathers whose inner being is screaming, "I need my time, too," and "Sometimes it's good for kids to wait," I agree, to a point. But the sports page?)

This time it's too late. I've let her down. The moment has passed, and I've allowed my inability to focus to push her away.

With the crazy schedules we keep and the myriad pressures we all face as parents, our daughters are often left behind to wait for us to make room for their seemingly inconsequential interruptions. I want to be the kind of father who is willing, whenever possible, to be available to my daughter. There must be thoughtful balance, for children can take advantage of a parent who unthinkingly allows no personal space or boundaries. But that is rarely my problem. I am far more guilty of not focusing on her than I am of allowing her to invade my necessary boundaries.

How about you?

CHAPTER SIX

"Who Am I?"
A Daughter's Search
for Identity

Dear Dad,

Last week when you asked me, "Who do you think you are, young lady?" I had no answer for you. I was so mad and frustrated and hurt that I wanted to scream and cry, but all I did was stare at you, then I turned and walked away. I wanted to say, "Do you know who I am?" I'm your daughter, and if you don't know who I am, who does? Then, when the words weren't there, I wanted to tell you that I have no idea who I am! But I couldn't tell you any of this. I was mad, you were mad, and we never talked about it. Now that I think about it, I really wish I knew who I am. And I really wish that you knew who I am.

—Sarah, 15, Georgia

"Who do you think you are?"

This worn-out query is most often spoken on an exhale of frustration. But what a question to ask a daughter in the throes of adolescence! In her seemingly endless search for a clear sense of self, a fifteen-year-old girl cannot hope to satisfactorily

———

When I was growing up, the world was a strange and cruel place. It seemed to shout so many messages at me:

- I had to be thin, fit, and confident to be popular.
- I needed to get a good education to succeed in life.
- I needed to stand tall as a woman and to forge new career trails for future women in the American workplace.
- I needed to be married and have children in order to be complete as a woman.
- I needed to be involved in the church, giving myself away to others, even before I knew for sure who that "self" was!

Every girl faces a similar list of expectations, voices, and opinions, and usually they are as subtle as they are powerful. They felt so overwhelming to me at times that I just wanted to give in, remain a kid, and avoid the whole adult thing all together.

———

respond to such a question. What is she supposed to say? Most girls at this stage of development are desperately trying to find out for themselves.

Much discussion has taken place lately over the exact meaning of the concept of *identity*. Some claim that it is our sense of self as we relate to others or to the roles we play. Others refer to identity as specific areas of behavior or lifestyle, such as sexual or familial identity. Still others seek to describe who we see ourselves to be underneath our behavior and beyond our self-expression. One thing is certain, Dad: Your adolescent daughter is on a quest to discover who she is, and she wants your help.

Sarah's letter reflects this key struggle in the life of every adolescent. The technical name for it is *individuation*. Basically, it is the process of becoming an adult. Contrary to much popular thought, the process of individuation does not mean that your daughter wishes to make a clean break from you and your family. It simply means that she wants (and needs) to become her own person within the context of your family. This is the essence of the adolescent journey—moving from being a child who is defined by her family to functioning as an independent adult member of the family system.

There are two aspects of individuation: the formation of personal identity ("Who am I?") and the development of personal autonomy ("My choices matter!"). This chapter deals with the first issue, identity. We'll talk about autonomy in chapter seven.

Marcia's Story

Marcia is sixteen. She's outgoing, polite, and very smart. She plays the piano, is a star soccer player, and has several guys wanting her to notice them. She appears confident and self-assured. She can look you in the eye and smile with genuine warmth each time she talks to you. Anyone who has been around her feels as though she's as solid a kid as they come. She's spent a lifetime making sure people in her life believe that. But there's more to Marcia's story.

When she was twelve, Marcia's parents went through a difficult time. Her dad left home for a few months "to think about what I need," he told Marcia. The day he left he told her, as the eldest of four kids, "I need you to take care of your brothers and sisters, Marcia. Your mom and I are going through a rough time right now, and she won't be much help. I need to live my own life for a while, so I need you to make sure that everybody is okay. I'm counting on you to be grown up. I know you won't let me down." With that, he turned and walked out the door.

During the next several months, Marcia's father came home to visit a few times, but he was virtually out of their lives. Those rare times when he did return, he talked to her mother and played with her little brothers and baby sister. Marcia was tall for her age and had developed to the point that she looked many years older. Her dad didn't seem to know how to react to her. He continued to admonish her to "keep holding the family together" and told her that he was proud of "how well you are doing." Yet he seemed distant from Marcia's perspective. She felt that he never wanted to talk to her and didn't seem to care what *she* was needing or how much she needed someone to watch out for *her.* She was forced to play a role—the mature, confident, self-assured, stable member of the family.

By now she was fourteen, a young woman growing up with the burden of having to be all things to all people but not having any idea who or what she was inside. No one had allowed her to take the time to figure out just who was hiding beneath that calm and cool exterior.

I met Marcia when I was speaking at a youth conference. I had mentioned during one message that often we try to find our identity in what we do, what we control, and what others say about us.[1] I went on to share that God has created each of us with a smile, and that each person is a precious masterpiece personally sculpted by the hand of the loving Creator.

Marcia was cautious as she approached me, but it was obvious that she wanted to talk. As she told me her story, I saw her countenance change from that of a confident student-athlete to a lost young woman. While she had become adept at creating and then living out a variety of roles, she had lost her sense of self somewhere along the way. She was lost in a family system that forced her to play responsible roles at the expense of exploring who she was. Although she was still young, the years had taken their toll on her and she was deeply wounded.

As she walked away, I couldn't shake the feeling that Marcia's journey will be a long and lonely one for years to come. But at least she had come to realize that she must allow herself to begin the process of finding herself.

Helping Your Daughter in Her Search for Identity

Although we hear much talk today about "sexual identity" and "gender identity," there is much more to your daughter's need to develop her own sense of personal identity.

Much of what a girl discovers about what it means to be a woman is in the modeling and attachment she receives from her mother (and other women). But true growth into womanhood needs to be much more about character, giftedness, passion, and heart than how a young woman lives out her "gender role." This is the gift a father can give his daughter. He can help her to discover and then celebrate the person God sees her to be.

Your daughter was created from the heart of the heavenly Father, knit together by the hand of the Son. By the Spirit, she has been stamped forever with God's image. As she strives to answer the question, "Who am I?", your daughter must continually be reminded that at the core of her being she is God's special child, dearly loved and created for a unique purpose.

A father's role in this process is to help his daughter see that she is already a unique and precious child of God. The search for her identity is more about discovering *who she already is* than about becoming something or someone else.

> ### From Dee
> ### Memories of an Adult Daughter
>
> ---
>
> There were times when I really missed having a dad around. I felt that I was on my own, trying to figure out who I was in the midst of the chaos. Somehow I had to filter through all those voices screaming at me and discover my own identity. I wonder how those years would have been different if I'd had a dad who loved me, talked with me, and blessed me as I grew up?
>
> ---

An old African proverb says, "There is a Dream dreaming us." Author Robert Benson takes this idea further by stating that many people today are "lost somewhere between the dreaming and the coming true."[2] This phrase is especially true for so many young people today. God is thinking about your daughter even as you read this. He has a plan for her—a "dream." Yet, if she's like most kids, she has no idea that she is that precious to the One who created her. Your daughter needs to know that she doesn't have to go on a search for her identity. It is readily available through a relationship with the One who made her. As Augustine said, "My soul was restless until I found my rest in Thee." You need to help her see that we discover who we are when we surrender to the love and chosenness of God.

A Historical Look at Identity

Developmentalist Erik Erikson, writing in 1950, described male identity as being built in terms of experience with the world. In contrast, he said that female identity is determined through relational intimacy. According to modern developmentalists, however, the latest research claims that "there are now fewer gender differences in identity than the earlier studies suggested."[3]

Both adolescent girls and boys need to discover who they are through relational intimacy *and* life experience. Throughout the history of developmental theory, it has been assumed that parents play some sort of role. But little attention has been given to this piece of the puzzle. Until just a few years ago, fathers were essentially excluded from the developmental formula. Social scientists now acknowledge that both mothers and fathers "are important figures in the adolescent's development of identity."[4] When placed alongside the research on father attachment, it's clear that during a child's quest for healthy identity formation, both the mother and the father are vital participants in the growing-up process.

Erikson's view that boys and girls discover their identities differently have largely gone unchallenged, even today. Therapist Patricia H. Davis does, however, make a distinction between Erikson's theory and modern views on adolescent girls' development in her book *Counseling Adolescent Girls*:

> Developmental psychologist Erik Erikson describes the ways in which both adolescent boys and girls work to find their own identities in his idea of the "identity crisis." For boys, Erikson's process describes the whole struggle; for most girls, Erikson's theory describes half of what she must accomplish. The second half of a girl's process of identity formation is described by Carol Gilligan; it is the process of coming to 'truth' about the self and how the self negotiates relationships. . . . For

girls this process of forming an identity often involves tricky negotiations. Not too many years ago . . . a girl's options were so few that the question of her adult identity was settled almost as soon as she reached puberty.[5]

While Davis falls into the secular trap of seeing identity solely in terms of roles, she does acknowledge that adolescent girls need a greater degree of sensitivity as they grow up. In terms of the roles women have been encouraged to fill as they flesh out their identity, women's roles today are much more open than even ten years ago. A girl's identity is no longer defined solely by the traditional roles of marriage and motherhood. This is now causing a crisis of sorts in adolescent girls as they seek the answers to the questions "Who am I?" "What do I do with my life, and how do I know?"

In our society girls are explicitly taught that they have both the right and the cultural power to choose their own identity and to create the roles they desire to live out. Implicitly, especially in the church, most girls are expected to go to college and prepare for the future, but always with an eye on finding fulfillment in marriage and in marital and maternal roles. Depending on your church, this message ranges from a subtle suggestion that nags at your daughter internally to an overt statement that reinforces a cultural stereotype no longer existing in our society.

There are still people and churches who teach that women are fully complete only when and if they get married. That teaching leads to a woman's primary identity being found exclusively within the context of that role. How does your daughter navigate such confusing waters? Who is right?

Messages, whether subtle or overt, that tell a young woman who she is by what role she takes on, often cause a struggle within the young woman who is seeking to discover who she is and how she fits in the world. The question is not a matter of "biblical roles," for the culture is so dramatically different today than it was during the life of Jesus and Paul. Some may long for "the good old days," when roles were clear and everyone knew what was expected of them. But this type of thinking will not be able to withstand the tide of cultural change. The current is too strong, and the waves are too powerful for the church to define for young women who they are to be and what specific roles they are to play.

In the meantime, as Christians debate over a woman's role in society, the church, and even the household, adolescent girls are being swept away, lost, insecure, without a place to land. Your daughter needs help as she attempts to discover who she is and how she is to order her life—all within a world that doesn't seem to care very much.

A Father's Role—Seeing Her as Unique

Daughters in today's world need mothers and fathers who are willing to trust God's creative handiwork when it comes to their identities. Society cannot dictate who your daughter is to be, nor is the church called to handle the task. Instead, a daughter needs a few select people in her life who have the conviction and ability to help her become *the person God created her to be!*

During the adolescent journey, a father has a unique opportunity to influence his daughter one way or the other. If he's stuck in the mire of philosophical and pseudo-psychological debate raging over "a woman's place," he may cause her to deny who she is simply to please him. God may have created her with unique and powerful gifts for furthering His kingdom, but this kind of father may also ignore his daughter's natural giftedness and push her into prescribed roles and relationships that can snuff out the creative spark offered her in the miracle of the way God created her.

On the other hand, a father who believes that God knew exactly what He was doing when He created his daughter waits expectantly to see the gift of God as she emerges from the cocoon of adolescence. That is the real joy of parenting—the wonder of seeing your child show signs of the beautiful majesty of God's creation as she discovers who she is in Christ! A father who is willing to love and willing to wait on the Lord; a father who is willing to trust that who his daughter has been created to be, is far better than what she is culturally predetermined to be will receive the reward he desires—a daughter who knows her God and who knows and likes herself.

The following letter came from a daughter whose father seemed to be more concerned with her fitting into cultural expectations than in allowing her to discover her created self.

Dear Dad,

I know you are disappointed in me, but I've been living a lie for many years, and I can't any longer. I don't know how to tell you this, and it's easier to write you than to talk to you, but I have decided that I'm breaking up with [my boyfriend] and dropping out of school [a Christian college]. I've been trying so hard to be the perfect little Christian daughter, and trying to be everything you ever wanted me to be, but I just can't anymore. I don't know who I am or what I want! I don't want to hurt you, but I have been hurting myself for so long, and I have to stop, now!

Dad, I'm still a Christian (you don't have to worry about that), but I don't know if my relationship to God is the same as your relationship to God. I want to follow Jesus, and I want to give my life to Him, but I also want to find out who I am, too! Please try to understand, and don't hate me. I still love you. I will always love you.

—Carol, 20, Salem, OR

The struggle in Carol's letter is obvious. We don't know if she ever gave her dad a similar letter or if she ever told him what she felt. One thing we do know: Carol loves her dad very much. And she feels like she's breaking his heart as she tries to figure out who she is and what she wants and needs out of life. The God she had grown to love, follow, and worship had not seemed the same to her as the God she was raised with. In discovering herself, Carol was also seeking to discover her faith. In the process, she felt that she needed to break away from the suffocating control of her father. He may be a gentle, loving man of God. But her perception of how he controlled her decisions and life made her feel as if she was denying who she was. The journey has been a hard one for Carol. Unfortunately, what she needed from her dad was encouragement in the process instead of a predetermined dictation of who he wanted her to be.

As developmental theorist Carol Gilligan writes:

> Developmental psychologists who are sensitive to the differences between girls and boys as they enter puberty and young adulthood are discovering that this time is often particularly difficult for the girls. Researchers find that in early adolescence, especially, girls are prone to depression and to losing hold of their precious newly emerged identities. This is not surprising in a culture that misunderstands and ignores their perceptions and visions, but is eager to exploit them for financial and other unethical gain.[6]

Harsh words, but a great deal of research supports Gilligan's position. Adolescence is a fragile time for your daughter. In a sea of strange, frightening, and wonderful emotional and physical changes, she is desperately trying to land somewhere safe and solid. She needs to know who she is and how she fits in this rapidly shifting world.

The Comparison Game

As she tries on various roles and pseudo-identities, it will be hard for your daughter not to become adept at the comparison game, measuring herself against everyone and everything.

Some theorists argue that such comparison is a healthy path to discovering identity because it differentiates who we are—our strengths and weakness, our gifts and talents, and our individual personalities and temperaments—from those around us. But common sense seems to scream out just the opposite. In comparing ourselves to others, we become equipped to identify differences, but our natural response to these differences is to see ourselves as lesser than those we are comparing ourselves to!

When we live by comparison, we constantly reinforce our inner conviction that we are not who we want to be. Therefore, we see ourselves as incapable and insignificant in the grand scheme of things. These seeds are sown during adolescence, and this tendency appears to be more pronounced in girls than in boys.

The game doesn't end at adolescence; many adult women continue to suffer from the comparison syndrome. A daughter needs to be told early on that she need not compare herself to others, because she is a valuable, gifted, talented person in her own right.

Mike Yaconelli, owner of Youth Specialties, once told an audience, "I've always thought that when I got to heaven, God would say to me, 'Mike, I'm glad you're here. But, Mike, why weren't you more like Moses? I liked Moses. He was *really* a servant of mine.' But I've only recently come to see that the greatest struggle for me has been to try and live as me! I am now beginning to see that God is more likely to say to me, 'Mike! Welcome, Mike. And, Mike, why weren't you *Mike?*'"

On paper it seems so obvious, almost trite. Yet in your daughter's daily struggle to find her own sense of identity, it's so hard for her simply to be herself. She barely knows who that is. She needs to be reminded that she's the person who hides alone inside her heart. That person has been created by God to soar as one set free to be completely herself.

A Father's Message

We have a ritual in the mornings at our house. When our kids head out the door for the day, we have a message for each one of them. I say, as each one leaves, "Let the Lord love you, and use that love to love others." Dee then offers this daily reminder: "Remember who you are. And, I love you." Our kids tend to respond with an "Okay" as they walk out the door. It's not a tightly controlled ritual, but it is a daily goal for us.

We know that we don't have the power to force our children to "let the Lord love them" or to "remember who they are." And rituals like this can turn into sappy, meaningless grunts if we're not careful. But we want our kids to go through adolescence being reminded every day that who they are and what they have to offer in the world comes from God, who loves them. We are His channels of that love or, as Philip Yancey writes, His "dispensers of grace." We pray that our lives reflect our words, and also that our children will experience the truth behind the words as they try to discover for themselves who they are.

As parents, and especially as fathers, the words we speak can be a potent reservoir of healing and empowerment. May the teaching of our Lord's best friend on earth spur us on to be good and wise stewards of what we say to our children:

> If anyone speaks, he should do it as one speaking the very words of God. If anyone serves, he should do it with the strength God provides, so that in all things God may be praised through Jesus Christ. To him be the glory and the power for ever and ever. Amen. (1 Peter 4:11)

Tell your daughter that she is loved—tell her every day. Remind her that God has made her beautiful, wonderful, and gifted. She is a masterpiece of the living God, and you get to be the messenger of that wild, wonderful truth!

CHAPTER SEVEN

Letting Go: Helping Her Become Autonomous

Dear Dad,
I know it makes you sad to see me grow up, but when are
you going to realize that I'm not eight years old
anymore?! I love you, but you can't seem to understand
that your "precious little baby" is gone forever!

Pam, 17, Orlando, FL

Every daughter is one of a kind. Child developmentalists, family researchers, and therapists all agree that when everything is said and done, every human being is absolutely and completely unique. And because no two children will ever be the same, each child brings to the world a brand-new mix of complex feelings, abilities, temperament, and responsive inclinations.

This great weakness of social science is rarely admitted. Yet, to codify, predict, or even to describe accurately what goes on in an individual's heart, soul, and mind—or how he or she is going to respond to a given set of circumstances—is extremely unlikely if not virtually impossible because no two people are

From Dee
Memories of an Adult Daughter

—

Growing up without a dad around, I can remember feeling as though I didn't have a protector. I was vulnerable to the world around me. I felt like I needed to learn how to take care of myself, stand on my own two feet, be independent and strong. As a result, I broke away from my mom and sister much earlier than I was ready. Although I felt a drive toward independence that I thought I could handle, in reality I lacked the maturity and experience to make healthy or smart decisions. No one could tell me differently, however, for I was on a quest to prove to the world that I was mature and capable.

In hindsight, I realize this push for independence was a defensive reaction to the very thing I needed and longed for the most—the loving safety of a father's arms that were big enough to hold me through the con-

(continued)

alike. God built this gift into us when he created humanity: Every life brings a fresh picture of the creative touch of the Master Artist. No one will ever be the same as someone else.

Oh, sure, genetics play a role in what our kids are like, as does environment. But two kids from the same parents in the same house will often turn out to be different in just about every way. This is especially true when it comes to boys and girls. Gender may not be the key issue in terms of how kids experience and report sibling differences within the family, but to many adolescent girls, it sure feels that way.

Dear Dad,

Don't you know that I need you as much as Ricky? Do you think he is the only one who wants to be with you? You say that you want to be with me, but when I try to talk to you, you just tell me what to do. Ricky got to get his permit when he was old enough, but I'm almost sixteen and you say I'm not ready! Ricky can stay out late with his friends, but you say you "don't know my friends." C'mon, Dad, wake up! You give Ricky so much more freedom than you give me, and yet you still won't talk to me about it!

—Sandra, almost 16, Denver, CO

Sandra's complaint is but a symptom of the core issue of her adolescent struggle — the perception she carries of her father's comparison of her with her brother Ricky. She believes that she's treated differently just because she's a girl and that triggers all kinds of emotions within her. Over time, this can foster an unstable sense of self.

Her letter is more a plea for her father to love her than it is a complaint about her brother. She wants to be listened to and taken seriously. She wants her father not only to love her but to value her. When she observes the relationship her brother and father have, she sees no option but to draw a comparison. Sandra needs her father to recognize her uniqueness in a world that is constantly comparing her to others who are better looking, faster, "cooler," and smarter than she thinks she is. This is tied up with an even more basic need — that her father see her as strong enough to make at least some of her own decisions.

fusion and pain of transition. Arms that responded with love when I made mistakes. Arms that offered me strength and wisdom. Arms that could help prepare me for the vast world and still be there when I wanted to come running back. Deep inside I wanted and needed that safety in order to become the woman God designed me to be. Without it, though I was still young, I was forced to be independent, and to walk my own path through adolescence.

——

The Search for Autonomy

The previous chapter detailed the first life task of an adolescent — the search for identity. Now we turn to the second life task of an adolescent daughter — the need to see her choices as making a difference. This has been called "developing an internal locus of control."

A sense of autonomy is rooted in a person's innate need and desire to stand tall through life as a unique individual. This need can only be fulfilled when it springs from a healthy sense of self. Identity and autonomy work together. Before a daughter can truly pursue a healthy sense of autonomy, she must first know who she is. Then she must believe in the person she sees herself to be.

Autonomy—the natural consequence of a healthy and growing identity—is not a battle for independence from family, even though it might look or feel that way. Certainly, your daughter may use words that sound like that's what she wants, and she may even seek such an arrangement. But a mature sense of autonomy is not simply a clean and total cut from those people who provide her with warmth, security, and love. It is the natural result of her need to become a fully functioning and equal member of those systems to which she is connected, especially of her family.

Interdependence is her real goal, not independence—a state in which she will ultimately feel isolated and alone. And the goal is not dependence—a state in which she feels less valued than others and ultimately a less important and less valued member of the system. No, she longs to discover herself as a gifted, unique person in her own right (identity), who is connected to the other members of the family while being able to function on her own by making some decisions and choices and then living with those choices. The truth is that your daughter cannot function without a belief that she has power over her life. While this may sound "worldly" to some Christians ("Isn't God in control?"), every healthy adult has at least some measure of personal autonomy. Without it, we would not have the confidence to get a job, obtain a mortgage, or get married.

The previous chapter dealt with a father's role in helping his daughter discover that her identity rests in her relationship to the heavenly Father. This chapter details what a father can do to help his daughter understand and experience autonomy. We will also discuss the difference between *identity* and *autonomy*. While they are related, identity—helping your daughter "find herself"—is much easier to help her achieve emotionally than helping her become autonomous. A daughter's search for autonomy is where a father's love, commitment, and concern are severely tested.

Are You Ready to Let Go?

> Dear Daddy,
> I hope you won't be mad at me, but I need to tell you to back off (there's no other way I can say it). I love you, and you are the greatest dad in the world, but I am not a little girl anymore. You need to let me go. I used to think it was neat when you would say how you hate it that I was growing up, but now I don't think it is. I want you to know that, whether you like it or not, I am growing up, and I am becoming a woman. It's now up to me to decide what I do, what I wear, who I date, and how I spend my time. If you don't let me or try to stop me, I'll do it anyway. I don't mean to hurt you, but I'm almost eighteen and then I really am on my own (legally). So, Dad, please let me go!
>
> —Karen, 17, Minneapolis, MN

It doesn't cost a father much to help his daughter find her own sense of self. Yes, you may be nervous as she goes through the process. There will be moments and seasons of experimentation with clothes and friends, especially in middle or junior high school. Hairstyles and music may push you to the edge of panic. But all in all, these are manifestations of an inner process, and they are usually relatively harmless. Generally speaking, a loving father who invests wisely in his daughter will soon feel proud and satisfied by the emerging young woman he loves.

In the case of autonomy, the process (and everything related to it) is a much different experience. A daughter's quest for a healthy sense of personal autonomy deals with issues that cut to the core of a father's historical role in most families. Autonomy has to do with control, choice, and sometimes painful consequences.

From a practical point of view, autonomy is the most

common point of contention and dissatisfaction between a daughter and her father. Most daughters want more freedom than they are given, and most fathers want to put off the inevitability of their daughters growing up. The reality is that by the time a girl is eighteen, her father has very little control over her choices. The father who wants to be confident that his daughter will handle the complexity of everyday life must learn how to give her more and more room to experiment, and even fail, *while she is still under his control and authority!*

Unfortunately, there is no secret to making it through your daughter's search for autonomy. We would love to tell you about "Six Surefire, Painless Ways to Ensure That Your Daughter Will Become a Confident and Well-Adjusted Adult" (for only $99.99). As long as you live by a certain set of principles, your daughter will move from childhood to adulthood painlessly and with little turmoil in the family. We'd love to say that all a daughter needs is love and support from her parents to always make the right choices. Perhaps some philosophies and styles of parenting promise such hogwash, but the truth is that all such statements are lies.

The first idea, that there's a formula that will produce the kind of results you want for your daughter is not much more than wishful thinking. We live in an age of popular programs that promise everything from easy weight loss to financial security. But life is much more a fluid process with complex pieces than a simple formula that works for everyone.

Right now you may be saying, "Wait a minute, you've included lists (or tips) to put these concepts into practice." We're using the lists as *supportive information* to help flesh out the ideas presented. When someone claims that a program is all that's necessary for raising children, life becomes more of a paint-by-the-numbers, fill-in-the-blank game than a wild dance of faith.

Raising kids is a tremendous opportunity for faith, surprise, and trust. Raising a daughter — while nerve-racking and exhilarating at the same time—is an adventure. And because no two daughters are alike and no two fathers are alike, a paint-by-the-numbers approach just won't cut it.

Second, helping your daughter move from childhood to adulthood is not simply a commitment to live according to a set of principles. Living by principles is a good, *general* way to live, and certainly there are principles laid out in Scripture that are helpful in many life circumstances when raising a daughter. But the greatest problem with a set of principles is the way they often subtly shift from principle to law.

As your daughter passes through adolescence, the last thing she wants (or even needs) is perceived rigidity on the part of her parents. There is no specific, clear-cut time when a daughter is ready to drive, increase her curfew, or be allowed to date. To help your daughter move through this process, in terms of her personal autonomy, the authority you grant her as she makes certain choices must be handed off over time, based upon a variety of negotiated factors.

When a parent establishes and then commits to a series of principles from which to operate, a daughter may sense a noose around her neck. In this perceived constriction, she may do one of two things: She either will leave the home (physically or at least emotionally and relationally), or she will buckle under. The first is bad enough; for if she "checks out" of the family to make her own choices without the support, guidance, love, and forgiveness of her father, she may make even more destructive behavioral choices. But if she shuts down and allows a father to control her by a rigid set of "principles," someday she will find herself bitter and angry over her father's need to control her just when she was needing to understand the notion of freedom and decision making. When she realizes this, she will become angry and rebel. Most likely this will happen when she's long gone from the protective and nurturing shield of father attachment.

Third, some parents are so concerned with the appearance

of love that they abdicate their responsibility to help their daughter as she begins to unfold her "autonomy" wings. Loving your daughter doesn't mean letting her do whatever she wants, whenever she wants.

By the late middle school years, modern North American parents seem to have capitulated their responsibility of offering help, guidance, and discipline to their children. In the name of love, some kids stay up as late as they want, even on school nights. In the name of acceptance, some children have no curfew. In the name of relational harmony, many parents think that discipline ceases when a girl hits adolescence, and their role becomes that of a counselor when and if she ever seeks out a "counseling session."

Love is a wonderful, tender word that carries different expectations to different families and households. How we define a father's love will ultimately dictate how we help our daughters become autonomous while still maintaining enough order and constraint to keep her choices from doing major damage.

Helping your daughter walk the tightrope of adolescence while offering her the safety net of attachment is no simple task. We've found three basic areas that are crucial to the father-daughter relationship if a father is to help his daughter make wise choices and stand on her own. These areas are an ability to understand, a weaning process, and a warm embrace.

Understanding

Researchers have discovered that as girls grow older they "seem to undergo a kind of crisis in response to adolescence and to the strictures and demands of the culture."[1] Although some parents (and especially fathers) may not recognize this, adolescence is a difficult process for most girls.

Historically, social scientists, educators, physicians, and even therapists have believed that the adolescent journey is roughly the same process for boys and girls. They have also believed that the process essentially described a child separating from her family. Many people who work with young people, even those who teach teachers, subscribe to this view. They continue to teach and counsel that it is healthy for young people to break ties with their parents and families. However, the simplistic nature of this view is dangerous, for it is observably accurate enough to appear true. However, over the last decade or so, social science has begun to affirm loudly that the opposite is true. The healthiest adolescent (or fledgling adult) is one who is intimately and joyfully connected to her parents and siblings.

Every father must be aware of a daughter's need for relational attachment to him during adolescence. As we have stated, and social scientists affirm, "healthy development throughout the adolescent period is a dual process of autonomy *and* family connectedness and attachment."[2] In other words, a developing sense of autonomy is not mutually exclusive with a need to be close to parents, and especially to a father. In fact, the reverse is true. A healthy sense of autonomy is more readily achieved and is an emotionally safer experience when a daughter feels connected to her dad. During and throughout adolescence the parental role shifts from authority figure to helping friend. This is why attachment is so crucial during this phase of development.

Dear father,
I need you to know I need you.

—Anonymous, Georgia

A Weaning Process

Patricia H. Davis, in *Counseling Adolescent Girls,* notes that adolescents need to know that their feelings and needs matter to their fathers.

One of the most frequent complaints girls have about their fathers is that they don't feel respected. During adolescence, girls are extremely sensitive to their fathers' feelings about them and may assume they know their fathers' feelings, even when they do not. When (or if) a father seems to be having trouble adjusting to his daughter's new and more mature identity, she probably interprets this state as rejection. Just as with her mother, a girl wants to feel valued by her father for being herself—the self she is becoming.[3]

The process of "letting go" must be carefully and sensitively controlled and monitored. Encouraging your daughter to take responsibility by making choices will entail a process of weaning her from your (and her mother's) authority to allow her the freedom to fail. This weaning process must be:

- intentional
- communicated
- negotiated

Try the following exercise with your daughter:

Daughter Autonomy Inventory

To fathers:
For each of the following areas, circle the number you think best represents your daughter's ability to be in control of her decisions. Then guess where she thinks her ability is.

1 = she's not ready yet   7 = no problem, she's in charge.

Choices	Father's view	Daughter's view
Watching television	1 2 3 4 5 6 7	1 2 3 4 5 6 7
Choosing movies to view	1 2 3 4 5 6 7	1 2 3 4 5 6 7
Choosing friends to talk to	1 2 3 4 5 6 7	1 2 3 4 5 6 7

Choosing friends to hang out with	1 2 3 4 5 6 7	1 2 3 4 5 6 7
Choosing friends to spend a weekend with	1 2 3 4 5 6 7	1 2 3 4 5 6 7
Having a curfew	1 2 3 4 5 6 7	1 2 3 4 5 6 7
Doing homework	1 2 3 4 5 6 7	1 2 3 4 5 6 7
Choosing activities and involvements	1 2 3 4 5 6 7	1 2 3 4 5 6 7
Picking college or a post-high school option	1 2 3 4 5 6 7	1 2 3 4 5 6 7
Finding and getting a job	1 2 3 4 5 6 7	1 2 3 4 5 6 7
Involvement at church (or other Christian activities)	1 2 3 4 5 6 7	1 2 3 4 5 6 7
Dating (choosing guys to date, choosing whether to date, et cetera)	1 2 3 4 5 6 7	1 2 3 4 5 6 7
Choice of music	1 2 3 4 5 6 7	1 2 3 4 5 6 7

To daughters:

For each of the following areas, circle the number you think best represents your ability to be in control of your decisions. Try to guess where your father would place your ability.

1 = I'm not ready yet   7 = no problem, I'm in charge.

Choices	Father's view	Daughter's view
Watching television	1 2 3 4 5 6 7	1 2 3 4 5 6 7
Choosing movies to view	1 2 3 4 5 6 7	1 2 3 4 5 6 7
Choosing friends to talk to	1 2 3 4 5 6 7	1 2 3 4 5 6 7
Choosing friends to hang out with	1 2 3 4 5 6 7	1 2 3 4 5 6 7
Choosing friends to spend a weekend with	1 2 3 4 5 6 7	1 2 3 4 5 6 7
Having a curfew	1 2 3 4 5 6 7	1 2 3 4 5 6 7
Doing homework	1 2 3 4 5 6 7	1 2 3 4 5 6 7
Choosing activities and involvements	1 2 3 4 5 6 7	1 2 3 4 5 6 7

Picking college or a post-high school option	1 2 3 4 5 6 7	1 2 3 4 5 6 7
Finding and getting a job	1 2 3 4 5 6 7	1 2 3 4 5 6 7
Involvement at church (or other Christian activities)	1 2 3 4 5 6 7	1 2 3 4 5 6 7
Dating (choosing guys to date, choosing whether to date, et cetera)	1 2 3 4 5 6 7	1 2 3 4 5 6 7
Choice of music	1 2 3 4 5 6 7	1 2 3 4 5 6 7

After both of you have completed this exercise, share your results with each other. Be prepared for your daughter to disagree with you, Dad. She may not, and you will know you're doing fine in this area. But for most father-daughter relationships, autonomy is not an easy issue. This exercise will at least get you talking! Now the door is open for future discussion and negotiation.

A Warm Embrace

A recent study found that adolescents have strong feelings when it comes to their fathers. One question, "What are your top suggestions for improving communication between fathers and adolescents?" garnered many suggestions. Here are the top nine responses.

1. Share feelings, not just thoughts
2. Learn to listen more than talk
3. Don't jump to conclusions
4. Learn to have an open mind
5. Tell the truth, no matter what
6. Be flexible
7. Control anger
8. Invest in me—spend time with me
9. Don't be critical[4]

Adolescents want their fathers to be real and to care about them.

Another factor that emerged from the same study showed that teenagers who perceived their fathers to be "emotionally available" scored nearly twice as high on the "Spiritual Wellness Inventory" (an instrument used to measure spiritual maturity, growth, and interest) than those who perceived their fathers to be "emotionally unavailable" (defined as "simply not close to their fathers").[5]

The authors infer from these two sets of data that there seems to be a connection between how close daughters feel to their fathers and the depth of their faith. While many factors undoubtedly contribute to such a nebulous notion as "spiritual wellness," the results of this study are significant enough to note.

The study did not show conclusively which factor was more responsible for the relationship between fathers and daughters—whether a daughter who takes her Christian faith seriously is more committed to a close relationship with her father or a daughter who has a father who has cultivated a close friendship with her enhances spiritual maturity and growth. Somehow, the relationship between a daughter's perception of father-closeness and her possession of a rich, deep faith is very strong. Therefore, it's safe to conclude that a father who is caring and connected to his daughter will likely see the fruit of that relationship in her own faith.

Your daughter wants you to be involved in her life. She wants to know that you care about her as a unique individual and that you ultimately trust her. Her ability to learn how to make wise choices, as well as how she will see herself in the future, is intimately connected with how close she feels to you.

What does she really want? A warm embrace. A hug. A flower. A card. A serious talk. A few questions. She wants her dad to treat her like a capable, smart, and gifted young woman who, although she will make mistakes along the way, knows that her dad is her greatest fan!

As you cheer your daughter on through her adolescent years, you will be handing her a great incentive to make the kind of choices that honor her, you, and God as she strives to develop personal autonomy.

CHAPTER EIGHT

A Father's Love as a Model of the Father's Love

Dear screw Up (Father),
I'd just like to say, thanks for being there for me when
I needed a dad! Because of you I have never had a real
father figure in my life since you left. Do you know
how hard it has been for my little brother? He has had
to grow up with three girls. How would you feel? My
little sister doesn't trust any adult males anymore
because of you.

—Mary, 15, San Antonio, TX

In March 1997, an episode of the television series "Chicago Hope" was dedicated entirely to the father-son relationship. The show ended with the two main character doctors sitting in a lounge area. One casually remarked to the other: "Why is it that we spend our lives trying to earn our parents' approval?"

The other doctor replied, just as casually, "And do you think they know it?" No answer.

Then the first asked, "Will we ever stop needing each other's approval?"

From Dee
Memories of An Adult Daughter

—

Young women respond in one of two ways concerning their faith as it relates to their relationship with their fathers. Some allow their own sense of a father's rejection to provide a reason not to trust the heavenly Father. For others, a sense of disconnectedness can actually drive them into a deep and rich faith experience. For these girls, however, the road to faith is often a long and painful journey. My life reflected this path.

Instead of transferring my fear of abandonment and loneliness to God, deep inside I was painfully aware of my need for the unconditional love God offered me in Christ Jesus. This awareness came about as a result of many painful years of independent, futile searching for my earthly father's love. The father-love I longed for was a love God the Father had designed to reflect His perfect love and to serve as a bridge to help me know Him. Unfortunately, my solo trek led me down paths of

(continued)

"I guess we'll just have to wait and see." The camera then panned back, and the shot slowly faded to black.

The truth of this interchange is a sober reminder to every parent. We have such power over our children. How we influence them can last their lifetime.

We've received far more letters from teenage girls expressing disappointment toward fathers and their failures than we did encouraging or positive ones. Many were addressed to fathers who had left home or perhaps still lived at home but were functionally absent. The pain in these girls runs deep.

By now, we hope we've made it clear that a loving father has a huge impact on the self-esteem and personal confidence of his adolescent daughter. The reverse situation, however, is true as well. An absent father, simply by default, often creates a deep insecurity in his daughter. She may have a hard time feeling worthy of love. Or she may feel unable to find any man—or any adult for that matter—who cares for her as a person. Daughters in this situation will often look for deep and intimate relationships with boys in order to fill the painful hole left by an inaccessible father. And a stern, distant, or abusive father has the potential to set loose even more devastation to his daughter's sense of self for years to come.

Whether you're a highly involved and

loving father or a distant, hard, and disconnected father, one consequence of your relationship with your daughter is sobering, at best: Whatever you have taught her about the notion of "fatherhood," chances are she will carry that into her understanding and practice of faith. While there is little solid research to prove it, there seems to be for most women a connection between how she views her father and how she feels and thinks about the heavenly Father. Take the case of Julie, a thirty-five-year-old counselor at a youth conference we spoke at.

Julie's dad was technically present, but when he was home he was distant at best and mildly abusive at worst. Julie didn't recall any serious beatings. But a tenseness existed around the house when her father was home, especially when he was drinking. I had delivered a message about God being our "biggest fan," using Romans 8:31 as a text: "If God is for us, who can be against us?" Julie approached me, knowing that we were writing this book on father-daughter relationships. She began bluntly: "My dad was no fan!"

She went on to share her story of a stern, distant father who still scares her to this day. The longer we talked, the more bitter she became. She worked hard at convincing me that she had been in therapy and was "clean" with him. But my observation was that she had allowed his claws

exploration with sex, drugs, and alcohol before I realized that the only One who could completely meet the needs of my life was my heavenly Father. To me, a bruised and broken daughter, this concept held incredible power and relief. It took years, but my ultimate response to God's offer of love was a passionate abandonment of my running heart to leap into the arms of protection and strength I had longed for as a child and now experience in my heavenly Father.

Some say parenting in the twentieth century is overrated. I believe that while our children ultimately belong to God, parents—especially fathers—have the responsibility and unique opportunity to flesh out the truth of God's constant, unconditional love. Don't worry, Dads, daughters don't need perfection. What your daughter wants and needs is the honest, open, and loving presence of a father who will help her walk through life. Have courage and step up to the plate of your daughter's world. It's an investment you will never regret.

---

to dig deeply into her soul. Her father was still a powerful, antagonistic figure in her life, even though Julie described herself as a happily married mother of three.

As I probed more deeply, she made an interesting statement: "I also have a hard time thinking of God as a father. If He's anything like my dad, I don't want anything to do with Him!" With that as a finale, she turned and walked away, saying that she had to go "spend time with her girls." I never saw her again. But her comment disturbed me and still does. Julie had been moved by the message of Romans 8:31, but she was torn apart by the image of a father who is a fan. Her heart had been so bruised by her own father that to imagine God as a loving, passionate, and active father was the ultimate contradiction.

I find it a frightening thought that how a father relates to his kids will affect how they will experience God. When Jesus brought the great and powerful, yet distant, Yahweh home by calling him "our Father," He placed a great deal of pressure on dads. We now carry the same title of the all-loving, all-powerful, and perfect Father in heaven. But once our Lord said it, we as fathers had to come to grips with the implications of such a comparison.

The Fatherhood of God

Jesus said these words: "And do not call anyone on earth 'father,' for you have one Father, and he is in heaven" (Matthew 23:9). What does it mean that God is our Father?

The first and most obvious issue when discussing the fatherhood of God is the nature of God Himself. Even the use of the male pronoun in that last sentence presents a rhetorical gender emphasis. Many people would not be offended by saying "He" when naming God. In fact, many would probably be more offended if we didn't use a masculine pronoun to refer to God. But in today's culture, some people are offended with the concept of God as solely masculine. The most theological argument is found in the Creation narrative in Genesis 1:27: "So God created man in his own image, in the image of God he created him; male and female he created them." If God *created* gender, then God must be *above* and *beyond* gender.

Although space and the intent of this book prohibit discussing this subject in depth, suffice it to say that theologians generally agree that God is indeed the author of gender. This means that God is not masculine. As noted theologians Bruce Demarest and Gordon Lewis state:

> Distinct from the physical aspects of human person-
> hood, God transcends the physical aspects of both male-
> ness and femaleness. However, since God created both
> male and female in his image, we may think of both as
> like God in their distinctively nonphysical, personal
> male and female qualities. Both male and female are per-
> sonal in the likeness of God who is personal. From this
> perspective, scriptural uses of masculine personal pro-
> nouns for God (and other male designations such as
> "Father") primarily convey the connotation of God's per-
> sonal qualities.[1]

This represents the mainstream of theological thought that God's apparent maleness is actually a way to describe God's personhood linguistically. Referring to God as Father is not to say that He is male but that His fatherhood is an invitation to intimate communion with Him as His children. In Henri Nouwen's masterful work, *The Return of the Prodigal Son,* he describes the heart of this Father in relation to His children:

> As Father, the only authority he claims for himself is the
> authority of compassion. That authority comes from let-
> ting the sins of his children pierce his heart. There is no
> lust, greed, anger, resentment, jealousy, or vengeance in

his lost children that has not caused immense grief to his heart. The grief is so deep because the heart is so pure. From the deep inner place where love embraces all human grief, the Father reaches out to his children. The touch of his hands, radiating inner light, seeks only to heal. . . .

Here is the God I want to believe in: a Father who, from the beginning of creation, has stretched out his arms in merciful blessing, never forcing himself on any-one, but always waiting.[2]

This is the same Father who spoke to Moses, grieved over Israel's rebellion, and sent His Son into the world as a baby. This is the Father to whom Jesus introduced us and called us to know, love, and serve. God our Father is our merciful, gentle, respectful, powerful, and patient Parent/King. As Paul wrote to the Corinthians, "for us there is but one God, the Father, from whom all things came and for whom we live; and there is but one Lord, Jesus Christ, through whom all things came and through whom we live" (1 Corinthians 8:6).

This same Father is the model and ultimate standard for every father. Again, Paul reminds us of this: "For this reason I kneel before the Father, from whom his whole family in heaven and on earth derives its name" (Ephesians 3:14-15). Our role as fathers, then, and the very structure of the family, are but pic-tures of true family as revealed in Christ Jesus and His relation-ship with the Father.

A Father Who Draws His Daughter to God
Recent studies have shown that the number-one predictor of children who go on in their faith is the lived-out faith of their parents. It is not the nature of the church community nor the denomination, and it is not even the quality of a church youth ministry, although those programs are a tremendous support to

parents. What makes committed young disciples is parents who consistently live out their faith both in words and in lifestyle.

If you have read this far, you know about the power and impact you have with your daughter as she is growing up. You know that her understanding of who God is, how He feels about her, and even how He has called her to live has a great deal to do with you. How you love your daughter and treat her will do far more for her future faith than years of "family devotions" and keeping religious rules and expectations. It may sound contradictory, but fathers who have strictly enforced "spiritual" rules and have structured the family around "religious" activities can sometimes cause the exact opposite response that they desire in their children.

> Dear Dad,
> Thanks for everything you have done for me. I really appreciate it. But there is one thing. Why do we have to do family devotions? It's boring! Everybody hates it, even you, it seems like, but we still have to do it.
> —Crystal, 13, Ft. Walton Beach, FL

It's true that faith is meant to be passed on to our kids. God is very clear about this:

> These commandments that I give you today are to be upon your hearts. Impress them on your children. Talk about them when you sit at home and when you walk along the road, when you lie down and when you get up. (Deuteronomy 6:6-7)

How we "impress them" on our children is the key. If we are loving and gentle with our daughters, and our faith penetrates deeper than mere activity and devotional duty, we communicate by our lives that God is real and He matters to us. This is what our children need to see.

Fathers who want more than anything else to draw their daughters to their heavenly Father would do well to heed these four characteristics of a godly father. He

- loves his wife
- lives and then dispenses mercy and justice
- fights against the seduction of power
- seeks to live an authentic life

Love Your Wife

In 1997, two professors from Abilene Christian University completed a ten-year study of church-raised adolescents' attitudes and perceptions of their fathers.[3] In the article titled, "How Do Fathers Help Turn Their Teenagers' Hearts Toward Christ?" the top issue mentioned was, "By setting an example for the family ('walk the walk')."

Today's young people, as Generation-X literature overwhelmingly affirms, are incredibly astute in their ability to judge the hearts and motives of people. For adolescent girls this is even more true. Their relational antennae are always active. If your daughter senses that her mother is not being cared for or treated with kindness, compassion, and respect by you, it's doubtful that you will be able to influence her positively for God's kingdom. If, on the other hand, she can feel that her mother is married to a man who honors and empowers her, your daughter will be far more open to allowing your faith to penetrate her life.

When you love your wife, you are loving each of your kids. You are also modeling the faith you profess.

Dispense Justice and Mercy

Both justice and mercy are aspects of the heavenly Father's character. God, in His justice, is good, right, honest, pure, and holy. Our God is passionate in His wrath against sin and His zeal for righteousness. In addition, God, in His mercy, is gentle, forgiving, and compassionate toward those who fail and fall down. Our God is equally passionate about His mercy, grace, and kindness. God is both holy and caring, righteous and forgiving, just and the One who justifies.

We, on the other hand, have difficulty balancing these characteristics. The father who tends toward kindness often has a hard time dispensing judgment and discipline when confronted with an offense. The father who esteems holiness may be less than merciful when his child fails. Both extremes are detrimental to a daughter's growth as a believer. She will be far better off with a father who seeks to balance justice and mercy and who lives them as a package instead of two polar opposites.

The high road of modeling God's character is difficult, but every father must train and discipline himself to humbly seek a balance between lofty moralizing and sentimental acquiescence. To model God's love, a father must clearly be committed to a life of truth, integrity, and purity. But he must also remember his own up-and-down spiritual journey. Yes, teach your daughter to seek goodness, to value righteousness, and to abhor sin as well as oppression. As you work hard to help train up your daughter in these things, recognize that God takes a lifetime with you — with all of us, patiently guiding and nudging us to the next level of lived-out righteousness. Therefore, you must discipline your daughter appropriately when she needs correction and carefully instruct and correct her without humiliating, defeating, or being relationally invasive toward her. As Paul writes, "Fathers, do not exasperate your children; instead, bring them up in the training and instruction of the Lord" (Ephesians 6:4).

Fight Against the Seduction of Power
Power is perhaps the greatest enemy of the truth. It lies to us: "You will truly *be somebody!*" It deceives: "You know better than

they do." It divides: "I am to be obeyed!"

Power rears its head in a variety of ways that can impact the father-daughter relationship. First, the need for power can cause a father to spend far more energy and effort in the workplace and in work-related relationships than with his family. Work's allure is easily rationalized: "This position (or person) will help my career, and that will be better for my family." But your daughter is far more concerned with knowing you as a person and watching how you view life.

In the workplace we feel that if we're going to carve out a niche that will impact our family, it's up to us. That's true, to a point. But when the drive to succeed at work spills over into a need for more power, prestige, or an evergrowing niche, or we allow ourselves to lose sight of what *really* is important, this striving is misplaced. It is up to God to build power and influence in our careers as we are faithful, kind, and diligent—but not obsessive—in our work.

Second, how a father wields power in the family sends a signal to an adolescent daughter about her father's desire to connect intimately with and love the other members of the family. If you are a father who needs to be in control, if you want the family to revolve around your life, your interests, and your schedule, then other family members—especially your daughter—may come to resent you. Yes, a father (along with his wife) must exert some form of leadership in the family. But godly leadership is more an exercise in empowering other family members than an inner drive to control them.

Third, how a father sees his power in the church will model for his family what it means to participate in the local family of God. How does your daughter see or experience your dissatisfaction, frustration, or anguish over the issues in your church? Do you present an attitude that is marked by humility, prayer, and healthy relationships? Or are you one who "makes known your position" and "speaks your mind"?

In our experience in the church and other Christian organizations, we've seen many people use power to control, divide, or even destroy ministries and relationships. Often, the children of these people are the losers, for they learn how to participate in churches and Christian institutions by throwing their weight around and vying to get their own way.

Teach your daughter not to seek power for power's sake. And when she is given power and influence, demonstrate how she can use it for God's glory and not her own.

Seek to Live an Authentic Life

Compartmentalization is perhaps the greatest single issue facing men of faith today. Modern men have perfected the art of pretense. On the inside they may feel fear and loneliness, but they learn at a young age to mask that fear behind a wall of superiority, busyness, and effective perseverance. They neatly package and shelve the things that bother them, hurt them, or cause them to feel insecure. *I'll deal with it later,* a man may think. But on the shelf these things fester, ooze, and drip, penetrating the soul like slowly burning embers. Still, our intrinsic bent is to ignore our pain. Fueled by the fear of being discovered, we move in and out of relationships, always subtly conscious that we are vulnerable to anyone who can see inside us.

Men involved in the church are not immune from this cultural malaise. In fact, they may suffer from it even more than others do. For many Christian men, the church is the most threatening place to be. They can easily feel that church is where they have to pretend the most. However, Christianity has only the power to heal those who can admit their brokenness, for Jesus Christ is Lord only when pretense is set aside.

It should be obvious by now that your daughter can tell what is real and what isn't. You can't hide from such a relationally intuitive machine as an adolescent girl who cares for you. How we fathers deal with our inner lives reveals the core honesty of our faith. Your daughter knows you well, and she loves you anyway. She can tell if you play at faith or if you really mean it. She can see if your prayers, your involvement in Christian activities, and your convictions flow from a soul that has been taken captive by the overwhelming grace of God. As author and speaker Brennan Manning has said, she will take notice if your heart has been "seized by the power of a great affection."

To live an authentic life means that you strive to live as one set free. Fear and failure can be your most strident adversaries when you empower them by concealment and denial. To live out authentic faith, you must consistently dredge the depths of your heart, experiences, values, and relationships. You must willingly present whatever you find to the God who quietly waits with healing compassion and fierce mercy.

For your daughter's faith to be set free, she needs to see *your* faith set free. Although never a father, St. Francis of Assisi knew what it meant to pass on the faith to our adolescent children. He said: "Preach Christ at all times — if necessary, use words!"

Dear Dad,

There are a great many things I could tell you but have never had the strength since I know we'd both be moved to tears so fast that nothing would come out right. My Father in heaven has so richly blessed me with the perfect father on earth. Without knowing it, you have shaped so much of my personality and built so much of my faith. I want you to know how much I truly love and appreciate you and every sacrifice, little and big, you have made for me throughout my life. Most of all, I am grateful for the loving, Christ-centered household in which you chose to raise a family. So much of your laughter and love lives within me. Thank you for the beautiful example you have set for my future household and family. Thank you for putting up with me and loving me unconditionally. Thank you for being my friend. You are an amazing man of God, Dad.

I love you with all of my heart!

—Teri, 21, Austin, TX

CHAPTER NINE

Being Her Teacher
When You Want to
Be Her Judge

Dad,
You've been an excellent dad, as much as you could. But
when I was a young child, you didn't seem to have enough
time for me. Now that I'm older, I don't have the time
for you. Now you need me. It's hard to build a father-
daughter relationship when I barely see you, and when I do
you act more like a strict priest than my father.

—Linda, 16, St. Louis, MO

Mr. Johnson was the best teacher our kids ever had. He was warm and friendly—the prototypical Teddy Bear. When a student went to talk to him, this fifth grade teacher stopped what he was doing, sat down on the edge of a desk to get on eye level with the budding adolescent, and listened with care and interest. When he got mad (as our kids tell it), he got mad! But just as quickly, he would turn around, smile, and offer a word of encouragement. He was a tough but fair grader. He would never overlook anyone, and he wouldn't allow himself to believe negative or harsh words that previous teachers had written

From Dee
Memories of an Adult Daughter

No daughter wants a judge as a father. Some don't even want a teacher! What a young woman does want in her dad is someone she can trust and believe in. To a daughter, her father is often like a judge who is distant, clear-cut, and lives by the book. I remember my dad acting this way, but by the time I was fifteen, I nodded and then did what I wanted to do. The judge "thing" didn't work for me, and I doubt that it works for many girls. A daughter just doesn't want to be parented by a distant judge.

A father who is a teacher will be welcomed if he's a good teacher. A good teacher listens first, *then* responds. A good teacher is able to laugh with his students and cares more about the final knowledge gained than about grades or tests. Every girl needs a father who is committed to being a good teacher.

My father was not a teacher, good *or* bad. He was *(continued)*

about one of his students. He was determined to bring out the best in every precious boy or girl he taught.

Miss Claypool was not the best teacher our kids ever had. She was all business, which is not necessarily bad. But she had a style that communicated a coldness you could almost feel when she entered the classroom. There was a poster on her wall that read, "Do it right the first time," and another, "School rules will be strictly enforced." Her students were orderly and well mannered. But there were few smiles, and some of the slower kids kept falling further and further behind those who were temperamentally suited to her way of doing things. Homework was handed in on time or it was not accepted. She was fair, consistent, and ruled with a heavy hand.

Mr. Johnson's kids were wild, fun, happy, and growing like weeds in every way. His class scores and marks improved in record numbers each year—across the board. Miss Claypool's kids were stiff and controlled. The best students, academically speaking, improved; the ones who struggled, regressed. Mr. Johnson was a teacher of individual kids on a journey. Miss Claypool was a controlling judge who maintained appropriate order. Every one of Mr. Johnson's students felt loved, supported, and encouraged. Miss Claypool's class felt structured, driven, and stereotyped. Each of the kids in Mr. Johnson's class went on to excel in middle school, but many of Miss Claypool's continued to scramble just to survive.

What makes a good teacher for someone who needs to grow but whose life seems to be in a constant state of turmoil? Does it take order, structure, and control? Or does it take a committed, concerned, and available fan?

a judge. I didn't want a judge, and I wouldn't listen to a judge. Now I know that I longed for a kind, gentle, smart, forward-thinking teacher!

A father who wants to give his daughter the best shot at a full life must resist the temptation to be a strict and rational controller or even a kind and benevolent judge. For her to realize fully what it means to live as an adult who knows and likes herself, and is responsible for her choices, dad must shift roles and become a gentle and focused teacher. A judging father tells his daughter right from wrong, instructs her on the way to live, and authoritatively dispenses rulings and directives. At this stage of her life, she is far more in need of a dad who teaches her how to distinguish for herself what is right and what is wrong.

In light of the concepts we have presented, look at the differences between a father-judge and a father-teacher:

Needs	Judge	Teacher
Identity	"Here's who I want you to be."	"Let's discover who you are."
Autonomy	"Here's what I want you to do."	"What do *you* want to do?" "How can I help you?"
Trust	"You trust me."	"I trust you."
Communication	"*I* will talk to you, and you speak when you are spoken to."	"I will listen to *you* and I will share with *you* my heart."
Closeness	"You are a part of this family; act accordingly."	"I love you and I believe in you." "I want you to know I'll always be there for you."

You have a choice every time you bump up against your adolescent daughter's needs in the areas of identity, autonomy, trust, communication, or closeness. You can either be a father-judge or a father-teacher. Let's look at what this means for each need.

Identity

When a convicted criminal faces a judge, he is at the directive mercy of that judge. It's not the *person* who wears the robe that matters. The criminal and the judge may be neighbors. They may volunteer in the same organization or even attend the same church. But an inherent authority and a certain style accompanies the role of judge.

In terms of a daughter's sense of identity, a father may love his little girl so much that he falls into playing the role of judge in her life. He may sense who she is, or what he perceives she ought to be, based on his love for her. He may even be correct in his assessment. But every time a father dictates to his daughter who she is, or even who she ought to be, he drives a stake right through the heart of their relationship. He also hinders her ability to discover who she is for herself.

On the other hand, a father who strives to teach, though he may care no more deeply than the judge, is aware and careful with his words and manner because he knows that his daughter's greatest need is to discover for herself who she is. The teacher-father is a helping, gentle instructor who listens to his daughter and gently pushes her to consider the best for her life.

This sounds so simple to do, but years of history as well as emotional and relational patterns are hard to discard. When a daughter hits adolescence, a father simply has to remember to leave the judge's robe in the closet. He must gently teach his daughter how to think about herself without controlling and dominating the process in an attempt to force her to see his view of her.

A father-teacher who wants to help his daughter in her quest for identity must keep the teacher's task foremost in mind. That task is to *instruct the student but not do the work of the student.* It is crucial that dads make this shift with daughters who are approaching adolescence.

When your daughter was young, you (and her mother) thought through all the options in a given situation or circumstance and told your child how she was to act or what she was to do. Now that she's an adolescent, the father-teacher's role is to listen to her, then gently but clearly remind her that she is still "in the classroom" and needs your input. It is equally important to communicate that the outcome of her thinking ultimately rests with her.

This change must take place incrementally over time. In terms of her identity, a father's goal is to help a daughter see herself in light of her relationship with God by focusing on His love demonstrated for her in creation and redemption. God made her unique. He loved her enough and found her precious enough to send His Son to die and rise again for her. The father-teacher's task is to continually bring his daughter back to this truth. He must strive, as respectfully and gently as possible, to help her see that all she is can only be discovered through the love and calling of Jesus Christ.

Autonomy

As a teacher, a father carries the responsibility to provide information for his daughter to act on. When it comes to autonomy, he has the advantage of having seen, over the course of a lifetime, the power of consequence. This depth of experience is a tremendous gift a father can give his daughter as she goes through adolescence, yet it must be handled with great care and savvy. When asked for input on a specific decision, for example, a father-judge may say to his daughter, "You can't do that! You should do this! When I was a kid. . . ."

In comparison, a father-teacher would probably respond with something like, "Think of a few different things that could happen with each of your options. Together, let's look at three possible consequences of each decision."

A father-teacher knows that unless his daughter learns how to make decisions, and understands and *even suffers the appropriate consequences herself,* she will not grow into healthy womanhood. She will constantly be looking for others to decide for her. That is far worse than most anything she will do under her father's loving tutelage.

It is vital to remember that the journey into adolescence is very difficult on a daughter, but especially in the area of autonomy. As Patricia H. Davis points out:

> Although gender roles are slowly changing, men's traditional 'natural' realm is the public; men have been expected to introduce girls to what it means to have competence and mastery outside of the home.

For this reason, a father's expectations of his daughter hold extreme importance for her. In the best cases, a father's support becomes the validation a daughter needs to confirm her own independent identity. A father who promotes his daughter's drive for achievement is telling her that a powerful part of her emerging identity is valued by those she loves. It is often difficult, however, in this androcentric culture, for fathers to figure out what it is they expect from (or for) their daughters.[1]

Your daughter is walking a tightrope between two worlds—one where she must completely rely on you (and your authority in her life) and another where she is completely responsible for herself. Imagine a daughter who has been told what to do, how to think, and how to act throughout her high school years. She graduates and leaves home for the large college two hundred miles away. In the first week she is accosted with invitations to drink and do drugs; she meets dozens of twentysomething young "dudes" with hyperactive hormones, who want to "spend the weekend" with her; and she has a roommate who has been a self-described "hard-core party-er" since age twelve. How do you think the daughter would fare in this environment?

Think of your own daughter. Is she prepared for the real world?

Dear Dad,
I'm not who you think I am. You still see me in my
sunday school dress and a cute ribbon in my hair. But
you have no idea what it is like at school. Everybody
drinks and has sex, and I am like everybody else. I don't
want to hurt you, but you never let me out of your "cage"
growing up. I didn't know what to expect. Well, I do now,
and I'm sorry. I feel bad even admitting these things, but
you had to know.
—Name and age withheld, youth worker conference in Anaheim, CA

As your daughter attempts to control her own life and make decisions, she needs you to teach her how and to encourage her in the process. For her own good, you really have no choice but to do this! A healthy, loving family becomes the adolescent's "life-laboratory" in which she has the relative freedom to test out her own way of making decisions and discovering for herself a value system she can use to guide her. This is difficult and may feel very risky, but the consequences in this type of an environment are generally not nearly so severe as they would be if she waited until she was on her own.

We're not saying that anything goes, and we're not advocating that you throw open the doors to her lifestyle and choices. Be a teacher, and treat her accordingly (even Mr. Johnson yelled and disciplined the students when they didn't behave responsibly). But teach her nonetheless.

A father-teacher will have a hard time watching his little girl flail and stumble, but he will be way ahead in the parenting game if he's there to pick her up and dust her off. As long as you are present and involved, like any good teacher, at least she has a chance.

Trust

The father-judge, even as his daughter grows older, remains primarily concerned that his daughter trusts him. This is just another way to get her to say, "You know better than me, Dad. I will always listen to you."

In contrast, the father-teacher is committed to moving beyond an authority-down style of parenting so that his daughter knows that, no matter what she does or becomes, he will always believe in her.

This is so hard for many fathers. For most men, trust is wrapped up in performance. We may feel like it's parental suicide to tell our sixteen-year-old that we trust her. If you still feel like that, after reading this far, we urge you to go back and reread chapter three.

Lifestyle, choices, consequences, even discipline are not intrinsic to the notion of trust. Trust is saying to your daughter that, no matter what, you know she will ultimately be the kind of person who knows who she is, makes wise choices, and takes control of her life.

A father-teacher, after his daughter makes a series of poor choices (or even when she is in the throes of rebellion), may say, "You will not be with friends for two weeks, and you've lost the car for a month. But I want you to know that I will walk through this with you as you try to learn from what happened."

Many Christian parenting experts would probably disagree with what we've just said. But we're *not* advocating an abandonment of parental concern or of an appropriate control of authority. *To do so would deny that your daughter still needs you to be her teacher when she is not yet an adult on her own!* But we also firmly believe that for a daughter's growth and future development, she must feel that her parents, and especially her father, truly believe in her, and trust her at the core, even when she fails or makes poor—even destructive—decisions. A father-teacher is not so concerned with the scores on the quizzes, or even the tests, in his classroom; he's in it for the lifetime score his daughter achieves.

Parenting is not for the fainthearted or for those who need to be in charge. (Of course, if you fall into this group, it's too late!) A parent's job is to wean his daughter off dependency on him and enable her to stand tall as an individual.

Communication

By now you know what your daughter needs from you as a father-teacher. But for most fathers, communication proves to be the biggest downfall. Research consistently affirms that fathers most often disappoint their daughters and sometimes even cause significant damage in this area.[2] Few dads are out to hurt their daughters. But many of us just don't know how to communicate with our daughters in a way that is meaningful for them. At the very least, we are simply uncomfortable when talking with them. Perhaps the problem is in our approach to the communication process.

A judge-communicator controls the communication. He dictates when and where the conversation will take place, the topic(s) to be covered, and the length of time set aside for the talk. "Speak when you are spoken to" is one of the most interpersonally destructive parenting statements ever uttered. A judge uses his gavel to get attention. A judge says, "I will talk, *you* will listen." *Ouch!* In writing this we can now feel ourselves righteously pounding that sacred hammer.

A loving, committed teacher-communicator gets on an eye

level, and a heart level, with his daughter. He watches for the nonverbal cues that map out the relational terrain. He gladly stops whatever he's doing when she raises a hand. He can tell when his instructions are confusing, or if he's gone too fast or too far, or when he's allowed a breach in the relationship by something said (or something not).

A father who seeks to be a teacher will do far more listening than talking. He will also never fail to answer the question "Why?" when misunderstood or even challenged, though it's up to him to ensure that the conversation stays on track and doesn't get too disjointed or emotionally out of hand.

He will give his daughter the benefit of his years of life — his experiences of pain and joy, failure and success, fear and victory — even before she asks. But he will also be keenly aware of timing, moods, and underlying issues that, although not mentioned, may be driving the conversation. In short, a teacher-communicator father will strive to maintain open lines of thought and intimacy through regular and sensitive communication whenever the opportunity presents itself.

Closeness

The judge's concern is with rules and directives. A judge, by role, cannot afford to get close because intimacy will cause a judge to rule with partiality. Yet a teacher is a better teacher when he or she cares. The teacher's main task is not evaluation, it is development and growth. He or she is concerned with care, instruction, and encouragement.

A father who tries to hold on to his role as the relatively distant and controlling father cannot hope to be close to his daughter. However, closeness is what she needs more than anything.

Dear Daddy,
You used to hug me, and now all you do is yell.
— Kim, 13, Montgomery, AL

Take off the robe, Dad. She's growing up, and she needs her father to love her, listen to her, and carefully — gently — instruct her in how she is to live.

CHAPTER TEN

Being Her Guide When You Want to Be Her Boss

Dear Dad,

This is hard to say (and I probably won't be able to even tell you), but I hate how you try to boss me around all the time. I know you love me, and you tell me that all the time, but I have a hard time feeling like you even know what love means. If you loved me, you would let me grow up. I'm fifteen now, and you treat me like I'm a little kid. I don't need a boss. I need someone to let me make my own decisions.

Remember when we went to the family camp last summer and we took that hike in the mountains? Remember Jeremy our guide? We all needed him and listened to him, but he made it fun for us. He didn't try and tell us where to go, he helped us pick our own trail. Remember how much we all liked that? Daddy, I need a guide more than I need a boss. I love you, but I'm sick of you being my boss. Can't you be my guide? Can't you at least try?

—Sharon, 15, Littleton, CO

From Dee

Memories of an Adult Daughter

I worked from the time I was fifteen until I got married. I've had some great bosses and a few others I would not wish on anyone. But as much as I liked the good bosses, no father, especially a father of a teenage daughter, will be effective as a boss.

My dad sometimes tried to be my boss. Whenever he did, I would chafe, argue, and fight. He wasn't very good at it (he'd made too many mistakes in our family), but he still thought that because he was the "father" he had the right to tell me (and the rest of his children) what to do. This only drove me further away from him. As long as he refused to get close, and to care about my life, I was determined not to allow him to control my life, *even when he thought he was!*

I have also been under the leadership of a guide. I remember sailing in British Columbia with a group of high school students. Our

(continued)

It's a hot day, almost sweltering. As you rush in from a bus that ran five minutes late, you can feel the eyes of the other employees, sharing your fear. You punch the time clock and clumsily rush to your station, hoping your tardiness will go unnoticed. Just as you sit and prepare your spool of coarse wool for the day's quota, you sense his approach. You aren't scared, really, but with a distinct sense of foreboding you glance up to face the duty manager. His eyes tell all. You are being "put on notice," and this is your last warning.

During the boss's speech you feel yourself wanting to run, to hide, or perhaps even fight back, regardless of the consequences. But as you sit and listen, you know you will just sit there, disengaged from the barrage of frustration and anger, waiting for it to end so you can get back to work. No sooner does he turn his back with a shake of his head than you find yourself whispering to a coworker, "I can't wait to get out of this place!"

Consider a second scenario: As the sun rises above the majestic peak of an ancient precipice, you can feel the anticipation of a new day in the wilderness. The crispness of the air, your still-visible breath, the song of a solitary bird having breakfast in a pine tree. "What does the day hold?" you ask. Your guide, a slim, bearded, wolf-like lover of the wild approaches with a warm smile and a warmer cup of coffee. "Where do you want to go today?" he says in reply.

You gaze at the distant peak but hesitate to form the words. "I don't know, really. But, well, that peak looks like fun. But I suppose it's too high, too far, and too difficult for a day's hike."

"Well," he says in a sober tone, "it is a tough climb. There's no easy route. It would take some risk and hard work to make it to the top." Then he is silent. He seems to be waiting for a response.

"I'd like to try, if we could."

A smile. "Okay, then, here are three options we need to discuss, and together we'll look for the best route."

Two types of leaders, as different in style as in function. A *boss* provides both the rules of the road and the instructions on how to get there. Guidelines, objectives, and discipline are the order of the day. A *guide* is a servant, available to offer advice for the journey and help in time of need. With a guide you can count on sincere questions, an attentive ear, and cautious yet gentle encouragement.

Which kind of father does an adolescent daughter need, a boss or a guide? Look at some of the differences between the two:

Boss	Guide
Controller	Advisor
Orders	Suggests
Talks	Listens
An authority	A friend

"captain" functioned more as a guide than a boss. He never took over, but he was ready to lend a hand or give some suggestions when we needed him (whether we knew it or not!). When it was stormy he stood by the helm, but he never panicked (even when we heeled over so far we thought we were going to capsize). When it was calm he would sit with us and talk about sailing, his love for the water, and he would instill in us the confidence we needed to carry on. I always wanted that kind of dad.

The dad I would have listened to—at least more than I did—was a dad who was willing to stand beside me as I made my way through adolescence, one who would have given me the boundaries I needed to keep from capsizing. I would have listened to a dad who was more interested in helping me navigate life's waters than in controlling my every move. A dad who guides will always be sought out when the wind is blowing. But a boss will not be summoned, even in a storm.

———

When your daughter was little, she needed a boss. She found comfort in a daddy who was in control. She needed and sometimes even wanted clear boundaries and disciplinary enforcement of the rules of the family. Your daughter may have been a compliant, obedient, and even happy little girl. But then, between ages ten and twelve, something began to change. As she entered the beginning stages of adolescence, your daughter instinctively knew that she was entering a phase of life where she was ultimately in charge of her own life. It's not that she sought this change. In fact, she may have tried to stall it. But the move from dependence to interdependence in the family was inevitable.

Perhaps you were not ready for such a change, but something had begun to click inside of her. She could sense that she needed to be more than a cute little girl who simply nodded at her mom and dad's ordering of her life. Her heart was aching at the loss of childhood, yet bursting with the hope of becoming a woman. She knew she had to grow up, and she needed her dad's help.

What kind of help does an adolescent daughter need? She needs the loving leadership of a guide!

The following chart represents the differences between how a guide and a boss might perceive their roles:

NEEDS	BOSS	GUIDE
Identity	"Here's the task before you— just do it."	"Who does God want you to become?"
Autonomy	"I am your father. The Bible says you must obey me."	"You will soon be an adult; the Bible says not to discourage you."
Trust	"I need to know that I can count on you."	"I need you to know that you can count on me."
Communication	"Be careful what you say to me."	"I'm always ready to talk about it."
Closeness	"Do what's expected of you and we'll always get along fine."	"Please don't cut yourself off; we need each other."

Let's take a look at how the two types of fathers—the boss and the guide—relate to the five key needs of an adolescent daughter.

Identity

A father-guide is a question asker; a father-boss is a question answerer. As a daughter walks through the changes that come with adolescence, she is constantly attempting to distinguish between the voices that compete for her attention. Some of these messages try to shove her into a box that may or may not fit her: "Be pretty"; "Be smart"; "Be like everyone else"; "Be different"; "Talk like this"; "Dress like that." Other messages seek to shape her identity in the roles she is expected to play and the things she's able to do: "Be a doctor"; "Go to college"; "Don't waste your athletic skill. You're a great dancer."

The voices may mean well; they may even think they're being loving and encouraging. But as the voices shout out the variety of roles, expectations, and desires your daughter is to fulfill, she will most likely feel overwhelmed instead of knowing who she sees herself to be. Each voice presents a path into the mist. With so many paths to choose from, your daughter may have a hard time deciding which way to go. The fog can get quite thick and foreboding. As the voices cry out, your daughter desperately needs a guide.

In terms of identity, a father-guide will repeat one message in a variety of ways and contexts: "As God's blessed and beloved child, who do you see yourself to be?" Your daughter may tire at being reminded of the same basic identity question, but the repetition serves two purposes: It lets her know that you care about her process of discovering who she is, and it constantly brings her back to seeing herself in light of who God sees her to be. Your job as a father-guide is simple and straightforward. You are to encourage your daughter to live as the one she knows herself to be. In this way, you will help her far more than if you tell her who she is to you.

Autonomy

It is a rare but smart boss who encourages those under his authority to make decisions and think for themselves. In management circles the tendency to overcontrol employees is called "micromanaging." A smart, well-trained boss will grant enough authority to match the responsibility required for someone under his charge.

Similarly, a good guide will not allow someone to do something dangerous or foolish. He knows how to steer those he is guiding away from danger, while still allowing and even encouraging them to call the shots.

For a father, conveying and commanding the ultimate authority of a boss and expressing the thoughtful and committed concern of a guide requires a delicate balance. When a father slips into the boss category, his daughter will likely sense his desire to control her, and she will pull back. The older she gets, the more important the role of father-guide becomes. Eventually, your daughter will be gone, and the only hold you'll have on her will be as a distant guide. And that's only if she allows you even that much of a role in her life.

Almost every daughter knows that she needs a guide and will, generally speaking, welcome a father who is committed to playing that role as she develops her own sense of autonomy. Most daughters will make decisions that a father-boss could not tolerate as they try out the wings of anticipated freedom. Many of their decisions will even make a father-guide nervous. One young woman wrote on the Internet to a group of youth workers in a youth ministry chat room about this very tendency:

> Teenagers are so confused. We don't know who we are
> or who we want to be. We want to see what else there is

in life. We want to try and dare to do the things that Mom and Dad always say no to.

We're dying for discussions that will bring us together to talk about real issues. We have hurts and worries and things we don't know exactly how to deal with. We want to talk about deeper things. To be honest with you, we want to know more about how God can really relate to us.

I ask one thing. I beg of you. Please do not ignore us, nor what we deal with.[1]

This young woman's letter was to Christian youth workers, and she was speaking to those who lead youth ministries across the country. But her cry must be heard by fathers, for the poignant call for relevant youth ministry is also a wake-up cry for fathers who want to help their daughters during this turbulent season of their lives.

The young woman claims that young people want to talk about deep, real, serious issues. If a father will invest time, energy, and care as his daughter moves through adolescence, she will have less need to find an outside person to be her guide.

It takes years of slowly building trust and weaning her off childlike dependence on you and her mother, but your daughter wants to have someone in her life who will help sort things out as she makes decisions that will affect her future.

Trust

Both a guide and a boss must have the trust of those they lead, and both need to know that they can trust those they lead. However, there is a difference in emphasis between a boss's view of leadership and a guide's. A guide knows that to be effective, it's more important that his client trust him than for him to trust his client. A boss is more concerned that he can trust his employee.

In the same way, a father-boss will always be questioning whether he can trust his adolescent daughter. But a father-guide focuses on convincing his daughter that he is trustworthy. When he violates that sense of trust, he must do the hardest thing of all on a father's list of duties—ask for forgiveness.

Dear Dad,

Have you ever been wrong? I don't think I have ever heard you say "I'm sorry" without somehow giving an excuse or reason why it wasn't your fault in the first place.

—Christine, 15, Palo Alto, CA

Why is it so hard for some parents to accept guilt and admit wrongdoing? When we've brought this subject up with kids over the years, most laugh and agree that it's nearly impossible for parents to take responsibility for their behavior.

You may be thinking, "At least here's one area that I have wired. It's not a problem with me." Well, perhaps you're right. But we would like to ask you to try something. Within the next day or two, take a few moments of down time (carve some out if you can't find it) and ask your daughter to respond honestly to the following three questions:

- Do you think I have a hard time admitting when I'm wrong?
- Do you think I am honestly sorry when I've apologized?
- How do you think I could improve in this area?

If your daughter hesitates to answer, even for a moment, then you know *right then* that she's carrying some baggage in this area. If she's afraid to say something, if she hems and haws, or sheepishly says, "No. You're fine," then there is, very likely, a block in her trust in you.

Most parents instinctively feel that they are fully trustworthy, and if their child doesn't trust them, it must be the child's fault. But it's understandable that if your daughter believes you have a hard time owning up to failure and weakness, she will allow that perception to cause a rift in her trust in you.

Communication

A boss wants his employees to know there are certain things they may and may not say to him. It is somehow tied to a skewed notion of respect for the position. A guide, however, needs information if he is to be a good guide. A boss may need information as well, but in a top-down organization, communication channels and protocol must be respected. A guide is more concerned with the task at hand and the adventure of the journey than he is about channels and modes of communication and appropriate protocol. A guide is in the service business. Therefore, his client needs to be encouraged to speak up and to speak loudly.

The ability to communicate is the greatest gift God has given to His people to build relationships. Communication allows us to have a thought, feeling, or emotion and then pass that same thought, feeling, or emotion on to someone else so they can experience it with us. Communication creates community, warmth, and intimacy. It is the centerpiece of every human activity, endeavor, and relationship.

Daddy:

This letter I've written you is sad because I could never really say these things to your face. I really wish I could be honest, but you are always shutting me off. You are either too tired or too busy or too mad or too whatever! I know it is partly my fault because I don't say things with the proper respect, or I get mad, or you really are tired. But you never want to listen to me, no matter what I do.

—Kelly, 13, South Bend, IN

Open lines of communication and the modes of communicating are the single most essential tool for the health and depth of the father–adolescent daughter relationship. Any rules, norms, or expectations that block communication will prove destructive to the core of that relationship. It's not just about talking; it's about how you talk, when you talk, and what you talk about that ultimately matters.

A father-guide wants communication wide open when it comes to his daughter. Of course, situations will occur when you need to draw a line in the sand; for instance, when you are overly exhausted or too emotionally charged to connect. But these episodes should be *few and far between and should be the exception, not the rule, to father-daughter communication.* If you recognize that ten o'clock at night is the time when she begins to open up, even though it's your time to go to bed, change your sleep patterns and see these late-night opportunities to talk as holy moments!

If your daughter is most honest when emotionally upset, then as a father-guide you may have to allow her to let off a little steam in order to get at the core of her frustration. Whatever it takes, the goal of the father-guide is to hear what his daughter feels, desires, fears, thinks, and needs. Whenever and however she needs to express that (and this will change over the course of her adolescence), your job is to open the door for her.

Closeness

A boss may mistakenly believe that he doesn't need his employees. But a guide is well aware that he's intrinsically connected to his client, whether or not the client knows it.

With patience and conviction, a father-guide realizes that he and his daughter are linked for eternity. There will be times when she seems to cut herself off from her dad or seems indifferent to him. A father who has read this book may occasionally get discouraged, sensing that his daughter doesn't like him like other daughters enjoy their dads. Or he may feel that his daughter is somehow different because of a season of time when she doesn't seem to want anything to do with him. But the father-guide knows that this season will pass. He knows it's just his daughter's way of trying to find herself apart from her mother and father.

Sometimes a father can push too hard as he seeks "closeness" out of *his* own needs and from *his* own perspective. But a father-guide must remember that his job is not complete until the very long journey is over. During adolescence, your daughter needs to know that you love her and are committed to her, *regardless* of how she behaves.

If your daughter is wandering away, this may be a sign of a serious problem that needs to be addressed with a qualified Christian elder, friend, or counselor. But it's more likely that distancing herself is just her way of working out something in her life. A father-guide is careful not to push. Rather, he listens and is consistent in his care, concern, and availability.

Dear Daddy,

Growing up in a divorced family was confusing sometimes, but your love for my stepmother was always constant. I was jealous sometimes because I knew you before she knew you. Now, as a young woman, I realize that your love for my stepmother was one of the greatest things you have ever given to me. You taught me how a husband should love his wife. I am very lucky to have a dad like you! I praise God for you.

I love you.

—Erin, 20, San Antonio, TX

CHAPTER ELEVEN

Being Her Friend When You Want to Be Her Protector

Dear Dad,
I'm not a baby. Stop calling me that!

—Steph, 13, Atlanta, GA

More than anything else I want to protect my kids—especially my daughter. I can tell this will be a lifelong struggle for me because, no matter how old she is, I want to keep her from anything that might possibly cause her harm. She's my "baby girl," and I'm her "provider and protector."

This feeling, however, shows the great danger of living life by short, snappy little platitudes. In this complex and rapidly changing world, the pithy answers may work most of the time, or even for a season of time. But rarely, if ever, do those clever sayings, created by people, hold up across the board. (The words of Scripture, on the other hand, can be quite pithy, and they are trustworthy over time. But even these must be read within their proper meaning and context, or misunderstanding and even harm can result.) Seeing my daughter as "my baby girl" as she moves through adolescence, and seeing myself as her ultimate

From Dee
Memories of an Adult Daughter

This chapter was hard for me because my dad was neither a friend nor a protector. I know it's important for a daughter to forgive and get past her father's weaknesses, recognizing that no one can be everything we need, but my dad filled neither role for me. And even had my dad been a protector, one who was more interested in socially strangling me than in walking beside me, that wouldn't have been helpful. For a variety of reasons, I was ready to spread my wings fairly young in my adolescence. But I'm convinced that as a girl, and then as an emerging woman, many times I definitely needed a friend.

I think this is true for most girls. The older we get, the less we want and need a father to bail us out or make sure we're shielded from the world. We daughters know that over time we must take our turn to learn how to take care of ourselves

(continued)

"provider and protector" are two such sayings that must be examined for the health and well-being of my daughter.

First of all, when your daughter hits adolescence, she is no longer a baby. To call her that, even in jest or as a favorite pet name, may actually place a ceiling on her growth as a young woman. I can hear groans of disagreement: "But it's just a nickname" or "She likes it when I call her that!" As endearing as one of these names may sound, there is a negative suggestive power in such words. Each time the word *baby* is applied to your daughter, the message is reinforced that she's precious to you only if she remains your little baby. Other terms and nicknames have similar consequences. The older your daughter gets, it's best to work hard at avoiding these self-limiting terms.

I recall a scene from an otherwise obscure movie from the 1960s in which a woman in her fifties was constantly referred to as "Baby" by her elderly yet feisty shut-in father. The obvious point of this subplot centered around the relational stranglehold her father used on her even after so many years. Sure, calling your thirteen-year-old "Baby" or "Sweetheart" may seem innocent. The truth is that every time you use those words—or words like them—to express your relationship to her, you are holding her back from becoming a mature adult peer. At thirteen, this may not seem important. But remember that your main job as a dad is to set your daughter free to become an adult and an interdependent member of the family system by the time she is eighteen or nineteen years old. Every advantage you can give her—even small ones like what name you call her—will be a valuable gift to advance her journey toward adulthood.

Ask yourself this question: "If my daughter were a CEO of a Fortune 500 company, would I call her the name that I now use for her?" She may like the name and even feel that it brings a certain sense of reassurance and comfort. But as she grows, your role in her life needs to change. It's important for you to become more of a valued friend who takes her seriously, and less of a father who protects her and holds the world together for her.

The second popular wisdom that can hinder a daughter's growth into healthy adulthood is the notion of her father being her ultimate "provider and protector." We are all too aware of the strong and positive emotions such a role brings to many fathers. After all, isn't that the father's job in the family? Doesn't the Bible tell fathers that they have the ultimate responsibility to lead, provide for, and protect their families?

Actually, the Bible is silent on the specific *nature* of the father's role. Most commentators acknowledge that, while this is an important relationship within the family,

(within reason, of course). The role of protector may be a father's first instinct, but being a friend is a father's first (and last) calling when it comes to raising his teenage daughter.

If your daughter doesn't feel like you are her friend, she will likely feel forced to look for a man to meet that need. I know this is true; I am living proof. I gave my heart and my life to an older guy when I was sixteen because *I was looking for a man to comfort me, care for me, and cherish me as a dear, intimate friend!* I was never fully satisfied in that relationship, and I often felt guilty, but I knew I needed a man.

Dad, your daughter needs you to be her friend. She needs a man who will encourage and comfort her as she goes through these years and beyond. The best protection you can give her is the love and tender care of a friend. This will be the shield she will take with her as she enters the world as an adult.

———

family, people in biblical times had a well-defined understanding of the various family roles. Fathers in the New Testament era knew what was expected of them and what role they played with their kids. Strong evidence suggests that in biblical times, dads were significantly involved with their children and cared deeply about their kids as people. For example, in Mark 5, the synagogue ruler Jairus was distraught over the impending death of his twelve-year-old daughter. His plea to Jesus for help was far more passionate and nurturing than that of simply a distant "provider / protector." It was the cry of a parent whose love and compassion brought agony and grief to know that his daughter was suffering.

Your daughter needs you to care, to be involved, and to connect with her like a friend as she goes through adolescence. The difficult but necessary balance of being a father as your daughter grows up is that she needs you to give her encouragement and room to grow as a woman, yet she also needs to know that emotionally and relationally she really matters to you. If the latter is not evident, you may see her trying to hold on to the "feel" of being your "little princess."

> Dear Dad,
> I love you so much but I feel like over the years we've lost a special connection between us. It seems like we never see each other anymore. Either I'm busy or you're busy. I just wish I could spend more time with you. I don't think it is fair to either of us.
>
> —"Pumpkin," 13, San Diego, CA

Here are four ways that you can reinforce your willingness and desire to help launch your daughter into adulthood:

1. *Have a monthly "check-in" time to allow her to evaluate your relationship.* This may be frightening at first, but as you develop rapport and can sincerely and honestly talk and lis-

ten to your daughter, these check-ins can be incredibly powerful times.

We believe that fathers should "date" their daughters on a regular basis. But this check-in "date" is more like a business meeting between beloved colleagues. Instead of talking about life, sharing experiences, and connecting as people and friends, sit down, perhaps at a restaurant or in a park, and talk about trust, openness, and how you both are feeling about your relationship with each other.

This is the time for your daughter to share how she feels about her friendship with you. She may be feeling smothered. Or she may say that she doesn't think you trust her. She needs to have such a forum to talk to you, and you need to listen without becoming defensive. Let her talk. Bite your tongue when you want to interrupt, and let her know with every fiber of your being that what she has to say matters to you.

This is also the time for you to share your hopes, dreams, and fears. Let her know—honestly but gently—how you feel she's doing. If you've convinced her that you truly care about her and her feelings and thoughts, she will want to listen to you. She probably won't be too excited about hearing even a mild critique of her, so go slowly. But remember that she expects your authenticity, and she honestly wants to know what you think and feel. She will probably argue, get defensive, and tell you all the ways in which any seemingly negative perception is false. Don't get discouraged. She's trying out life, testing various values and patterns of behavior, and she's scared that she may be failing. She needs you to believe in her and encourage her.

2. *Look for positive signs that she's moving toward independence, and tell her you've noticed.* Because your daughter wants so badly to be affirmed by you, make it a habit to find specific and practical areas to affirm. If she's starting a new school year, ask her to tell you about her classes and let her know you'll be praying for her. When she hints at something new that she's

learned, or if she shows special interest in a specific subject, write her a note, telling her how terrific it is that she's growing up. It's the little things she's looking for as she seeks your approval and love.

3. *Ask her how you can help her.* Your daughter will appreciate a sincere attempt to care for her. But be careful. It's easy for this to appear fabricated or even loaded with unfair or overly protective expectations. You know your daughter. Trust yourself to know what will cause her to get defensive and what she will openly receive. Ask her, for example, how you can relieve some of the pressure she may be under. You may feel that she needs to "handle her own affairs" in order to learn, but she also needs to know how to let other people walk with her through life. It's an American — not Christian — value that claims we must "stand on our own two feet" and "make our way in the world" completely independent of others.

A healthy adult is not *independent* but *interdependent,* able to give and receive help from others throughout life. You can help your daughter to achieve this state. And if you really want to see her light up, ask her to help you! You type a paper, she makes some calls. As you work together as a team, she learns that she can help you as much as you can help her!

4. *Pray with and for her as often as possible.* As much as you want to protect your daughter, it is the Lord who is Protector and Provider *throughout her life!* Many dads believe their role is to be their daughters' protector until she gets married, and then they relinquish that responsibility to a husband. This philosophy — neither culturally universal nor even biblically sound — has the potential to do much more harm than good as a girl grows up. Proverbs 31 would not have been written if the woman described there had been raised by a father who was more interested in protecting his daughter than preparing her for life.

Earl Palmer, of University Presbyterian Church in Seattle,

once made the statement, "We as parents are not called to prepare the road for the child, but the child for the road." This is the task of a father with his daughter: He is to slowly remove his protective hand as she grows up, while replacing it with the loving advice of a friend. This is the only way she will learn how to protect herself from the wiles of a dark and aggressive culture. Prayer is the great reminder that we must relinquish our daughters to the protective and guiding hand of the heavenly Father.

What does it look like to move from being a protector to being a friend? Take a look at the following chart:

Need	Protector	Friend
Identity	"I will take care of you; where would you be without me?"	"I like who you are."
Autonomy	"When you fail, I'll get you out of trouble."	"I'll be there if you need me, but I have confidence in you."
Trust	"You can count on me."	"I know you can handle it."
Communication	"Listen to me, I know what's best for you."	"I am here to listen to you; I will be your sounding board."
Closeness	"Stay close to me, I'll be your protector."	"Walk beside me, I'll be your friend."

In looking at the five key needs of an adolescent daughter, here's what it means to be a friend instead of a protector:

Identity

Most dads struggle with "letting go" of their daughters. You've watched your daughter grow up right before your eyes. As she's gone from a tiny and beautiful infant to a bouncing Brownie, she has always needed protection from a cold world that sought to do her harm. As hard as it is to set her free to live her life and make her own choices, she *needs* to be set free, and she longs for her dad to help cut the cord.

Do you like who your daughter is and who she is becoming? Tell her! Write her a poem or a story. Send her a card. Buy her a flower or an ice cream cone. Let her know that to you she is smart and wonderful, talented and lovely. As you do, continue to proactively hand this budding young woman off to the God who has pledged to be her *true* Protector, her faithful Lover, and all-sufficient Savior.

Autonomy

A father-friend doesn't rescue his daughter every time she gets into trouble or difficulty. He encourages her to have the confidence to initially try to make it out of the hard time on her own. A father-friend is more concerned with his daughter learning how to navigate treacherous and frightening seas than he is about grabbing the wheel just in the nick of time.

Many parents secretly enjoy the power of knowing that their children would be in trouble without them. Some adults even continue to receive an allowance well into their adult years, *even when they have families of their own!* This dependency is neither healthy nor smart for the child and the parents. A child who has been allowed to run to her parents whenever things get tough is held back from truly becoming an adult.

We're not suggesting that you force your child to live on her own or that you never provide financial or other assistance as she grows up. In fact, once children have realized what it means to be an adult and are living responsibly and with a healthy sense of autonomy, occasional help can be an invaluable way of reminding them that, although they're adults, your relationship with them remains *interdependent*. Your daughter will always be a member of your family, and family members tangibly express their love and care for one another during both times of crisis and celebration.

A father-friend does not cut all ties and abandon his daughter as she gets older. We are suggesting a *balance* between two extremes, avoiding both the temptation to overprotect and rescue and the tendency to "cut her off." Your role must change from the father who protected and watched out for his little girl to a friend who is committed and available to love her, listen to her, and help her see that she's a capable young woman.

Sometimes a father can forget how much his daughter needs him as a friend during this process. A dad might, in trying to encourage his daughter's growing sense of autonomy, treat her as if she were really on her own. Such a strategy will backfire. If your daughter feels that she must be autonomous in order to receive encouragement, affirmation, and friendship from you, she will likely try to perform as an adult in external ways while she's not yet ready on the inside. Remember your goal as a father, which is to set her free as one who walks through life with a sense of inner confidence.

Dad,

I love you, Dad, and I just wanted to tell you some feelings I've had for quite some time now. I want you to know I'm very proud of all that you have done for me. I thank you for teaching me how to be responsible, to strive for better and better every day, and most important, to put God first in my life. But, Dad, there were so many times all I wanted was a simple hug or just words of encouragement. I see you play with our nieces and nephews, and the love and affection you show them, and I wonder, where did I go wrong? I always have tried to be everything you ever wanted and I find myself still trying and never feeling good enough. I know you love me because Mom tells me, but sometimes that isn't enough.

—Cathy, 25, Alexandria, VA

Cathy has spent a lifetime trying to win her dad's approval and affection. Because her effort was not developed from a healthy sense of self and in the knowledge that she was freely loved as she was, she never really developed a sense of personal autonomy at all. Cathy's father still had emotional hooks in her that held her back from becoming a healthy adult woman. If Cathy's father had worked to prove his friendship apart from her behavior and performance, and constantly reminded her that she was fully capable to make good decisions, she would be a different woman today. The good news is that if you are or were like Cathy's father—even if your daughter is grown—you can still affirm her ability to function as an adult (though it will take the same hard work we've outlined in this book).

Trust

A friend trusts, a protector demands trust. A father-friend trusts his daughter, a father-protector expects his daughter to trust him.

While trust is a two-way street, and this duality is important in any intimate relationship, the giving of trust is also the defining of a new status in a relationship. Trust granted is a symbol that the relationship has achieved a level of equity and mutuality. When a parent demands trust, or even seeks it, "trust me" sounds more like a command of parental control, power, and authority than a desire for an intimate relationship.

We have talked a great deal about trust. It all comes down to a few simple questions. Do you believe that your daughter, as she nears the latter stage of adolescence, can handle her own life? Or do you feel that she still needs you and maybe her mother standing in the wings, ready to jump in and take over should she fall? To build the kind of friendship that will last a lifetime, and to develop a young woman who is capable and confident, you must believe that your daughter has the ability to take care of herself. Naturally, you will face times—as with any friendship—when you will need to "jump in and help bail." But most of the time you must seek to encourage her as a friend and allow her to increasingly live her own life. Your friendship, prayers, and support will provide her with a tremendous reservoir as she grows into womanhood.

Communication

Fathers love to be consulted. In the psyche of the modern Western male, there is an innate need to be taken seriously. This means being viewed by others—especially our families—as a kind of Wizard of Oz, the All-Wise Answer Man.

What father doesn't envision himself offering eternal wisdom and spiritual insight? Yet every father is human, fallible, flawed. Whether or not he is willing to admit it, he knows it, his wife knows it, and his adolescent kids know it!

At a deeper level, most men would rather be themselves than carry the burden of being the "perfect" dad—whoever that is. We would like the relief of simply being travelers on the rocky road of life, along with our wives, our kids, our friends and neighbors, and the rest of the world. As such, we fathers need others every bit as much as they need us.

As your daughter grows up, you are the ultimate loser if you and she have not learned how to talk and share as people. Being her friend means letting her into the places in your life where few are allowed to go.

It's important not to reveal too much too soon because she is still in the transition period between being a girl and being a woman—a developmental peer. But you have the beautiful opportunity to *begin the process* during these vulnerable years. You can help her to see inside you—maybe just a little at first, until she is old enough to deal with you as a peer. This will enable her to trust you as more than a protective, authoritarian controller and see you as a person she can trust.

Dad, she longs to know you and to hear from you. A day will come when you will wish you'd spent more time simply talking from the heart. As your daughter proceeds through adolescence, she's ready for you to do that now.

Closeness

We have stated that closeness is hard to describe and harder to define. However, the goal in your daughter's journey toward adulthood is for her to feel close to you. No one truly feels close to a protector, however kind and warm that protector may be. Rather, we feel close to those who have proven their friendship.

The little things you do as your daughter is growing up—taking her seriously, investing time and energy into caring for her, listening and talking with her, helping her find herself, and giving her permission to spread her wings and make her own choices—will all add up to her feeling close to you. It's not something you can order or schedule or turn on and off like a switch. It's not even a technique to follow, a kind of "five easy steps to becoming closer to your daughter" program. Everything we've been talking about in this book is more concerned with a mindset than a technique, a commitment than a strategy, a driving force than a calculated methodology of parenting.

Do you love your daughter? Be her friend. In turn, she will stay close to you. And you both will be the winners.

CHAPTER TWELVE

Setting Her Free

Dear Dad,

I'm sitting here on the beach at camp thinking about how lucky (blessed, I guess) I am, and I keep thinking of you (and Mom). You've always been such a great dad! Even when you were mad or upset you always made sure that I knew how much you loved me. Your constant praise for me, the way you believed in me (even when we both knew I'd made a mistake), and the friendship we shared, I took for granted all those years. Now I'm off to college in a few weeks, and it's suddenly hitting me how well you prepared me for the "big, bad world!" Until tonight, I don't think I'd ever really thought about what a gift you've given me as I've grown up. I'll always be grateful to God for the way you've cared for me, listened to me, given me advice without making me feel stupid or silly, and for how you've treated me like a close and precious friend. You are my friend, Daddy. Thank you for that!

—Mimi, 18, Cleveland, OH

From Dee
Memories of an Adult Daughter

God powerfully met me as a broken and lost twenty-year-old woman who needed a father's touch. As you have read, my own father, because of many issues in his own life that he has yet to address, did not "set me free." In fact, at times I have thought that I've been even more powerfully set free by the mercy and compassion of my heavenly Father because my biological father left me to drift on my own. God has a way of healing the broken-hearted and fixing the mistakes and neglect of others.

But that, Dad, is not God's plan for your daughter. His desire is to have you be His channel of love, forgiveness, and empowerment for your little girl, now grown up. To set your daughter free, you must communicate three things to her with your life, your heart, and your words:

■ You are my beloved child, and I will always be grateful for you.

(continued)

In the Lewis and Dodd study of adolescent attitudes toward their fathers, they listed the "Top Ten Things My Father Did Right":[1]

10. Loved my mother
9. Was always there for me
8. Frequently told me he loved me
7. Always told the truth
6. Apologized when wrong
5. Really listened
4. Boldly talked about the Lord
3. Always had a sense of humor
2. Showed me how to be a Christian
1. Always put God first

Nearly every father wants to be the kind of man his daughter will be proud of. This list is a good reminder of that sort of dad. Love for your wife, commitment to your daughter, and genuine verbal and authentically fleshed-out faith are but markers that point to a man who cares deeply for his daughter.

Even when these adolescents reported "always put God first" at the bottom of the list, the rest of the list portrayed a father who is more concerned about living his faith than preaching it. The list describes the father who loves his daughter enough to be her friend, her teacher, and her guide.

A Father's Role in the Adolescent Journey

By now you're familiar with the two key tasks that drive every adolescent: The search for personal identity ("Who am I?") and the development of autonomy. As each young person deals with these tasks, there's no escaping the process of moving from being a dependent child to an interdependent adult. The ones who emerge from this trying and difficult season with the greatest sense of satisfaction and health will be those who have been supported by a strong perception of attachment to their parents. In most cases it is the father who holds the key to how well an adolescent handles the transition.

This seems to be harder for girls than for boys. Boys need to attach, or feel close, to their dads every bit as much as girls. But how they experience the relationship with their fathers is far different from girls. Boys want to be close, but that means they want to *do things* with their fathers and spend time with them in mutual activities.

A girl also wants to feel emotionally and relationally *close* with her dad, and she may accept activities with him as meeting part of that need, for a while. But what she's really interested in is having their hearts and souls connect. Boys want and need this at some level too, but few in our culture are aware of it. Girls are so in touch with relational dynamics, hidden meanings, and psychological innuendoes that from a daughter's perspective a father will either do a great job as a dad or he will fail miserably (there seems to be little middle ground). His daughter, by the nature of what she wants and needs, and how she sees the world, will not let the process happen any other way. Eventually a girl who has grown up disappointed in the way she

> - You are a gift of God, and I cherish the honor of being your father.
> - You are now a woman, and my role will change. From this day forward I will be your friend, your ally, and your champion.
>
> As you celebrate your daughter's movement into womanhood, you are handing her back to her true Father, who will be her Guide, Teacher, and Friend. It has been your task to be His ambassador, but when you set her free she becomes your peer in Christ.
>
> You will always be "Daddy," but she now needs to be able to look you in the eye and say, "I am a woman, called by God, blessed by family, and set free by my dad."

perceived her father ignoring her growing up may come to the conclusion that "that's just the way dad is," and internally make peace with her disappointment. But the years of trying to connect, to please him, and then the behavioral reactions when snubbed are difficult to erase. It can take women years to undo what a father did simply through ignorance or neglect.

Either way, a father has great power over his daughter. For most daughters, he holds the key to such life issues as self-esteem, career choices and ambition, relational stability, behavior and expectations in dating and marriage, and the ability to see herself as a fully functioning adult. Although most women can compensate to eventually overcome the gaps left by an indifferent or non-existent father, some are scarred for life. A loving, involved, attentive father can save his daughter from a lifetime of painful and destructive experiences. A girl who grows up with the perception that her father loves her, believes in her, trusts her, and celebrates the unique person that she is has a much better chance at reaching her God-given potential than one who is left to fend for herself.

One girl sent us a paper she had written for a class that described such a father:

My Father's Footsteps
I'm not sure my father understands how much he has made an impression on me. I live my life following his footsteps and trying to make each imprint fit. He is my guide and my most loved mentor.

I watch carefully the paths my father takes. With love and understanding, he works hard to see his children grow up to be successful, full of life, confident, and kind. The most important thing to him is knowing that his children understand the value of having an open and kind heart.

"Strive for your goals the way you know how, the way you know is right," he constantly tells us. It's simple, but not easy. Through struggles and hard times, my dad is a model for stability and peacefulness. He makes my worries vanish even during difficult times. His arm around my shoulder calms me and I feel safe. It is then that I can go out and do my best. He trusts in God, in himself, and in his decisions, and he leads his family to do the same.

A Father's Driving Goal: Setting His Daughter Free

The ultimate goal of a father is to set his daughter free to be an adult peer in the family system. Some do this too early by pushing their daughters into adult-like roles and responsibilities before they are ready. Your daughter may seem ready to be treated as an adult, but you must be careful not to allow her to be pushed too quickly—even if she's the one doing the pushing! In our culture, many parents see maturity before it is actually there. As child psychiatrist David Elkind writes:

> The [historical but no longer culturally true] perception of adolescent immaturity, though it may have done a disservice to adolescents in some respects, nevertheless reinforced the unilateral authority of parents and adults. This authority guaranteed that adults would play a responsible role in helping young people meet the psychological, sexual, occupational, and cultural demands of their transition to adulthood. For [today's] postmodern generation, however, the perception of adolescent sophistication has encouraged mutual authority between young people, parents, and other adults. As a result, postmodern adolescents have much less support from the older generation in meeting the demands of the transition to a secure adulthood. And this, despite the fact that the demands for today's adolescents are much more difficult to satisfy than were those of the [earlier] modern era.[2]

The goal of parenting during this transition is to watch for the markers that indicate growth in the individuation process, specifically watching for identity formation and a growing and healthy sense of autonomy. The greater the growth observed, the more you should treat your daughter as an adult peer. Always be on the lookout for granting too much freedom, which can easily cause her to eventually feel lost and abandoned. The balance is difficult, but through careful observation, open communication, and genuine intimacy, common sense and intuition will be a reliable guide.

Portrait of a Healthy Adult Daughter

There are six marks of a young woman who has been rooted and established by a father who is involved, attached, and caring.

1. She is confident. A daughter who has been raised by a father who takes seriously her needs of identity formation and autonomy, and who builds a relationship of trust, communication, and closeness will walk tall as a grown woman. She will believe that she can be whoever God calls her to be and do whatever God asks of her. She will take responsibility for her choices, recognize and admit fault when she is wrong, and expect everyone in her life to treat her with respect. This will most likely be true because that is how her father lived and how he taught her to live.

2. She is compassionate. A daughter who has been raised with a healthy sense of self will not be an adult who is overly preoccupied with herself, but instead cares about those who are hurting, unfortunate, oppressed. She will see life as a mission and calling. Her goal will not be self-fulfillment. Rather, she sees her life in light of who God is. Therefore, His priorities will be her priorities.

3. She trusts and is trustworthy. A daughter who has experienced adolescence in a two-way trust relationship with her father will reap the benefits of such a relationship firsthand. As an adult, she will know the power of trust and will be more likely to give herself to others who are likewise trusting and trustworthy. This is an invaluable asset when it comes to her future relationships. Her marriage, her friendships, and her career will be greatly enhanced because she understands loyalty and trust.

4. *She is a communicator.* A daughter raised to share her mind and heart with her father—who has experienced intellectual and verbal intimacy with a dad she trusts and loves—will have the ability to both expect and elicit the same from the future men in her life.

At some level, every man wants to connect with someone he loves, but many have been allowed to hide who they are for so long that they have lost the ability or skills to effectively communicate. A daughter who has lived with a communicating father will know how to draw out a man she cares about. She will also have enough self-respect to demand that he not hide from her. The chances of broken relationships in her life, due to poor communication, are far less than for a daughter who was raised by a silent or distant father.

5. *She will be a great parent.* The daughter who is attached to her father during adolescence will know the joy of intimate, relational parenting. Because she has lived with someone who saw her as important, valuable, and worth time and effort, she will follow that model into her parenting. She will also have the commitment to her own children that enables her to work with her husband to be the kind of father their children need.

6. *She will always be a connected daughter.* The greatest benefit of a daughter raised with an eye on father attachment is that the bond developed during these crucial years will be strengthened over time. As she grows into a woman, her appreciation for her father will only increase. And as the years progress, she will be able to see how deeply he loved her, even when she didn't seem to respond to him. She will be his number-one fan for the rest of their

lives. As she becomes more confident in who she is, she will also reconnect with her mother, and she will see her parents' partnership and love as the most powerful influence in her life.

The Greatest Gift: What Teens Treasure Most in a Father

In Lewis and Dodd's study, teens were asked, "What do you treasure most in a father?" Included in this list was time spent together: "He's my best friend" and "He went out of his way to make memories." The list, however, can best be summarized by two simple phrases, "our mutual respect" and the "ability to talk about everything."[3]

These two statements are what we have tried to communicate throughout the pages of this book. To become the person God has created her to be, your daughter must know that you're there for her. She needs to know that you are calling her true self out, freeing her to learn how to make choices and live with them as she moves through adolescence. She needs to have a relationship built on mutual trust, communication, and a sense of closeness. As you love her, listen to her, and gently guide her through these years, you will provide her the best possible shot at life.

The last step in launching a daughter into adulthood is acknowledging to her that you now see her as an adult woman. There is no specific age when this happens; it may slowly evolve over time. One day you may be talking on the phone to your daughter and realize that she's no longer dependent upon you. She has developed into a person who knows who she is and is comfortable with herself and committed to taking responsibility for her life. When this happens, you will know that your daughter has crossed the line from child to healthy adult, from "little princess" to grown woman.

It's time to celebrate!

Notes

Chapter One: My Princess Is Growing Up

1. For supporting studies, see L. Yablonski, *Fathers and Sons* (New York: Gardner Press, 1990); D. M. Alameida and N. L. Galambos, "Examining Father Involvement and the Quality of Father-Adolescent Relations," *Journal of Research on Adolescents* 1(2) (1991): 155-172; M.E. Lamb, *The Father's Role* (Hillsboro, N.J.: Lawrence Erlbaum, 1987); and J. Demos, "The Changing Faces of American Fatherhood: A New Exploration in Family History," in S. Cath, A. Gurwitt, and J. Ross, eds., *Father and Child: Developmental and Clinical Perspectives* (Boston: Little, Brown, 1982), pp.431-443.

2. Dr. Bruce Narramore, *Help! I'm a Parent* (Grand Rapids: Zondervan, 1995), p.15.

Chapter Two: "I Need You, Daddy!"

1. Terry Apter, *Altered Loves* (New York: St. Martin's Press, 1990), pp.74-75.

Chapter Three: Trust: The Glue That Holds Relationships Together

1. Doug Webster, *Dear Dad: If I Could Tell You Anything* (Nashville: Thomas Nelson, 1995), p.187.

Chapter Four: Closeness: The Adolescent Safety Net

1. W. A. Collins and S. A. Kuczaj, *Developmental Psychology: Childhood and Adolescence* (New York: Macmillan, 1991), p.108.
2. J. S. Turner and D. B. Helms, *Contemporary Adulthood* 4th ed. (Fort Worth, TX: Holt, Rinehart & Winston, 1989), pp.176, 178.
3. John W. Santrock, *Adolescence* (Dallas, TX: William C. Brown Publishers, 1990), p.227.
4. Carol Gilligan, *In a Different Voice: Psychological Theory and Women's Development* (Cambridge, MA: Harvard University Press, 1982), pp.156-157.
5. L. M. Brown and C. Gilligan, *Meeting at the Crossroads: The Landmark Book About the Turning Points in Girls' & Women's Lives* (New York: Ballantine Books, 1992), p.49.

Chapter Five: Communication: The Heart of Father-Daughter Intimacy

1. The research consistently affirms that a father is important in the life of his daughter (Turner & Helms, 1989; Papini, D. R. Roggman, L. A., 1992). Adolescent perceived attachment to parents in relation to competence, depression, and anxiety: A longitudinal study. *Journal of Early Adolescence,* 12(4), pp.420-440; Papini, D. R. Roggman, L. A. and Anderson, J. (1991). Early adolescent perceptions of attachment to mother and father: A test of emotional distancing and buffering hypotheses. *Journal of Early Adolescence,* 11(2), pp.258-275. Yet there is little focused research that attempts to understand how and why a girl's father is an important figure in her life as an individual. This is a question that has yet to be asked by family researchers on a systematic and consistent basis. One area, however, that surfaces in many of the studies on the parent-daughter relationship is a father's inability to communicate with his daughter in a manner as satisfying as communication

with her mother. Studies have found that there are some general communication problems between fathers and adolescent daughters (S. A. Anderson, 1990. Changes in parental adjustment and communication during the leaving home transition. *Journal of Social and Personal Relationships* (vol. 7), pp.47-68; D. M. Alameida & N. L. Galambos, 1991. Examining father involvement and the quality of father-adolescent relations. *Journal of Research on Adolescence* (vol. 1, number 2), pp.155-172.) Fathers are reported to possess less communication skill than mothers and to have, overall, more difficulty when engaging in interaction. But these data, again, are couched within father-child or parent-child studies and so often lump together boys' and girls' attitudes and perceptions. Nonetheless, studies do reflect this communicative attention in the father-daughter relationship. In studying parental attachment, for example, J. E. Paterson, J. Field, and J. Pryor (1994) (Adolescents perceptions of their attachment relationships with their mothers, fathers, and friends. *Journal of Youth and Adolescence* (vol. 23, number 5), pp.579-600) found that both sons and daughters "interact less with their fathers and report a lower quality of affect with them than with their mothers" (p.595). In a study on parental styles of parental communication, Reese and Fivush (1993) (Parental styles of talking about the past. *Developmental Psychology* (vol. 29, number 3), pp.596-606.) found that fathers put more "communicative pressure" (p.597) on their children than do mothers, although the authors believed this to be a positive parental strategy, helping the child to "prepare for communication with the outside world" (p.597). These and other studies found, in general, that fathers are less communicative with their daughters than are mothers (Bellinger & J. B. Gleason, 1982. Sex differences in parental directives to young children. *Sex Roles* (vol. 8), pp.1123-1139. R. W. Larson, 1993. Finding time for fatherhood: The emotional ecology of adolescent father interactions. *New Directions for Child Development*, (vol. 62) pp.7-25. B. McLaughlin, D. White, T. McDevitt, and R. Rasking 1983. Mothers' and fathers' speech to their young children: Similar or different? *Journal of Child Language* (vol. 10), pp.245-252. M. Malone and R. Guy, 1982. A comparison of mothers' and fathers' speech to their three year old sons. *Journal of Psycholinguistic Research* (vol. 11), pp.599-608.) As with much of the literature in this field of study, others have found no significant difference between mothers and fathers in adolescent communication (V. F. Haigler, H. D. Day, and D. D. Marshall, 1995. Parental Attachment and gender role identity. *Sex Roles* (vol. 33, number 3,4), pp.203-220.)

2. Henri Nouwen, *The Return of the Prodigal Son* (New York: Doubleday, 1992), p.90.

Chapter Six: "Who Am I?" A Daughter's Search for Identity

1. I had received this way of describing the Christian life from Henri J. M. Nouwen, who details this in his book *In the Name of Jesus*.
2. Robert Benson, *Between the Dreaming and the Coming True* (San Francisco:HarperCollins, 1996).
3. Santrock, *Adolescence*, p.386; see also study by H. P. Grotevant and C. R. Cooper, 1986. Individuation in family relationships. *Human Development* (vol. 29), pp.82-100.
4. Santrock, p.386
5. Patricia H. Davis, *Counseling Adolescent Girls* (Minneapolis: Augsburg Fortress, 1996), pp.30-31.
6. As quoted by Patricia Davis, *Counseling Adolescent Teenagers*, citing the work of Fine, Mortimer, and Roberts, 1990, p.13.

Chapter Seven: Letting Go: Helping Her Become Autonomous

1. F. Prose, "Confident at 11, Confused at 16," in W. A. Collins and S. A. Kuczaj, *Developmental Psychology: Childhood and Adolescence* (New York: Macmillan, 1991), p.385.

2. P. H. Mussen, J. J. Conger, J. Kagan, A. C. Huston, *Child Development and Personality*, 7th ed. (New York: Harper & Row, 1991), p.599.
3. Patricia H. Davis, *Counseling Adolescent Girls* (Minneapolis: Augsburg Fortress, 1996), p.56.
4. David Lewis and Carley Dodd, *"How Do Fathers Help Turn Their Teenagers' Hearts Toward Christ?"* (Abilene Christian University, 1997), p.80. The study was conducted with teenagers who were generally active in the Church of Christ. Although the findings cannot be universalized to all young people, or even to other denominations, as the Church of Christ is a tightly knit, historically uniform group, Drs. Lewis and Dodd detail some very important self-report data from the teenagers.
5. Lewis and Dodd, p.51.

Chapter Eight: A Father's Love as a Model of the Father's Love

1. Gordon R. Lewis and Bruce A. Demarest, *Integrative Theology* (Grand Rapids: Zondervan, 1987), pp.195-196.
2. Henri J. M. Nouwen, *The Return of the Prodigal Son* (New York: Doubleday, 1992), p.90.
3. David Lewis and Carley Dodd, "How Do Fathers Help Turn Their Teenagers' Hearts Toward Christ?" (Abilene Christian University, 1997), p.81.

Chapter Nine: Being Her Teacher When You Want to Be Her Judge

1. Patricia H. Davis, *Counseling Adolescent Girls* (Minneapolis: Augsburg Fortress, 1996), p.56.
2. Studies have consistently affirmed that communication problems exist between fathers and adolescent daughters. Fathers are reported to possess less communication skills than mothers and to have overall more difficulty when engaging in interaction with their adolescent children (see S. A. Anderson,

1990). Changes in parental adjustment and communication during the leaving home transition, *Journal of Social and Personal Relationships,* 7, 1990, pp.47-68; and D. M. Alameida and N. L. Galambos, "Examining Father Involvement and the Quality of Father-Adolescent Relations," *Journal of Research on Adolescence* 1(2) (1991): pp.155-172.

Chapter Ten: Being Her Guide When You Want to Be Her Boss

1. *Youthworker Journal* (March / April 1997): p.6.

Chapter Twelve: Setting Her Free

1. David Lewis and Carley Dodd, "How Do Fathers Help Turn Their Teenagers' Hearts Toward Christ?" (Abilene Christian University, 1997), p.76.
2. David Elkind, *Ties That Stress: The New Family Imbalance* (Harvard, Mass.: Harvard University Press, 1994), p.169.
3. Lewis and Dodd, p.75.

Authors

CHAP CLARK is associate professor of youth and family ministries and director of youth ministry at Fuller Seminary. He earned his doctorate in human communication from Denver University where he specialized in organizational systems and family relationships. He is the author of numerous books, including *Next Time I Fall in Love*, *The Youthworker's Handbook to Family Ministry* (both Zondervan), *Boys to Men* (Moody), and *The Performance Illusion* (NavPress), which was nominated for Christianity Today's 1993 Reader's Choice Book of the Year.

DEE CLARK is currently working on her master's degree in counseling at Denver Seminary. She has extensive experience in counseling and discipleship ministry with families, couples, women, and teens. She is a frequent conference speaker and has lectured at marriage, family, women's, and youth conferences across the country. With Chap, she is the author of *Let Me Ask You This* (NavPress), a marriage devotional.

The Clarks have been married for seventeen years and have three children. They live near Pasadena, California.

A New Europe in the Changing Global System

A New Europe in the Changing Global System

Edited by Richard Falk and Tamás Szentes

United Nations University Press

TOKYO · NEW YORK · PARIS

United Nations University Press
The United Nations University, 53-70, Jingumae 5-chome,
Shibuya-ku, Tokyo 150, Japan
Tel: (03) 3499-2811   Fax: (03) 3406-7345
Telex: J25442   Cable: UNATUNIV TOKYO

UNU Office in North America
2 United Nations Plaza, Room DC2-1462-70, New York, NY 10017
Tel: (212) 963-6387   Fax: (212) 371-9454   Telex: 422311 UN UI

United Nations University Press is the publishing division of the United Nations University.

Cover design by Takashi Suzuki

UNUP-934
ISBN 92-808-0934-2

Contents

Introduction

Richard Falk

The shared premise of this volume is that the end of the Cold War initiated a new political era globally, and most dramatically, in Europe. After all, the central East/West encounter was situated in Europe, with its primary expression being the division of Germany into two states, each belonging to an alliance that was ideologically and geopolitically antagonistic to the other. This centrality of a divided Germany was epitomized by a divided Berlin, the former capital city of a unified Germany and embodiment of the German cultural and political spirit. Is it any wonder, then, that the collapse of the Berlin Wall in 1989, and the human surge from East to West, represented both the symbolic ending of the Cold War and the victory of the West, or more accurately, perhaps, the collapse of the East.

After a brief and natural interlude of euphoria, the countries formerly part of the Soviet bloc embarked on the hard work of transition, each in its own way repudiating its communist past and aspiring to become, as rapidly as possible, a political and economic replica of its co-regionalists in Western Europe. This homogenizing impulse, an expected sequel to liberation, included as a high priority participation in the integrative process so impressively carried on over a period of decades within the framework of the European Community.

The challenge of this new era was also felt in the West, most immediately and intensely by Germany, at once the most extreme beneficiary of the events of 1989, but also the most tested and strained, discovering that the dynamics of reunification were expensive and divisive, and, in their own way, as traumatic as the ordeal of disunity and confrontation. The far more severe test for Europe after the Cold War was associated, however, with the breakup of Yugoslavia and the Soviet Union, giving rise to ethnic and ultra-

1

nationalist strife. The cruel, ongoing war in Bosnia raised serious doubts about the capacity of Europe to evolve a coherent regional security framework in the absence of the sort of overriding threat posed by Soviet power and ideology. While Serbian efforts to destroy Bosnia went forward, including genocidal policies and practices, it became evident that the various European states each conceived of the conflict by reference to its own conception of national interests, heavily shaped by Balkan memories of intra-European rivalries. As well, the United States, the long-accustomed leader of Europe on security matters, was unwilling to commit itself much beyond a posture of concern.

Also drawn into question by the events in former Yugoslavia was whether NATO could be adapted to the new agenda of security concerns in Europe, or was essentially linked in function and viability to the bipolar structure of the Cold War years. By 1995 developments in Russia, especially the disturbing rise of the ultra-nationalist Vladimir Zhorinovsky, a more assertive foreign policy by the Yeltsin government, and a brutal campaign of repression in Chechnya led to renewed European apprehensions. These were expressed both by the intensified wish on the part of the countries in Eastern and Central Europe to join the wider European economic and security structure as soon as possible, and by the Western European governments abruptly, if temporarily and uncertainly, rediscovering the rationale for unity by way of NATO. In the background, as well, was the allocation of emphasis between inclusive conceptions of Europe that encompassed Russia, as by way of the CSCE mechanism, as distinct from those that were building from their earlier identity as a Western bloc of countries united by their opposition to communism and their commitment to contain Soviet expansionism.

Often during periods of adjustment in international political life, contradictory developments occur side-by-side, and are generally too puzzling to comment upon. In this regard, simultaneous with the reemergence of Russia as a valuable partner of the United States in shaping the destiny of Europe. During the Cold War this partnership took the form of confrontation in a hostile climate, but, even then, tacit shared interests were present, although rarely acknowledged: maintaining the division of Germany as a means to ensure that a third war for control of Europe would not arise from the interplay of intra-European ambitions and rivalry and a shared resolve by the two superpowers that the countries of Europe should be reduced to passivity when it came to the forging of security policy, with European governments pressured into playing subordinate roles in the offsetting alliances of NATO and the Warsaw Pact, so much so that the sovereignty-oriented France couldn't swallow its loss of political independence even as its leaders shared a concern about Soviet expansionism with other Western European countries.

There was an essential symmetry here, and in view of the ineffectual European response to the crises generated by a disintegrating Yugoslavia during the last several years, there is now a renewed prospect of some Russian/American cooperation in resolving the crisis, as well as managing the Middle East peace process, but not on the basis of parity, with Russia's claim to great power status fading quickly. It is now doubtful that Russia as active partner of the United States will define the security of Europe in the years ahead, but even the possibility of entertaining such a suggestion shows how rapidly change occurs in this post-Cold War world. More likely, especially in the aftermath of Chechnya, the evident weakness of Russia's government and the disarray of its military forces, is some new version of East–West tensions, not a Cold War to be sure, but a geopolitical alignment that regards Europe, as a whole, again vaguely threatened by developments in Russia and the surrounding countries that have emerged out of the ruins of the Soviet Empire.

There have also surfaced in this period of the 1990s other European concerns that had long been deflected. First of all, there were tensions associated with international economic policy, specifically the degree to which Europe would pursue protectionism on a regional scale in relation to the United States and Japan, especially given domestic pressures in several countries that are reluctant to embrace free trade on a global scale, despite the eventual success of the Uruguay Round negotiations in replacing GATT with the World Trade Organization, a big step, at least potentially, in the direction of global economic governance. Whether the reality of governance, or even economic autocracy, will emerge is uncertain. There is even the possibility of a stillborn World Trade Organization and reliance on robust economic regionalism and nationalism.

It is difficult to decide whether continued economic integration is leading to a coordinated world economy, to a tripolar rivalry in the form of antagonistic trading blocs that pitted Europe against the Pacific Basin and North America, or is producing a confused cauldron of statist regionalist and globalist ferment, in effect a crisscross of economic arrangements. Implied also was a rethinking of the relevance of relations with the South in the new era. The state/society tensions that surfaced in Europe in relation to the approval process for the Maastricht Treaty, with its ambitious plans for a common European currency and a European central bank before the end of the century, suggested deep divisions between capital-driven and people-oriented economic policy. High and seemingly persistent unemployment in most European countries, including those most prosperous, indicates the likelihood that no strong consensus on the rate and depth of European economic integration is likely to take shape in the immediate future.

Europe since 1989 has not experienced a serene, moderate aftermath to the decades of Cold War tension. An upsurge of xenophobic and chauvinistic politics has produced violence against foreigners, as well as the reemergence of right-wing political parties with proto-fascist orientations. The encounters between the West and Islam have also been played out in several arenas, encouraging calls for secularist conformity by European public opinion. As well, some non-European cultural practices, such as female circumcision, have been criminalized. In several respects, the future of secularism is being called into question by "ethnic cleansing" in Bosnia. Not since the Spanish Civil War has the notion of non-intervention in for-eign societies generated such intense controversy. Then, as now, critics of non-intervention are claiming that the failure to challenge Serbian aggres-sion embodies a diplomacy of appeasement, both inherently immoral and dangerously encouraging to other repressive political tendencies in Europe.

This book of essays brings together a series of much revised papers origi-nally presented at a conference in Velence, Hungary, organized by the United Nations University in 1991. The chapters have been grouped together to suggest dominant themes, but there is some inevitable overlap. Although authors attempted to update their presentations, developments in Europe have, in some instances, overtaken parts of the analysis offered here. Nev-ertheless, this volume as a whole seeks to explore as fully as possible the newly emergent Europe, its internal dynamics and its bearing on the world as a whole. So much historical consciousness has been Euro-centric, but our aim here has been to link Europe to wider dynamics of the global setting.

The chapters by Árpád Göncz and Domokos Kosáry are strictly intro-ductory, presenting perspectives on the undertaking that reflects the outlook of the authors, but not developing coherent substantive arguments.

The chapters in Part Two attempt to depict from various angles the over-all post-Cold War circumstance of Europe. Björn Hettne develops a chal-lenging systemic account of Europe as a region leading the way into a new world order constituted increasingly by regions. Hettne regards regionalism as a functional stage of economic integration that softens inter-state rivalry and allows new forms of political community to take shape. In this regard, Hettne favors what he calls "benign mercantilism" to strengthen the global tendency to move from the militarism of geopolitics to the functionalism of geoeconomics.

Samir Amin is less hopeful about the present global setting, perceiving the new reality as one in which the North is using its technological and military power to sustain its hegemony over the South, causing severe human suffering in the marginalized regions of the world. In this regard, Amin regards the new Europe as once more focused on resuming its role as part of a global hegemony. The prospects for resistance are related to the rise of transnational social movements that bypass state structures, and promote grassroots developments that facilitate delinking from the global economy.

Robert Cox adds an interpretation of Europe caught up in a struggle to adapt to an increasingly globalized pattern of production, which provides the occasion for redefining state/society relations on the basis of more radi-cal forms of democracy that embody true socialist ideals, that is, ideals at odds with what was falsely labeled as socialism during the period of com-munist rule.

Finally, in this part, Richard Falk's chapter situates the new Europe in a world order that is far less Euro-centric, one that is also confronting a new type of geopolitics. Europe's future security is endangered more by "black holes" resulting from "weak states" than from traditional projections of military power by "strong states." As the Bosnian ordeal demonstrates anew, the means of addressing such an array of challenges is not available, nor likely to be; in this regard the Gulf War represented the old geopolitics, while the Bosnian War represents the new geopolitics.

The next group of chapters, in Part Three, come to terms with Europe as a region internal to itself, and especially addressing problems in Eastern and Central European countries that are derivative from Soviet indirect rule and its reliance on bureaucratic centralism.

George Schöpflin's chapter considers the condition of nationalism in contemporary Europe, and the sort of impact that it is likely to have in the near future. Schöpflin addresses the special problems that could arise for Europe from nationalist tendencies and tensions in Eastern and Central Europe, the reemergence of the nationalist and ethnic factor after a long period of ruthless denial.

In Tibor Palánkai's chapter the question of bringing the countries into the European Union is addressed. The opportunities and obstacles are explored both from the perspectives of these liberated countries caught up in internal reform and in relation to the interests of Western Europe. This chapter also explores whether this process of Europeanization should be carried on within the looser framework of "commonwealth," thereby taking continuing account of the unevenness of economic and political development in the two halves of Europe.

Charles Cooper's chapter examines whether this unevenness can be mitigated in Eastern and Central Europe through an accelerated process of technological transfer. Cooper evaluates both the burdens of the communist, statist approach and the possibility of learning from the efficient statism of the newly industrialized countries on the Pacific Rim. In effect, Cooper argues that the statist legacy of communist rule may lend itself, with suitable assessment of specific growth and export opportunities, to a rather successful process of adaptation, making the prospect of transition not quite so disruptive, nor so dependent on superseding the inherited structures with the sort of market-led orientations of most Western European countries.

This kind of inquiry is continued in the chapter by Vladislav Kotchetkov, which examines the functionality of the science and technology establishments in Eastern and Central European countries. Kotchetkov explores reform priorities in the post-communist settings, and, as with Cooper, considers whether and how to borrow from success stories elsewhere.

The final chapter in Part Three is by Lal Jayawardena and considers the complex effects on North–South relations in trade and finance that are likely to result from the democratization and marketization of Eastern and Central Europe. Jayawardena is relatively reassuring that this shift in Europe doesn't have to be at the expense of countries in the South, and that if undertaken with due awareness can achieve mutually beneficial results for all sectors of the world economy. In essence, Jayawardena argues that Eastern and Central European countries are not likely to be trading rivals of developing countries in the South, and are more significantly likely to be valued trading partners. Thus, if financial flows are equitably sustained to both sets of recipient countries there is no basis for the growth of market economies in Eastern and Central Europe to be seen as a threat to poor countries in the South.

In Part Four the emphasis shifts back to the general level of concern relating to the future of Europe as a whole. In Carlos Blanco's chapter European evolution and impact are assayed in broad strokes, drawing upon a concern about the significance of emergent Europe for Latin America. Blanco is sensitive to the dual heritage of Europe as hegemon and as inspiration.

Mihály Simai's chapter also surveys the broad contours of Europe's evolution and prospects, informed by an acute awareness of the historical experience of Europe. Simai is preoccupied with how well is handled the integration of post-communist Europe, especially the implications of a unified Germany, and of economic and political reconstruction for Eastern and Central European countries. Simai considers the correlation between the pace of development of Eastern and Central European economies and their incorporation in the wider, regional integration process. In effect, Simai explores what rate of integration is mutually beneficial for sustaining democracy and fostering economic progress for the members of the former Soviet bloc.

In the next chapter Albert Bressand examines the various European relationships to economic integration and disintegration in the early phase of the post-communist era. In this chapter, Bressand also interprets the past and present interplay between Europe as an economic region and Europe as a player seeking market-share in the world economy. From this perspective, then, there is a tension between inward-looking strategies of economic policy that did not exist when Europe was divided into blocs, and only Western Europe was seeking to consolidate its capabilities to address the challenges posed by the United States and Japan.

In the final chapter Gianni Bonvicini explores the formal institutional evolution of the European Union, seeking to discover the most beneficial path to the future for the whole of Europe. Bonvicini by focusing on the Single European Act is more concerned with Western Europe than other authors, although he discusses, as well, institutional reform in light of marketization taking place in the countries of Central and Eastern Europe.

Taken as a totality these chapters survey the horizon of the future, with particular attention to the challenge and opportunity posed by the post-Communist circumstances of Eastern and Central Europe. Whether this transition will be handled successfully is a momentous question for the years ahead. It is likely to be more influenced than this volume suggests by the analogous dynamics taking place in Russia and the former republics. Europe also seems to be faced by a growing Islamic challenge being mounted on the southern shores of the Mediterranean, but spilling over in various ways into Europe.

1

Opening Address: Who Are We Europeans?

Árpád Göncz*

I find it characteristic that, while speaking about the changing world and our place in it, we Europeans keep asking our age-old question: who are we actually?

The problem of our identity bothers us so much first of all because, if anyone, we are aware of the fact that our culture is not autochthonous. The ideas that struck root on our continent were mostly imported from the Near East, the principal exporter of religions of the world. The imported ideas were then further shaped, thus becoming characteristic of Europe alone.

That is how Christian Europe took shape, preceded by the Greek and Latin cultures, upon which our European identity was built. Thank God, a number of barbarian tribes also added their own features to it; some of them became Europeans being pushed to the West by us Hungarians, until we, too, got a foothold in this region.

European Christianity having thus been established out of various imported components, and our continent having lived it through most of its Medieval Age, the Renaissance Man appeared on the scene. Very characteristically, this kind of European began asking questions about himself. And when he seemed to be on the verge of finding the answer, the advent of Reformation split the common basis of the query. But the fundamental division gave rise to a new type of human being: the autonomous man.

Europe, that successful importer of ideas, became from then on a major exporter of this new type of man; in the final analysis, even the United States of America is an export product of Europe.

* Árpád Göncz is the President of the Hungarian Republic.

This European man produced the French Revolution and the first Industrial Revolution, and has invented human rights. Not that these rights had not been deeply rooted in the European mind for ages, but it was only then that they were distinctly articulated and solemnly declared. In such a manner, Europe created the best cement of the 19th and 20th centuries, mighty enough to keep the global village together, including the Atlantic shores, Asia and the Pacific Region.

Nowadays, with the European characteristics becoming world heritage or mass products, it is insufficient to speak about Europe. But if we want to know more about the impetus inherent in this achievement, as well as the driving force behind it, and look for the common feature of the widely different types of human beings that make up the European species, it turns out that these beings all ask questions. And this is what makes us European, rather than some ability to come up with ready-made answers.

I dare say that the European Man who invented professional philosophy can be considered anything but wise. He was incessantly bothered by the problem of his identity, and could not come to a rest in his relationships with nature and the human world around him. In that struggle he was very unlike the Oriental Man who merged into Nature, and was one with the world.

European Man believed in his ability to change this world. Instead of adapting himself to the world, he wanted to transform the world to the liking of his own self. What were his motives? Our climate, I think; he had to wrestle with Nature for his daily living and to fight with his alter egos, since Europe is made up of many small nations.

Just like elsewhere in the world, centrifugal and centripetal forces were present simultaneously in Europe, but I feel the former was more effective, more crystallizing. Nowadays, it seems that the forces of unity can overcome those of disunity. And this holds true in spite of the fact that, on our half of the Continent, disunity seems to prevail right now. That could be put to the account of the time-lag in history. But unity can be rightly called "European" only if based on differences expressed, instead of differences glossed over or suppressed.

Thus, Europe has always been, and will most likely remain, a continent of peoples. But it should be added that it will also be a continent of regions. Even the present process of unification will surely be implemented by and through regions.

In these very days we are witness to the Mediterranean peripheries coming abreast of the Western and Northern parts of the continent that were the classical regions of European development in modern times. And I, as a Central European, now trust that our turn has come in closing the gap. What is more, in my view we could hardly miss the opportunity – not that it would be sufficient to look on events with folded arms. And I do believe that there will be no second-class countries to the East of us, for Europe would not be true to itself if anybody were excluded from it.

Europe by definition has always been something that accepts and assimilates. My unshakable optimism is based on that perception. On exporting its character to the whole world, Europe is likely to act in the belief of transforming the world into Europe. The very nature of our culture ensures the contrary, because the Global Village about to appear will not be Europe any more. While assimilating the world, Europe also becomes similar to it, expanding into a world itself. And in the final outcome the right question will not be "What is Europe, as distinct from the rest of the world?" but rather "What is the world?" And should everything go well, no question will be necessary since the unity of the world will be so natural. The only thing that bothers me is that I shall not see the day, and, since I do not even hope that I will, I have every right to be optimistic.

2

Keynote Address:
Europe and the World System
in a Historical Perspective

*Domokos Kosáry**

The historian can perhaps promote, to a certain measure, the understanding of the problems of our age by pointing out the way in which we have proceeded and arrived at this stage, and by presenting the main tendencies that could be observed and the experiences gained. But the historian also has to warn his or her contemporaries – decision-makers first of all – to avoid not only the mistakes of the past, but, if possible, also their own mistakes.

If we wish to understand the relation of Europe to the world from a historical perspective, we first have to speak about the dramatic history of European expansion, its evolution and decline, about the gaining of supremacy and then its loss, about colonization and subsequent decolonization. Historians seem to agree that this process of overseas expansion was, from the perspective of world history, perhaps the most important single phenomenon of the modern times, many consequences of which survived when the process itself had come to an end. It is no surprise, therefore, that in 1986 a special project was launched by the European Science Foundation, under the direction of Professor H. J. Wesseling in Leiden, on the History of European Expansion. Its program emphasized that this overseas expansion had dramatic consequences not only for Europe's own history, but also for the history of the rest of the world. It started in the 15th century with the so-called "discoveries." The Treaty of Tordesillas in 1494, which divided the non-European world into a Portuguese and a Spanish sphere, denoted the beginnings of four centuries of colonization by rival powers, a process which culminated in the period of imperialism in the late 19th and early 20th

*Professor, academician, historian, Dr. Domokos Kosáry is the President of the Hungarian Academy of Sciences.

centuries. It durably defined Europe's historical relation to the other parts of the world and to peoples of remote regions.

It was mainly through Europeans that contacts were established between other, mainly isolated cultures of the world. The expansion led to the conquest of parts of the Americas and Asia, Africa and Australia, and to the migration, voluntary or forced, of great masses of people. It created white-dominated societies in Africa, and black and mixed societies in North and South America. More recently, in the wake of decolonization, these were followed by massive reverse migratory flows from Asia and Africa into Western Europe.

Some kind of expansion – economic, religious or political, military – was of course characteristic of several other cultures, too. Suffice to mention here the Asian nomadic empires, the Arab merchants, the Islamic and the Ottoman conquest. Europe's case can therefore be marked off from the others not by the mere fact of expansion, but rather by being more far-reaching, and varied, as well as being of a greater efficiency and more stable than those non-European counterparts. The scope and impact of European expansion were hardly in proportion to the relatively small dimensions of the continent. Looking for the cause of this, an American author, Sidney A. Burrel, came to the conclusion that this external expansion of Europe was a later phase of an earlier, internal European expansion that began about the turn of the 10th and 11th centuries. In fact, it was in those times that quite a number of new peoples and countries established contact with European culture, in a huge semicircular arc ranging from Scandinavia to East–Central Europe. The Kingdom of Hungary, too, was founded at this time.

This internal expansion was marked by the growth of the population, the rise of cities, the colonization of unsettled areas, the development in the techniques of production and transportation, and finally a growth of wealth, exhibiting a relatively steady increase of European capacities. Thus, by the end of the 15th century, Europeans satisfied the conditions which indirectly made outward expansion possible. But Europe still had to be motivated to make the great effort involved in its overseas expansion. Christian missionary zeal no doubt played a great role; this seemed especially true of the Spanish and the Portuguese pioneers in the big adventure, although the thirst for precious metals and the desire for conquest had been present in the background of European slogans from the very beginning. But, in this author's view, a "consciousness of the unknown" was a supplementary factor that moved Europeans to take action.

In reality, European evolution did not of course follow such a straight line. The spectacular boom of the 13th century was followed – right in Western Europe – by a period of crisis. From the East, in the Mediterranean basin and in the Balkans, respectively, toward the Danube region, Ottoman expansion set off, which quickly cut many important links. This setback, too, spurred Europeans to look for new possibilities and adventures, affecting mainly peoples living on the Atlantic coast, for whom vistas much wider than the Mediterranean area opened up.

It is not necessary to enumerate here the different phases of expansion, to describe the wars waged – also between themselves – by rival powers succeeding one another, thus Spain, Portugal, the Netherlands, France, or the taking hold of new colonies, or to describe the special role of England, finally outstripping all of them, by achieving economic, commercial, trading predominance.

In the 18th century, the protagonists of the Enlightenment turned with ever growing sympathy toward the peoples of remote colonies, and applied the lessons drawn from their experiences overseas in criticizing the society of their homeland. On the one hand they created, on the basis of the news they learned about peoples living at an undeveloped level, the image of the "commonsensical savage," capable of recognizing, with his disingenuous mind and instincts, the troubles of the more evolved social and political systems. But, on the other hand, these Europeans also formulated – in the manner of Raynal and Diderot – a trenchant criticism of the powers competing in the subjugation and plundering of the world outside Europe, a critique alluding also to the actions of these powers in their own country. There were also warnings that these distant conquests would have a dangerous effect on the political system of the European states themselves. However, these reflections did not hinder the countries interested in expansion from continuing their actions. The dynamics of the Industrial Revolution in the 19th century resulted in a race for control over undeveloped regions, in order to secure raw materials for exploitation and sales opportunities, as well as to alleviate problems of impoverishment and over-population in Europe by overseas emigration.

Special mention should be made of the fact that the forces of European expansion exerted an ever growing pressure also on the Asian and Far Eastern feudal empires, which they encircled from both the sea and land – with Russia already entering into the new colonial game. By this time the development of these non-European empires had already slowed down; stopped short, their traditional structures seemed to be increasingly backward and inappropriate. The Ottoman empire was gradually forced to give up South East Europe. India fell under British rule. China, with its ancient civilization, was another distinct and huge, separate world, and was able to resist European penetration for a somewhat longer time. China's capacity to resist was also enhanced by the relative stability of its political system.

Among the Asian and Far Eastern state organisms, Japan, this closed insular world, was the one which proved to be the most capable of development. Japan succeeded, more than any other of those Asian countries, in developing also an urban bourgeoisie vis-à-vis feudal lords. But even in Japan internal forces alone were not able to make capitalism develop. Asia and the feudal states of the Far East first encountered capitalism as the concomitant of European conquest.

We can in fact speak, also in the case of other countries outside Europe, about social-political systems based upon privileges and which can be more or less grouped under the notion: feudalism. And, so it seems, capitalism, as a new economic and social system, could come into being in a spontaneous way, that is, from the society's internal forces, only in Europe, or, more exactly, in the more developed epicentre of the European continent; whereas in other regions, capitalism unfolded under the impact of the European challenge and in relation to the already existing initiative, and by this means gained ground throughout the world as the economic foundation of society.

Of course, it can be presumed, in principle, that this transformation, with its concomitants, might well have also come about spontaneously in other regions at some future point. But such a speculative possibility cannot be sustained, or rather does not alter the historical experience and facts that non-European capitalism was derivative in its actual origins.

Europe conveyed to the world what it actually disposed of. It subjugated Latin American local civilization by means of its more developed military techniques. Later on, Europe gained control over other points in the world by economic penetration, trade, commerce, by the range of capitalistic methods. The latter were compatible, if it was found necessary, with the use of force, oppression, arms. But, in the last analysis, the spread of capitalism implied after a time the dissemination of political ideas and institutions, the technical equipment of a new social system. The expansion of Europe brought with it Western ideas, legal concepts. European civilization was transplanted, adapted and imitated to a greater extent than any previous civilization in the world's history. This also allowed other societies and cultures which proved to be strong enough and suited for this undertaking to bring themselves to a further stage of development while at the same time defending themselves from European penetration.

Hence, in the course of its expansion, Europe also facilitated – although often through painful interference and at a severe cost – a process by which the different cultures of the world adopted for themselves the capitalist way, and associated methods of civilization. Of course such countries as those in North America were even stronger instances of this dynamic, but their reality is best considered as transplanted parts of European civilization. Today such countries are put together with Europe to constitute Western civilization.

The break-up of the colonial system was facilitated by the great recurrent, internecine European wars, in which often other parts of the world were also more and more involved. Some more advanced colonies had succeeded in liberating themselves long before the process of colonization reached its final phase. American independence was preceded by the defeat of France in the Seven Years War (1763) and by the elimination of French power in the New World, thereby removing a common threat to both the colonies and the British alike. Latin American countries gained independence as a result of the Napoleonic Wars in Europe early in the nineteenth century. Finally, after the two world wars, the gradual process of decolonization became virtually inevitable. Europe, recovering from its ruins, had to start a new life and to find its place in the changed and changing global world system.

This system is characterized by the globalization of economic, political and environmental problems, by the impact of new technologies, by the discrediting and collapse of outmoded social and political concepts including the Soviet socialist utopia, by the growing importance of the United States and of some new, rising powers in the Far East, and, last but not least, by deepening impoverishment of large portions of the Third World. Of course, Europe has neither the possibility nor the intention of trying to recapture, in any form, its previous role, vanished in the mist of the past. Nor can it try to withdraw into isolation in order to avoid the pressures both of the pre-dominance of the stronger partners and of the misery of the weaker ones. As the example of the late socialist system shows, either type of experiment can only end in a complete fiasco. For Europe there is only one alternative: to find an active role in the global system, and to take part in the building up of a new system of cooperation and coordination capable of managing conflicts between the stronger partners as well as between them and the weaker ones, that is, between the North and the South.

To fulfill the opportunity of this new role, however, Europe has to be united. The well-progressing integration of the Western countries has to be completed by the joining of at least a considerable part of the recently freed Eastern zone, by a new internal expansion of Europe; not only – and not mainly – in order to make Europe bigger and stronger, but also for the more cogent reason of preventing the Eastern zone from becoming a permanent source of dangerous trouble: poverty, unrest and inevitable conflicts, a sore wound on the body of Europe. It is certainly in the interest of Western Europe to avoid this eventual danger. And it is certainly in the interest of the countries of the East Central zone – such as Poland, Czecho-Slovakia or Hungary – to join the European Community. It is, therefore, in the interest of both parties, the Western and the Eastern regions alike, to promote the integration of the whole of Europe. This task, however, will be far from being easy.

Europe is, of course, not only a geographical term. It also denotes a historical culture, one of the civilizations which came into existence on the earth in the course of the history of humanity. European culture is, however, so manifold, so divided by various ethnic, natural, linguistic, religious, political and regional etc. differences, that a British historian, Alan Sked, recently declared that this alleged unity was only a myth, an arbitrary notion retrospectively applied to the past in the service of our recent political endeavor to make Europe united. In reality, of course, this somewhat pro-vocative statement can easily be refuted by pointing out that the existence of a common European culture was recognized by many people long before our time with its contemporary character and that its diverse colors still belong to the same spectrum. This very diversity is in itself one of the main characteristics of European culture. The same author also argues that it was precisely the lack of European political unity that helped European nations to maintain their strength and freedom for many hundreds of years, while the forced unity of the great Asian empires had never been a lasting one.

According to another British author, E. L. Jones, the "European miracle" that is the exceptional historical role of Europe was mainly due to the inefficiency of the great unified Asiatic empires.

The comparison, however, is evidently false. European integration has nothing to do with the centralized uniformity of the Asiatic empires. If it happens, Europe will emerge as a free association of existing states and nations which will each preserve their own identity within the greater framework still characterized by traditional diversity.

In the West, existing states more or less coincide with the existing nations. There are, of course, some well known exceptions, but local adjustments were and will probably be able to cope with this problem.

In a great part of the Eastern zone, however, states and nations do not coincide in the same way. Ethnic groups and fragments of nations are often intermingled in such large numbers that it becomes nearly impossible to separate them by drawing a distinct geographical line. The multinational character of certain parts of this zone cannot be overlooked, and cannot – and must not – be corrected by the use of brutal force. Consequently, integration will inevitably demand in the Eastern zone a modification of the traditional 19th century concept of nation state. This concept allowed a ruling nation of a certain state to consider the entire territory, including its people, as its own national state exclusively, as its own property, without much regard to other ethnic groups or national minorities residing within its international boundaries. The present national conflicts, which appeared in some of these states after the collapse of the communist regimes, are mostly due to this fact. Without changing the existing political frontiers, the old concept of the nation state has to be modified, not only on the upper level, to make sovereignty adapted to the requirements of integration, but also on a lower level, in order to assure minorities, ethnic groups, religions the possibility of using and developing their own languages and cultural institutions without discrimination or fear. This assurance is part of their human rights, which are, of course, in principle, also protected as individual rights. In order for these rights to become effective for groups it will be sometimes necessary to have individual rights complemented by collective rights, including a guarantee of cultural autonomy from the state in which they are living. In East Central Europe no individual would on his or her own have the means to organize a network of educational institutions, including a university. The establishment of education reflective of ethnic and national identity is central to the demands being made by almost every important minority in Europe. A solution for these problems would certainly help to overcome some of the gaps between East Central Europe and the West, gaps which currently hinder the process of integration for the whole of Europe. With its internal structure strengthened, this new, integrated Europe will certainly be more able to locate its new place and clarify its new role in the emergent global system taking shape in the aftermath of the Cold War.

3

Europe in a World of Regions

*Björn Hettne**

1. The New Regionalism

Despite the current military dominance of the remaining superpower, there are indications that, with the ending of the Cold War, a more multipolar world is taking shape, facilitating the development of a new kind of regionalism as one possible structural pattern of a new world order. It is the argument of this paper that this process has been triggered by the European integration process and that Europe serves both as a positive example for offensive regionalism and as a threat leading to a defensive regionalism in other world regions.

The principal argument for regionalism is not new. In 1945, the famous Hungarian economic historian Karl Polanyi developed a regionalist scenario against what he feared was to become a fruitless attempt to reshape a liberal world order. In the post-war world there were, in his view, two options: the utopian line of regionalism and planning. It was the policy of the USA to pursue the first. Polanyi mistakenly asserted that the new pattern of world affairs would rather be one of regional systems coexisting side by side. (Polanyi, 1945, p. 87) The current dramatic world order changes, constituting what Polanyi called an "opportunity structure," nevertheless make it worthwhile to consider this proposition afresh. (Hettne, 1991a)

More recently, but in a similar situation of impending structural changes, Dudley Seers, in a posthumous work, argued in favor of a more introverted

---

*Dr. Björn Hettne is Professor and Director of the Department of Peace and Conflict Resolution at the University of Gothenburg, Sweden.

Europe in a more regionalized world. His "Eurocentric scenario" would, however, benefit the Third World as well:

Our contribution to overseas development may well have been on balance negative, even since decolonization.... There is a growing demand for "self-reliance" in the Third World. Our correct response is to respect this, and – so far as we can – reduce, not increase, our contacts. (Seers, 1983, pp. 181 and 182)

This is basically a "dependentista" argument, but applied to regions rather than to states. Seers also refers to it as "extended nationalism." I shall use the term "the new regionalism," which implies a *multidimensional regionalism* going far beyond the "common market" concept. Most significantly, it should include an autonomous capacity for conflict resolution.

Seers believed that Europe may prove to be the first of a new series of regional blocs, largely economically self-sufficient and with a significant degree of cultural cohesion in terms of common ethnic origins, customs, and historical experience. The new regionalism would be quite different from the existing or emerging regional systems of trade. There would be a stronger political element, including not only protectionism but also a regional welfare policy.

In the emerging tradition of international political economy, this is essentially what elsewhere has been called the "benign" view of mercantilism:

The benign view sees a mercantilist system of large, inward-looking blocs, where protectionism is predominantly motivated by considerations of domestic welfare and internal political stability. Such a system potentially avoids many of the organizational problems of trying to run a global or quasi-global liberal economy in the absence of political institutions on a similar scale. (Buzan, 1984, p. 608)

The purpose of this paper is to continue the discourse on regionalism initiated by Polanyi and revived by Seers, applying an international political economy perspective. My approach is also rather Eurocentric, since the process of "Europeanization" constitutes the point of departure, and the other world regions will be discussed mainly from a European perspective.

Promises

The New Europe, emerging after 1989, is the model case of the new regionalism. Here we find a trend towards political and economic homogeneity, paving the way for a deepening process of economic and political integration.

In the Third World, regionalism seems to be on the rise as well, although unevenly and rather embryonically in comparison with Europe. However, in the post-Cold War order there is a certain room-for-maneuver and there are no longer any really important external constraints upon "the new regionalism." The problems are rather internal to each region: economic problems, regional hegemonism, national conflicts, and ethnic rebellions influencing the regional security systems. The regions of the world have not become more peaceful in the post-Cold War era, rather some old problems frozen in the Cold War complex are reemerging. One example is the issue of "balkanization."

On the other hand, without being a panacea, "the new regionalism" may in fact provide solutions for some of these problems:

- Self-reliance was never viable on a national level (for most countries) but could be a feasible development strategy on a regional basis (collective self-reliance).
- Collective bargaining on the level of the region rather than on the abstract level of "the South" could improve the economic position of various groupings of Third World countries in the world system, and collective strength could make it possible for them to resist political and strategic pressures from the North.
- Certain conflicts between states could be more easily solved within an appropriate regional framework without being distorted by the old Cold War considerations. For instance, ethnic conflicts often spill over into neighboring countries and are thus perceived as threats to national security. The way states commonly deal with these issues is normally the most certain way of perpetuating them. Therefore a regional solution is often the only realistic option.

The arguments for regionalism make sense today as in 1945, but, as history shows, the future is pregnant with surprise. Regionalism or interdependence is an open question. The crucial point is the strength of social actors which are the carriers of competing "social projects." (Hettne, 1986) Are there existing or emerging world regions to fill an emerging vacuum of power, or will an eventual trend towards multipolarism lead to an intensification of anarchic conditions? A political transformation of dormant world regions into acting subjects also implies substantial changes within the various regions.

Preconditions

The history of regional integration in the different areas of the world after World War II shows the working of many disparate and conflicting impulses. In the first wave, regional cooperation was largely a hegemonically imposed phenomenon in the context of the Cold War. Gradually regionalism became a force propelled mainly by *internal* factors. (Väyrynen, 1984) This is the most important precondition for "the new regionalism," although regional formations necessarily operate in the context of a global system and, thus, the one cannot be understood in isolation from the other.

One essential precondition for the process of regionalism from below to gain momentum is increased political and economic homogenization among the countries of a particular region. In the formation of regions the security imperative, in both its negative and positive impact, is of particular importance.

The positive and negative aspects of the security imperative are simultaneously in operation, in the sense that integration within a region can be both positively related to cohesive factors within that region, as well as negatively related to threat factors from outside the region. If regional integration is defined by its predominantly voluntary character (Haas, 1970), it cannot be primarily caused by coercive factors within the region. This would imply empire-building rather than regional integration. The principle of voluntariness underlines the need for a certain balance of power, as well as a reduction of threat factors within the region. Successful integration generates a positive-sum-game and also a transformation of the security order from a "security complex" to a "security community."

In a "regional security complex" the national securities of the involved states are deeply interwoven. (Buzan, 1991) In a "regional security community" (Deutsch, 1957) the institutional development has succeeded in eliminating even the thought of using force as a means of conflict resolution. Also the threat perceptions are becoming more homogenized and externalized.

Thus, in order to be a peace factor, the regional organization should coincide with the security complex as a whole, not only with a particular subcomplex. Furthermore, it should provide some countervailing force to the local great power. The ultimate criterion for a successful process of regionalization is, as was stressed above, the development of an efficient internal mechanism for regional conflict resolution.

2. Hegemonic Succession in the Capitalist World

A market, whether national or global, presupposes some kind of political order in order to function. The crucial issue in the case of any transnational market is how economic exchange and even economic cooperation can take place under conditions of anarchy, or, differently put, how the "anarchy" becomes orderly enough to permit economic transactions of different types. This is of course particularly difficult when we are dealing with "the world market," i.e. those national markets which are linked to each other under some kind of free trade regime. Recent debates in international political economy have focused on the role of hegemonic stability in the functioning of the international economy, as well as the implications of the decline of hegemony for its smooth working. (Keohane, 1984)

The Meaning of Hegemony

Hegemony should be distinguished from a mere dominance based on force. It can be seen as a comprehensive kind of power, based on several different but mutually supportive dimensions, which fulfills important functions in a system lacking formal authority structure. Consequently, hegemony is by definition more or less voluntarily accepted by other actors. This implies that hegemony can decline simply as a consequence of a legitimacy deficit, even if the power resources should remain intact. In such a case hegemony is peeled off and only dominance is left. It also implies that a reduction in power resources is compatible with a continued hegemonic position – to the extent that the leadership role of the hegemon is accepted by other states in the system. Hegemonic power is relational and contextual, and carries little meaning in separation from the system of which it forms part, and which it helps define.

The *theory of hegemonic stability* purports to explain the creation, functioning and disintegration of a liberal world economy – nothing more and nothing less. It is obvious that a powerful state with socialist inclinations would not support a liberal world economy. In fact the concept of hegemony loses its established meaning in such a highly hypothetical situation.

The theory assumes a free trade orientation of the hegemon, as well as a willingness to pay the necessary costs for keeping the world economy open.

Increased rivalry and conflict among capitalist countries concern the problem of succession, i.e. the question of the potential new hegemon. From a historical perspective this problem has been resolved through wars. (Modelski, 1978; Gilpin, 1981; Kennedy, 1987) The current situation seems different. The likelihood of a "succession war" is reduced for reasons of military technology – war is simply too destructive. The new battleground is rather economic competition, which most likely will take place among the emerging trading blocs (the Triad). There is, furthermore, no obvious candidate for the role of a new hegemon, but Japan and the new Europe are two potential candidates. Their weakness lies in their low military profile up until now, as was clearly illustrated during the Gulf War.

The crucial question is whether the decline of hegemony automatically leads to a disintegration of the liberal international economy. This concern with the liberal order and the preconditions for its smooth functioning explains the focus on the issue of US hegemony – and the consequences of its alleged decline.

The USA in Decline?

Based on its more multidimensional hegemonic power, the USA has provided the general rules for the world economy. These rules are summed up in what usually is referred to as the Bretton Woods system, which has constituted the framework for economic interdependence for the last several decades. Consequently a decline in US hegemonic power seems to imply a world governance crisis, for instance in the form of nationalist and protectionist policies, challenging the existing rules of the game and making the world economy more fragmented. There is one debate on the theory of hegemonic stability as such, and another dealing with the issue whether a persuasive case for US decline really can be made.

Here we are primarily concerned with the second debate. The theory of hegemonic stability implies that hegemonic power is temporary and subject to what Paul Kennedy in an often quoted phrase called "imperial overstretch." Is this what now ails the USA? Before we enter this debate it should be stressed that even "the myth of hegemonic decline" is real in its consequences, as it forms part of a political climate conducive to the development of a strategy to cope with hegemonic decline. At the same time, the fact that Pax Americana is called into question indicates a weakening of the ideological dimensions of hegemony. (Cox, 1991)

Turning to the empirical issue, the question of decline depends, of course, on our definition of hegemonic power. The more multidimensionally the hegemonic power is defined, the more difficult it is to answer the question about rise or decline in precise quantitative terms. Decline may characterize one dimension and revitalization another. A stable hegemony would, however, necessitate a convergence of power dimensions: military strength, industrial capacity, financial solvency, political and social stability. On some of these dimensions the USA is getting weaker. We must therefore distinguish its phase of multidimensional hegemonism (the 1950s and 1960s) from the recent phase of unidimensional hegemonism (or dominance?).

The thesis of US decline has been seriously challenged by quite a few observers from different perspectives. (Strange, 1988; Russet, 1985; Huntington, 1988; Krauthammer, 1990) The Gulf War certainly demonstrated that the USA is the only state with a global military reach, but also underlined the financial problem of sustaining the exercise of such power, raising the question of "imperial overstretch." A hegemonic power should, arguably, be able to move militarily without "passing the hat." (Hormats, 1991)

The cracks in the alliance behind the UN military action in the Gulf, particularly in the messy aftermath of the war, illustrate the limitations of US ideological leadership. Neither Japan nor Germany felt the military action to be really necessary and had reasons to suspect that US dominance in the Middle East also implied dominance over them, in view of their oil dependence. France at times acted against the US strategy but remained isolated in the European context. A lot of rethinking is going on in Europe regarding a common security policy, ultimately leading to some form of European military cooperation. The Grand Alliance with the USA as undisputed leader is thus explained by rather unique political circumstances, not likely to be repeated.

The opinion in the USA is today, as has been true before, split between isolationists and globalists. The latter argue in favor of a unipolar world with the USA unilaterally imposing its solution upon various regional conflicts, solutions that are consistent with "the national interest" of the United States. (Krauthammer, 1991) For the isolationists the prospect of a North American region, consisting of the USA, Canada, and possibly Mexico (NAFTA), would be a proper response to the development of a "European fortress."

A European Candidacy?

During 1989–90 there were several signs of increasing European independence vis-à-vis the USA. The Gulf War in the spring of 1991 dramatically reversed this perception of eroding US influence. (Hadar, 1991) Whether this reversal is temporary or not is being debated, but there are few doubts about the new Europe's intentions to deal with its own crises, as for instance the events in former Yugoslavia.

I shall assume that hegemonic decline and multipolarism in the post-Cold War period will result in a more autonomous Europe as a whole. The future security system will reflect this broader integration pattern, often referred to as the "Europeanization" of Europe. The essential meaning of this concept is embodied in the process toward increasing political homogeneity, the elimination of extremes. (Hettne, 1991b)

The more recent process of homogenization in Europe has gone through three phases: in the South, the disappearance of fascist regimes in the mid-1970s; in the West, the self-assertion of the Atlantic partners in the early 1980s; and in the East, the downfall of the communist regimes in the late 1980s. Fascism and communism (some countries have tried both) can be seen as nationalist "catching up" ideologies in a historical context of Western technological superiority over Eastern and Southern Europe. The elimination of the Mediterranean dictatorships removed some anomalies from the European scene and put the continent on the road towards political homogeneity, a basic precondition for substantial economic integration. As far as Eastern and Central Europe is concerned, the orientation simply had exhausted its potential, not least as a model of development.

The political homogenization also implies an increased similarity as far as economic and even social policies are concerned. The course toward economic union and a common financial structure is now firmly set. Thus, Europe began more and more to appear as one single actor in world politics, albeit gradually and not without birth-pangs. Europe is *outgrowing* the integrative framework of the EC and this makes it necessarily more concerned with "domestic" issues. There are forces which want to make Europe a global power, but these forces are countered by other interests and movements favoring a non-hegemonic world system. There are thus several Europes and, consequently, several possible future scenarios, regarding both internal developments and external policies.

3. The New Political Landscape of Europe

The process of homogenization has led to a state of liberal hegemony in Europe, and democracy and market will therefore provide the basis for future integration. This political homogenization of Europe is and will be expressed in the enlargement of the EC, unless the twelve present members take a protectionist attitude toward the rest of Europe, which would be an untenable position, as it would imply different degrees of European citizenship.

The attitudes concerning deepening vs. enlarging among the twelve are, however, very mixed, while an increasing number of countries are queuing up (Austria, Sweden, Malta, Cyprus, Turkey) and more can be expected to turn up in the near future (Norway, Finland, Iceland, Hungary, Poland, Czechoslovakia, the Baltic countries). We may also face a situation when completely new nations approach the EC (Slovenia, Slovakia). As long as an applicant is a capitalist democracy with a European culture, it would seem hard to draw a line between the welcome and the unwelcome. In the course of the 1990s, the number of members could thus reach perhaps twenty and beyond that the EC will coincide with Europe as a whole. This raises the question of a viable security order for Europe.

Towards a European Security Order

There is already a certain competition between existing institutions regarding their respective roles in an emerging security order for Europe. This evolution will take place in the context of crisis rather than orderly planning. The Gulf War was one of such crises, another has been associated with the breakdown of the Yugoslav federation and the disintegration of the Soviet internal empire, a third the desperate pressure for immigration from the Balkans and from North Africa across the Mediterranean. Thus, due to this pressing time factor, the actual organizational solutions may be suboptimal.

So far three organizational possibilities have emerged:
(a) NATO with a strengthened European leg. This is basically a continuation of the old Atlantic partnership, but with a stronger role for Europe. This option would imply continued US control over Europe and the maintenance of the essentially economic character of the EC.
(b) The EC takes on a politico-military role, perhaps through the cooptation of the WEU. In a more moderate version of this scenario, WEU remains outside EC to provide a bridge between NATO and EC. At present only nine of the twelve are members of the WEU, and some of the current candidates for EC membership are sensitive about security cooperation.
(c) The Conference on Security and Cooperation in Europe (CSCE) becomes more institutionalized and provides a collective security system for Europe, a kind of European UN. In a longer time perspective, it may also be provided with some military capabilities. This all-European security structure would guarantee the continued presence and participation of both the ex-superpowers.

CSCE will operate only in a peace order, which is more or less distant, depending on the nature of crisis management in the short run. If the purpose of NATO was to "keep the Americans in, the Russians out and the Germans down" that purpose has now been lost. My assumption is that NATO will fade away, and instead the EC will take upon itself a stronger political and military role. The internal divisions surfacing in connection with the Gulf War revealed the problems involved in creating a new security order for Europe, but also the need for a common European political (and consequently military) front. However, security orders are not really *created*, they emerge from responses to real challenges and therefore they cannot be predicted.

Regional Conflict Resolution: The Case of Yugoslavia

Without doubt, successful regional conflict resolution is the ultimate test for an autonomous regional security system. Yugoslavia provided the first test, and few observers would consider this an unqualified success. EC crisis management, however, shows a significant improvement between the Gulf and the Yugoslavian crises, not only because the latter was an "internal" European crisis, but also owing to real changes in political attitudes in preparation for the controversial but unavoidable political and military union.

It should be kept in mind that, despite Bosnia, Slovenia has been spared fighting, and that other explosive regions (Kosovo, Macedonia) remained largely peaceful. It was the EC troika of foreign ministers, neither NATO nor the CSCE, which did the acting. The process was not without internal differences, however. Austria and Germany were more sympathetic to the aspirations of the secessionist republics, whereas other countries, among them France, were more anxious to retain the Yugoslav federation. The important point was not to encourage secessionism, while at the same time not to let the federal government or the military establishment believe that a violent solution would be acceptable. Opinions also differed with regard to a possible military intervention, if and when mediation failed. As the crisis deepened, public opinion turned increasingly against Serbia, which was in line with Croatian strategy.

The crisis underlined the power vacuum in a Europe still searching for a viable security order. An uncontrolled and violent dissolution of the Yugoslav federation has had farreaching consequences for the whole of the Balkans, the most turbulent of the European subregions, if not for the whole European project.

A failure does not necessarily imply an impotence on the part of the EC. It should be recognized that no easy resolution to this conflict existed. Lessons will nevertheless be derived, and the necessary constitutional and institutional adaptations will be made. Perhaps the next challenge will be "the Magyar question" (the numerous restive Hungarian minorities in Romania, Czechoslovakia, Yugoslavia, Ukraine, and Austria). Whatever the outcome, the crisis will be a milestone on the road to a European political and military union.

The Internal Pattern of Europeanization: Subregionalism

In the new European landscape several subregions, which transcend the old Cold War division, are emerging. Some of them reflect old historical formations: the Swedish Baltic Empire, the Habsburg Empire, and the group of Balkan countries once part of the Ottoman Empire. Bilateral relations, which under Cold War conditions had a pioneering significance in these three contexts, are Finland–Estonia, Austria–Hungary, and Greece–Bulgaria.

One interpretation of this new trend is that we are witnessing a return to classic balance-of-power politics in a new subregional form, where the sources of power are more economic than military. The objective need for such a pattern is obviously in response to the emergence of a unified Germany as the predominant regional political and economic power. The German threat is an evident factor behind attempts to form a Central European Union.

On the other hand, Germany with its strong federal traditions may itself form part of various subregional formations. Hamburg/Bremen cultivates a "Hanseatic" project to revive the old medieval trading system in northern Europe and give it a modern shape. The purpose is to provide a challenge to the southern German growth pole centered on Munich, which together with Milan and Barcelona constitutes a strong economic triangle in southern Europe.

The Baltics are swiftly building up economic relations with the Nordic countries, and may enter the EC through the less cumbersome EFTA route. At the same time they will provide a gateway for trade with the republics of the former Soviet Union, above all Russia.

Turning to the Balkan subregion, the immediate unifying threat seems to be Turkey rather than Germany. From the point of view of peace-building, subregional cooperation should therefore preferably include Turkey, which in view of Turkey's application for EC membership by no means should be ruled out. Against this, however, stands the fact that European identity took shape in reaction to an alleged "Asiatic Despotism," for which Turkey was the first model.

Thus, Europe will grow, and as it grows it will turn inwards. New levels of economic and political action will appear: subregions, transnational growth zones, and ethno-nationalism. The latter will be legitimized and might become less destructive in the setting of the new Europe. Movements creating tensions in the context of present state structures will partly achieve their purpose in a Europe without borders, e.g. the Hungarians, the Tyroleans, the Basques, and the Macedonians and other minorities living in several states, but not permitted to create a state of their own.

The External Impact of Europeanization

What will be the future European role in other regions? A new aggressive hegemonic superpower or a "Fortress Europe" closing its doors to the Third World? Or will it become a responsible actor organizing massive transfers of resources, as argued in the Brandt Commission's reports?

The external effect of the process of Europeanization differs depending on alternative "domestic" developments. Below follow some scenarios:

The Orwellian or "Fortress Europe" scenario perceives Europe as a regional security state, inspired by autarkic mercantilism and in latent or manifest conflict with other regional systems. A European Fortress will build fences against an excluded "thirdworldized" Europe and a possible "great march" from a marginalized Third World. From the poor parts of the Third World there will thus be increasing migration pressures, reinforcing the trend towards "Fortress Europe." Many European newspapers have drawn the conclusion that the drama of the Albanian refugees in Italy could be a mere foretaste of what can be expected in the future. I call this rather dreadful scenario Orwellian, because of its similarity to the way Orwell described a future world in his "1984." It is a darker conception of "Fortress Europe" than the assumption simply of increasing protectionism, although a connection is often made. (*IM*, December 1988)

The *"European Superstate" scenario* views Europe as an extroverted regional state, which is inspired by a mixture of liberalism and some elements of mercantilism. Internally, it will be organized in the form of concentric circles with a core, semiperiphery and periphery. Externally, the new superstate centered on the core will aspire to a hegemonic position, or at least a shared, trilateral, hegemony. This means that Europe should take a more active role in global security structures, relying on its own regional security/coercive capabilities. It will cultivate selective relations with the more dynamic parts of the Third World, for instance the emerging regional powers. It will also continue to provide some development assistance to the poor within the Lomé framework.

The *Neo-Atlanticist scenario* perceives Europe as a more open trading system consisting of sovereign nation-states, protected by a modified Atlantic security system: NATO with a European leg. The economic inspiration for this scenario comes from neoliberalism, the dominant development ideology of the 1980s, particularly in its British "new right" form, and in Reaganism, combining a belief in market miracles with jingoist nationalism. The Gulf War was a revival of this project after a decline following the events of 1989. The major international contradiction according to this worldview is what is called "Euro-America" vs "Islamistan." This Europe will create an unstable situation, which sooner or later will transform itself into one of the other scenarios, depending on which social forces emerge in the different countries, and how they relate to one another.

The *"European Home" scenario* views Europe as an introverted regional state in a world of regional blocs, a neomercantilist state inspired largely by the values of the left-liberal, social democratic and Euro-communist welfare ideology. It thus includes a substantial element of interventionism in order to protect the welfare system, as well as nurtures supportive links to Third World regions. Such links would primarily promote collective selfreliance on a regional level, such as the so called "Nordic initiative" towards SADCC.

The *"Greening of Europe" scenario* envisions Europe as a loose, undefined informal structure of regions and local communities within a world order of similar decentralized structures, which would be characterized by "third system politics." The role of the state would be drastically reduced in this rather anarchistic scenario which, judging from some recent elections, has lost some of its earlier attraction.

None of these scenarios will have a monopoly on the future; rather they constitute parallel and complementary political tendencies, influencing and modifying a mainstream model in which the probable core will be a compromise between the "European Home" scenario and the "European Superstate" scenario. The actual compromise will depend on internal European forces, which at least at present favor the former scenario.

None of these scenarios will, furthermore, provide good news for the Third World. A North–South structure is now emerging within Europe. This undoubtedly means that the importance of the Third World will diminish in economic as well as in political terms.

Evidently, the EC will take note of the human rights record in its dealings with individual developing countries (the 68 ACP countries). Environmental concerns will play an increasing role. Further obstacles are created by the EC's anti-dumping policies. Reciprocity will be a key issue in the EC trade policy. (*South*, Nov. 1990–Jan. 1991) In the immediate future, at least, poor Third World countries will have to rely more on their own resources. EFTA contains a core of "likeminded countries" with a tradition of more generous assistance, but EFTA is rapidly harmonizing the Euro–South relations to EC standards. One obvious response to this emerging situation is Third World regionalism: South–South cooperation and collective self-reliance.

4. Soviet Decline and the Formation of a Post-Communist World

The US and Soviet hegemonies were altogether different species: liberal versus imperial. Soviet hegemony rested on the ideological primacy of the Communist Party of the Soviet Union within the socialist world system but this primacy was backed by the militarized Soviet state. This situation is therefore more akin to the old type of imperial dominance, and in fact there was a striking continuity between the tsarist empire and the now dissolved Bolshevik state. Although described as a "socialist federation" which included the right to secession, there was no procedure for how this should be realized.

Thus, compared to Pax Americana, Soviet hegemony was more coercive and less related to technological superiority and economic strength. (Dibb, 1986; Kaiser, 1988) For that reason the rules of the capitalist world economy also applied to the socialist world system, insofar as its external relations were concerned. As long as the socialist system was relatively closed, however, the Soviet dominance reigned supreme.

From Hegemonic Power to "Chaos Power"

The sources of Soviet ideological hegemony were several:

Firstly, Russia experienced an indigenous revolution, and therefore enjoyed ideological supremacy among subsequent revolutionary societies. The culmination of this prestige was the Great Patriotic War against fascism.

Secondly, the existence of Soviet Russia provided a revolutionary space to be utilized by revolutionary movements all over the world. Successful movements, which subsequently were transformed into state power, naturally felt gratitude to the leader of world revolution.

Thirdly, by its sheer size, the Soviet Union stood out as the dominant power "on the other side" and therefore constituted a natural political alternative. This "side," however, never was a symmetric counterpart in structural terms, but a rather heterogeneous constellation of rebels, which under the conceptual umbrella of "socialism" tried to catch up with advanced capitalism – or escape dependence. At present, this socialist world system, with some important Asian exceptions, has dissolved, a process obviously related to the withdrawal of the Soviet Union from its traditional geopolitical spheres of interest. The "revolutionary societies" had survived mainly through external support.

The erosion of Soviet ideological hegemony started at the same time as its consummation, i.e. during the years after the Second World War. First to question it was Tito's Yugoslavia. More widespread East European disturbances followed after the death of Stalin, and in the late 50s China embarked upon its own road to socialism (or wherever this road will lead). The open Sino-Soviet break in 1964 put an end to the illusion of a unified socialist world system under Soviet hegemony. Ten years later the Soviet Union, after a long defensive struggle, grudgingly gave up its ideological monopoly. This was also the time of the birth of Eurocommunism. The Western communist parties became irreversibly autonomous. Again, after a little more than a decade, the Soviet Union unilaterally lifted the "overlay" over Eastern and Central Europe, and the socialist countries were turned loose, free to abandon socialism. We are now in the last phase: the dissolution of the Soviet empire.

The erosion of Soviet hegemony of course also had its material causes, or what in a somewhat different context has been termed "imperial overstretch." The military build-up, started in the 1960s, reached an economic ceiling ten years later, when severe economic stagnation set in. Add to this the growing discontent among national minorities throughout the Soviet empire, and the picture of an irreversible hegemonic decline is fairly complete. Gorbachevism should in fact be understood as a "diplomacy of decline" (Sestanovich, 1988) and, as Hans Magnus Enzensberger expressed it, Gorbachev was the "master of retreat."

Since a military threat to the external world would be suicidal, what remained of Soviet power was "chaos power," the power to produce havoc in the rest of the world. The problem was that this power cannot be used repeatedly, it is quickly exhausted. The G7 meeting in London (July 1991) restricted the Western support for Gorbachev's reforms to association with and advice from the IMF and the World Bank. Judging from other countries' experiences, these are not very stabilizing measures, as later developments in the Soviet Union also confirmed. The increasingly negative reactions to Soviet appeals were based on the external judgment of the viability of the Soviet federation and the realization that it was time to deal directly with the emerging states that were arising in place of the old republics. This change in attitude of course reinforced the process of dissolution.

The Soviet Region: An Eastern EC?

Homo Sovieticus is a disappearing species. Instead there are emerging states which, in order to avoid economic fragmentation and political tensions, will have to sort out their relations within some kind of regional framework. As in Europe, there is a need for some kind of balance between one major regional power and smaller subregional groupings. Therefore, in the future, we will perhaps look upon the Soviet Union as "an Eastern EC." Devolving substantial authority from the center to the republics and regions has proved to be the only way to save some kind of federation or confederation. (Kux, 1990) This method may not necessarily succeed, but then there is no solution apart from war.

There is thus a great likelihood that what has already happened to the external empire now will happen to the internal. Some countries of the external empire will presumably escape the region by "de-Easternization" and consequently join the more wealthy "Western EC," but for most countries in the internal empire, perhaps with the exclusion of the Baltics, a poorer Eastern version of the EC is the best that they can hope for. Economic nationalism on the level of the fifteen republics would be a catastrophe. Russia produces 63 percent of the union's electricity, 91 percent of its oil, 75 percent of its natural gas, 50 percent of its meat, 85 percent of its paper. Direct trade relations among individual republics would therefore be a cornerstone in structural reform and for a "renewal" of the federation.

A loose economic commonwealth based on political decentralization would be an obvious solution. As a matter of fact the EC has been explicitly used in the internal reform debate as a model to copy. Obviously the Eastern EC will, like an expanded rather than deepened Western EC, become more introverted, and, in the long run, the two will probably form part of a larger more or less spontaneous integration process. Europe will ultimately become a "House," if not a "Fortress," but, either way, a solution must be found to the increasing instability within the former "Soviet Region." Moscow may learn to prefer friendly neighbors to restive ex-republics, and the smaller countries must somehow come to terms with geopolitical realities, including their highly interdependent Russian economy. There are strong reasons to find a better balance between function and territory but provincial autarky is, as president Bush explained in the Ukrainian legislature, no option. Nor is a union kept together by coercive means. In the current turbulence, a somewhat utopian project is to build a new union, based on new foundations, one of them being a functioning civil society. Valery Tishkov, director of the Institute of Ethnology, makes this analysis:

In developed societies ethnicity, economics and politics represent three weakly interrelated and largely independent systems. In such societies the members of cultural, linguistic, and religious groups typically protect their interests and ensure their groups' autonomy on the basis of individual rights and general democratic principles. Nationalism and exclusive ethnic loyalty arise in the absence of these safeguards, in societies that lack mechanisms for the articulation of collective aspirations and interests, and where ethnicity, economics and politics interpenetrate in one poorly functioning system. Clearly the Soviet Union still belongs to this second category. (Tishkov, 1991: 21f.)

As far as the reorganization of the union is concerned, nine of the fifteen former republics did initially agree on the basic principles (the Nine-plus-One formula), while six (apart from the Baltic republics they were Armenia, Georgia and Moldavia) refused to participate in any negotiations that did not imply full independence. Thus the foundations for a new union were indeed shaky from the beginning and the resulting confusion triggered the failed military coup in August 1991, which again changed completely the preconditions for the union–republics relationship. What is emerging is a loose framework coordinated by an interrepublican economic committee, an embryonic EC.

What matters from now on will be the relationship between an increasingly nationalist and self-confident Russia and more or less "independent" ex-republics. Geopolitics and comparative economic strength will shape relations. As in the Western EC, the objective of long-run stability will stimulate subregional groupings countering the influence of the regional great power.

5. Third World Regionalism: The European Factor

Regional integration outside Europe has not been a great success so far. Two reasons are evident:
1. *the structure of the world economy*, which under hegemonic control has tended towards interdependence rather than regionalization, and
2. *the common-market concept of regional cooperation*, which in a situation of asymmetry has reintroduced the global hierarchy of dependency relations in the region.

In this overview of Third World regionalism, I shall focus on the European factor. What negative or positive influence has Europe exercised over the integration process in different regions? It is true that the EC, or rather its Commission, is spreading the gospel of regional integration over the globe, but Europe's role will have to change substantially if a new, better, and more symmetric interregional exchange pattern is to take shape. Not only must the content of the interregional relations (Europe, or subregions within Europe, on the one hand, and various Third World regions, on the other) change, but Europe must also take a more active part in promoting regional cooperation and integration in the Third World. The "regional dialogue" carried out by the EC is explicitly intended to stimulate regionalism in the Third World. However, as long as the world order remained hegemonic and politically polarized, the whole exercise was necessarily mainly symbolic.

In a post-Cold War world order, on the other hand, the old pattern of cultivating friendly regimes, intensifying and creating divisions within different regions, could be replaced by a more active European policy of promoting resolution of indigenous and region-specific conflicts on the regional level, and stimulating regional cooperation through region-based development programs. This policy should be distinguished from solutions which are enforced upon the regions from above.

In this context I am referring mainly to the EC and EFTA countries. The former Eastern bloc is disappearing as an actor, as far as the Third World is concerned, and the links between the former Soviet Union and its previous clients, already dramatically redefined in "the new thinking," are becoming increasingly weak, owing to both the economic and political turmoil, as well as the political transformation within these former client states. (Duncan & McGiffert Ekedahl, 1990)

Let's consider some current trends in the main regions of the world so as to identify the European factor to the extent possible.

Latin America and the Caribbean

At present Latin America is becoming marginalized or, as some would say, "Africanized" in the world economy. Its crisis is simultaneously a debt and development crisis. (Griffith-Jones & Sunkel, 1986) The disappearance of the socialist alternative means that Latin America will become even more dependent on the USA and even more arrogantly treated. Not only the Soviet but also the European counterweight has evaporated. (Castaneda, 1990)

Some even argue for a "Fortress America" as the best Latin America can hope for. Mexico, which had some potential of becoming a regional power, now seems to draw the conclusion that joining North America is the only possible way out of stagnation. *Central America* is also tilting towards the north. The small Central American states, to the extent that they are not yet part of North America, will have little choice but to follow Mexico's example.

The economic and geopolitical change in the north of Latin America puts a certain pressure on the *Southern Cone*. The treaty signed by Argentina and Brazil in 1985 put fresh life into the integration process in the region. In March 1991 a free-trade agreement was signed between these two countries and Uruguay and Paraguay (MERCOSUL). This new kind of cooperation, designed to prevent further marginalization of Latin America in the world economy, is modeled on the EC.

The *Caribbean region* has a 500-year relationship with Europe, a relationship which has formed it, and continues to form it as a region. (Sutton, 1991; Thomas, 1988) The earlier attempts at regional cooperation occurred in a colonial context, which is one reason for their failure. The CARIFTA arrangement of 1968 was a minimal form of integration since its principal integration mechanism was the phased freeing of interregional trade. In 1973 CARIFTA was replaced by the more ambitious CARICOM. It had from the start an explicit political element, namely coordination of foreign policy. This idea seems to have grown out of experiences of negotiating with the EC (Thomas, 1988, p. 317). There were statements condemning destabilization and criticism of CBI, but, after the invasion of Grenada, controversial foreign policy issues have again been avoided.

Asia

In *South Asia*, the world powers, especially the USA, but also Russia and China, are promoting their interests by forging alliances with local states, while Europe in spite of its historical role had taken a rather low profile. The region is internally dominated by one "regional power," although Pakistan and India had a kind of competitive relationship before the splitting up of Pakistan in 1971. The problem of regional hegemonism is thus present (Hettne, 1988).

Thus the security situation in South Asia cannot be understood unless the ethnic, regional and religious conflicts within the states – and the way these affect interstate relations – are carefully considered. In a situation of geopolitical dominance by India, ethnic strife, secession and disintegration could be the main vehicles for changes in the interstate system. Over the years the security situation has grown more and more complicated. (Buzan & Rizvi, 1986) India is strengthening her position in relative terms due to the growing regional disorder, but this also means a high risk of external penetration. Regional cooperation would mean a change for the better, at least as far as economic security is concerned. The economic rationale is not overwhelming at present, rather it has to be created. (Adiseshia, 1987)

It is both a strength and a weakness that SAARC contains all the South Asian states (India, Pakistan, Bangladesh, Sri Lanka, Bhutan, Nepal and the Maldives). It is a weakness because the conflicts in the region will paralyze SAARC for a long time to come, confining its scope to non-controversial marginal issues like tourism and meteorology. It is a strength precisely because controversial problems can be handled within one organization and at least a framework for regional conflict resolution has been created and exists. Put differently, the regional organization coincides with the regional security complex and can be seen as an embryo of a security community.

Southeast Asia, like Europe, has been divided in two economic and political blocs: ASEAN (Indonesia, Thailand, Singapore, Malaysia, the Philippines and – since 1984 – Brunei) and the Indochinese area (Vietnam, Kampuchea and Laos). The latter subregion is under communist rule with Vietnam exercising subregional hegemony.

Vietnam and, behind it until recently, the Soviet Union have been seen as a threat by the ASEAN countries, which is precisely the reason why ASEAN as a regional organization has worked rather well. The source of common cause and identity is thus negative, a threat. Thus, it is a case of negative rather than positive peace. As in Europe, the dismantling of the Cold War system will change the pattern of conflict rather than eliminate conflicts. We can expect more relaxation between the two subregions and more conflicts within them.

The countries in ASEAN could be described as capitalist in economic terms and conservative in political terms. The national economies are outward-oriented, and the political systems are formally democratic but in practice more or less authoritarian. Problems on the international market usually reinforce domestic authoritarianism owing to the strong two-way causal relationship between economic growth and political stability. Economic growth and redistribution are preconditions for ethnic peace, political stability is a precondition for the economic confidence expressed by international capital flows into the region.

Peace in the larger region, the formation of which now seems to be under way, would however change the basic parameters of the way ASEAN operates. As the superpowers pull out, old rivalries are emerging, at the same time as the objective preconditions are improving for cooperation that could encompass the whole region in the longer run.

The rationale behind regional dialogue initiated by the EC comes out clearly in the following statement by Roy Jenkins:

From the formation of ASEAN we in the Community have always sought to treat with ASEAN as a region since we from our own experience have learnt that an external stimulus can often support internal cooperation. (Edwards & Regelsberger, 1990, p. 15)

East Asia is the most dynamic of the world regions, containing a technologically highly developed country with possible hegemonic ambitions (Japan), an enormous "domestic" market (China), three NICs (South Korea, Taiwan and Hong Kong) and a "socialist" autarky (North Korea), preparing itself for major changes which may alter the pattern of cooperation within the region. Reunification of Korea, democratization of China, and a more independent Japanese role in foreign policy would release an enormous regional potential. These changes are admittedly not immediate prospects, but on the other hand their occurrence is quite feasible.

Korean unification is, of course, the key to regional cooperation. Considering the economic superiority of South Korea and the political lag in North Korea, it will probably be a spontaneous process of the German type, an

"Anschluss." South Korea, together with the other NICs, is facing changes in those objective conditions which originally made them into NICs, and their strategy in the 1990s will probably concentrate on the domestic market, preferably a regional market. The regional framework is still, however, in flux. South Korea and Taiwan are traditionally dependent on Japan but may have more to gain by orienting themselves towards Southeast Asia. The ending of the Cold War opened up new possibilities for inter-subregional contacts, thereby widening the potential for regional cooperation.

Perhaps the most complex issue in the region is the future international role of Japan: will it remain number two in Pax Americana or take a more independent role? The latter, and perhaps more likely option, would imply the accumulation of military strength and a break with the introverted Japanese worldview. After the break-down of the GATT negotiations in 1990 the Malaysian prime minister Mahathir Mohamad invited Japan to act as a leader of an East Asian Economic Grouping (EAEG), which would create an East Asian and South East Asian super-bloc with a Sino-Japanese core. Japan then rejected the idea of an "East Asian EC," but the idea is still being discussed as an insurance policy, should the European and North American "fortresses" take shape.

Africa

In Africa there has been little regional integration, simply because there is so little to integrate. The need is rather for "integrated economic development" on a regional level (Thisen, 1989), an element conspicuously lacking in Africa's Structural Adjustment Programs. (WA, 22–28 July, 1991) Regionalism, however, has been a highly politicized issue, which tends to create suspicion in the national center of decision-making in Africa. Little remains today of Nkrumah's pan-Africanism, but what was then a dream has now, nevertheless, become a necessity. At the OAU summit in Abuja it was repeatedly stressed that the ongoing integration of Europe requires a collective response from African states, in the form of an African Economic Community.

The most important experience so far is SADCC (Southern Africa Development Cooperation Conference). The main function of SADCC was originally to reduce dependence of the subregion on South Africa, the regional power with evident designs of regional control. Thus, it is a fairly clear example of the "new regionalism," not simply based on a common market concept, but having wider political objectives. With the elimination of apartheid in South Africa, the agenda for regional cooperation in southern Africa will change fundamentally – and the incentives will perhaps become positive rather than negative. Much depends on the character of a post-apartheid regime, but in any post-apartheid scenario regionalism will play a larger role.

The prospects for regional cooperation begin to look brighter, partly as a result of the weakening of African nation-states. In the summer of 1990, in the shadow of the Kuwait crisis, ECOWAS, for instance, intervened in the Liberian civil war with the explicit purpose of preventing a general massacre of the population. Although not a highly successful operation in terms of conflict resolution, it was unprecedented in the history of African regional cooperation. From now on the more stable regimes within a specific region may feel obliged to rely on regional frameworks to avoid plunging neighbors into conditions of anarchy.

In the *Maghreb* region harsh realities lead to new attempts at stimulating regional integration. In February 1989 the Arab Maghreb Union was created in order to tackle both peace (the Western Sahara conflict) and development (the debt crisis) issues. There is great fear in the region that the traditional European markets will close after 1992. At one stage Morocco even signaled its interest in joining the EC. The aim is now to stimulate trade between member states, increasing non-traditional exports, and cutting imports. (*South*, May 1989) The southern European countries are deeply concerned about the stability in Arab North Africa and have developed the project of creating a Conference on Security and Cooperation in the Mediterranean (CSCM) modeled after the CSCE, but based on an even broader concept of security, including, for instance, water scarcity as a security risk. This is significantly different from the US/Middle East paradigm. (Hadar, 1991)

The Middle East

The Middle East region is in many ways the most complex. It covers territories in two geographical continents, Asia and Africa, and is extremely diverse in ethnic terms, at the same time as it is largely dominated by one religion and one linguistic culture. Therefore it is no coincidence that great ambitions towards regional unity coexist with constant conflicts between states and ethnic groups. Of great importance is the frustrated but yet surviving idea of an Arab Nation.

The present political boundaries of states were externally imposed by the European colonial powers and lack emotional significance, since they so often have been changed in the past. Centers such as Cairo, Damascus, Baghdad and Istanbul have possessed a regional significance far beyond their present national roles. The artificial boundaries and the lack of democratic tradition make the power play between heavily armed states as close to Machiavelli's world as one can come. It is thus the region of "realist thinking" *par préférence*.

For obvious economic and strategic reasons, the superpower involvement in the region has been fundamental. In the most recent political crisis in the region, triggered by Iraq's conquest and occupation of Kuwait in August 1990, attempts at finding a regional solution were halted by US intervention. This produced a polarization within the region between conservative and radical currents. As the then faltering Soviet Union opted out, the USA with the help of frustrated potential regional influentials established itself in the region – nobody knows for how long, since the threatening break-up of Iraq could be the beginning of a long struggle for regional power, in which external interests headed by the USA are likely to play a major role.

The old Europe gave up its Middle East ambitions in 1956. The Gulf crisis was a moment of truth for the new Europe (the EC), as far as its external posture was concerned, and an embarrassing lack of unity was actually revealed. After some initial protests led by France, Europe again gave up its independent policy towards the Arab world, at least for the time being. To restore its image and counter US influence, the European strategy now involves a major rule for Iran. (*ME*, July, 1991) The intervention of regional influentials such as Egypt, Turkey and Syria was not necessarily popular among the people of these regions, which opens the door for unexpected domestic repercussions.

It is thus very difficult to foresee what a new security system in the Middle East may look like. Ironically, Sadam Hussein is still needed since no alternative military government is coming forward to guarantee the fragile balance of power. The problems to be solved are many: first of all to contain the power and influence of Iran, to find and sustain a solution to the Palestine question, and to reduce the gap between the rich Gulf states and the poor Arab masses. Then there is a host of minority and human rights problems of which the most urgent is the Kurdish question. In terms of our criteria for regionalism – economic and political homogenization, and institutions for regional conflict resolution – the "new regionalism" in the Middle East is at best embryonic.

6. The Promise of Benign Mercantilism

Taking the continuation of the trend towards multipolarity as its point of departure, this paper has explored the potentials of a world order beyond hegemonism, a world order in which the regions constitute a crucial role. This "new regionalism" is characterized by a rather high degree of economic self-sufficiency and a capacity for autonomous conflict resolution. Such a perspective is different from the "new world order" presently in vogue, for the reason that long-run economic trends here are seen as more important than are shows of force based on military dominance.

The Trend towards Multipolarism

There is a theoretical possibility of a multilateral order based on interstate cooperation, but it seems more likely that some kind of fragmentation of the world economy will take place. The military dimension is the ultimate and now unchallenged pillar of US dominance, but the political costs of making use of military means to solve political problems will increase. The contradiction between global military power and domestic poverty, eroding the domestic social fabric, will in a democratic setting work towards continued decline and the reallocation of resources in the direction of domestic needs.

The Soviet decline is definitive, and not in dispute. But is it hegemonic decline or something more? We have underlined the difference between the Soviet hegemony over the socialist subsystem and the global hegemony of the United States. Yet, as long as there were local bridge-heads and the communist ideals had some appeal, the socialist system was not simply a coercive dominance system. Soviet domination had hegemonic intentions but suffered from the contradictions of an imperial system. The new détente is based on peaceful coexistence no longer but on a liberal transnational hegemony.

The trend towards multipolarism will not be arrested by a European bid for hegemony. Rather the emergence of a European regional state and the essentially introverted orientation of such a state, together with the negative threat of "Fortress Europe" and the positive policy of "group to group dialogue" of the EC, will stimulate a global process of regionalization. A question mark must, however, be added as far as the post-communist world is concerned. Here, in the wake of hegemonic decline, balkanization rather than regionalization is the predominant trend.

Patterns of Fragmentation

One rather obvious and already visible pattern of fragmentation is the development of a few major trading blocs: the EC, North America/Mexico (NAFTA), and the East Asia Economic Group (EAEG). This paper has dealt more with a possibly less conflictual regionalized world order: "The New Regionalism."

"The New Regionalism" could be compared to traditional nation-building with the difference that the coercive political/administrative center is lacking. Rather its emergence is related to imperatives in the international political economy, including ecological concerns. This process evolves by its own internal logic, unevenly in different regions. Far in advance is Europe, where the trend now is toward a regional state. This could be the only way of saving the European welfare state, which no longer can be maintained as a national project. In an era of global market hegemony and market expansion, regionalism could perhaps be seen as the self-protection of global society: a reenactment of Polanyi's double movement.

In terms of our criteria, i.e. political and economic homogenization and a regional framework for autonomous conflict resolution, Europe is on its way to achieving "The New Regionalism." The EC model is also a possible way out of the mess in Yugoslavia and the former Soviet Union, if organized efforts to go this way can be successfully organized.

Other regions may want, or become forced, to follow the European example of internalizing the sources of growth and make use of a "domestic" regional market, although there may be a long step to security cooperation. Our survey exhibits a very uneven picture.

In all cases there is a European factor of varying significance, rather weak in Latin America, stronger in Asia, potentially very strong in Africa and the Middle East. There is no doubt about what the intentions are. In a preface to a recent book on Europe's global links, Hans-Dietrich Genscher says:

The community takes all possible steps to promote voluntary regional associations in other parts of the world ... The path of political dialogue and economic cooperation embarked upon by the EC in a spirit of true partnership is proving to be the path of the future ... towards greater regional stability and more calculable international relations. (Edwards & Regelsberger, 1990, p. VII)

The new role of Europe can be seen in the case of Maghreb, where the CSCM concept implies a comprehensive regional approach quite different from the US/Middle East paradigm for the area. If it works it will be expanded to conflicts in the Middle East region, even helping to resolve the Palestine issue.

A Regionalized World System

Although the preconditions for "extended nationalism" thus differ substantially between regions, I would nevertheless bet on this "neomercantilist" scenario as the best world order the world can hope for. Many observers probably feel uneasy about this concept. Mercantilism is the ideological expression of the nation-state logic, operating in the economic arena and violating the liberal principle that free trade in the long run is for the benefit of all. Neomercantilism retains the same suspicion which the old mercantilists harbored against free trade. It transcends the nation-state logic in arguing for a segmented world system, consisting of self-sufficient blocs large enough to provide "domestic" markets and make use of economies of scale and specialization in production, on the one hand, without falling prey to the anarchy of the world market, on the other.

Such a regionalized world system would evidently be more stable and peaceful than a liberal world order, which historically has revealed an inherent tendency towards collapse. Most regions in a regionalized world system would be large enough to have a reasonable degree of economic efficiency, in accordance with the principles of comparative costs, economies of scale and other conventional economic efficiency arguments. At the same time, perversions generated by excessive specialization and an overly elaborated division of labor could be avoided. Interregional trade will of course continue to take place, but somewhat subordinated to the "territorial" principle of regionalism, rather than the "functional" principle of the world market.

There is a difference between this new form of protectionism and the traditional mercantilist concern with state-building and national power. What we could call "neomercantilism" is a transnational phenomenon. Its spokesmen do not believe in the viability of closed national economies in the present stage of the development of the world economy. On the other hand, they do not believe in the viability of an unregulated world economy either. Nor do they – in contrast with the Trilateralists and the Interdependentists – put much faith in the possibility of managing such a world economy. Rather the neomercantilists argue in favor of the regionalization of the world into more or less self-sufficient blocs. These blocs would be introverted and maintain symmetric relations between themselves.

The "benign view" of mercantilism coincides with what I call The New Regionalism. It must be emphasized that such a "neomercantilist" vision faces serious problems of acceptance owing to the strong historical association of mercantilist thinking with extremist nationalism, and because of its periodical revivals (in the form of protectionism) in connection with economic crises. This "guilt by association" argument can, however, be rejected, since no real efforts have in fact been made to construct a world order on the basis of neomercantilist ideas. The established view that such ideas tend to reemerge in the context of world depressions and collapsing world orders should not be held against them. Constructive propositions must be distinguished from desperate responses in a situation of crisis. They should be judged on their own merit, in a situation characterized by normalcy.

REFERENCES

Adiseshia, M. (1987), "The Economic Rationale of SAARC." *South Asia Journal.* Vol. 1, No. 1.

Buzan, B. (1984), "Economic Structure and International Security." *International Organization.* Vol. 38, No. 4.

Buzan, B. (1991), *People, States and Fear.* Brighton: Wheatsheaf.

Buzan, B. & Rizvi, G., eds. (1986), *South Asian Insecurity and the Great Powers.* London: Macmillan.

Castaneda, J. G. (1990), "Latin America and the End of the Cold War." *World Policy Journal.* Vol. VII, No. 3 (Summer).

Cox, R. W. (1991), *Perspectives on Multilateralism.* Tokyo: United Nations University.

Deutsch, K. W., et al. (1957), *Political Community and the North Atlantic Area.* Princeton: Princeton University Press.

Dibb, P. (1986), *The Soviet Union: The Incomplete Superpower.* London: Macmillan.

Duncan, W. R. & McGiffert Ekedahl, C. (1990), *Moscow and the Third World under Gorbachev.* Boulder, Colo.: Westview Press.

Edwards, G. & Regelsberger, E., eds. (1990), *Europe's Global Links. The European Community and Inter-Regional Cooperation.* London: Pinter.

Gilpin, R. (1981), *War and Change in World Politics.* Cambridge: Cambridge University Press.

Griffith-Jones, S. & Sunkel, O. (1986), *Debt and Development Crisis in Latin America.* Oxford: Clarendon.

Haas, E. B. (1970), "The Study of Regional Integration: Reflections on the Joy and Anguish of Pretheorizing." *International Organization.* No. 24 (Autumn).

Hadar, L. T. (1991), "The United States, Europe and the Middle East." *World Policy Journal.* Vol. VIII, No. 3, pp. 421–449.

Hettne, B. (1986), "An Inventory of European Social Projects for Peace and Development." In E. Làszlo, *Europe in the Contemporary World*. New York: Gordon and Breach, Science Publishers Inc.

Hettne, B. (1988), "India." In J. Carlsson and T. M. Shaw (eds.), *Newly Industrializing Countries and the Political Economy of South–South Relations*. London: Macmillan.

Hettne, B. (1991a), "Europe and the Crisis: The Regionalist Scenario Revisited." In Marguerite Mendel and Daniel Salée (eds.), *The Legacy of Karl Polanyi, Market, State and Society at the End of the Twentieth Century*. London: Macmillan.

Hettne, B. (1991b), "Security and Peace in Post-Cold War Europe." *Journal of Peace Research*. Vol. 28, No. 3, pp. 279–294.

Hormats, R. O. (1991), "The Roots of American Power." *Foreign Affairs*. Vol. 70, No. 3.

Huntington, S. P. (1988), "The US – Decline or Renewal?" *Foreign Affairs*. Vol. 67, No. 2.

Kaiser, R. (1988), "The USSR in Decline." *Foreign Affairs*. Vol. 67, No. 2.

Kennedy, P. (1987), *The Rise and Fall of the Great Powers*. New York: Random House.

Keohane, R. O. (1980), "The Theory of Hegemonic Stability and Changes in International Economic Regimes, 1966–77." In O. R. Holsti, R. M. Siversen, and A. L. George (eds.), *Change in the International System*. Boulder, Colo.: Westview.

Keohane, R. O. (1984), *After Hegemony: Cooperation and Discord in the World Political Economy*. Princeton, NJ: Princeton University Press.

Krauthammer, C. (1990), "Decline Theory Lives on Undeterred by the Facts." *International Herald Tribune* (March 15).

Krauthammer, C. (1991), "The Unipolar Movement." *Foreign Affairs*. Vol. 70, No. 1.

Kux, S. (1990), "Soviet Federalism." *Problems of Communism*. Vol. XXXIX (March–April).

Modelski, G. (1978), "The Long Cycle of Global Politics and the Nation State." *Comparative Studies in Society and History*. Vol. 20 (April).

Polanyi, K. (1945), "Universal Capitalism or Regional Planning." *The London Quarterly of World Affairs* (January).

Russet, B. (1985), "The Mysterious Case of Vanishing Hegemony, or Is Mark Twain really dead?" *International Organization*. Vol. 39, No. 2.

Seers, D. (1983), *The Political Economy of Nationalism*. Oxford: Oxford University Press.

Sestanovich, S. (1988), "Gorbachev's Foreign Policy: A Diplomacy of Decline." *Problems of Communism*. Vol. XXXVII (January–February).

Strange, S. (1985), "Protectionism and World Politics." *International Organization*. Vol. 39, No. 2, pp. 233–259.

Strange, S. (1988), *States and Markets*. London: Pinter.

Sutton, P., ed. (1991), *Europe and the Caribbean*. London: Macmillan.

Thisen, J. K. (1989), "Alternative Approaches to Economic Integration in Africa." *Africa Development*. Vol. XIV, No. 1.

Thomas, C. Y. (1988), *The Poor and the Powerless. Economic Policy and Change in the Caribbean*. London: Latin American Bureau.

Tishkov, V. A. (1991), *The Soviet Empire Before and After Perestroika*. UNRISD.

Väyrynen, R. (1984), "Regional Conflict Formations: An Intractable Problem in International Relations." *Journal of Peace Research*. Vol. 21, No. 4, pp. 337–359.

4

A World in Chaos

*Samir Amin**

1. Global Rationality or Chaos with New Globalization and Polarization?

We all live on a planet whose destiny we collectively determine, or so we are told. And it is undeniable that the globalization which began five centuries ago with the European conquest of the Americas has passed into a new stage during the past forty years, as the consequence of a heightened intensity of international exchanges of all sorts and a global spread of the means of destruction. Shall we conclude from this observation, banal though it is, that all societies on the planet must subordinate themselves to the criteria of rationality that govern the global expansion of capital? This view, though it is dominant today, is not merely illogical and erroneous but infinitely dangerous.

(1) Capitalism has always been a world system. As such the process of accumulation which governs its dynamic – itself shaped by a law of value operating on a world scale on a truncated basis, i.e. to the exclusion of labor power – necessarily leads to the polarization of the world into centers and peripheries. Polarization is therefore immanent in capitalism and does not need to be explained by diverse and contingent factors peculiar to the social formations that make up the system. The recognition of this essential aspect of "actually existing capitalism" evidently has consequences that are as decisive for theoretical analysis as they are for the definition of progressive political action. For everything is subordinate to the logic of world polarization: the social struggles that develop in the various local areas, the

*Dr. Samir Amin is Director of the African Office of the Third World Forum, Dakar, Senegal.

conflicts between states at the center, the forms of differentiation at the peripheries, and much more.

This permanent trait of capitalism does not exclude change, which marks the successive phases of its expansion. For example, the long "Britannic" phase (1815–1914) was based on the building of a world market, particularly between 1848 and 1896, structured by the contrast between the industrialized centers, historically constituted as the bases of the national bourgeois states, and the non-industrialized peripheries, gradually subjected to a colonial and semi-colonial status. The world market under the hegemony of Britain went into crisis at the end of the period, owing to the accentuation of rivalry from Germany and the United States. The system was gradually restructured by retreats of the older imperial powers and their replacement by newer rivals in the crusade to carve up the world. But this process led to war.

The break-up of the old system precipitated by the Russian revolution and accentuated by the Chinese seemed to have established two systems, one which styled itself socialist, although what really happened was basically the delinking of immense parts of the periphery. This long phase (1917–1980) divides itself into two periods. From 1914 to 1945 the center stage was occupied by the violent conflict of the two world wars. Beginning in 1945, the world market reconstructed itself under the hegemony of the United States, in an atmosphere of military and ideological bipolarization and Cold War. During this entire phase the East–West conflict presented itself as a struggle between socialism and capitalism, although it was never anything but the conflict between the peripheries and the center, manifested in its most radical form. This particular state of the world system provoked liberation struggles throughout the peripheries, largely bourgeois in their orientation and capitalist in their aspirations. It was "the era of Bandung" (1955–1975), in which North–South conflicts were acted out within the logic of the East–West confrontation. (Amin, 1988)

The requirements of globalization during the postwar years, 1945–1970, were expressed in terms of a two-part paradigm. Within the developed countries it was thought that Keynesian interventions could assure steady growth for the benefit of all, dampening the business cycle and reducing unemployment to a minimum. This vision was all the more remarkable in that it simultaneously envisioned the reconciliation of national politics and the forward march of globalization. In the Third World, the ideology of Bandung asserted that national development could be open to the advantages of economic interdependence. By contrast, the socialist countries were walled off in the ghetto of autarky.

The crisis of capitalism beginning in 1970 put an abrupt end to the illusions of Keynesianism and to what I call the ideology of development in the Third World, while the "socialist" countries had certainly not found the solution to their problems. But into the void created by this double crisis jumped the ideological offensive of neoliberalism, with its reductionist remedy for all ills, the market. Yet the blind pursuit of this dogma could lead only to the break-up of the world system and the renewal of clashes between unbridled nationalisms, that is, to the opposite of its promised result.

(2) Globalization, which re-established itself in 1945 and is now in a new phase, has assumed particular characteristics that sharply distinguish it from its earlier manifestations. The new globalization is characterized by a tripolar constellation of the United States, Japan, and the EEC that is without precedent. This tripolarity entails not only an intensification of trade among the poles but also and especially an interpenetration of capital. Up until now capital has always been national, but now apparently a dominant international capital is emerging at an incredible rate. However, the alleged relationship between the change which operates on the level of property relations and that which calls itself a "revolution in technology" is, in my estimation, little studied, if indeed it really exists. Each of the successive stages in the history of capitalism is defined simultaneously by its specific forms of domination of labor by capital and by the forms of existence of the bourgeoisie that correspond to them. One distinguishes, therefore, the stage of manufacture (1600–1800) and of large-scale industry (1800–1920), both analyzed by Marx, then of Taylorism–Fordism (1920–1980), analyzed by Harry Braverman (1974). The new stage, called "informatics," awaits its analysis. I call attention to the pioneer work of Coriat (1990). But if each of the three preceding stages operated in the frame of an "international economy" made up of central nations, in reviving the thesis of Michel Beaud I shall say that the new stage marks the emergence of a "world economy" of a much deeper degree of integration. (Beaud, 1989)

The consequences of this change are major. Accumulation in the central nations was formerly regulated by national political and social conflicts that structured the hegemonic alliances. But today there exists no analogous mechanism that could structure a hegemonic alliance on the grand scale of the economic decisions that are being made – not even for the USA–Japan–EEC tripole. Political analysts who see the dwindling scope of national decisions and the widening effects of an autonomous global economy are quite aware of this new fact. But there is no solution to the problem it raises, since no supranational state is visible on the horizon. This is the first major source of the chaos that the new globalization will bring in its train.

But it is not the sole source, by any means. The tripolar penetration does not marginalize the periphery, as the glib and superficial discourse of the economists supposes. The politicians, who are much more in touch with reality, refute this claim every day. The Gulf War startlingly illustrates its error. With four-fifths of the world's population – the vital reserve army of labor – and indispensable natural resources, both well appreciated by politicians, the periphery must without question be preserved and subordinated to the expansion of capital, however polarizing this may be. Here one finds a second source of the chaos for which the coming decades are destined.

In a brilliant analysis of the history of globalization, Giovanni Arrighi (1991) contrasts the contradictory tendencies of capitalist accumulation: at one pole the growing power of the active army of labor, at the other the growing misery in the ranks of the reserve army. The first tendency paved the way to social democratic strategies on the part of the masses, the second for revolutionary outbreaks of the Leninist type. I shall not go into this thesis at length here, but I accept its essential claim. I only remark that Arrighi is too optimistic about the globalization that is under way, because he believes that it is going to draw together the active and reserve armies in the various regions of the system – the more advanced centers as well as the peripheries and (especially) the semi-peripheries. I do not believe it. On the contrary, it seems much more probable that geographic separation will continue to be dominant because the reserve army will remain concentrated at the periphery and semi-periphery. It follows that the ideological separation between social democracy at the centers and revolutionary at the periphery is not yet ready to disappear, even if the political forms of delinking were to produce something other than Leninist movements. As always, social democracy will remain limited in its capacity to move beyond the point it has reached and achieve the substitution of wage-earners' hegemony for the hegemony of capital. (I shall return to this very important matter at a later point.)

Polarization, in my opinion, is a permanent and basic characteristic of really existing capitalism. It is not a cyclic phenomenon, as Arrighi suggests. He distinguishes, in effect, a sequence of periods: 1848–1896 (globalization); 1896–1948 (fragmentation of the world system); 1948 to the present (reconstruction of the world system). Be that as it may. But I observe that the first of these periods is marked not by an attenuation of contrast between the centers and peripheries, but on the contrary by the emergence of the modern form of the periphery, which becomes colonial and semi-colonial. This development in itself leads to the fragmentation that follows.

2. The Empire of Chaos

(1) The world system is in crisis. There is a general breakdown of accumulation, in the sense that most of the social formations of the East (formerly so-called socialist) and the South (Third and Fourth World) are unable to reproduce on an extended scale, carry on reproduction or even in some cases to hold their own. The latter is the situation in the Fourth World countries of Africa. The crisis in the Third World manifests itself as an insufficiency of capital accumulation. In the developed centers it takes apparently opposite forms which classical economics would have called an excess of supply of loanable funds relative to the demand for productive investment. This excess is wasted in a wild orgy of financial speculation, creating an unprecedented situation.

The crisis reveals that the polarization of the world really constitutes an historical limit for capitalism. A genuine resumption of accumulation calls for a re-allocation of capital that is unattainable under the short-term profitability criteria that govern the market. The solution of the market is bound to generate growing national and international social imbalances which will turn out to be unbearable. There is no scientific value in neo-liberalism, because it pretends not to see that the unregulated market can only reproduce and deepen such negative consequences, and that an analysis of the advantages of the market for a particular society is valid only to the extent that it starts from the real parameters of that society's situation: the level of its development, its historical place in the world division of labor, and the social and political links that it has forged and maintained. A critical analysis must then ask what might make it possible to carry off a daring escape from the vicious circle of the market. From this point of view the considerable differences between various regions of the world forcefully imply specific political positions that cannot be derived from the postulated rationality of the market. To these objective factors one must add a quite valid recognition of the economic relevance of the cultural, ideological, and political history of the various peoples. The real imperatives of our epoch imply therefore the reconstruction of the world system on a polycentric basis.

To any narrow political and strategic conception of the world order, such as that which centered on the Big Five (the United States, Europe, USSR or Russia, China, Japan), it is vital to oppose one that gives a real place to the nations and great regions of the Third World. Third World countries and regions have to control their relations with others and subordinate them to the imperatives of internal development, and not the opposite, which they must do if they are compelled to adjust to the world expansion of capital. This primacy of the internal imperative is the concept to which I apply the term "delinking" – one which evidently has nothing to do with exclusion or autarky.

Without a doubt this historic, fundamental limit to capital is tied in with others whose manifestations are quite plain to see, since they express themselves in certain "new" forms of social protest, rising sometimes to the point of questioning the legitimacy of the ideological and political systems of the advanced societies. The first such challenge is the refusal of workers and others to submit themselves to the demands of economistic alienation. This refusal, clamorous during the revolts of 1968, lies dormant for long periods and then bursts out in dramatic and often destructive ways. The second is a response to the wastage of natural resources and degradation of the natural environment by capital. It has also produced a movement, international in reach, and even "green" political parties in some countries.

The crisis manifests itself along both geopolitical and cultural lines: in conflicts between states on the one part, and in clashes of civilizations on the other. The response will therefore imply massive political changes: both the creation of new political organizations within the West, East, and South, and the organization of relations among them, i.e. a new interstate system. None of these changes is on the agenda of actual political action. The historical drama of our epoch is situated precisely here, and has its roots in the failure of social consciousness to imagine positive and progressive alternatives.

(2) The chaos results from a lack of correspondence between the geography of power on the one hand and the effects of the global expansion of capital on the other. The analyses of globalization that I have proposed above have defined the two spaces in which this non-correspondence expresses itself – the relationships between the centers and the relationships of these centers to the peripheries. In my opinion, however, the intensity of the conflicts that arise in these two spaces is not of the same order.

The struggles for eventual leadership among the centers – between the United States and its counterparts: Japan and Germany, between NATO and such military elements as survive in the former USSR, among the Europeans themselves – will remain limited. I can hardly imagine that they will lead to armed conflicts like those of 1914 and 1939. But neither will they find amicable solutions, for want of a coincidence between the space of economic power and that of political and social decisions. Neither the Group of Seven nor its veritable directorate (the USA, Japan, and Germany), even with all the infrastructure of institutionalized cooperation that exists in today's world, can render the social and political consequences of globalization unconditionally acceptable to all the participants. Nonetheless, because the conflicts of the developed West are not dramatic, they will solve themselves by changes in the hierarchy of powers without questioning fundamentally the internal social order in the way it had been in Europe during the inter-war period (through the rise of fascism), for instance, in North–South relations, in the characteristic conflict of "actually existing" capitalism, which irreconcilably opposes the peoples of the periphery and the expansion of world capitalism. In this context, who will win? The forces that would have a united North prevail over the South (as we have seen to a startling degree in the Gulf War)? Or those who would advance the cause of a polycentric world, in the sense in which I have used the term? The future of humanity depends on the outcome. Either an order more savage than ever, or an order that will attenuate the intolerable contrasts between centers and peripheries, and in doing so will enable a humane perspective for future generations.

We are now marching down the wrong road. There is no doubt of this. "Liberal" globalization will lead only to greater polarization, and through this process will summon up from the peoples of the peripheries resistance movements that can only be massive and violent. But Western political thinking will ask only one question: how may one manage that which is intolerable? In this frame of thought, the economic order produced by the world market (a grand disorder, in fact) must be topped off with a military order that assures the efficient repression of the revolts of the South. The position of the Western powers on the reform of the international order, of which the Gulf War multiplied the opportunities for expression, continues to be nothing but a refined hypocrisy, in which "morality," "law," and "justice" are invoked repeatedly in a futile attempt to mask the defense of unspeakable interests.

A NATO strategy corresponding to this vision of the world order already exists. It is based on a two-part program: on the one part to permit to fester the situations in the Third World that do not threaten the imperialist order; on the other to smash by the most violent means – as we have seen in the Gulf War – the emerging powers of the Third World that for whatever reason are rebelling against this order.

Conflicts within the Third World must be examined in this framework, for they are not all alike. There are conflicts that are the products both of the objective impasses in which the societies of the Third World are trapped by globalization and of the deficiencies of a social consciousness that is unable to respond constructively to such challenges. The drifts toward inter-ethnic conflicts are of this type. The mediocre political games of the dominant local classes feed on these drifts, and powers that are on the defensive turn their energies in just such directions. These conflicts do not menace the capitalist order. With a cynicism quite evident in their theory of "low-intensity conflicts," the capitalist powers encourage such situations to develop. But some conflicts oppose the North directly to the South, either the authentic popular forces of the challenge, or, for some reason, its state powers. Here, as we have already seen in the Gulf War, the rapid deployment tactical forces of NATO may be inadequate, and the strategy then taken by the Pentagon is violence in the extreme, even, as necessary, to the point of genocide.

The efficacy of such strategies of intervention by the North requires the maintenance, the reinforcement, of Atlantic solidarity. But nothing beyond. The recognition of American hegemony, perhaps restricted along strictly military lines, leaves the field of economic competition open. The tacit accords with Japan, Germany, and after them the other European powers, strengthened by the immobilization of the former USSR and China, are enough. We see clearly now how the North–South conflict, an expression of the fundamental conflict of "actually existing capitalism," returns to the front of the stage. For the détente and the rallying of the former USSR to the tenets of the West provide no opportunity for the solution of regional conflicts, as the NATO propagandists proclaim. The North–South conflict has never been the product of the East–West conflict, its projection outside Europe, even though the support of the USSR for certain Third World nationalist forces had sustained this impression. The North–South conflict is anterior and primordial; it has defined for five centuries capitalism as a polarizing world system, intolerable for this reason to the majority of the peoples of this planet.

This is why I shall express my conclusion on this theme in a manner brutal and simple in the extreme: the intervention of the North in the affairs of the South is – in all its aspects, at every moment, in whatever form, and *a fortiori* when it takes the form of a military or political intervention – negative. Never have the armies of the North brought peace, prosperity, or democracy to the peoples of Asia, Africa, or Latin America. In the future, as in the past five centuries, they can bring to these peoples only further servitude, the exploitation of their labor and the expropriation of their riches, the denial of their rights. It is of utmost importance that the progressive forces of the West understand this.

3. Problems Specific to the Different Regions of the World

In the pervasive chaos of the present, one can distinguish problems of a general nature and problems that are specific to the regions that comprise the contemporary world. The dominant discourse of the moment accents those of the first sort, ecology for example. Gorbachev himself, in the manifesto that initially established his popularity in the West, understood clearly the returns he could get by putting his deposits in this account. And these problems are real. But the fact remains that a response to the challenges they pose must be mediated by correct responses to the specific – and dramatic – problems of the diverse regions of the world, particularly of the South and the East.

(1) The countries of the East – the former USSR and China – have launched reforms that assure the market and foreign trade a greater importance than they have had in the past. Their problem has nevertheless two faces that are inseparably linked: the democratization of society on the inside and the control of the overture to the outside. There is every reason to believe that the solution of this double problem is not reducible to the neoliberal recipe, but the right path to follow is difficult to discern in the disorder of the moment. The uncertainty itself is double, on the level of the social content of the system when it has regained its equilibrium and on the level of its place in the hierarchy of the world. There is, to be sure, a direct link between these two levels, but it is difficult to establish that link until the prior question of "what it all means" has been answered. Will the critique of "Stalinism" work itself out in a full return to capitalism, as the objective attitude of Gorbachev and Deng would lead us to conclude, or will it be derailed by a critique from the left, as Mao attempted in his day?

In the case of a return to capitalism, are peripheralization and the degraded international position that must accompany it inevitable? And how will the peoples of the former USSR and China react? In the case of a progressive, national–popular advance, how will "conflicts in the bosom of the people" be managed and how will this management express itself in the face of objective economic laws, whether outside of or beyond "actually existing capitalism?" Such questions have yet to be answered.

I content myself here with enumerating such problems, to return to them at a later time. However, I think it is useful to call attention to one point. In my previous analyses of the "Soviet Mode," I had placed my emphasis on three components of this system: capitalism, socialism, and statism. I now believe that the breakdown of this system leaves room for only two alternatives: (1) capitalism pure and simple or (2) a national–popular evolution which establishes a balance between the forces and tendencies of capitalism and those of socialism. The dominant statism will by then have proven itself to be historically unstable, as Mao foresaw.

(2) The developed societies of the West do have serious problems in common, although they lack the dramatic dimensions of those of the East and South. I propose to analyze them in terms of a crisis of Western democracy: how to assure within a democratic framework that the popular forces have access to political power?

This question has not yet been answered. The forms of social democracy we have seen until now have permitted workers to achieve important social rights, although these are now the object of a capitalist offensive aimed at dismantling them. However, in accepting the double consensus on which Western society rests – the regulation of political life by pluralist elections, and that of economic life by private property and the market – social democracy has not challenged the hegemony of capital, but only tempered it with the power of the workers in the political arena. On this level I do not share the optimism of Giovanni Arrighi, who seems to me to overestimate the strength and scope of this power.

This Western democracy, even now, is seriously troubled. With good reason the working classes judge with increasing severity what the pundits now call the "political class," whose right and left wings busy themselves with protecting the double consensus, draining all real content from "pluralist" politics. Systematic control and manipulation by the media, intended to prolong the life of the consensus, direct Western society on its gentle descent into a sort of "sweet-tasting" fascism, paralyzing all hopes for a progressive evolution.

This objectively necessary evolution should aim at substituting the hegemony of the salaried classes for the present historical compromise between labor and capital. (Lipietz, 1989) This will necessarily call into question the systems of ownership of the means of production and of economic decision making, and at the ideological and cultural level will challenge the technocratic vision of social control, as the Frankfurt school has called it for half a century. This is a long way off.

(3) In the heart of the Western world, Europe faces challenges of its own. The building of the Europe of the EEC has been limited until now to the progressive widening of the market. But if in the phase of take-off during the 1950s and 60s, social adjustments to this widening could be made fairly easily, today it is quite evident that entire regions and sectors will be unable to reconvert in the face of agonizing competitive challenges. As they become socially and politically intolerable, these challenges will raise the possibility that the whole project of the EEC may come tumbling down. Unless it is accepted that the market must be supplemented by plans for reconversion based on a common progressive social policy, failure will result. If such initiatives are undertaken by the European left, it will clearly demarcate its politics from neoliberal dogma and gain widespread support. But this seems also a long way off.

This first challenge had hardly been raised before the changes in the East confronted Europe with an equally grave challenge. The old European project, the EEC, supposed that the economic power of Germany (then only the West) would be counterbalanced by the political power of Great Britain and France. This possibility was foreclosed by the unification of Germany. The German choice – to invest its efforts in economic expansion toward the east and otherwise to stay in the shadow of the United States – emptied the European project of all its meaning.

The European project had from the outset been an attempt to forestall the danger of "communism," which has now utterly gone, if indeed it ever existed. In this sense this project had been conceived as part of the wider economic, political, military, and ideological undertaking of US domination. An economically integrated Europe, never intended to be on a par with the United States, was to be just a subsector of the world system, open to militarist "Atlanticism" and to the economic penetration of American corporations. Europe continues to believe it needs the military umbrella of the USA and could therefore not afford to break with Atlanticism. From this viewpoint, the tendencies toward autonomy, which by all evidence had the sympathies of de Gaulle, never got beyond the status of impulse. Eventually Europe has chosen to rally behind the United States in its resolve to resubjugate the Third World. NATO thereby became the instrument to breathe new life into Atlanticism.

With an exceptional lucidity, de Gaulle had seized the two essential features of the problem. Right away he had understood that from 1945 Great Britain had made an historic choice, probably irreversible, to align itself with the United States come what may. He had equally understood that it was necessary to conceive of Europe "from the Atlantic to the Urals," that is to say, on a scale that would provide a counterbalance to French–German relations. The changes in Eastern Europe should have given a new vigor to this necessity. But "European integration" cannot be reduced to the expansion of the EEC to the East. The specific problems of the East are too grave for this limited vision. Surely Gorbachev's proposal of a "common European home" responded to these complex problems. Even if his formula was vague, it implied the development of institutions that reconcile European integration with an autonomy that allows individual states to respond to their particular situations.

In my opinion, therefore, the only terms of a real alternative are the following: either there will be a move toward the construction of this common home, or Europe will come further apart – Germany going its own way, with or without the EEC, emptied of any real content. It is my impression that we are firmly embarked on this path for now.

(4) The problems of the Third World are major, and the new globalization accentuates them further. Can the development path taken by certain semi-peripheries continue to be followed? In those that are already semi-industrialized, the development strategy is confronted with a decisive choice. Based on a distribution of income less and less egalitarian, such a path will clash more and more with emerging democratic aspirations. Whether or not

these countries pursue progressive responses to their social problems, it is manifest that they will run head on into the simple logic of globalization through the market. In case they do nothing but succumb to "adjustment," democracy will collapse before having taken root. In other words, a "stabilizing" democracy along Western lines accompanying a capitalist path of economic development seems to me an illusion. Is it, moreover, a real objective of the Western powers? Or only a tactical diversion of the moment? The pursuit of industrial "take-off" in the semi-peripheries implies adjustment to a higher technology and containment of the class struggle within a democratic matrix. I do not believe that this will be easy or even probable in any concrete situation I can think of.

The option of delinking, then, has no real alternative. To say it is not a genuine option is to say that there is no possibility but disintegration. Would it not be better to search for forms of delinking appropriate to the present circumstances than to succumb to chaos?

(5) The prospects are even more somber when one considers the African and Arabic South. When in the nineteenth century Great Britain and France were dividing this region between them, they had no suspicion that one day they would have to accept its decolonization, as they did in the aftermath of the Second World War. The French could conceive of nothing better for their former empire in Black Africa than to place it at the disposal of the capitalists of the Community of Six, with France reserving particular privileges for itself by means of the franc zone, Francophonism, and a system of defense agreements with client states. Neocolonialism thus took the place of colonialism of the older type.

The European plan for the Arab world and North Africa hardly went further, save that Europe has worked harder to keep the allegiance of the local ruling classes who have found themselves in a stronger historical position here than South of the Sahara. The implicit European strategy enmeshed the Arab nations in the impasse of a capitalism peripheral to European expansion. Although the petroleum-exporting nations could mobilize their financial means to accelerate industrialization, their ruling classes could only conceive of an industrialization which opened new outlets for the products of developed capitalism – European in particular, but also American and Japanese. This could not but reinforce the tendency toward globalization, and was not in any sense progress toward autocentered national or regional development. When the crisis came, this deepened integration in the global system showed itself to be catastrophic. Witness the foreign debt, whose effects were brutally aggravated by stagnation and the American counter-offensive. Saudi Arabia, a traditional client of Washington, opted for unconditional surrender to the financial and monetary instruments of American hegemony. Attempts at autocentered development had been partial, limited by the nature of the ruling classes of the nations that had begun them. Although a few gestures in this direction were made (and supported by the USSR), they were strenuously fought by the West, Europe included.

To what can we attribute this refusal of the Europeans to conceive of any relations with the Arabs and Africans other than those of neo-imperialism?

An examination of the structural and conjunctural position of Europe will clarify this issue. Europe covers the deficit in its trade with the USA and Japan by means of a surplus in its trade with the Third World and the East. In order to play the game of globalization, therefore, it needs to maintain unequal relations with its own dependencies. Europe has found the principal opening for its expansion in modernizing its Southern European peripheries and its own industries. Unlike the United States and Japan, which predominantly exported capital in order to dominate in the Third World the industrial delocalization that this export generated (notably in Latin America and Southeast Asia), Europe had opened itself to massive importation of the manual labor it needed to fuel its own internal expansion. It is no accident that the immigration flows precisely from the European dependencies most damaged by this strategy: the Arab countries, Africa, and the Caribbean. One also knows to what degree such immigration has created in Europe a political ambience hostile to the Third World. Finally, since it is poor in natural resources relative to the United States, Europe attaches a great importance to the security of its provisioning. Having renounced autonomy in its military forces, it has condemned itself to depend on the good will of the Americans and to content itself with auxiliary rapid deployment forces (directed against the Third World) to complement the main US intervention forces. This seems to constitute the extent of its military vision.

None of this gives credence to European pronouncements about the Third World. In fact the Europe of the EEC carries a heavy load of responsibility for the "Fourth-Worldization" of Africa. For the unequal relations renewed in the association of the EEC and the ACP (African, Caribbean and Pacific countries associated with the EEC) hardly constitute the liberation of Africa and the development of its peoples, but on the contrary, their incarceration in mining and agriculture, as before. In this sense, Europe carries an important responsibility for the crystallization of the new dominant classes and the economic, social, and political disaster of the continent. The ultimate alignment of Europe with the politics of "adjustment" advocated by the United States through the IMF and the World Bank illustrates Europe's conceptual mediocrity in this domain and shows clearly that the conflicts between the USA and Europe do not extend beyond narrow limits of commercial rivalry. Is this recolonization dressed up as charity anything more than the expression of the failure of the so-called development policies advocated and supported by the West in its entirety in these regions of the Third World?

Europe's responsibility for "the Arab impasse" is no less negligible. Here too Europe has refused to depart from the strategy of the United States and its faithful instrument Israel. The Gulf War tragically illustrates the consequences of this European choice. The objective is quite simply to maintain the Arab world in a state of maximal fragility and vulnerability by rejecting categorically even the idea of Arab unity (painted as a nightmare), by guaranteeing against winds and tides the survival of the archaic regimes of the Gulf, by assuring absolute military superiority of Israel, by refusing the Palestinians the right to exist as a sovereign people. Such unconditional support for Atlanticism and Zionism finally played into the hands of the USA by placing exclusive control over oil under the control of Washington. This ought to make one reflect on the limited capacity of Europe to rethink its perception of the Arab world. For a time, the Europe of the EEC, at the initiative of France and its Mediterranean partners, had toyed with the idea of "breaking" the Arab world by bringing the Mahgreb into its orbit. The spontaneous reactions of the peoples of the Mahgreb to the Gulf War put an end to this unrealistic project.

There remains the failure of political and social consciousness that the Arabs share with other peoples who respond inadequately to the Western challenge: flights of archaic religious illusion, weaknesses of the forces of democracy, and the persistence of military autocracies are the results of the blockage of alternative progressive perspectives in the Arab world. In that perspective the building of a "common European home" should find its natural complements in a united Arab world and a united Africa – the fundamental elements of a polycentric world. The way to such an evolution is long, and in the meantime chaos will persist.

4. The Way out of the Impasse

In the preceding exposition I have tried to show that in all regions of the world the problems are serious, sometimes grave or even dramatic, and for now the deficiencies of political and social consciousness are such that the responses that are taking shape are not adequate to the challenges and can do nothing but aggravate the chaos and barbarism. These deficiencies constitute the backdrop of the crisis of the left throughout the world.

The opposition of left and right reflects in the developed capitalist world a double historical heritage: the Enlightenment (conservative ideology versus progress and movement; authoritarian rule versus democracy) and the workers' movement (regulation subject exclusively to the rationality of capital versus socialism). Neither the one nor the other of the elements of this heritage enjoys a decisive presence in the societies of the periphery. Here the right–left boundary is drawn by acceptance or rejection of "actually existing capitalism," that is to say, the globalization that has peripheralized the Third World. For this reason the national liberation movement, in all its historical forms – bourgeois, popular, and "socialist" – constitutes a force on the left side of the world ledger and the most active social force in the Third World. The adversary it faces there is the class of ruling subalterns and compradors, whose qualifications are those of "collaborators," "traitors," or "colonial lackeys," according to current modes of enactment. There is no consensus here comparable to what exists to give structure to Western societies. In the conjuncture of the moment local power is in reactionary hands, either well established or shaky, or else it reverts to the forces of nationalist movements. The West invariably opposes such movements. In some manner one ought therefore to oppose the real monolithic quality of these Western societies – behind their glued-on facades of pluralism – to the genuine pluralism of opinion in the peripheral societies of the South and East, whose oppositions are too explosive to be managed by a "Western" democracy.

Contrary to a tenacious prejudice, the ideologies of national liberation movements do not attribute responsibility for their countries' situations to "external" factors. Quite the contrary, the emphasis is usually placed on combatting the local forces and ideas that constitute the obstacles to progress. But it goes without saying – at least that is the general opinion among national liberation movements across widely diverse places and times – that all progressive movements enter into conflict with forces that impose themselves from outside. The world capitalist system is not therefore considered to be a neutral or ambiguous factor, and *a fortiori* it is not positive. It is an obstacle, whose name, imperialism, while it is often dismissed in the West as an "unscientific" term, is in the peripheries usual, banal, and general, and whose ever-present influence is regarded as self-evident. The internal quarrels that animate the movements of national liberation concern the concrete nature of this imperialism in each of the phases of the world expansion of capitalism since its origin, the forms of expression of the laws of its movement, the means of its intervention, the social alliances that it forges and the means by which it reproduces polarization. There is no doubt of its existence among its victims.

We know how difficult it has been and continues to be to establish a constructive dialogue between left forces in the West and those of the Third World. Despite this fact, alas quite evident, the segments of the left most aware of the global nature of the challenge that humanity faces and committed to a universalist perspective have always engaged in this dialogue whose vision extends well beyond the immediate results that are sometimes given prominence.

A humane and progressive response to the problems of the contemporary world implies the construction of a popular internationalism that can engender a genuinely universalist value system, completing the unfinished projects of the Enlightenment and the socialist movement. This is the only way to build an effective front against the internationalism of capital and the false universalism of its value system.

On the internal level, social alliances which define the content of progressive strategies will necessarily produce alternatives for different regions. In the West, their bourgeois dimension – based on a long history that has led to advanced development – will remain prominent for quite a time. This does not preclude progressive socialization of the system and, in time, the emergence of the hegemony of the salaried strata. In the countries of the East, they will call for the liberation of society from the yoke of statism and a dialogue between socialism and capitalism. But in the Third World, they will almost always imply a reversal of tendencies that are more radical than evolutionist, and the outright rejection of bourgeois subalternism. If, therefore, one is right to envision the substitution of popular control, national and regional, for the bourgeois vision of exclusive control by the market, the intense feeling of crisis which this choice implies will be more dramatic in the South and East than in the West. Failure to recognize this is sure to close off the response of people trapped in the hopelessness of antediluvian nationalisms and traditionalisms, whether religious or not.

The present crisis should be the occasion for the progress of critical thought, if one understands by that the calling into question of all dogmas. There is not much of this, perhaps among other reasons because neither the academic economist nor the administrative mind-set that it engenders encourages questions. The leaders of social movements and other progressive political men and women are well aware of this need to question. The world polycentrism whose principles are outlined here is the only realistic basis for a new internationalism. Only the deep understandings that flow from this paradigm will make us able to recognize the objective diversity of our conditions and problems, to lay the foundations for reconstructing our world, and to acknowledge the common destiny of the peoples of our planet.

REFERENCES

Amin, Samir (1988), "Il y a trente ans, Bandung." In *L'échange inégal et la loi de la valeur*. Economica.

Arrighi, Giovanni (1991). In: Amin–Arrighi–Frank–Wallerstein, *Le grand tumulte*. La Découverte.

Beaud, Michel (1989), *L'économie mondial dans les années 80*. La Découverte.

Braverman, Harry (1974), *Labor and Monopoly Capital*. Monthly Review Press.

Coriat, Benjamin (1990), *L'atelier et le robot*. Christian Bourgeois.

Lipietz, Alain (1989), *Choisir l'audace*. La Découverte.

5

Structural Issues of Global Governance: Implications for Europe

*Robert Cox**

1. Global Governance in the Transition from the Twentieth to the Twenty-first Century

This paper will focus on three broad issues of global governance in the transition from the twentieth to the twenty-first century: (1) the globalization of the world economy and the reactions it may provoke; (2) the transformation of the inter-state system as it has been known since the Westphalian era; and (3) the problematic of a post-hegemonic world order. In discussing these issues, three levels of human organization have to be considered in their interrelationships: the level of social forces, the level of states and national societies, and the level of world order and global society. The aim of the paper is to sketch out a framework for understanding the problem of global governance, using these three issues and three levels, and then to consider its implications for Europe, and for Europe's choices in relation to the world.

Globalization

The two principal aspects of globalization are (1) global organizations of production (complex transnational networks of production which source the various components of the product in places offering the most cost advantage and also the advantages of political security and predictability); and (2) global finance (a very largely unregulated system of transactions in money,

* Robert Cox is Professor Emeritus of Political Science at York University, Toronto, and UNU Programme Coordinator.
  This chapter is reprinted, with changes, by permission of the author and Cambridge University Press, from *Gramsci, Historical Materialism and International Relations*, ed. Stephen Gill.

credit, and equities). These developments together constitute a *global economy*, i.e. an economic space transcending all country borders, which coexists still with an *international economy* based on transactions across country borders and which is regulated by inter-state agreements and practices.[1] The growth of the global economy and the progressive subordination to it of the international economy are widely seen among liberal economists and politicians as the wave of the future – on the whole a "good thing" to which everyone sooner or later must adapt through the pressure of global competition.

Globalization has certain consequences, which are less often pointed out, but which have serious implications for the future structure of world order.

One of these consequences is a process that can be called the internationalization of the state. If you think back to the inter-war period and especially the depression years of the 1930s, the role of states was primarily to protect national economic space from disturbances coming from outside. The Bretton Woods system moved towards a different balance. It sought to achieve a compromise: states still had a primary responsibility to safeguard domestic welfare and levels of employment and economic activity; but they were to do this within rules that precluded economic aggression against others and aimed at a harmonization of different national economic policies. Since the mid-1970s, with the demise of Bretton Woods, a new doctrine has achieved preeminence: states must become the instruments for adjusting national economic activities to the exigencies of the global economy – states are becoming transmission belts from the global into the national economic spheres. Adjustment to global competitiveness is the new categorical imperative.

The effect of this tendency is differentiated by the relative power of states. Indebted Third World states are in the weakest position. Here, states that are weak in relation to external pressures must become strong enough internally to enforce punitive adjustment measures on vulnerable social groups. States in "developed" countries discover that sensitivity to foreign bond markets, fiscal crisis, and the transnational mobility of capital have effectively diminished their autonomy in determining national economic policy. The United States, despite being the world's biggest debtor, retains a relative autonomy in determining national economic policy. Other states must adjust their economic policies to situations very largely determined by the United States.

Another consequence of globalization is the restructuring of national societies and the emergence of a global social structure. Globalization is led by a transnational managerial class that consists of distinct fractions (American, European, Japanese) but which as a whole constitutes the heart of what Susan Strange has called the "business civilization." (Strange, 1990) The restructuring of production is changing the pattern of organization of production from what has been called "Fordism" to "post-Fordism."[2] That is to say, the age of the large integrated mass production factory is passing; the new model is a core/periphery structure of production with a relatively small control-center core and numerous subsidiary component-producing and servicing units linked as required to the core. Economies of scale have given place to economies of flexibility. More flexibly decentralized production facilitates border-crossing relationships in organizing production systems; it also segments the labor force into groups segregated by nationality, ethnicity, religion, gender, etc., such that this labor force lacks the natural cohesion of the large concentrated workforces of the old mass production industries. Power has shifted dramatically from labor to capital in the process of restructuring production.

The geographical distinction of First and Third Worlds is becoming somewhat blurred. Third World conditions are being reproduced within "developed" countries. Mass migrations from South to North combine with the reemergence of "putting out" production, sometimes of a "sweatshop" variety, and the expansion of low-wage employment in services in the "developed" countries of the North, to produce a phenomenon called the "peripheralization of the core." The terms "core" and "periphery" are losing their earlier exclusively geographical meaning to acquire gradually the meaning of social differentiation within a globalizing society – a differentiation produced in large measure by the restructuring of production.

Karl Polanyi's analysis of nineteenth-century Britain suggests a paradigm for present-day global changes. (Polanyi, 1957) Polanyi wrote of a "double movement." The first phase of this movement was the imposition upon society of the concept of the self-regulating market. To Polanyi, as economic historian and anthropologist, the notion of an economic process disembedded from society and set over and above society was an historical aberration, a utopian idea that could not endure. The disintegrating effects that the attempt to impose the self-regulating market had upon society generated during the later nineteenth century the second phase of the double movement: a self-protective response from society through the political system reasserting the primacy of the social. This second phase took form with the legalizing of trade unions and collective bargaining, the construction of social security systems, the introduction of factory legislation, and ultimately recognition of government's responsibility to maintain satisfactory levels of employment and welfare.

One can well hypothesize today that the present trend of liberal deregulation and privatization which appears to carry all before it in global economics will encounter a global response. This response will endeavor once again to bring economic process under social control, to reembed the economy, now at the global level, in society and to subordinate enhanced economic capacities to globally endorsed social purposes.

Transformation of the State System?

As mentioned, economic globalization has placed constraints upon the autonomy of states. More and more, national debts are foreign debts, so that states have to be attentive to external bond markets and to externally influenced interest rates in determining their own economic policies. The level of national economic activity also depends upon access to foreign markets. Participation in various international "regimes" regulates the activities of states in developed capitalist countries, achieving conformity with global economy processes, tending toward a stabilization of the world capitalist economy.[3]

Apart from these constraints inherent in the existing global economic order, there are new tendencies within this order producing two new levels of participation, one above and one below the level of existing states. These new levels can be named macro- and micro-regionalism.

As counterweights to the dominance of the US economy and its prolongation into a North American economic sphere, two other macro-regional economic spheres are emerging, one in Europe and the other in the Western Pacific centered on Japan. Europe and Japan confront separately the challenge of enlarging their autonomy in the global economy in relation to the dominance of US economic power.

At the same time, the opening of larger economic spaces, both global and macro-regional, coupled with the weakening autonomy of existing states, has given scope for sub-state entities to realize greater autonomy or independence, to seek direct relationships to the larger economic spaces, escaping subordination to a weakened existing state. Catalan and Lombard micro-regionalists aspire to a more affluent future in the Europe of post-1992, free from Spanish or Italian central governmental controls and redistributive policies. Quebec *indépendantistes* are the most enthusiastic supporters of a North American economic space. The former Soviet empire and former Yugoslavia are collapsing into a multiplicity of political entities most of which can hardly hope to control their own destinies but all of which will seek some form of relationship with the large economic spaces now in formation.

Globalization is generating a more complex multi-level world political system, which implicitly challenges the old Westphalian assumption that a state is a state is a state. Structures of authority comprise not one but at least three levels: the macro-regional level, the old state (or Westphalian) level, and the micro-regional level. All three levels are constrained by a global economy which has means of exerting its pressures without relying upon formal authoritative political structures.

There is an increasingly marked duality and tension between the principles of interdependence and territorially based power. Interdependence (most often a euphemism for relationships of dominance and dependence) is manifested in the economic sphere. Territorial power is ultimately military. The United States is at the heart of the tension between the two principles. Global economic interdependence requires an enforcer of the rules – just as the self-regulating market of the nineteenth century had as enforcers at the local and global levels Robert Peel's police force and British sea power. Today the United States plays the role of global enforcer; but at the same time the US economy is rapidly losing its lead in productivity.

The trade deficit and budget deficit in the United States have been bridged by foreign borrowing, in recent years mainly from Japan. The internal reforms that would be necessary to reverse this process by reducing the deficits are blocked by the rigidity of the US political system and the unwillingness of politicians to confront the public with unpleasant choices. For the time being, foreign finance sustains a level of military and civilian consumption in the United States that US production would otherwise not allow.

The Gulf War underlined on the military side (as Germany, Japan, Saudi Arabia and Kuwait were obliged to pay for a war decided and directed by the United States) what has quietly become the case on the civilian side for some years. The United States does not pay its way in the world, while its structural power, resting increasingly on its military strength, continues to bias the global system in its favor. This is a far cry from the post-World-War-II world in which the United States provided the resources for recovery and the model of productivity for the rest of the world.[4] What was a system of hegemonic leadership has become a tributary system.

Hegemony and After

There is an active debate about whether or not the hegemony of Pax Americana is in decline.[5] (See Keohane 1984, Kennedy 1987, Nye 1990, Strange 1987, Gill 1990) What remains unclear in this debate is a failure to distinguish between two meanings of "hegemony." One meaning, which is conventional in international relations literature, is the dominance of one state over others, the ability of the dominant state to determine the conditions in which inter-state relations are conducted and to determine the outcomes in these relations. The other meaning, informed by the thought of Antonio Gramsci, is a special case of dominance: it defines the condition of a world society and state system in which the dominant state and dominant social forces sustain their position through adherence to universalized principles which are accepted or acquiesced in by a sufficient proportion of subordinate states and social forces. (Cox, 1983) This second meaning of hegemony implies intellectual and moral leadership. The strong make certain concessions to obtain the consent of the weaker.

The Pax Americana of the post-World-War-II era had the characteristics of this Gramscian meaning of hegemony. The United States was the dominant power and its dominance was expressed in leadership enshrined in certain principles of conduct that became broadly acceptable. The economic "regimes" established under US aegis during this period had the appearance of consensual arrangements. They did not either look like the crude exploitation of a power position or resemble a hard bargain arrived at among rival interests. Moreover, the founding power behaved more or less according to the rules it established.

The recourse of US policy during the 1980s to unilateralism and the more manifest divergencies of interest among the United States, Europe, and

Japan, together with the subordination of Third World countries to western economic and military pressures, have changed the nature of global relationships. US power may not have declined either absolutely or relatively, but the nature of the world system can no longer be described as hegemonic in the earlier sense.

Past hegemonies – the Pax Americana of the mid-twentieth century – have been based on universal principles projected from one form of western civilization. A civilization is an intersubjective order, that is to say, people understand the entities and principles upon which it is based in roughly the same way, stimulated and confirmed by their own experiences of material life. By understanding their world in the same way, they reproduce it by their actions. Intersubjective meanings shape the objective world of the state system and the economy.[6] The fashionable prediction that we have arrived at the "end of history"[7] (a notion stimulated by the collapse of Soviet power and the end of the Cold War) celebrates the apotheosis of late western capitalism. It is, however, in the nature of history not to have an end, but to move ahead in zig-zag manner by action and reaction. If the consensual basis of Pax Americana is no longer so firm as it was in the 1950s and 60s, then we must ask what intersubjective basis there could be for a future world order.

A post-hegemonic era would be one in which different traditions of civilization could coexist, each based on a different intersubjectivity defining a distinct set of values and a distinct path towards development. This is a difficult challenge to common ways of thinking. It would imply building a mental picture of a future world order through a mutual recognition and mutual understanding of different images of world order deriving from distinct cultural and historical roots, as a first step. Then, as a second step, working out the basis for the coexistence of these images – creating a supra-intersubjectivity that would connect or reconcile these culturally distinct intersubjectivities.

2. Europe's Choices: Forms of State and Society

How do these global tendencies and issues appear in the European context? How will Europeans respond in shaping their society and their form or forms of state?

It has become a commonplace on both left and right of the political spectrum that the capitalist state has both to support capital in its drive to accumulate and to legitimate this accumulation in the minds of the public by moderating the negative effects of accumulation on welfare and employment. During the post-war years, a neo-liberal form of state took shape in countries of advanced capitalism based on a negotiated consensus among the major industrial interests, organized labor, and government. It was "neo" in the sense that classical liberalism was modified by Keynesian practices to make market behavior consistent with social protection of the more disadvantaged groups.[8]

As growth stagnated in advanced capitalist countries during the 1970s, governments in effect denounced the social contract worked out with capital and labor during the post-war economic boom. Governments had to balance the fear of political unrest from rising unemployment and exhaustion of welfare reserves against the fear that business would refrain from leading a recovery that would both revive employment and enlarge the tax base. In this circumstance they bent before the interests of capital.

In the neo-liberal consensus it had become accepted wisdom that society would not tolerate high unemployment or any dismantling of the welfare state. If these things were to occur, it would, it was said, cost the state the loss of its legitimacy. The truth of this statement has not been demonstrated uniformly. Indeed, it would more generally seem to be the case that the legitimacy of state welfare and of labor movements has been undermined in public opinion, not the legitimacy of the state. Large-scale unemployment has produced fear and concern for personal survival rather than collective protest. The unions are in strategic retreat, losing members, and unable, in general, to appeal to public opinion for support.

The disintegration of neo-liberalism was prepared by a collective effort of ideological revision undertaken through various unofficial agencies – the Trilateral Commission, the Bilderberg conferences, the Club of Rome, the Mont Pelerin Society and other less prestigious forums – and then endorsed through more official consensus-making agencies like the OECD. A new doctrine defined the tasks of states in relaunching capitalist development out of the depression of the 1970s. There was, in the words of a blue-ribbon OECD committee, a "narrow path to growth," bounded on one side by the need to encourage private investment by increasing profit margins, and bounded on the other by the need to avoid rekindling inflation. (McCracken Report, 1977).

The government–business alliance formed to advance along this narrow path ruled out corporative-type solutions like negotiated wage and price policies and also the extension of public investment. It placed primary emphasis on restoring the confidence of business in government and in practice acknowledged that welfare and employment commitments made in the framework of the post-war social contract would have to take second place.

It would be premature to define the outlines of a new coalition of social forces likely to achieve a certain durability as the foundation of a new form of state. Two principal directions of change in political structures are visible in the erstwhile neo-liberal states of Western Europe: one is exemplified by the confrontational tactics of Thatcherism in Britain (and by Reaganism in the United States) toward removing internal obstacles to economic liberalism; the other by a more consensus-based adjustment process as in West Germany and some of the smaller European countries.

Hyper-liberalism

The Thatcher–Reagan model can be treated ideologically as the anticipation of a hyper-liberal form of state – in the sense that it seems to envisage a return to nineteenth-century economic liberalism and a rejection of
the neo-liberal attempt to adapt economic liberalism to the sociopolitical
reactions that classical liberalism produced. It takes the "neo" out of neo-
liberalism. The whole paraphernalia of Keynesian demand-support and
redistributionist tools of policy are regarded with the deepest suspicion in
the hyper-liberal approach.

Hyper-liberalism actively facilitates a restructuring, not only of the labor
force, but also of the social relations of production. It renounces tripartite
corporatism. It also weakens bipartism by its attack on unions in the state
sector and its support and encouragement to employers to resist union
demands in the oligopolistic sector. Indirectly, the state encourages the
consolidation of enterprise corporatist relations for the scientific–technical–
managerial workers in the oligopolistic sector. State policies are geared to
an expansion of employment in short-term, low-skill, high-turnover jobs that
contribute to further labor market segmentation.[9]

The political implications are a complete reversal of the coalition that
sustained the neo-liberal state. That state rested on its relationship with
trade unions in the oligopolistic sector (the social contract), an expanding
and increasingly unionized state sector, readiness to support major busi-
nesses in difficulty (from agricultural price supports to bailouts of industrial
giants), and transfer payments and services for a range of disadvantaged
groups. The neo-liberal state played a hegemonic role by making capital
accumulation on a world scale appear to be compatible with a wide range of
interests of subordinate groups. It founded its legitimacy on consensual
politics.

The would-be hyper-liberal state confronts all those groups and interests
with which the neo-liberal state came to terms. The government–business
alliance generates an imposing list of disadvantaged and excluded groups.
State-sector employees made great gains as regards their collective bargaining status and their wages during the years of expansion and have now
become front-line targets for budgetary restraint. Welfare recipients and
non-established workers, socially contiguous categories, are hit by reduced
state expenditure and unemployment. Farmers and small businessmen are
angry with banks and with governments as affordable finance becomes
unavailable to them. Established workers in industries confronting severe
problems in a changing international division of labor – textiles, automobiles, steel, shipbuilding, for example – face unemployment or reduced real
wages.

So long as the excluded groups lack strong organizations and political
cohesion, ideological mystification and an instinctive focus on personal survival rather than collective action suffice to maintain the momentum of the

new policy orthodoxy. If at least a small majority of the population remains relatively satisfied, or even a politically dominant minority, it can be mobilized to maintain these policies in place against the dissatisfaction of an even very large minority or slim majority that is passive, divided and incoherent.

State Capitalism

While the hyper-liberal model reasserts the separation of state and economy, the alternative state form that contends for relaunching capitalist development promotes a fusion of state and economy.

The visible hand of this state capitalism operates through a conscious industrial policy. Such a policy can be achieved only through a negotiated understanding among the principal social forces mediated by the state in a corporative process. This process produces agreement on the strategic goals of the economy and also on the sharing of burdens and benefits in the effort to reach those goals.

The state-capitalist approach is grounded in an acceptance of the world market as the ultimate determinant of development. Unlike the neo-liberal approach, the state-capitalist approach does not posit any consensual regulation of the world market. "Regimes" may survive from the neo-liberal era, but state capitalism is not the most fertile ground for their formation. States are assumed to intervene not only to enhance the competitiveness of their nations' industries but also to negotiate or dictate advantages for their nations' exporters. The world market is the state of nature from which state-capitalist theory deduces specific policy.

The broad lines of this policy consist of, in the first place, development of the leading sectors of national production so as to give them a competitive edge in world markets, and, in the second place, protection of the principal social groups so that their welfare can be perceived as linked to the success of the national productive effort.

The first aspect of this policy – industrial competitiveness – is to be achieved by a combination of opening these industrial sectors to the stimulus of world competition, together with state subsidization and orientation of innovation. Critical to the capacity for innovation is the condition of the knowledge industry; the state will have a major responsibility for funding technological research and development.

The second policy aspect – balancing the welfare of social groups – has to be linked to the pursuit of competitiveness. Protection of disadvantaged groups and sectors (industries or regions) would be envisaged as transitional assistance for their transfer to more profitable economic activities. Thus training, skill upgrading, and relocation assistance would have a preeminent place in social policy. The state would not indefinitely protect declining or inefficient industries but would provide incentives for the people concerned to become more efficient according to market criteria. The state would, however, intervene between the market pressures and the groups concerned so that the latter did not bear the full burden of adjustment. (By contrast, the hyper-liberal model would let the market impose the full costs of adjustment upon the less fit.)

The state-capitalist form involves a dualism between, on the one hand, a competitively efficient world-market-oriented sector, and, on the other, a protected welfare sector. The success of the former must provide the resources for the latter; the sense of solidarity implicit in the latter would provide the drive and legitimacy for the former. State capitalism thus proposes a means of reconciling the accumulation and legitimation functions brought into conflict by the economic and fiscal crises of the 1970s and by hyper-liberal politics.

In its most radical form, state capitalism beckons toward the prospect of an internal socialism sustained by capitalist success in world-market competition. This would be a socialism dependent on capitalist development, i.e. on success in the production of exchange values. But, so its proponents argue, it would be less vulnerable to external destabilization than were socialist strategies in economically weak countries (Allende's Chile or post-carnation-revolution Portugal). The more radical form of state-capitalist strategy presents itself as an alternative to defensive, quasi-autarkic prescriptions for the construction of socialism which aim to reduce dependency on the world economy and to emphasize the production of use values for internal consumption.[10]

Different countries are more or less well-equipped by their historical experience for the adoption of the state-capitalist developmental path with or without the socialist coloration.[11] Those best-equipped are countries in which the state (as in France) or a centralized but autonomous financial system (as in Germany) has played a major role in mobilizing capital for industrial development. Institutions and ideology in these countries have facilitated a close coordination of state and private capital in the pursuit of common goals. Those least well-equipped are the erstwhile industrial leaders, Britain and the United States, countries in which hegemonic institutions and ideology kept the state by and large out of specific economic initiatives, confining its role to guaranteeing and enforcing market rules and to macroeconomic management of market conditions. The lagging effects of past hegemonic leadership may thus be a deterrent to the adoption of state-capitalist strategies.

The corporatist process underpinning state-capitalist development, which would include business and labor in the world-market-oriented sector and workers in the tertiary welfare-services sector, would at the same time exclude certain marginal groups. These groups have a frequently passive relationship to the welfare services and lack influence in the making of policy. They are disproportionately to be found among the young, women, immigrants, minority groups, and the unemployed. The number of the marginalized tends to increase with the restructuring of production. Since these groups are fragmented and relatively powerless, their exclusion has generally passed unchallenged. This process does, however, contain a latent threat to corporatist processes.

This threat could take the form either of anomic explosions of violence or, more seriously, of political mobilization of the marginals, which would pit democratic legitimacy against corporatist economic efficiency. These dangers are foreshadowed in the writings of neo-liberal ideologues about the "ungovernability" problem of modern democracies. (Crozier, Huntingdon & Watanuki, 1975) The implication is that the corporatist processes required to make state-capitalist development succeed may have to be insulated from democratic pressures. To the extent this becomes true, the prospects for internal socialism sustained by world-market state capitalism would be rendered illusionary. In the medium term, state-capitalist structures of some kind seem a feasible alternative to the hyper-liberal impasse. The long-term viability of these forms is a more open question.

Western Europe has, in its different national antecedents, propensities tending toward each of these forms of state and society. It might be said that in its present power structure the dominance of capital in the opening of the Europe of 1992 favors hyper-liberalism. However, the social corporativist tradition is strong, especially in continental Europe, and may compensate in politics for the dominance of hyper-liberalism in economic power. The concept of "social Europe," an anathema to Thatcherism and more covertly rejected by some elements of continental capital, is promoted by a social democracy more deeply rooted than in other major world regions. The encounter between hyper-liberalism and state capitalism will be tested first in Europe, and Europe's answer will serve as a model or at least as an alternative for North America, Japan, and perhaps other regions in a future world.

Social Forces Counteracting Globalization

Hyper-liberalism is the ideology of globalization in its most extreme form. State capitalism is an adaptation to globalization that responds at least in part to society's reaction to the negative effects of globalization. We must ask ourselves whether there are longer-term prospects that might come to fruition following a medium-term experiment with state capitalism. This is best approached by enquiring how the conditions created by globalization could generate a *prise de conscience* among those elements of societies that are made more vulnerable by it.

If the state-capitalist solution were to be but an interim stage, the prospect of turning around the segmenting, socially disintegrating, and polarizing effects of globalization rests upon the possibility of the emergence of an alternative political culture that would give greater scope to collective action and place a greater value on collective goods. For this to come about, whole segments of societies would have to become attached, through active participation and developed loyalties, to social institutions engaged in collective activities. They would have to be prepared to defend these institutions in times of adversity.

The condition for a restructuring of society and polity in this sense would be to build a new coalition of social forces capable of becoming an alternative basis of polity. Europe's social history has known such movements. They have influenced the shaping of society and state, even though they have never fulfilled their aims. These aims could in any event hardly be achieved in one national society alone; movements of this kind would have to grow simultaneously in several countries. The merging of European political processes inherent in the project of 1992 could provide a broad arena in which this struggle could be pursued.

The revolution in Eastern Europe could further stimulate popular movements in both Eastern and Western Europe. Economic globalization, however, suggests that such movements could not succeed in one macro-region alone. These processes would have to draw sufficient support in the world system to protect their respective regional base or face the consequences of a relative military and economic weakening unless competing macro-regions were experiencing comparable developments. The existing globalization grounded in the economic logic of markets would have to be countered by a new globalization that reembedded the economy in global society.

3. The Sequel to "Real Socialism"

If the options for the Europe of western capitalism can be expressed in relatively clear terms, the situation of the countries of erstwhile "real socialism" approaching the threshold of the twenty-first century is more complex.[12] Yet the long-term future of Europe implies an accommodation between these two regions. It is easy in the early 1990s to proclaim real socialism a failure. It is more difficult to envisage the effacing of the history of two generations through which social structures have been formed. The Eastern part of Europe is not a *tabula rasa* on which Western capitalism may be simply inscribed. The options for the region, whether for the parts that may anticipate total integration within the West (the former GDR), close association with the European Communities (Poland, Hungary, and Czechoslovakia), or an autonomous evolution with a degree of integration into the world economy (the former USSR), have realistically to take account of existing social structures. Both capitalist and socialist societies have grown by extracting a surplus from the producers. In market-driven capitalist societies, this surplus is invested in whatever individual capitalists think is likely to produce a further profit. In socialist societies, investment decisions have been politically determined according to whatever criteria are salient at the time for the decision-makers, e.g. welfare or state power. The social structure of accumulation is the particular configuration of social power through which the accumulation process takes place. This configuration delineates a relationship among social groups in the production process from which a surplus is extracted. This power relationship underpins the institutional arrangements through which the process works.[13] It also shapes the real form of political authority.

To grasp the nature of the social structure of accumulation at the moment of the crisis of existing socialism in the late 1980s, one must go back to the transformation in the working class that began some three decades earlier. The new working class composed largely of ex-peasants that carried through the industrialization drive of the 1930s in the Soviet Union and the war effort of the 1940s worked under an iron discipline of strict regulation and tough task masters recruited from the shop floor. During the 1950s a new mentality reshaped industrial practices. Regulations were relaxed and their modes of application gave more scope for the protection of individual workers' interests. Managerial cadres began to be recruited mainly from professional schools and were more disposed to the methods of manipulation and persuasion than to coercion. The factory regime passed from the despotic to the hegemonic type.[14]

An historic compromise worked out by the Party leadership included a *de facto* social contract in which workers were implicitly guaranteed job security, stable consumer prices, and control over the pace of work, in return for their passive acquiescence in the rule of the political leadership. Workers had considerable structural power, i.e. their interests had to be anticipated and taken into account by the leadership, though they had little instrumental power through direct representation. This arrangement of passive acquiescence gave rise over time to cynicism expressed as: "You pretend to pay us. We pretend to work."

The working class comprised an established and a non-established segment. One group of workers, the established worker segment, were more permanent in their jobs, had skills more directly applied in their work, were more involved in the enterprise as a social institution and in other political and civic activities. The other group, the non-established worker segment, changed jobs more frequently, experienced no career development in their employment, and were non-participants in enterprise or other social and political activities. The modalities of this segmentation varied among the different socialist countries.

Hungarian sociologists discerned a more complex categorization of non-established workers: "workhorses" willing to exploit themselves for private accumulation (newly marrieds for instance); "hedonists" or single workers interested only in the wage as the means of having a good time; and "internal guest workers," mainly women, or part-time peasant workers, or members of ethnic minorities allocated to do the dirty work. (Hungarian Academy of Sciences, 1984) In practice, labor segmentation under "real socialism" bore a striking similarity to labor segmentation under capitalism.

This differentiation within the working class had a particular importance in the framework of central planning. Central planning can be thought of in abstract terms as a system comprising (a) redistributors in central agencies of the state who plan according to some decision-making rationality, i.e. maximizing certain defined goals and allocating resources accordingly; and (b) direct producers who carry out the plans with the resources provided them. In practice, central planning developed an internal dynamic that defied the rationality of planners. It became a complex bargaining process from enterprise to central levels in which different groups have different levels of power. One of the more significant theoretical efforts of recent years has been to analyze the real nature of central planning so as to discern its inherent laws or regularities.[15]

Capital is understood in Marxist terms as a form of alienation: people through their labor create something that becomes a power over themselves and their work. Central planning also became a form of alienation: instead of being a system of rational human control over economic processes, it too became a system that no one controlled but which came to control planners and producers alike.

A salient characteristic of central planning as it had evolved in the decades just prior to the changes that began to be introduced during the late 1980s was a tendency to overinvest. Enterprises sought to get new projects included in the plan and thus to increase their sources of supply through allocations within it. Increased supplies made it easier to fulfill existing obligations but at the same time raised future obligations. The centrally planned economy was an economy of shortages; it was supply constrained, in contrast to the capitalist economy which was demand constrained. The economy of shortages generated uncertainties of supply, and these uncertainties were transmitted from enterprise to enterprise along the chain of inputs and outputs.

Enterprise managers became highly dependent upon core workers to cope with uncertainties. The core workers, familiar with the installed equipment, were the only ones able to improvise when bottlenecks occurred. They could, if necessary, improvise to cope with absence of replacement parts, repair obsolescent equipment, or make use of substitute materials. Managers also had an incentive to hoard workers, to maintain an internal enterprise labor reserve that could be mobilized for "storming" at the end of a plan period. Managers also came to rely on their relations with local Party officials to secure needed inputs when shortages impeded the enterprise's ability to meet its plan target.

These factors combined to make the key structure at the heart of the system one of management dependence on local Party cadres together with a close interrelationship between management and core workers in a form of enterprise corporatism. From this point, there were downward linkages with subordinate groups of non-established workers, with rural cooperatives, and with household production. There were upward linkages with the ministries of industries and the state plan. And there was a parallel relationship with the "second economy" which, together with political connections, helped to bypass some of the bottlenecks inherent in the formal economy.

Several things can be inferred from this social structure of accumulation. One is that those constituting its core – management, established workers, and local Party officials – were well entrenched in the production system. They knew how to make it work and they were likely to be apprehensive about changes that would introduce further uncertainties beyond those that they had learned to cope with. Motivation for change was most likely to come from those at the top who were aware that production was less efficient than it might have been, and who wanted to eliminate excess labor and to introduce more productive technology. (Those at the core of the system had a vested interest in existing obsolescent technology because their particular skills made it work.) Motivation for change might also arise among the general population in the form of dissatisfaction with declining standards of public services and consumer goods; and among a portion of the growing "middle class" of white-collar service workers. The more peripheral of the non-established workers – those most alienated within the system – were unlikely to be highly motivated for change. There was, in fact, no coherent social basis for change but rather a diffuse dissatisfaction with the way the system was performing. There was, however, likely to be a coherent social basis at the heart of the system that could be mobilized to resist change.

Economic Reform and Democratization

Socialist systems, beginning with the Soviet Union, have been preoccupied with reform of the economic mechanism since the 1960s. The problem was posed in terms of a transition from the extensive pattern of growth that was producing diminishing returns from the mid-1960s onward, to a pattern of growth that would be more intensive in the use of capital and technology. Perception of the problem came from the top of the political-economic hierarchy and was expressed through a sequence of on-again off-again experiments. Piece-meal reform proved difficult because of the very coherence of the system of power that constituted central planning. Movement in one direction, e.g. granting more decision-making powers to managers, ran up against obstacles in other parts of the system, e.g. in the powers of central ministries and in the acquired job rights of workers.

Frustrations with piece-meal reforms encouraged espousal of more radical reform; and radical reform was associated with giving much broader scope to the market mechanism. The market was an attractive concept insofar as it promised a more effective and less cumbersome means of allocating material inputs to enterprises and of distributing consumer goods. It was consistent with decentralization of management to enterprises and with a stimulus to consumer-goods production. The market, however, was also suspect insofar as it would create prices (and thus inflation in an economy of shortages), bring about greater disparities in incomes, and undermine the power of the center to direct the overall development of the economy. Some combination of markets with central direction of the economy seemed to be the optimum solution, if it could be done.

Following in the tracks of the reform movement came pressures for democratization. These came from a variety of sources: a series of movements sequentially repressed but cumulatively infectious in East Germany, Poland, Hungary, and Czechoslovakia; the rejection of Stalinism and the ultimate weakening of the repressive apparatus installed by Stalinism; and the consequences of the rebirth of civil society and of the recognition by the ruling cadres that the intelligentsia was entitled to greater autonomy. The two movements – *perestroika* and *glasnost* in their Soviet form – met and interacted in the late 1980s.

Some economic reformers saw democratization as a means of loosening up society which could strengthen decentralization. Some of these same people also saw worker self-management as supporting enterprise autonomy and the liberalizing of markets. Humanist intellectuals tended to see economic reform as limiting the state's coercive apparatus and as encouraging a more pluralist society. For these groups, economic reform and democratization went together.

Other economic reformers recognized that reform measures would place new burdens on people before the reforms showed any benefits. There would be inflation, shortages, and unemployment. The social contract of mature real socialism would be discarded in the process of introducing flexibility into the labor market and the management of enterprises. The skills of existing managers would be rendered obsolete, together with those of many state and Party officials engaged in the central planning process. Anticipating the backlash from all these groups, "realist" reformers could conclude that an authoritarian power would be needed to implement reform successfully. Without it, reform would just be compromised and rendered ineffective, disrupting the present system without being able to replace it.[16] The economic Thatcherites of real socialism could become its political Pinochets.

The initial effects of both economic reform and democratization produced some troublesome consequences. Relaxing economic controls towards encouraging a shift to market mechanisms has resulted in a breakdown of the distribution system, with a channelling of goods into free markets and black markets, rampant gangsterism, and a dramatic polarization of new rich and poor. Among the new rich are members of the old nomenklatura well placed to adapt their knowledge of how enterprises worked to the new opportunities of market capitalism.

The relaxing of political controls gave vent to conflicts long suppressed, mobilizing people around ethnic nationalisms, various forms of populism, and, at the extreme, right-wing fascist movements. Furthermore, the outburst of public debate, while it severely undermined the legitimacy of the Soviet state and its sustaining myths, also demonstrated an inability to come to grips with the practical reorganization of economy and society. The reform process itself made things worse, not better in practical material terms.

The legitimacy of real socialism was destroyed by Stalinism and the anti-Stalinist backlash. Civil society is reemergent but its component groups have not achieved any articulate organized expression. This is a condition Gramsci called an organic crisis; and the solution to an organic crisis is the reconstitution of a hegemony around a social group which is capable of leading and acquiring the support or acquiescence of other groups. What does our analysis of the social structure of real socialism tell us about the prospects of this happening?

Two routes towards democratization in recent Eastern and Central European experience have been, first, a movement from outside a moribund Party, led by an independent workers' movement to which an intelligentsia attached itself (Poland); second, an enlargement of scope for independent decision-making in the economy through a strategic withdrawal by the Party from direct control over certain aspects of civil society (Hungary). Both of these routes now in retrospect are deliberately leading towards a restoration of capitalism. The former GDR shows a third route to capitalism: total collapse of the political structures of real socialism and full incorporation of its economy into West German capitalism.

Three Scenarios

For the remaining European countries of real socialism, options for the future can be grouped broadly into three scenarios. Each of these should be examined in terms of the relationship of the projected form of state and economy with the existing social structure of accumulation.

The first scenario is economic liberalization leading towards market capitalism and the integration of the national economy into the global capitalist economy. In its "pure" form, this project includes a "shock therapy" in the Polish mode to free market forces. By implication, this course could lead its exponents to conclude, after an initial period of troubles, that dictatorial powers will be needed to prevent elements of existing civil society, notably workers and segments of the bureaucracies, from political protest and obstruction in response to the bankruptcies of enterprises, unemployment, inflation, and polarization of rich and poor that occur as its accompaniment and consequences. This is the option encouraged, wittingly or unwittingly, by the Western consultants pullulating through the world of real socialism as the whiz-kid offspring of private consulting firms and agencies of the world economy. It is encouraged paradoxically by the revival of von Hayek's ideas in Eastern and Central Europe, by a mythology of primitive capitalism, and by a pre-environmentalist fascination with Western consumerism.

More moderate and mature political leadership might hesitate before enforcing the full measure of market-driven adjustments upon the more resistant and the more vulnerable elements of civil society. The compromise envisaged by this leadership would likely be a form of corporatism that would aim at co-opting core workers into the transition to capitalism, separating the more articulate and more strategically placed segments of the working class from the less articulate and less powerful majority. The enterprise-corporatist core of real socialism's social structure of accumulation would thus lend itself to facilitating the transition to capitalism – to something like the state-capitalist option for Western Europe discussed above with a possibly more authoritarian political aspect.

Some intellectuals (including some Western economic advisers) have entertained the possibility of a transition to capitalism combined with a liberal pluralist political system. This vision most probably underestimates the level of conflict that would arise in formerly socialist societies undergoing the economic stresses of a transition to capitalism in the absence of a corporatist compromise. The choice then would become which to sacrifice, democracy or the free market? The historical record, as Karl Polanyi presented it in his analysis (1957) of Central Europe in the 1930s, suggests that democracy is first sacrificed but the market is not ultimately saved. This setting was, for Polanyi, the opening of the path towards fascism; and some observers from Eastern and Central Europe raise again this specter as a not unlikely outcome of the social convulsions following the breakdown of real socialism.[17]

The second scenario is political authoritarianism together with a command-administrative economic center incorporating some subordinate market features and some bureaucratic reform. This would leave basically intact the enterprise-corporatist heart of the former planning system, which would also constitute its main political roots in civil society and its continuing source of legitimation in the "working class." The "conservatives" of Russia (with the backing of some influentials in the military and the KGB) may be counted among its supporters. The long-term problem for this course would be in the continuing exclusion of the more peripheral segments of the labor force from any participation in the system, though these elements might be calmed in the short run if the revival of authority in central planning were to lift the economy out of the chaos resulting from the collapse of authority in both economic management and political structures. The short-term problem for this scenario would be the unleashed cacophony of the liberal intelligentsia with its international audience.[18]

The third scenario already fading away is the possibility of democratization plus socialist reform. This could take the form either of producer self-management, or of a democratization of the central planning process, or conceivably of some combination of the two. Of the three scenarios, this one, with its two variants, was the least clearly spelled out and least favored. One reason for this may be that the power of the media in the former Soviet Union was monopolized by the adherents of the first two and especially by the radical market reformers. (Mandell, 1990)

Self-management has been claimed by both economic liberals and socialists. It has lost ground among the liberals without noticeably gaining conviction among socialists. Some of those economic reformers who once thought of self-management as a support to economic liberalization, now appear to have drawn back from this option.[19] Nevertheless, from a socialist perspective, the possibility must remain that self-management, in the absence of some larger socialist economic framework, might conceivably evolve toward a form of enterprise corporatism within a capitalist market, i.e. the moderate variant of the first scenario.

The position of workers in relation to these three scenarios remains ambiguous and fragmented. In this there is a striking resemblance to the position of workers under capitalism since the economic crisis of the 1970s. The same question is to be raised in each case: does the unqualified term "working class" still correspond to a coherent identifiable social force? The potential for an autonomous workers' movement was demonstrated in Poland by *Solidarnosc*; but in the hour of its triumph that movement fragmented. The Soviet miners' strike of July 1989 revived the credibility of a workers' movement; but it has not definitively answered the question.

Projects for managing and reorienting the working class that emanate from members of the intelligentsia are more readily to be found than clear evidence of autonomous working-class choice. It appeared that the former Soviet government had tried to channel the miners' strike towards demands for enterprise autonomy, only subsequently to abandon self-management as part of market reform. (Mandell, 1990, p. 18) Academician Zaslavskaya, in a famous internal Party document, advocated a policy of manipulating worker attitudes "in an oblique fashion" through incentives. (Novosibirsk Report, 1984, pp. 95–96.) Some economic liberal reformers, no longer interested in self-management, entertained the notion of collective bargaining by independent trade unions as a counterpart to a capitalist economy.

Workers, it seems, may not have very much of an active, initiating voice in the reform process. They may continue as previously to be an important passive structural force that reforming intelligentsia will have to take into account. Their attitudes might be remolded over time as Zaslavskaya and others envisaged. For the present many of them are, as a structural force, likely to remain committed to some of the basic ideas of socialism: egalitarianism in opportunities and incomes, the responsibility of the state to produce basic services of health and education, price stability and availability of basic wage goods. (In this respect, they would have to be classified, in the vocabulary in which *perestroika* has been discussed, as "conservatives.") Workers like other groups are critical of bureaucracy and irritating instances of privilege. These are the basic sentiments that future options for socialism could most feasibly be built upon.

4. Europe and the World

The future of Europe has been considered here in terms of the options for forms of state and society as they are conditioned by existing social forces within Europe – forces which are the European manifestation of global tendencies discussed in the first part of this paper. Europe's relationship to the rest of the world will depend upon how Europeans define their own social and political identity by making their choices among these options; but at the same time external influences from the world system are affecting the internal European balance of social forces in the making of these choices.

The emerging European macro-region will have a formal political structure different from the more informal authority structure of the other two macro-regions, the US and Japanese spheres. Whereas the United States and Japan are economically and politically dominant in their spheres, the European core area in economic terms is a corridor running from Turin and Milan in the south through Stuttgart in the east and Lyon in the west up to the Low Countries and the southeast of England, spanning seven states. In political terms authority rests in a consultative confederalism in which participant states often differ in their policy preferences and micro-regions are asserting various degrees of autonomy. This makes it less likely that Europe can speak in a unified way, especially on foreign policy matters – witness the divergences over the Gulf War – although pressure from the other macro-regions could become a recurrently unifying force.

The central issue in defining the future European identity will be the extent to which it is based on a separation of the economy from politics. Strong forces urge that this separation become the basic ontology of the new European order; and that a European-level political system be constructed that would limit popular pressures for political and social control of economic processes left to a combination of the market and a Brussels-based technocracy. These forces have the initiative within Europe, and they have the external backing of the United States as the enforcer of global economic liberalism. (Gill, 1991) Europe has, however, a deeply rooted tradition of political and social control over economic processes, both in Western social democracy and in Eastern real socialism. This is why the transformation of Eastern and Central European societies can be so important, despite their current weakness, in the overall balance of social forces shaping the future. East and West are no longer isolated compartments. Political processes will flow from one to the other; and although now the dominant flow is from West to East, a counterflow may be anticipated in migration and in political movements. Despair generating right-wing extremism in the East could both challenge and encourage right-wing extremism in the West. The emergence of a firmly based and clearly articulated democratic socialism from the transformation of real socialism in the East, if it were to materialize, could likewise strengthen Western social democracy.

Europe's relations with the United States will in the long run be redefined as Europeans recreate their own identity. The Gulf War and President Bush's "new world order" placed Europe in an ambiguous position. Britain and France followed the US lead, intent on regaining a position near the center of global politics as it was envisaged in the 1940s. Neither country appears to have gained status or other rewards as a consequence. Germany held back, conscious of a divided domestic opinion and of the overwhelming need to give priority to absorbing the impact of the collapse of real socialism in the East. Italy, to a certain extent, followed both courses.

Will Europe continue to accept the role of the United States as enforcer of global economy liberalism? Will Japan continue to subscribe to the US deficit? The United States, despite its unquestioned economic and political power, is moving into the same kind of difficulties as had earlier beset the Soviet economy – declining rates of productivity, high military costs, and an intractable budgetary deficit. The role of enforcer is not sustainable by the United States alone; and there is a real question whether Europeans and Japanese would want to perpetuate and to subsidize this role for long.

Reconsidering Europe's relationship to the United States directly affects Europe's relationship to the Third World. The Gulf War was, in one of its manifold aspects, an objective lesson to the Third World that the global political economy was capable of mustering sufficient military force to discipline and punish a Third World country that sought to become an autonomous military power and to deviate from acceptable economic behavior. The subsequent decision by NATO to establish a rapid deployment force under British command can be read as a reaffirmation of this lesson.

This is consistent with a view that sees the Third World from the perspective of the dominant forces in the global economy: some segments of the Third World become integrated into the globalization process; other segments which remain outside must be handled by a combination of global poor relief and riot control. Poor relief is designed to avoid conditions of desperation arising from impoverishment which could threaten and politically destabilize the integrated segments. Riot control takes the form of military–political support for regimes that will abide by and enforce global economy practices, and, in the last instance, of the rapid deployment force to discipline those that will not.

Europe, in historical and in geopolitical terms, has a particular relationship to the Third World: the relationship of Islamic to Christian civilizations. Europe's vocation for unity can be traced to the medieval *Res publica Christiana*, a concept of unity that had no corresponding political authority. Islam's vocation for unity looks back to an equally distant past and to the ephemeral political authority of the caliphate. Its unity also transcends states. Islam is for Christendom the great "Other." In contemporary terms, Islam also appears as a metaphor for the rejection of western capitalism as a developmental mode.

The bridging of the schism between East and West in Christendom, symbolized by the collapse of "real socialism," leaves unresolved the European confrontation with Islam. The global economy perspective sees the Third World as a residual, marginal factor, a non-identity. The historical experience and perspective of Europe confront Islam as a real identity, a different civilization, one which returned to Europe its origins in Greek philosophy, taught it science and medicine, and showed it a cultivated style of living; but which remained fundamentally alien. Not only is this confrontation external, across borders and the Mediterranean sea. It is also becoming internalized within European societies, e.g. in migration and its response in such political phenomena such as the *Front national* in France. The new Europe is challenged to free itself from the view of the Third World as residual and marginalized, and to confront directly the cultural as well as economic and political issues in a recognized coexistence of two different civilizations.[20]

Europe, in sum, can be a proving ground for a new form of world order: post-hegemonic in its recognition of coexisting universalistic civilizations;

post-Westphalian in its restructuring of political authority into a multi-level system; and post-globalization in its acceptance of the legitimacy of different paths toward the satisfaction of human needs.

Notes

1. On this distinction between international and global economies see Madeuf & Michalet (1978).
2. These terms have been used by the French *"regulation school"* of economists, e.g. Robert Boyer (1990). A similar approach to the transformation of industrial organization has been taken by some US economists, e.g. Michael Piore & Charles Sabel (1984).
3. On the role of "regimes" see especially Keohane (1984).
4. See in this regard the perceptive essay by Charles Maier (1977).
5. I am borrowing from the titles of two very different books (Carr, 1945 and Keohane, 1984), each of which has nevertheless something relevant to say.
6. On intersubjective meanings in politics, see Taylor (1976).
7. See Fukuyama (1989).
8. This section is based on two earlier publications of the author. See Chapter 8 in Cox (1987) and also Cox (1991a).
9. On the segmentation trend, see, *inter alia*, Wilkinson (1981).
10. Some French writers have probed these questions, e.g. Stoffaes (1978) and Kolm (1977).
11. Some recent US studies that have compared the institutional characteristics of leading capitalist countries include Peter Katzenstein (1978) and John Zysman (1983).
12. "Real socialism" is a direct translation of *Realsocialismus* which is used here in place of the cumbersome and now anachronistic term "actually existing socialism" that became current in English-language discourse about Communist Party regimes following the publication of the English translation of Rudolph Bahro's book (1978). This section is largely based on Cox (1991b).
13. I have taken the concept of social structure of accumulation from David Gordon (1980). My use of it focuses more specifically on the relationship of social forces, whereas Gordon uses it more broadly to encompass e.g. the institutions of the world economy. I have applied the concept to the capitalist world economy in Cox (1987).
14. The terms are taken from Michael Burawoy's use of Gramsci's concept of hegemony. See Burawoy (1985).
15. Prominent among those who have opened up this line of theoretical enquiry are Wlodzimierz Brus (1973) and János Kornai (1980 and 1982).
16. The positions of various groups in Soviet society with regard to reforms are reviewed in R. W. Davies (1990).
17. E.g. Milan Vojinovic (1990). Ralf Dahrendorf, while arguing the possibility of capitalism with liberal pluralism, is also concerned by the possibility of a fascist revival (1990, pp. 115–116).
18. This was written prior to the aborted putsch of August 1991 in Moscow, but is not because of that event to be ruled out as a possible future scenario.
19. Davies (1990) reported this of e.g. the economist Aganbegyan.
20. A thoughtful introduction to such a perspective can be found in Yves Lacoste (1984).

REFERENCES

Bahro, Rudolph (1978), *An Alternative in Eastern Europe*. London: NLB.
Boyer, Robert (1990), *The Theory of Regulation: A Critical Analysis*. New York: Columbia University Press.

Brus, Wlodzimierz (1973), *The Economics and Politics of Socialism*. London: Routledge and Kegan Paul.

Burawoy, Michael (1985), *The Politics of Production*. London: Verso.

Carr, E. H. (1945), *Nationalism and After*. London: Macmillan.

Cox, Robert W. (1983), "Gramsci, Hegemony and International Relations. An essay in method." *Millennium*. Vol. 12, No. 2.

Cox, Robert W. (1987), *Production, Power, and World Order: Social Forces in the Making of History*. New York: Columbia University Press.

Cox, Robert W. (1991a), "The Global Political Economy and Social Choice." In Daniel Drache and Meric S. Gertler (eds.), *The New Era of Global Competition*. Montreal: McGill Queen's University Press.

Cox, Robert W. (1991b), "Real Socialism in Historical Perspective." In Ralph Miliband and Leo Panitch (eds.), *The Socialist Register 1991*. London: The Merlin Press.

Crozier, Michel, Huntingdon, Samuel P. & Watanuki, Joji (1975), *The Crisis of Democracy. Report on the Governability of Democracies to the Trilateral Commission*. New York: New York University Press.

Dahrendorf, Ralf (1990), *Reflections on the Revolution in Europe*. New York: Random House.

Davies, R. W. (1990), "Gorbachev's Socialism in Historical Perspective." *New Left Review*. No. 179, January–February.

Fukuyama, Francis (1989), in *The National Interest* (US), Summer.

Gill, Stephen (1990), *American Hegemony and the Trilateral Commission*. Cambridge: Cambridge University Press.

Gill, Stephen (1991), "The Emerging World Order and European Change: The political economy of European union." Paper presented to the XVth World Congress of the International Political Science Association, Buenos Aires, July.

Gordon, David (1980), "Stages of Accumulation and Long Economic Cycles." In Terence K. Hopkins and Immanuel Wallerstein (eds.), *Processes of the World System*. Beverly Hills, Calif.: Sage, pp. 9–45.

Hungarian Academy of Sciences (1984), "Wage Bargaining in Hungarian Firms." *Institute of Economic Studies*, Nos. 23 & 24.

Katzenstein, Peter, ed. (1978), *Between Power and Plenty: Foreign Economic Policies of Advanced Industrial States*. Madison: University of Wisconsin Press.

Kennedy, Paul (1987), *The Rise and Decline of the Great Powers*. New York: Random House.

Keohane, Robert O. (1984), *After Hegemony*. Princeton, NJ: Princeton University Press.

Kolm, Serge-Christophe (1977), *La transition socialiste. La politique économique de gauche*. Paris: Editions du cerf.

Kornai, János (1980), *Economics of Shortage*. Amsterdam: North-Holland.

Kornai, János (1982), *Growth, Shortage and Efficiency: A Macrodynamic Model of the Socialist Economy*. Berkeley.

Lacoste, Yves (1984), *Ibn Khaldun. The Birth of History and the Past of the Third World*. London: Verso. (First published in French by Maspero, Paris, 1966.)

Madeuf, Bernadette & Michalet, Charles-Albert (1978), "A New Approach to International Economics." *International Social Science Journal*. Vol. 30, No. 2.

Maier, Charles (1977), "The Politics of Productivity: Foundations of American international economic policy after World War II." *International Organization*. Vol. 31, No. 4.

Mandell, David (1990), "A Market without Thorns: The ideological struggle for the Soviet working class." *Studies in Political Economy*. Vol. 33, Autumn, pp. 7–38.

McCracken Report, The (1977), *Towards Full Employment and Price Stability*.

Novosibirsk Report (1984), Trans. published in *Survey*. Vol. 128, No. 1, pp. 88–108.

Nye, Jr., Joseph S. (1990), *Bound to Lead. The Changing Nature of American Power*. New York: Basic Books.

Piore, Michael & Sabel, Charles (1984), *The Second Industrial Divide*. New York: Basic Books.

Polanyi, Karl (1957), *The Great Transformation*. Boston: Beacon Press.

Stoffaes, Christian (1978), *La grande menace industrielle*. Paris: Calmann-Levy.

Strange, Susan (1987), "The Persistent Myth of Lost Hegemony." *International Organization*. No. 41.

Strange, Susan (1990), "The Name of the Game." In *Sea Changes*. New York: Council on Foreign Relations.

Taylor, Charles (1976), "Hermeneutics and Politics." In Paul Connerton (ed.), *Critical Sociology*. Harmondsworth, Middlesex: Penguin.

Vojinovic, Milan (1990), "Will There be a Palingenesis of Extreme Rightist Movements." Paper prepared for the conference "After the Crisis," University of Amsterdam, 18–20 April.

Wilkinson, Frank, ed. (1981), *The Dynamics of Labour Market Segmentation*. London: Academic Press.

Zysman, John (1983), *Governments, Markets, and Growth*. Ithaca: Cornell University Press.

6

Failure in Europe: Regional Security after the Cold War

Richard Falk*

It is far more difficult to compare the Europe of the 1990s with the Europe of the 1980s than could have been anticipated just a few years earlier. With the euphoria of 1989 came expectations of steady progress toward peace and stability for the whole continent of Europe, but the realities that have emerged, and should to some extent have been anticipated, are far more problematic: the breakup of Yugoslavia has unleashed a prolonged challenge to European security that has not been met and, whatever the outcome, will leave ugly scars from waiting too long and doing too little; the flow of refugees and other foreigners into Western European countries is severely threatening to a politics of moderation and tolerance in several countries, especially in Germany; the emancipation of Eastern Europe from Soviet hegemony and communist rule has inflicted many hardships on these societies in the course of their transition to market economies; the collapse of the Soviet empire has generated a cycle of vicious ethnic politics in several of the former republics, as well as producing a continual constitutional and economic crisis in the Soviet Union; the Soviet collapse has caused a new series of anxieties about nuclear weapons proliferation and civil strife in a country possessing nuclear weapons; and most daunting of all in some respects, at this moment of great historical choice, the leadership of virtually every European country seems both mediocre and unpopular, even beleaguered, with the Italian state confronted by the deepest crisis of legitimacy since the onset of fascism.

There is, of course, some tendency to be so preoccupied with the grue-

*Dr. Richard Falk is the Albert G. Milbank Professor of International Law and Practice at Princeton University.

some character of this array of challenges as to forget the important positive aspects of a comparison with the prior decade of the 1980s: Europe is no longer mobilized for apocalyptic warfare, or endlessly engaged in divisive debates about deploying new weapons systems; there is no longer an ideological fault-line in Europe, and the peoples of the Eastern countries have gained political independence and substantial protection of their human rights; several countries in Eastern Europe are making strides toward improving the living standards of their populations, as well as providing a safer and more life-sustaining environment; also, despite a rather deep recession, the affluent countries of the West, especially Germany, have heavily subsidized the transition of the countries of the East, especially the former Democratic Republic of Germany, suggesting some measure of commitment to a wider European identity.

In this essay emphasis is placed upon the problematic side of this emergent situation in the 1990s. The Cold War is definitely over, at least for Europe, but in its place no appropriate architecture of regional security has yet emerged, despite the severity of the new agenda of threats.[1] Indeed, there has been a seeming regression in terms of cooperative capacity in the security domain highlighted by the ordeal of Bosnia, but preceded by the geopolitical irresponsibility and gross mismanagement of the breakup of Yugoslavia.[2] As well, the inability to bring peace to the Middle East has to be understood, at least in part, as a failure of overall Western diplomacy. How are we to understand this European failure? Is it linked to the decline of the United States and to a consequent wider failure of American leadership? What kind of positive steps can be envisaged for Europe in the security domain during the remaining years of this last decade of the second millennium? How should the so-called Atlantic Alliance be reconceived in light of the changed circumstances of the 1990s?

1. A Time for Humility and Reassessment

Experts and public opinion have been continually taken by surprise by international developments in the course of the last decade. As a result, there is a definite loss of confidence by observers about their capacity to grasp the formative social forces that are shaping the historical situation.[3] Such attitudes of bewilderment contrast with the solidity of the Cold War decades that followed closely upon the end of World War II. Since the emergence of the Gorbachev leadership in the Soviet Union, our previous interpretative guidelines have been of little use. To begin with, who could have expected that the stolid Soviet bureaucracy would elevate to power a transformative political figure, especially during its own period of internal crisis? And who could have anticipated that when Gorbachev began to reverse the course of Soviet foreign and domestic policy he would not have been quickly removed from authority or killed by either the Communist Party machinery or the KGB? And why was there not more of a disposition among the citizenry in the West and elites to respond to these shifts by way of drastic demilitarization?

It seems quite likely that this extraordinary dynamic of change, in the first Soviet instance, occurred only because the main actors underestimated the effects of their innovations. There is considerable evidence that Gorbachev thought he was "saving" socialism and reviving the Soviet Union, not preparing the Soviet system for capitalism, much less setting the stage for Soviet disintegration. On the other side, it seems evident that Soviet enemies of reform did not realize, at least not soon enough, the depth of Soviet discontent within and without the post-Stalinist state, or the irreversibility of the momentum for change that had been released.

Also on the wider international stage, there emerged a kind of geopolitical turmoil that superseded the discipline of bipolarity and deterrence, a circumstance that seems to have triggered Iraqi aggression against Kuwait, and recourse to the UN Security Council as the appropriate framework for retaliatory warfare; the Gulf War, with its high-tech display of United States military superiority, was the sort of large-scale battlefield encounter that had been avoided during the long period of ideological confrontation between East and West in the Middle East. The Gulf Crisis that emerged in 1990 has to be understood, in part, as a reaction to the collapse of the restraint side of Cold War geopolitics. Earlier, both sides were exceedingly cautious about pushing inter-bloc relations in crisis directions, and, as the Cold War experience ripened, this caution became engrained in the style and substance of superpower policymaking.

There was some degree of anticipation of hyper-nationalist activity in the immediate aftermath of the Soviet collapse, but not on the level of intensity that has emerged in the former Yugoslavia. (Snyder, 1990) There was also a disquieting sense of disproportion that emerged in light of the rapid, devastating response to Kuwaiti aggression and the desultory response to the terrifying violence set loose in Bosnia, mainly, but not exclusively, provoked by Serbian aggressive initiatives. Unquestionably, part of this sense of disproportion was "innocent", that is, the Gulf Crisis presented a clear military option in a setting where the leading countries shared a strategic interest in safeguarding oil reserves. In contrast, the military option in the post-Yugoslav crisis has been controversial and the strategic effects of action and inaction are not perceived symmetrically by the leading states, or even by elites in a given state. It is, thus, both difficult to know what to do, and almost impossible to build a collective consensus, except belatedly and inconclusively. Nevertheless, the refusal of Europe, with or without the United States, to act decisively on behalf of the victim peoples of Bosnia has been widely condemned as the worst instance of accommodating political evil in the region since a diplomacy of appeasement greeted the expansionist militarism of Nazi Germany.[4]

There are two intertwined claims being made here: first of all, the series of unexpected developments in the European region since Gorbachev's ascent to power in 1986; secondly, the bloody conflicts in the Gulf and Bosnia as illustrative of the failures of post-Cold War regional security.

2. Explaining the Yugoslav Failure: The Ascent of the Weak State

Geopolitics in the Cold War era was preoccupied with the containment of the strong state, that is, seeking to deter the projection of military power beyond national boundaries.[5] Both superpowers, with their respective blocs, threatened their adversary with catastrophic damage in the event of unacceptable provocation. By and large, deterrence "worked," and what has been described triumphantly as "the long peace" resulted, especially for Europe. (The phrase was introduced by the diplomatic historian John Lewis Gaddis, 1987; for a controversial "reading" of the implications for Europe of the end of the Cold War, see Mearsheimer, 1991.) There are different ways of evaluating the costs of this "peace," both for Europe and for the Third World, but it is certainly an achievement that interstate violence was avoided in Europe for a period of over four decades, and that even intrastate violence resulted in relatively few casualties, and was in no instance prolonged except in Northern Ireland.[6] The Gulf War itself can be understood, at least its "successful" aspects (restoring Kuwaiti sovereignty; defeating Iraq's armies of aggression), as an instance of containment applied against a regionally strong state (that is, Iraq was an obvious threat to project its military power beyond its borders, and was in no serious danger of an internal breakdown of order). The unsuccessful aspects of the Gulf War are particularly associated with the failure to restructure the Iraqi state along more democratic lines or to protect sufficiently its victimized Kurdish and Shi'ia minorities from an oppressive backlash orchestrated from Baghdad.

This unsuccessful experience resembles in some respects the Yugoslav debacle. Taken in the context of earlier interventionary diplomacy and a wider phenomenon of proliferating claims of self-determination, some understanding of the difficulty of positive action begins to emerge. It should be noted that the record of intervention during the Cold War is a long string of failures; if containment of strong states achieved the long peace, it can only be acknowledged that interventionism produced "the long war."[7] That is, the attempt to use military means to restructure politically foreign countries was a persistent feature of the Cold War period, often resulting in prolonged warfare of a highly destructive character, and generally failing to achieve its intended results. The American experience in Indochina, the Soviet experience in Afghanistan were paradigmatic. In the face of determined nationalist resistance, it is exceedingly difficult to translate military superiority into political outcomes except through total victory on the battlefield (an elusive outcome in a guerrilla war) and subsequent military occupation.[8] Successful resistance is especially likely if nationalist identity has been effectively appropriated by the political forces that are opposed to foreign intervention.

There is a closely related series of developments associated with the ascendancy of the weak state (that is, the state that cannot control the play of antagonistic nationalist and ethnic forces within its boundaries or defend its borders against interventionary probes by its neighbors). Lebanon of the mid-1970s disclosed both the character and the magnitude of weak-state problems in a turbulent region, producing a horrifying civil war that was cynically manipulated to a large extent by antagonistic neighbors, Syria and Israel; the state of Lebanon was too weak either to impose internal order or to raise the threshold of intervention for its foreign antagonists to unacceptable levels. This pattern suggests the relevance of implosive conflict, geopolitical black holes that cause great human suffering and draw into question the peacekeeping capacities of "the new world order" of the 1990s. The Yugoslavian breakdown has been the dominant illustration, but the unfolding situation in several former Soviet republics and in Somalia, Sudan, Liberia, and Cambodia suggests the generality of weak-state challenges and the difficulties of fashioning appropriate regional and global responses.[9]

Two types of difficulty that became prominent during the Yugoslav breakdown are worth considering in greater detail, what will be called here *logistical* and *motivational*. Logistical difficulties arise as a result of the limits of constrained military power to achieve political outcomes in militarily weaker states. These limits on effectiveness are not intrinsic. If a militarily superior state or coalition of states defines its goals unconditionally, and especially if it is prepared to occupy the defeated country for a prolonged period, then a political solution can be imposed, at least temporarily. This dynamic of unconditional victory is best illustrated by a reference back to the outcome of World War II, including the occupation of both halves of Europe, but especially the countries defeated in the war. These logistical considerations also reflect the rise of nationalism and the dissemination of sophisticated weaponry and military doctrine. Interventionary diplomacy in the early phases of the colonial era was not logistically constrained, as in contemporary reality, because nationalist sentiments were generally inert or limited to a tiny fraction of the population and there was often little intrinsic capacity to resist outside intrusions.[10]

These considerations are accentuated by a combination of additional elements, especially the memory of past attempts and the nature of the risks attendant upon including political goals in the definition of the military mission. The United States in the Gulf War was definitely influenced by its long anguishing attempt to impose a political solution on Vietnam, the so-called "lost crusade," and, perhaps even more vividly, by the failure of its efforts to support the political restructuring of tiny Lebanon in 1983.[11] The US military, particularly the army, was reluctant to take on such political assignments in interventionary settings where support was constrained by considerations of costs and an ambivalent domestic public opinion. These factors weigh more heavily in situations where the terrain is supportive of irregular warfare and the indigenous population, or a substantial portion of it, is likely to be hostile to any foreign military presence and effectively mobilized for resistance. Even Israel, with total control and military dominance, has found it daunting to face a mobilized, hostile population over time as in southern Lebanon after the 1982 war, and even in "the occupied territories" of the West Bank and Gaza.

There is a further logistical constraint of a normative character that is especially operative in relation to a liberal democratic society that engages in interventionary diplomacy. The intervening state has to act as if it is respectful of legal and moral prohibitions, and if it neglects these prohibitions it will encounter a rising tide of opposition at home that will in time extend to the military forces themselves as occurred in Vietnam. With the universal espousal of respect for the laws of war, human rights, and particularly the right of self-determination, a ruthless occupation is a costly and politically dangerous option. Add to these factors a transnational learning process by resistance movements, ranging from an appreciation of the political potency of massive nonviolent resistance (the intifada) to the traumatic effectiveness of terrorist tactics (hizbollah). The British inability to stamp out IRA violent resistance in Northern Ireland over a period of decades suggests the quality of difficulty involved even when the material relation of forces is so one-sided.

There are additional technological factors relating to military capabilities. It is now possible to inflict battlefield destruction on a one-sided basis in situations where the target country is unable to escalate effectively, as again the Gulf War illustrated.[12] The prospects of unacceptable escalation in a Cold War setting both might have inhibited Iraq in the first instance, and would almost certainly have led the United States to seek a negotiated, rather than a military, solution to the crisis. Here is the logistical point: in the post-Cold War political environment it is possible in some settings to inflict destruction without fearing either the quagmire effects of prolonged entanglement or significant losses of life or equipment. The whole military effort can be stage-managed from a distance, and generally completed so rapidly that no serious political opposition can be mounted, especially if, as has been the case in recent uses of military force, the media are throttled and effectively controlled.

The application of these logistical factors to Bosnia is evident, although the precise relevance is bound to be controversial. Each situation is so complex that reasoning by analogy and the invocation of lessons from the past can never be conclusive. But certain factors seem obvious: the Bosnian terrain is well-suited for irregular warfare and the various contending parties, especially the Serbs of nationalistic persuasion, are mobilized to fight and die around an extremist creed that includes the prospect of acute vulnerability in the event of an unfavorable outcome.[13]

Furthermore, the main incentives and pressures for intervention are "humanitarian," "moral," and "legal," not strong motivators in the domain of geopolitics. Such strategic factors as concerns about a war spreading further South in the Balkans, and beyond, as well as about massive refugee flows to the North, have emerged late in the conflict and were not sufficiently clear in effect to alter sufficiently the calculus of costs and benefits of military action. All along the American model of intervention has been based on the possibility of military action being taken from the safety of the air with no disposition to establish a ground presence as a dimension of even such limited goals as protecting safe havens. Such an insistence shifts the debate to a very slippery set of technical (what can be achieved militarily by a given tactical plan, say bombing Serbian gun emplacements around Sarajevo, and what would be the likely Serbian political and military response) and psychological conjectures (are the Bosnian Serbs passionate extremists who would be likely to take strong countermeasures against UN peacekeeping forces seeking to ensure that relief gets through to the civilian population even at high costs to themselves? or cowardly bullies likely to be accommodating once challenged militarily?).[14]

The nature of the undertaking also has confused the appreciation of logistical obstacles. Those who had been generally opposed to military intervention in the Third World during the Cold War, and are generally dubious about geopolitical arguments favoring a military option, were often in the Bosnian setting the most outspoken champions of interventionary action on humanitarian grounds. Their advocacy was also influenced by the institutional auspices of the UN Security Council or NATO. In effect, the benevolent character of the interventionary operation was somehow assumed to be sufficient to waive any logistical objection as merely expressive of a lack of commitment, and thus not genuine. Part of the interventionary mindset was the view that it was unacceptable to do nothing in the face of genocidal ("ethnic cleansing") practices and such atrocities as the systematic rape of Moslem women. Such an enthusiasm for coercive intervention overlooked the experience of failure even when a major military commitment of a sustained kind was brought to bear by a superpower that had staked its prestige on victory. The presumption that somehow the interventionary task was easier because it was for a good cause and under the UN banner remains exceedingly unconvincing.[15] The UN experience in Somalia up through mid-1993, seemingly a far easier instance of humanitarian intervention, confirms these skeptical views.

Such logistical concerns are strongly reinforced by motivational factors. The stakes in Bosnia for outsiders do not strike leaders or the publics of leading countries as sufficient to justify life-and-death risks of any substantial extent. Also, the Yugoslavian breakdown is not perceived as linked closely to any issue of major strategic importance.[16] Indeed, to the extent that strategic concerns can be identified, their bearing is mixed. For instance, anti-Serbian action has been neutralized to various degrees by a traditional Russian affinity with Serbs and by the indirect Western interest in the survival of Yeltsin in his struggle with more archly nationalist Russian rivals.[17]

The economic dimension of interventionary diplomacy also inhibits appropriate action in at least four ways. Firstly, the United States, the central intervening state, has been committed to a domestic focus during the whole period and, even aside from the expenses of intervention, the distracting impact on the governmental priorities also operates as an inhibition. Secondly, the post-Cold War setting puts questions of economic competitiveness and global market shares on the top of the *geopolitical* agenda, which makes an investment in intervention seem far less attractive than when rival superpowers were competing for ideological allegiance. Thirdly, there are no longer many illusions among policymakers and military planners that cheap interventions can achieve their objectives, and thus no intervention seems preferable to one that is likely to end in inconclusiveness and resentment. Fourthly, the foregoing considerations, when added to the general recessionary condition of the world economy, make it much more difficult to appropriate additional funds for such marginal security purposes.[18]

The motivational impetus is also linked to the problematic logistical circumstances. No credible military option can be discerned that will have both a reasonable probability of success and an assurance that entrapment in a Bosnian quagmire will not result. It is not like Panama 1989 where a scenario of destroy and abandon, coupled with a distinct mission of capturing Noriega, could be carried out with predictable rapidity at almost no risk. In Bosnia, a first step is likely to provoke a punishing reaction against either the UN presence or the Muslim civilian population, and then the pressure to take a bigger interventionary step would be almost irresistible. Also, it would not be enough to bomb and abandon, as the essence of any interventionary effort is to promote a fairer political outcome than is resulting from the internal play of forces, and this would almost certainly require some sort of continuing presence on the ground and vigilance over a period of years if the whole operation is to have any credible prospect of being regarded as "a success."

The strength of the arguments against intervention are formidable, especially against meaningful intervention. There is still the possibility in the midst of 1993 that the pressures of President Clinton's campaign rhetoric, reinforced by the deteriorating situation in Bosnia, will yet lead to some kind of intervention, likely with only a symbolic bearing on the eventual "settlement." But the more fundamental reality is that a tragic predicament is presented by the Bosnian ordeal: to refuse intervention is morally and legally unacceptable, yet to intervene is logistically and politically impossible. Because Bosnia is in Europe this stalemate is inevitably damaging to the future of regional security within the setting of an integrated Europe. It is generally interpreted as revealing the persistence of statist rivalries in Europe, and as casting doubt on how far the dynamics of European integration can and will be carried. Especially when connected with the unrelated difficulties associated with the Maastricht treaty-making process and with bringing East European countries into the system, the whole response to the dismantling of Yugoslavia is giving Euro-skeptics a fieldday. Perhaps more seriously, a precedent has been established for the violent creation of an ethnically cleansed state that is sure to be heartening to ultra-nationalists and the politics of bigotry everywhere.[19]

3. Lessons for Europe and Their Limits: The Menace of Geopolitical Regression

The complexity of the current situation, its fluidity and contradictory tendencies, make it especially difficult to draw conclusions, even if qualified as "preliminary." In this regard, what is here being called "lessons" should not be understood in a didactic spirit. The intention is to highlight certain features of the existing situation and offer some tentative recommendations of a prescriptive sort.

Both in response to secessionism in Yugoslavia and in relation to the monetary dimensions of the European Community project, the supposedly slain dragon of European geopolitics has reemerged in the immediate aftermath of the Cold War. The question now raised is whether the Cold War, with its blocs and superpower occupation, was merely a lull in the history of European interstate and internation rivalry, especially among the leading states and the Balkan nations.[20] The Cold War had repressed the capacity and will of these governments to think in traditional statist terms, focusing their conflictual energies almost exclusively on the East–West phenomenon, which was essentially an extra-European conflict that used Europe as the ultimate geopolitical stage, a theater suited only for continuous rehearsals, with an almost absolute priority attached to avoiding the performance. (Kaldor, 1990)

One among several elements was the acceptance of American leadership in this period as a substitute for statist initiative in the most crucial domain of public policy – namely, national security.[21] In this regard, Western European states relinquished their sovereignty almost to the same extent as was the case in a more blatant, less voluntary, form in Eastern Europe. The post-Cold War situation is somewhat paradoxical: the East European countries with their new orientations are preoccupied with internal matters, while the more successful West Europeans are engaged more fully in matters of regional scope. Such engagement is seen as a virtual necessity, given the prospect of a gradual US withdrawal and loss of a geopolitical rationale to entrust to a single state a leadership role in security matters.

In this transitional setting, there are three possibilities, none of which has proved satisfactory in relation to the Yugoslav challenge. The first is to allow Germany to take on the role of regional hegemon, grounded on its relative economic strength, diplomatic ambition, and military potential. This direction seemed also to accord with US government preferences at the beginning of the 1990s. The Yugoslavian experience has discredited, temporarily at least, this reliance on German leadership. In retrospect, deference to German diplomatic assertiveness in the 1990–91 period, the outright encouragement of the breakup of the Yugoslav federation, Genscher's heavyhanded promotion of an independent Slovenia and Croatia, had the inevitable sequel, Serbian anxieties and defensiveness coupled with the recognition of Bosnian claims of self-determination in an atmosphere already roiled by ethnic strife.

This German role revived concerns about "the German Problem," as well as revealing a continuing German attachment to throwing its weight around in the Balkans, especially in Croatia. The subsequent disaster in Bosnia, possibly unfairly, both set back German claims to exert regional leadership and led Germans themselves to question their readiness for such an expanded diplomatic role. This set of perceptions have been reinforced by Germany's statist (as distinct from Community) approach to monetary policy, giving clear priority to domestic concerns about inflation when in conflict with wider regional requirements for lower German interest rates so as to overcome recession by stimulating business and high unemployment.

The end of the Cold War burdened Germany with the enormous problematique of reunification, causing a deficit and inflation, thereby making it psychologically difficult to give much deference to French (and other) concerns.[22] Thus, a combination of circumstances has made the option of relying on tacit German hegemonic leadership in Europe unavailable in the near future.

The second possibility is the accelerated expansion of the European Community role in the political and security areas, a real move in the direction of Euro-federalism. The Maastricht Treaty when signed in late 1991 created an initial sense that wider integrative steps were entirely plausible, and could be undertaken with considerable political support among elites; the Delors' vision of the future of Europe seemed to be riding an historical wave of credibility. But subsequent developments have changed this atmosphere. Maastricht itself encountered much more resistance than anticipated, evoking territorial concerns about yielding sovereignty to the bureaucrats in Brussels and bringing to the fore inter-elite tensions. The recessionary condition of Europe added greatly to these difficulties, as did the unevenness of European economic conditions, leading to the severe disputes about currency flows, and interest rates that sapped confidence in the capacity of the Community to move at the pace dictated by the Maastricht Treaty even with respect to monetary integration (common currency, central bank), much less take on the touchier agenda of regional security. Such a loss of confidence was further reinforced by the unanticipated severity of domestic backlash against refugees and immigrants, as well as the seriousness of ethnic strife that engendered inconsistent partisan responses on the part of Community members. The inability to act early and effectively in relation to criminal violence in Bosnia underscored the inability of Europe to act in unity within the broad domain of regional security in post-Cold War circumstances, but it also reminded leaders and citizens that despite the disappearance of the Soviet threat it was not possible to treat security concerns as matters of "low politics."

The third option was to adapt the Cold War framework, keeping the

United States centrally involved, thereby retaining a credible leader for security policy that could transcend European rivalries and yet had a record of effective action. Such reliance had, to some extent, worked in the Gulf War, with the old framework adapted to new realities: the United States led diplomatically and controlled the exercise of the military instrument, but the Europeans (and Japanese) agreed to pay the costs of the operations and to participate in peripheral ways, and the UN Security Council provided a mantle of legitimacy to justify war in a political context no longer informed by Cold War demonology. Such an option may be available in settings where major shared strategic interests are at stake, as is the case with oil reserves, but elsewhere the United States, for reasons suggested in the previous section, is unwilling, and possibly unable, to provide reliable leadership, and, even if it were in a position to do so, the requisite European consensus might not be forthcoming. This latter possibility has materialized in relation to the role of NATO in relation to the Bosnian strife.

This unwillingness to lead on this scale has now been confirmed by successive US presidents of somewhat differing political persuasion in relation to Bosnia; despite Clinton's campaign promises to rectify Bush's passivity in Bosnia, his presidential approach has resembled that of his predecessor, being strong rhetorically, weak when it comes to action, conveying an impression of uncertainty and ambivalence. Whatever eventually happens in Bosnia, it seems evident that European regional security, especially arising from intra-regional sources, will have to fashion a European solution, with a much diminished role for the United States. How diminished will be shaped by debates about the future of NATO and the CSCE, as well as WEU, but also by the rate of US military withdrawal from the continent, especially Germany. It will also be influenced by developments in Russia, including the success of efforts to reverse nuclear weapons proliferation attendant upon the Soviet breakup. If Russia were to convulse, or pose a new kind of strong state menace, then the prospect of greater US involvement in European affairs and a big NATO future would increase dramatically.

These observations suggest by implication a future course of action in and for Europe:
- greater German sensitivity to wider European concerns, rebuilding some confidence that Germany might be given in time the role of *primus inter pares*;
- realization that statist geopolitics in Europe will reproduce such conflict formations that eventuated in extremist politics and two disastrous wars;
- appreciation that the new global setting calls for a more independent Europe, and that Europe's economic prospects in the global marketplace rest on its capacity to manage regional security;
- acknowledgement that suppressed nationalist sentiments must be addressed by way of human rights, but not by acceding to claims that the right of self-determination is a mandate to establish ethnically pure polities;[23]
- commitment in principle to achieve balanced regional demilitarization in

Europe; including as complete denuclearization as other nuclear weapons states would agree upon, and supplemented by positive security relationships with neighboring countries, especially Russia and Turkey.

– commitment to strengthen the conflict-resolution and preventive diplomacy roles of regional institutions, including CSCE, WEU, and possibly NATO; also, on a longer-term basis, enhancing participation of citizens' associations in security-related institutions, and strengthening the role of the European Parliament in the conflict-prevention domain, thereby strengthening an already nascent European civil society.

Notes

1. The Asian reality is different, better and worse; locked in some of the old patterns, but ironically not confronted with anything comparable to either breakdown in Yugoslavia or the various eruptions of violence in the Middle East.

2. Leading European countries contributed to the breakup of Yugoslavia, giving aid and comfort to secessionism in Croatia and Slovenia, despite strong evidence that such steps, unless prudently taken, would induce intense ethnic anxiety and nationalist passions. The United States was non-committal and semi-detached, almost reverting to a sphere of influence approach, apparently regarding the future of Yugoslavia to be primarily a regional matter in the early stages of crisis during 1990–91, and deferring to the primacy of German diplomatic goals in Europe.

3. Arrogance of viewpoint in the face of the disappointing record of specialists in either explaining and predicting is one mask that ignorance wears.

4. This textual assertion is not meant to place all the blame on the Serbs. All sides have contributed to the breakdown, followed by atrocities and ethnic politics of the most extreme sort, and it is this dispersed responsibility that has made it simplistic, and inflammatory, to blame only Serbia. Of course, Slobodon Milosevic invited such reactions by his use of chauvinistic nationalism to play on Serbian fears in Croatia and Bosnia, and to build support for the establishment of a Greater Serbia in the new fluid situation. Further, Bosnian Serbs have intensified the situation by launching their campaign of "ethnic cleansing."

5. Euro-centricism, given the persistence of many Cold War features of Asian politics.

6. Although oppressed.

7. This is the main theme of a forthcoming book written in collaboration with Amin Saikal.

8. Germany and Japan after World War II are indicative of "successful" political restructuring in the direction of constitutional democracy. In each case questions are being posed as to whether the reforms went deep enough, or whether, with the lapse of time and mounting domestic pressures, new anti-democratic tendencies are likely to become stronger.

9. To describe the weak state syndrome is not to explain these tragic situations in a purely deterministic way, as unfolding without human capacity to exert influence; there are strong reasons to believe, for instance, that German diplomacy in the 1990–91 period, pushing for immediate recognition of secessionist claims by Slovenia and Croatia, set in motion a train of events that eventuated in ethnic strife that might have been avoided or mitigated by a clearer historical appreciation of the dangers being created, especially in Croatia, and then, in light of Serb action there, in Bosnia as well; the difficulty of addressing breakdowns of order in weak state situations does not relieve domestic and international actors of responsibility, even criminal responsibility for ensuing behavior. As William Pfaff suggests, in the course of a competent article, "the West's passivity and incompetence in dealing with the Yugoslav crisis [was] hardly inevitable ..."; choices were made at every stage. (Pfaff, 1993)

10. Such an assertion is not meant to overlook the many efforts at colonial resistance by peoples of the non-Western world, including heroic struggles. (Wolf, 1982) Also, perhaps, high-tech dominance enables a new interventionary potential.

11. Although Bush strongly signaled his efforts to gain freedom from "the Vietnam syndrome," his refusal to be drawn into the internal politics of Iraq after Desert Storm was both a tragedy for the Iraqi people that extended beyond the debate about the war itself and an acknowledgment of a US reluctance to associate political conditions with the definition of military victory; also operative in the Iraqi setting was a degree of political ambivalence arising from a concern that Iraqi dismemberment could result from any further intervention in Iraqi internal affairs, and that such a development would strengthen Iran's position in the region, which would be adverse to US views of regional stability, as well as extending the interventionary mandate beyond the coalition consensus, especially on the part of the Arab participants.

12. Saddam Hussein made two desperate attempts at escalation: ecological devastation and Scud attacks on Israel; both failed – the coalition was willing to live with the risks of ecological damage, although the extent of damage was uncertain at the time, and Israel was only lightly damaged and induced not to respond, thereby keeping the coalition intact.

13. The media also reinforce the perception that Serbs are extremist, ignoring the relevance of a substantial nonviolent democratic opposition among Serbs.

14. It is instructive to recall that planners in Vietnam consistently underestimated the "pain" that the North would endure for the sake of maintaining its war aims.

15. Good causes are not generally strong motivators; even after the Cold War, the UN remains either a fig leaf for great power action or ineffectual; there has also been a failure of political imagination all along by those advocating humanitarian intervention, neglecting the courageous efforts to mount nonviolent and democratic oppositional forces within Serbia and Bosnia.

16. In contrast, the Gulf War had at least four: oil, Israeli security, survival of pro-Western Gulf regimes, especially in Saudi Arabia, and nonproliferation of nuclear weapons.

17. This latter interest has had the effect of discouraging more forceful action in the Security Council, such as lifting the arms embargo of Bosnia; not that such an action would actually help the Bosnian cause, but might actually accelerate the level of destruction, inducing the Serbian forces to intensify their military efforts, which seems well within their capabilities.

18. In the background may be a further unacknowledged economic factor: the reluctance to spend money and take risks on behalf of Muslim victims; there is likely to have been a different response all along if the religious identity of principal perpetrator and victim had been reversed.

19. Again, after a certain point, such a dynamic in the former Yugoslavia was almost inevitable.

20. State is used here to designate political units that enjoy the full status of sovereignty, including membership in the United Nations; nation is used to designate a people whose ethnic identity is distinct, and who seek varying degrees of autonomy. Most states are multination, especially if the political identities of indigenous peoples are taken into account. When captive nations aspire to be states, tension inevitably results.

21. Soviet leadership was more comprehensive in Eastern Europe, and far more resented, depending on imposed rule reinforced by periodic interventions. The Soviet military overthrow of the government of Imre Nagy in 1956 established the pattern.

22. As with other conservative governments, the more constructive option of higher taxes to pay the costs of reunification was avoided for political and ideological reasons.

23. This is the implication of "ethnic cleansing" in theory and practice; the Bosnian outcome is, in this regard, an ominous precedent; the whole conception of self-determination in international law needs to be reformulated, moving from the statist conceptions that governed until the end of the Cold War to the ethno-nationalist conceptions that have prevailed since the Baltic states achieved their independence in 1991.

REFERENCES

Gaddis, John Lewis (1987), *The Long Peace: Inquiries into the History of the Cold War.* New York: Oxford.

Kaldor, Mary (1990), *The Imaginary War*. Oxford: Blackwell.

Mearsheimer, John (1991), "Back to the Future: Instability in Europe after the Cold War." *International Security*. Vol. 15, pp. 5–56.

Pfaff, William (1993), "Invitation to War." *Foreign Affairs*. Vol. 72, pp. 97–109, at p. 107.

Snyder, Jack (1990), "Averting Anarchy in Europe." *International Security*. Vol. 14, pp. 5–41.

Wolf, Eric R. (1982), *Europe and the People without History*. Berkeley: University of California.

7

Nationalism and Ethnicity in Europe

George Schöpflin*

1. Nationhood and Nationalism

The 1990s have clearly seen a major shift in the functions, perceptions and effects of nationalism in Europe.[1] Whereas, in the immediate postwar years, nationalism was for all practical purposes a kind of political pariah, a phenomenon that was regarded with maximum disfavor, and the emphasis was all on integration, federalism and the long vision of a United States of Europe, the last two or three years have seen a seemingly sudden and a not altogether welcome change in the eyes of those who have never sought to understand the nature and functions of nationhood.

The suddenness is, in part, an optical illusion. In reality, under the surface of events, ethnicity and nationhood not only remained in being, but contributed significantly to the pattern of politics, though it was seldom understood in this way. (Rothschild, 1981) The argument that will be developed in this paper is, in simple terms, that nationhood became an inescapable fact of political life in Europe in the 19th century, that, far from disappearing or even weakening, it retained its key functions in the 20th, and that for the foreseeable future it will have a considerable saliency, whether it is conceived of in these terms or not. Hence, as far as policy-making is concerned, it is important that the true nature of nationhood and the political doctrine built on it – nationalism – be understood rather than dismissed.

A number of assumptions will be made in what follows without any attempt to argue them in detail. Nationalism is a political ideology that claims that the world is divided into nations and only into nations; and that

* Dr. George Schöpflin is lecturer in East European Politics at the University of London.

each individual belongs to a nation and to only one nation; nations may be defined by various characteristics, but crucial among them is their relationship to a particular territory and their claim to exercise political control over that territory in the name of the nation. In other words, nationalism is inextricably involved with the political process and must be interpreted in the same way as other facets of politics are.

Nationhood: The Ethnic Factor

The definition of nation used in this paper is connected with, but conceptually separate from, nationalism. (Armstrong, 1982) Nations are a modern development, dating by and large from the late 18th century, and can be located at the moment when loyalty to nation became the primary cohesive force to cement the relationship between rulers and ruled. Prior to this, various ethnic phenomena with political consequences did, in fact, exist and influence political actors, but they were secondary to religion or dynasticism or late feudal bonds of loyalty. It is only with the modern period that nationhood emerged as the most important legitimating principle and has remained that way.

The emphasis in this definition, therefore, is on the legitimating functions of nationhood. From the end of the 18th century in Europe, states could claim to be authentic states only if they were the expression of the aspirations of a particular nation. Previously, states were legitimated by reference to loyalty to a secular ruler or by religion. The rise of nationhood as the primary agent of legitimation was not confined to international politics, but was central to the newly reformulated relationship between rulers and ruled. Under dynastic or religious legitimation, that relationship, while involving elements of reciprocity, was one-sided and non-secular. Ultimately dynastic legitimation was grounded in the divine right of kings to rule and with religion the proposition is self-evident.

The 18th century, however, saw an altogether different pattern emerging, which was derived from secular propositions, namely the idea of popular sovereignty, that legitimacy was a two-way relationship, giving both rulers and ruled rights and duties towards each other. The bond between the two, then, had also to be reformulated, because the nature of community was something qualitatively different. This switch from religious to secular legitimation was not as sudden as it might appear with hindsight; secular aspects in the definition of kingship had been intensifying steadily since the Middle Ages.

This was where nationhood came in. Nationhood became the tissue that was to connect the entire population of the state with its political institutions and claim to exercise power or control over it in the name of popular sovereignty. This process is the civic core of nationhood, its channel into politics. Nationhood, then, should be conceptualized as simultaneously having a political (civic) and a cultural (ethnic) dimension. Of course, the role of ethnicity in politics had been present and understood previously.

Various pre-modern references to the idea of a single ethnic group existing in one territory and the significance of this can be found in history, but this misses the point. Ethnicity was at best only one and not the most important source of legitimacy, whereas with the reception of nationalism the nation is the single overarching basis of political community, one that has never been superseded.

Nationhood: The New Legitimation of States

This is not intended to diminish the continuing significance of ethnicity in the construction of nations. On the contrary, it is evident that modern nations benefit enormously from an ethnic base, but that ethnic base was not sufficient on its own to constitute the political community. It is one argument to say that ethnicity is significant in the constitution of states; it is something radically new that ethnicity should be the single most important factor in the equation, yet it is this transformation that took place with the end of the 18th century – the French revolution is a suitably symbolic marker.

The explanation for the sea-change lies in the unintended consequences of various historical processes and their particular conjuncture in time. The growing perception of the insufficiency of the neo-feudal bonds of rule, with their particularisms and exceptions cutting across new commercial patterns, the awareness that outdated principles of legitimacy could not satisfy the demands of the newly conscious strata, especially the emerging bourgeoisie, for more access to power and the consequent quest for alternative links, all played their role. Perhaps the cry of the American colonists against George III, "no taxation without representation," illustrates this most vividly. It constituted a demand for the construction of polities on a new civic (that is, "rational") basis. In effect, the new demands were cutting across old loyalties and eroding them rapidly. The Napoleonic wars, which temporarily destroyed old-established verities and undermined their claim to traditional legitimation in the Weberian sense, carried this process through the length and breadth of Europe.

In this situation, the states with a well-established centralized power, which had not undergone major territorial adjustments, profited most clearly. The so-called core states (England, France, Holland, Sweden), where territory, political power and community had largely coincided for several centuries and where there were no major ethnic discontinuities, like ethnic minorities, were best placed to benefit from the new dispensation. (Tilly, 1975; Orridge, 1981)

For the last two centuries in Europe, polities have subsisted on a mixture of civic and ethnic elements, sometimes in competition, sometimes overlapping, as a continuous process, with the relationship between the two being constantly defined and redefined. (Smith, 1991) It is important to understand that both these factors have been present, for there is a strong tendency in Western Europe, where democracies have been established and functioning for a considerable period of time, to ignore, if not indeed to decry, the ethnic aspects of nationalism and deny them any function. Yet the argument that the central constitutive element of any political community is the set of affective bonds derived from a shared culture, the basis of nationhood, is difficult to refute.

Democracy, therefore, rests on the strongly cohesive identities provided by nationhood – there is no democratic state that is without this, Switzerland included (see below). On its own, democracy is not capable of sustaining the vision of past and future that holds polities together, because it does little or nothing to generate the affective, symbolic and ritually reaffirmed ties upon which community rests. The collection of individuals, the supposed actors in the liberal theory of democracy, who share interests and are supposedly in a contractual relationship with each other and the state, is insufficient for this purpose. (Keens-Soper, 1989)

What has happened in Western Europe is, as suggested already, that nationhood was pushed out of sight and effectively ignored in the post-1945 period, in what should be regarded as an epic battle between liberalism and Marxism. Now that this conflict is over, with the defeat of the latter, the constraints on nationalism have loosened and there are many signs that nationalism has not only reemerged into the daylight, but may in fact be an ideology with a future.

Nationhood: The Historical Aspects in Western Europe

The reasons why this displacement from consciousness should have taken place lie in a particular coincidence of events. In the first place, the dominant problem in Western Europe, indeed in Europe as a whole, for well over a century, from 1848 say, was popular participation. How could the newly urbanized middle and working classes be given access to political decision-making without destroying the existing edifice of power, which did provide for a degree of stability and predictability in politics? The French revolution was a terrible warning as to what would happen when this process was accelerated or when extremists gained control of politics. Indeed, the negative legacy of the French revolution for the spread of democracy could hardly be exaggerated, not least because it legitimated revolution as a desirable agent of change, rather than seeing it as a consequence of the failure of the political system. (Bibó, 1991)

For much of the subsequent century-and-a-half, the problem of integrating the working class into democratic politics was fought out along two broad axes – the liberal and the socialist. Both liberalism and socialism should be seen as answers to the challenge of modernity – the involvement of the mass of the population in dynamic and continuous change, growing complexity and widening choice, and implications of this for the redistribution of political power. Conservatism failed to produce a coherent philosophy to tackle these issues head on, rather it tended to sweep the problem to one side and, at best, concerned itself with the consolidation of the *status quo ante* or sought to ally itself with organic, at times nationalist, theories of community. The dominant innovative lines of thought were the liberal and socialist, however. What these share is a difficulty in the understanding of nationalism, because they both derive their first principles from economic rationality, rather than cultural. Consequently, as long as the discourse in Europe was dominated by these two currents, nationalism was marginalized and political conflicts tended to be seen primarily in the terms defined by these two. Of course, nationalism remained on stage and numerous conflicts had their nationalist aspects, predictably so given the importance of nationalism in legitimation, but in these contexts nationalism was embedded in other conflicts and was perceived as only the first level of explanation (for example, the Franco-Prussian War).

The period after the First World War saw a massive loss of faith in building on the existing European tradition, understandably so in the light of the terrible devastation that Europe had undergone. The problem of broadening popular participation remained, coupled with a weakening of the self-legitimation of the ruling elites. This inevitably produced a gap in the fabric of thought and through this gap there emerged two broad radical alternatives – the fascist and the communist. Both these radical currents denied the viability of incrementalism and meliorism and demanded sudden, radical transformation. Fascism failed first, with the defeat of 1945, but this exacted a terrible price. It left Europe more exhausted than ever before and under the hegemony of the two extra-European superpowers, which had their own agendas for the future. At the same time, by having linked itself closely to the organic-nationalistic currents of the right, fascism did much to discredit nationhood as well as nationalism. For a period after 1945, reference to either was of little use in legitimating ideas. It was not until the success of Gaullism, in the 1960s rather than the 1950s, that any change could be discerned.

The division of Europe also had far-reaching implications for the new European identity that began to emerge in the transformed circumstances. Europe was now essentially redefined as Western Europe. As long as the countries of Central and Eastern Europe remained under Soviet overlordship, there was little point in considering the countries east of the Elbe as parts of Europe and the construction of the new Europe went ahead without them. Besides, the onset of the Cold War constrained the Western Europeans to redefine their identities in terms of integration rather than rivalries, a process which was enormously aided by the memories of the devastation of the Second World War. The Cold War, the fear of and rivalry with the Soviet Union, had far-reaching ramifications for the new European identity. It meant that Europe would be defined against communism and by the criteria of liberalism, Christian democracy and a degree of étatism. But the commitment to pluralistic democracy and market economics was firm and grew firmer with success – political stability and economic prosperity.

The process of Western European integration, from the Schuman plan, Messina, the Rome treaty to the effective functioning of the Common Market, must be regarded not only as a major success story in its own right, but also as a significant redefinition of the European identity. From that time on, the identity and agendas of Europe were inextricably intertwined with the EC and the entry of six new (Western European) members confirmed this. There was no Europe other than the one centered on Brussels. This, however, had a marked impact on nationhood and nationalism. Political integration was perceived primarily as an economic, administrative and technological process, from which the national-cultural element could be omitted. It was assumed that, once the new structures were in place, nationhood would simply lose its relevance or at any rate its political saliency. This attempt to divorce political community from its cultural-affective elements had a certain political attractiveness in the immediate circumstances of the post-1945 period, when reconstruction and redefinition were the order of the day, but, once that task was accomplished and the outlines of the civic elements of a new Europe were in place, the ethnic elements were bound to resurface.

The new European identity received support and nurturing from another source, from the international order as a whole. In part, this was derived from the overriding need for stability under conditions of the superpower rivalry, which could not tolerate minor conflicts with their origins in nationalism. Memories of the futility of the League of Nations, and its endless debates on frontier questions and irredenta, also played a role here, given that the inter-war period was the dominant experience of the ruling generation of politicians until the 1970s. The new order, as encapsulated in the United Nations, was deeply antagonistic to the emergence of new states by secession. (Mayall, 1990) Indeed, until the recognition of the independence of the Baltic states in 1991, only Bangladesh was successful in gaining recognition of its independent status. And even at that, great care was taken by the West in according recognition to the Baltic states to define them as a special case, because these countries had already enjoyed independence between the wars, and to distinguish them from other republics of the former Soviet Union, for which recognition would not be immediately forthcoming as long as the latter existed. Biafra was an earlier example of an attempted secession that was not widely recognized. The Helsinki process was as strict on this as the UN.

Decolonization was another matter. New states could and did come into being by this route, but this was hardly applicable to Europe, where only Malta and Cyprus were decolonized states. On the other hand, until the completion of decolonization it is also true that the Western European colonial powers were deeply involved with ridding themselves of empire, a process that ended with the collapse of the Portuguese empire in the 1970s. The abandonment of territory is always a traumatic experience for a state; the loss of empire and the proliferation of new states in the Third World probably helped to strengthen the general presumption that, as far as Western Europe was concerned, nationalism, irredenta, frontier revision and the like were unacceptable.

Mention must be made here of the role of the United States and its values. The United States was consistently hostile to Europe's overseas empires (for example, Suez) and was, equally, supportive of the Western European integration process, seeing in it a kind of embryo United States of Europe. On the other hand, Washington has never been particularly sensitive to questions of ethnicity in international politics, tending to regard them as a tiresome distraction. As long as European agendas were heavily determined by United States influence, the role of nationhood in European politics would be strictly circumscribed. The West Europeans accepted this willingly and happily or reluctantly and with reservations, like General de Gaulle, who, in contrast to his contemporaries, fully understood the meaning of nationhood, at any rate as far as France was concerned.

Finally, mention must be made here of the ethnic revival of the 1960s and after. The causes of this resurgence can be located in a variety of factors – dissatisfaction with the increasing remoteness of the state, particularly in its technological–technocratic manifestation in France and Britain, the renewed self-confidence of greater prosperity, the narrowing of horizons with the end of empire, and the demand for greater democratic control based on the cultural community rather than the state where these two did not coincide. It is worth adding that no European state is ethnically homogeneous except Iceland, so that there is no complete congruence between ethnic and civic elements anywhere in Western Europe. Solutions to this question were, therefore, important.

Nevertheless, the new ethnic movements were characterized by one crucial difference from previous nationalist upsurges – they did not call the integrity of the state into question. This was true even when the political rhetoric of some neo-nationalist movements, like the Scottish National Party, did demand independence. In reality, these movements were looking primarily for access to power within the confines of the existing state frameworks and they tended to limit their demands to local, cultural or regional issues, which could be solved through devolution or better provisions for minority languages and so on. With one or two exceptions, the democratic systems were able to cope with these movements fairly successfully – Northern Ireland and the Basque country represent the main failures. Elsewhere a variety of techniques were employed to integrate these new demands for power – new in that they based their demands for power on existing cleavages but ones which had not previously been used to legitimate claims to political power – and thereby absorbed any possible shock to stability that might have arisen. This is not to suggest that this process took place entirely without some political conflict, but major upheavals were avoided.

Crucially, Western political systems and societies had become highly complex and were becoming increasingly so. This meant that ethnic identities, while salient, were only seldom allowed to dominate agendas; both groups and individuals found themselves caught up in a network of competing interests and identities, which tended to downgrade the impact of ethnic mobilization and permitted the operation of compromise mechanisms. Above all, where remedies for ethnically based grievances are feasible within the existing political framework, reductionist mobilization does not take place. Reductionist mobilization is the state of affairs where all questions, problems, arguments, demands, etc. are interpreted exclusively in ethno-national terms and political articulation is reduced to this one cleavage. Evidently in a situation of this kind, the normal arrangements, compromises and deals that democratic systems bring into being do not take place, for when deep-level cultural issues come to the foreground they cannot be bargained away and material concessions or incentives will be useless. Northern Ireland illustrates a case where reductionism of this kind, along an ethno-religious cleavage, has taken place.

2. "Consociationalism"

The most significant of the techniques used to integrate multi-ethnic populations is "consociationalism."[2] Consociationalism is a way of governing deeply segmented polities. In states where there are major and strongly persistent cleavages (ethno-national, religious, racial, linguistic), majoritarian politics will clearly be a recipe for disruption, as each group looks to maximize its advantage to the disbenefit of others. Indeed, if relations between two ethno-national communities deteriorate and reductionist mobilization takes place, separation and possibly territorial realignment will be the only solution. But, short of that, the techniques of consociationalism are worth discussing, especially as they have been fairly successful in several multi-national states in sustaining a democratic order.

The key aspect of consociationalism is that it is anti-majoritarian and thus completely alien to the Anglo-Saxon tradition of political organization. Notably, it recognizes the collective rights of groups, both as against other groups and as against their members.[3] They may certainly derogate from individual rights and seem contrary to the principle of the equality of all before the law, but are nevertheless desirable if the alternative is disruption or low-level civil war (viz. Northern Ireland, where the consociational solution was attempted too late, after reductionist mobilization made its chances of success futile). In fact, of course, European political systems recognize that combinations – group rights – are a part of modern social and political life and extending these to ethnic or religious groups, subject to certain safeguards, can hardly be termed undemocratic.

The adoption of consociationalism, however, imposes a major burden on the majority. By and large nation-states are regulated by the moral-cultural codes of the majority and it is precisely this that makes the position of the minority so difficult – it has to compromise its own codes in too many respects. When this happens, the minority will look for alternative ways to put its aspirations into effect, conceivably to separation. Consequently, the majority must accept that its own codes will have to be compromised for the sake of maintaining the state. This is very much what has been put into effect in Switzerland, the ultimate consociational success.

Consociational systems seek to draw all the different segments into the decision-making process through elite representation, a kind of grand coalition, although other institutional forms can also be envisaged, like regular consultation with all groups by the president. The basic elements of a consociational system include consultation with all groups in order to build support for constitutional change; a veto by all groups over major issues affecting them; a proportionate sharing of state expenditure and patronage; and substantial autonomy for each group to regulate and control its supporters. The bureaucracy should develop an ethos of ensuring that policies are implemented accordingly, the government should keep much of its negotiation behind closed doors in order to prevent popular mobilization around a particular issue which can be related to group identity, and a set of tacit rules of the game should be adopted.[4]

Consociationalism, however, imposes two essential conditions in order for it to work. In the first place, all the groups concerned must be willing to work towards accommodation and be ready to bargain and that, in turn, means the creative use of both substantive and procedural solutions that will help all the parties. In other words, all groups must work to avoid zero-sum game situations, even at the risk of ambiguity. Above all, there must be no major winners or losers. Second, the leaders of a group must be able to secure the support of their followers, otherwise the consociational bargains will fall apart; the success of this will depend on the confidence of the members of the group in the system as a whole – a recognition that their interests will be taken into consideration in the bargaining. Thus the leadership of the group must be able to sell solutions to the membership. Society, as well as leaderships, must be sophisticated for consociational solutions to work well.

Other factors important to the success of consociationalism include a readiness to delegate as much as possible to the groups themselves, that is, extensive self-government. This is complicated in modern societies by the erosion of the territorial principle; on the whole, in dynamic societies, members of different segments will tend to be dispersed throughout the entire area of the state and it would be fatal to consociationalism to base devolution of power solely on territory. Next, the principle of proportionality should be observed rigorously, with if anything an overrepresentation of smaller groups; the minority veto is, of course, the ultimate resource for the protection of small segments. Overrepresentation, however, should not be confused with affirmative action strategies, which have the different objective of promoting the equality, not the stability, of minorities.

There are various helpful though not essential preconditions for the success of consociationalism. These include the relative equality in the size of the segments and the absence of a group with a majority; a relatively small total population, for this means a smallish elite, in which there is a strong chance that members of that elite will share values through similar or identical educational and other experiences. There should be an overarching loyalty to a legitimating ideology of the state and a corresponding moral-cultural outward boundary towards other states. In addition, a tradition of political accommodation can be very useful indeed. It should be noted that these preconditions are neither necessary nor sufficient for the success of consociationalism, but they are useful.

3. The Central and Eastern European Pattern

In Central and Eastern Europe the pattern was in many respects substantially different. This had both historical and contemporary political aspects. Historically the single most important factor in this context was backwardness and its consequences. Whereas, as argued, in Western Europe the state developed more or less coextensively with the cultural community and indeed was important in forming it, in the East, the state and polity, together with the economy, were subordinated to external rule. The fact of foreign overlordship was crucial, in as much as it separated the civic and the ethnic elements from one another and precluded the continuous interrelationship between the two that proved to be so significant in the evolution of nations in the West.

The weakness of the civic elements of nationhood and the corresponding emphasis on ethnicity had a number of results with further consequences of their own. In the first place, at the threshold of the modern period the Central and Eastern European countries had singularly lopsided social-political structures when contrasted with Western Europe. The politically conscious sub-elites were small, certainly well under 10 percent of the population, and they were not politically masters of their own fate, because of alien, imperial rule. By and large, these sub-elites were divided in their attitude to empire. Some accepted the benefits, whether personal or communal, to be derived from service, others did not; loyalty to the dynasty was in some cases given willingly, in others only grudgingly or with resentment. What was shared throughout the area was that some awareness survived of the community's previous political economy and was used as a reference point by those looking for greater freedom from the imperium. In some instances, the legacy of the past may have involved legal provisions (for example, the rights of the Bohemian crown) (Kolarz, 1946), in others it might only have been a memory of past statehood or it could have been statehood combined with religious separateness.

This was the background against which nationalism was received at the beginning of the 19th century. The new imperative of political legitimacy, that ethnic and civic elements of nationhood coincide, ran up against the obstacle of the ruling empires, which rejected any thought of redistributing power. The Holy Alliance was, in effect, devised specifically with the aim of preventing the reception of nationalism from being pursued to its logical conclusion – the creation of new states legitimated by nationhood and not by dynasty. The system devised at the Congress of Vienna held together for a century, with only the Ottoman Empire crumbling in the Balkans and permitting the emergence of a series of new states. The decline of Ottoman power from within and the sense that it was not wholly appropriate for Moslem rulers to govern Christian subjects, which informed repeated Western interventions in favor of granting independence to new Balkan states, accelerated this process.

In Central Europe and Russia, on the other hand, the existing empires' control was broken only by defeat in war and the determination of the victors to redraw the political map along ethno-national lines – this was the essence of President Wilson's Fourteen Points. The belt of new states that came into being, however, proved to be weak in both ethnic and civic terms. They were unable to integrate their deeply segmented polities and lacked the cultural and economic bases necessary to create effective civil societies. In fact, they were caught in a near-classic vicious circle, in as much as they sought to use the instruments of the state to bring civil society into being, found that this ran into various impediments deriving from backwardness, intensified state control and made it even more difficult for civil society to come into being. The ethno-national cleavages were among the most intractable. These ethno-cultural communities, different from the majority, found the attempts to integrate them into what they perceived as an alien polity unwelcome, and responded with resentment and hostility. The terms of the integration were, inevitably, loaded against the minority, in that no distinction was made between loyalty to the state as citizen (and taxpayer) and loyalty to the cultural community. Ultimately this meant that members of ethnic minorities were *eo ipso* suspect and that the terms of loyalty demanded of them amounted to the complete abandonment of their own moral-cultural codes, something that communities as a whole would seldom do, though individuals might.

The state of affairs in Central and Eastern Europe after the Second World War was felt to be deeply unsatisfactory by all participants. This was exacerbated by the introduction of the collective principle in dealing with non-majority ethnic communities, in an attempt to bring about ethnic purification. This intensified anxieties and did little to contribute to the integration of the population.

The backwardness of Central and Eastern Europe gave rise to a further feature which characterizes the area. In Western Europe, the protagonists of the new doctrine of nationalism, the intellectuals, defined and proclaimed their ideas in relatively complex societies, in which the contest for power took place among various social groups, like the declining representatives of the old order, the rising entrepreneurs and the emerging working class, with the result that power was diffused and the intellectuals could not establish a preeminent position for themselves. Indeed, much of the 19th century was characterized by an ever more desperate critique of the bourgeois order on the part of intellectuals. (Steiner, 1971) In Central and Eastern Europe, however, the older order was stronger and societies were far weaker, so that intellectuals came to dominate the scene and acquired an authority which they deployed in the definition of nationhood.

At the same time, because the political challenge to intellectuals was weaker, their claims were not contested and, indeed, to an extent they could define their terms independently of society, imposing a concept of nationhood on it. The drive for intellectual purity was thus added to the various nationalist ideologies that were formulated and, as a result, nationalism in Central and Eastern Europe acquired an exclusive, messianistic quality that it did not have in the West. (Bauman, 1987) This high-profile role of intellectuals and the particular expression of nationalism have proved to be an enduring part of Central and Eastern European politics. In this respect, the nations that came into being in the area can be termed "nations by design" and many of their characteristics differ from those of the West. In particular, there is a long tradition of using or rather abusing nationalism for political purposes not connected with the definition of nationhood, like delegitimating political opponents by calling them "alien" or resisting the redistribution of power on similar grounds. (Schöpflin, 1974)

The Coming of Communism

The arrival of communism transformed the situation in many respects. At the level of theory, communism and nationalism are incompatible. Communism insists that an individual's fundamental identity is derived from class positions; nationalism that it derives from culture. In practice, however, the relationship between the two doctrines, both of which, as argued in the foregoing, were partial responses to the challenge of modernity, was much more ambiguous. Initially, communist rulers sought to expunge existing national identities and to replace them with what was termed "socialist internationalism," a crude cover-name for Sovietization. Gradually, and especially after the second de-Stalinization of 1961, they found themselves impelled to come to terms with the national identities of their subjects and made a variety of compromises with it, regardless of the fact that this diluted and undermined the authenticity of their communist credentials. There are countless examples of communist parties using nationalism in this way.

For societies, communist parties could never be authentic agents of the nation, given the parties' anti-national ideology, but this did not preclude their taking advantage of the new post-1961 political dispensation and to express national aspirations in the space provided. It was this meeting of the two agendas, that of the rulers and ruled, that helped to explain the initial success of, say, the Ceauşescu regime's mobilization in the 1960s and 1970s, when there was a coincidence between the aims of communists and societies.

Where there was no direct overlap, nationalism could be the expression of social autonomy, that is, a demand for strengthening the civic elements of nationhood, and of the hope that society would gain greater access to power. This raised a problem, however. Nationalism may be an excellent way of determining identity, but it has little or nothing to say about political participation (the functions of nationalism are discussed below). In this sense, the demands for autonomy expressed through nationalism – "we should have the right to decide for ourselves because we are members of the Ruritanian nation" – were another illustration of the confusion of codes to which this area is subject. Theoretically the demand for, say, freedom of the press or assembly cannot be anything like as clear. In this respect, nationalism came to be entrusted with a function that it could not really discharge and tended to point societies towards confusion and frustration, as well as expectations that could not be met.

The communist period had further implications of major relevance to the current period. By sweeping away all other competing ideas, programs and values, which the communists insisted on in order to sustain their monopoly, they made it much easier for an undiluted nationalism referring solely to ethnicity to survive more or less intact, more or less conserved in its original state. This meant that some, though not all, of the national disputes and problems of the pre-communist period were simply pushed under the carpet, so that with the end of communism these have automatically reappeared.

In addition, the reflexivity of modernity, that "social practices are constantly examined and reformed in the light of incoming information about those very practices, thus constitutively altering their character" (Giddens, 1990, p. 38), has been much impeded by communism, which claimed to be guided by absolute standards. Thus the kind of relativization that has made nationalism a manageable problem in Western Europe, where the demands for power on the basis of nationhood compete with demands based on other identities (class, economic interests, gender, religion, status, etc.), has not really taken place or is only now beginning to emerge. The propensity to see all matters as involving ethnic nationhood, whether properly related to nationhood or not, is one of the key characteristics of the contemporary Central and Eastern European scene and will not change until nationalism is "desacralized" and subject to other influences, thereby reaching an equilibrium with the civic elements. In effect, what is essential is that post-communist polities develop cross-cutting identities, rather than cumulative ones. (Dunleavy and O'Leary, 1987) This will take time.

One-sided Modernization

Communist rule forced these countries through a one-sided modernizing revolution, which has had a considerable impact on two areas directly affecting nationalism. In the first place, the particular virulence of nationalism in the pre-communist period can be attributed at least partly to the fact that large sections of the population were backward and were subjected to the initial impact of modernization, whether through the market or the state, in being brought into a new kind of community. This is always a traumatic process as traditional communities are swept away, and Central and Eastern Europe was no exception. The communist transformation effectively liquidated the traditional peasantry of the area, of the type bound by the village, illiterate and suspicious of the city and urban life. This applies with minor modifications to Poland (and Yugoslavia), for, despite the absence of collectivization, the agricultural population was as closely enmeshed in the control system of the state as elsewhere.

Inevitably, those who were forced to leave the land looked for answers to their newfound existential problems and generally discerned these in ethnic nationalism, although for some sections of society the communist answer of utopia, hierarchy and authoritarianism was quite acceptable. The failure of the communist system to integrate these societies meant that nationalism continued to provide answers, especially after communism was manifestly seen to have failed. However, this factor is not entirely negative. If the extremes of nationalism are to be associated with the trauma of modernization, the gradual assimilation of the Central and Eastern European peasantry into urban ways should see the long-term abatement of the kind of nationalistic excesses that are so feared.

Second, even though the communist revolution was a partial one, it did very effectively extend the power of the state over society and constructed a modern communications network that has allowed the state to reach virtually the whole of the population, in a way that was not true of the pre-war era. The use of television to spread a message, whether this is communist or nationalist, is far more effective than what was available before electrification. In this respect, Central and Eastern Europe has been globalized, which makes the reception of the global message of material aspirations easier to transmit, though its reception will be slow. The absolute claims of nationalism will be relativized only when the processes of reflexivity and globalization are advanced. No national community can be secure in its nationalistic claims if these are constantly examined and redefined under the impact of ever more information.

The Functions of Nationalism

At this point, it will be useful to look at the functions of nationalism, both as a means of explaining its persistence and to offer perspectives on the future. The historical antecedents of nationalism in Central and Eastern Europe help to explain some of its more intractable features in the contemporary period, but what this sketch of the antecedent processes does not answer is the question of why nationalism survives at all. Its Marxist and liberal opponents have written it off countless times, yet it lives on, despite having been dismissed as "irrational." This implies that nationalism must have a function that no other body of ideas has been able to supplant and, contrary to the claims of its detractors, it remains a living and authentic experience, unlike, say, feudalism, and operates by rules of its own that are rational in its own context.

These functions must be sought in the cultural origins of nationalism, rather than in its political expression. (Schöpflin, 1991b) The proposition in this connection is that every community looks for its moral precepts – the definitions of right and wrong, pure and impure – in its storehouse of cultural values and seeks to defend these from challenges, whether real or perceived. In this way, communities construct the rules of a moral-cultural universe, which then defines them. If this were to disintegrate, the community itself would be threatened. Crucially, it is by the moral-cultural universe that communities define the bonds of loyalty and cohesiveness that hold it together. These bonds, in turn, create the basis of identity which is at the center of a community. Reference is made to these whenever questions of communal existence and belonging are on the agenda. Furthermore, communities also use this moral-cultural resource to articulate the affective dimension of politics. This is not in itself a pathology; all groups possess emotional as well as rational expression in their collective activities. Finally, it is through these cultural traits that the boundaries of a community are constructed, whether these are external boundaries or internal ones. External boundaries define the community in question against other communities. Internal boundaries refer to the acceptability or unacceptability of certain patterns of action or thought. (Barth, 1969)

The problems raised by nationalism in the political realm can be derived from the foregoing. Thus although in politics nationalism has universalistic claims, in reality these are not true. In broad terms, nationalism is excellent in defining the identities of members against non-members of collectivities, but it says nothing about the distribution of power within a community or the allocation of resources.[5] But, because nationhood taps into the emotions underlying collective existence, it is easy enough to confuse the codes relating to political power and those governing political identity, something that has happened repeatedly in the last two hundred years.

In this sense, nationalism can be used as an instrument to legitimate political demands that are entirely unconnected with, say, the distribution of power, but this lack of a logical and causal nexus is muddied by the reference to the affective dimension that nationhood conjures up. Thus in concrete terms, Slobodan Milosevic has (for the time being) successfully convinced the Serbs that the reason for their economic plight is not that the Serbian economy is run badly, but because various aliens (the Kosovo Albanians, the Croats, etc.) are threatening the integrity of the Serbian nation, although in fact the two factors have nothing to do with each other.

4. Perspectives on the Future

There is every indication that nationhood and nationalism will play a growing role in the internal and international politics of Europe, though with different implications for the different halves of the continent. In Western Europe the strength of the civil elements of nationhood, as expressed in the multiple and cross-cutting identities and interests of individuals and groups, coupled with the attractiveness of the integration process, is likely to be substantial enough to offset occasional upsurges of ethnic or even ethno-national mobilization. This does not mean to say that it will be easy, but the traditions of compromise and bargaining over resource allocation, the commitment to democracy and the perception by these societies that they have a direct interest, political as well as economic, in the maintenance of democracy should be sufficient to ensure that nationalist conflicts do not seriously destabilize any state.

The particular trouble spots of Northern Ireland and the Basque country are likely to fester on for a while, but in both these instances the status quo is, in effect, a kind of solution, in as much as any alteration would – at this stage – be likely to intensify difficulties rather than alleviate them. Elsewhere regular adjustments in the distribution of power should be sufficient to absorb ethno-national demands.

However, the end of communism in the former Soviet Union as well as in Central and Eastern Europe has resulted in two major changes. In the first place, the (re)unification of Germany has legitimated the national principle in Europe for the first time since 1945. Essentially, there were no civic grounds for German unity, only ethnic ones. There was no particular reason for Germans to unite in one state other than the fact that they were Germans; in other words it was the ethnic factor that fuelled this move. A democratized East German state could, presumably, have continued in being, in much the same way as a democratized Hungarian or Polish state has done, if it had had the ethnic underpinnings, but, despite the best efforts of the Honecker regime to construct a separate East German ethnicity, this never acquired much authenticity and the application of the ethnic principle has unequivocally pushed it into a single German state.

The broader significance of this has not escaped others. If Germans can claim to eliminate state boundaries by reference to nationhood, there is no reason why this is not applicable elsewhere and, indeed, German unification has become an off-stage reference point for those seeking independence in other parts of Europe. At the same time, there is more than a suggestion that the sympathy entertained by German opinion towards Croatian and Slovenian independence derived at least in part from Germany's own experience.

The knock-on effect of both German unification and the recognition of the Baltic states has been felt elsewhere, obviously in Yugoslavia, but also in Spain, where the difference in status and powers between Catalonia and the Basque country on the one hand and the other provinces on the other poses a growing problem. (*Financial Times*, 16 September 1991.) The Yugoslav question requires more detailed discussion than can be attempted here, but it is worth noting that the central reason why the state collapsed as a single entity is that, after 1945, it was reconstituted by Tito as a communist federation with an explicitly communist legitimation. The collapse of that communist legitimation has brought about the decay of the state as such and the corresponding reversion to the much stronger nationalist legitimations of Serbian, Croatian, and Slovenian nationhood. It appears unlikely in the extreme that attempts to put Yugoslavia together again can be successful, provided that those looking to keep it as a single state are committed to consensuality. A non-consensual Yugoslavia, however, would be highly unstable, because it would fly in the face of both the civic and the ethnic elements of national legitimation.

The end of communism is likely to have other fallout in the area of identity. For the last four-and-a-half decades, Europe has tacitly or sometimes expressly defined itself against communism, insisting that what is European is not communist and to some extent vice versa (only to some extent, because commitment to democracy involves offering some political house-room to anti-democrats like communists). In this respect, the end of communism will require a reappraisal of what Europe stands for, what its identity is. This will also include a redefinition of the socialist agenda, seeing that the defeat of communism will have reverberations for democratic socialism as well.

Post-communism and Ethno-national Questions

In the post-communist countries of Central and Eastern Europe, the construction of democracy inevitably means coming to terms with the resurgence of nationalism and, equally, finding the necessary instruments for integrating ethnic elements into the new systems. This poses a number of problems, some of which can only be touched on in this chapter. The states of Central and Eastern Europe are all to a greater or lesser extent ethnically heterogeneous and will, if they intend to maintain their commitment to democracy, have to make provision for the well-being of minorities. Centrally, this will oblige them to accept and practice democratic self-limitation, something that will require considerable restraint on the part of the new governments. There is little evidence to date that consociational solutions, clearly the most effective in making provision for consensus across segmented societies, have been taken on board. However, the political mood in the Central European states – Poland, the Czech Republic and Hungary – suggests that there is, in fact, some readiness to avoid the worst excesses of majoritarian policies. (Schöpflin, 1991c and 1991d)

Furthermore, self-limitation will also involve an understanding of the proposition that in a democracy the state is not the instrument of the ruling majority for the implementation of certain ideals and utopias, but the agent of governance for the whole of society, regardless of ethnicity. By the same token, the sacralizing of territory, the belief that the particular frontiers that have come into being are in some way above politics, is harmful, because it can lead the majority into the dubious perspective of regarding all minority claims as an infringement upon the sacred territory. There is more than a hint that attitudes of this kind inform Romanian and Serbian thinking, concerning Transylvania and the Kosovo. Any attempt to insist that civic rights should be denied to those who claim different ethnic rights leads directly to major violations of human rights.

Finally, there is the broad problem of integration. In order for democracy to operate effectively, the great majority of the population must feel committed to it and must have an active interest in sustaining it. Without this, democracy will become the affair of the elites and thus be vulnerable to popular upsurges of an anti-democratic nature. Various scenarios illustrating this can be written, notably the rise of an authoritarian leader using nationalist slogans to divert the attention of the population from economic privation. The Milosevic model or "Latin-Americanization" comes very close to being a paradigmatic case, but the model is potentially applicable throughout the area, even given a relatively favorable international environment. Any such development, overemphasizing the ethnic elements of nationalism against the civic ones, is liable to result in growing instability and friction between ethnic groups and undermine the best chance of building democracy that Central and Eastern Europe has ever had.

Notes

1. Some of the arguments in this paper appeared in George Schöpflin (1991a).
2. There are others, like assimilation and integration, cantonization, federalism and arbitration. (See O'Leary, 1991.)
3. Consociationalism has nothing whatever to do with the minority treaties of the interwar period, which sought to guarantee certain protection to national minorities, and generally failed, because the state – dominated by the majority nation – rejected these attempts. Consociationalism deals with a situation where the majority accepts that the minority must play an active role in the political life of the state and should do so on the same terms as itself.
4. The classic exposition of consociationalism is Arend Lijphart (1977). See also Powell Jr. (1982, pp. 212–218).
5. In many national ideologies, there are elements of self-perception that claim particular democratic virtue for the nation in question; however, these are contingent and are in no way necessarily connected with the definition of nationhood.

REFERENCES

Armstrong, John (1982), *Nations before Nationalism*. Chapel Hill, NC: University of North Carolina Press.
Barth, Fredrik, ed. (1969), *Ethnic Groups and Boundaries: The Social Organization of Culture Difference*. London: Allen & Unwin.
Bauman, Zygmunt (1987), "Intellectuals in East-Central Europe: Continuity and Change." *Eastern European Politics and Society*. Vol. 1, No. 2 (Spring), pp. 162–186.
Bibó, István (1991), "Reflections on the Social Development of Europe." In *Democracy, Revolution, Self-Determination: Selected Writings*. Boulder, CO: Atlantic Research, pp. 421–526.
Dunleavy, Patrick & O'Leary, Brendan (1987), *Theories of the State: The Politics of Liberal Democracy*. London: Macmillan.
Giddens, Anthony (1990), *The Consequences of Modernity*. Cambridge: Polity Press.
Keens-Soper, Maurice (1989), "The Liberal State and Nationalism in Post-war Europe." *History of European Ideas*. Vol. 10, No. 6, pp. 698–703.

Kolarz, Walter (1946), *Myths and Realities in Eastern Europe*. London: Drummond.

Lijphart, Arend (1977), *Democracy in Plural Societies: A Comparative Explanation*. New Haven, CT: Yale University Press.

Mayall, James (1990), *Nationalism and International Society*. Cambridge: Cambridge University Press.

O'Leary, Brendan (1991), "Nine Grand Methods for Dealing with Ethnic Conflicts." Conference Paper, Bálványosfürdö, July; in Hungarian: "Erdély = Észak-Irország?" *Világ*. Vol. 2, No. 37, 11 September, pp. 41–43.

Orridge, Andrew (1981), "Varieties of Nationalism." In Leonard Tivey (ed.), *The Nation-State: The Formation of Modern Politics*. Oxford: Martin Robertson, pp. 39–58.

Powell, Jr., G. Bingham (1982), *Contemporary Democracies: Participation, Stability and Violence*. Cambridge, MA: Harvard University Press.

Rothschild, Joseph (1981), *Ethnopolitics*. New York: Columbia University Press.

Schöpflin, George (1974), "Nationalism, Politics and the European Experience." *Survey*. Vol. 28, No. 4 (123), pp. 67–86.

Schöpflin, George (1991a), "Nacionalizmus a posztkommunista rendszerekben" ("Nationalism in Postcommunist Systems"). *Világosság*. Vol. 33, No. 7–8 (July–August), pp. 481–491.

Schöpflin, George (1991b), "Nationalism and National Minorities in Central and Eastern Europe." *Journal of International Affairs*. Vol. 45, No. 1 (Summer), pp. 51–66.

Schöpflin, George (1991c), "Central and Eastern Europe over the Last Year: New Trends, Old Structures." *Report on Eastern Europe*. Munich: RFE/RL Research Institute, Vol. 2, No. 7 (15 February), pp. 26–28.

Schöpflin, George (1991d), "Post-communism: Constructing New Democracies in Central Europe." *International Affairs*. Vol. 67, No. 2 (April), pp. 235–250.

Smith, Anthony D. (1991), *National Identity*. London: Penguin.

Steiner, George (1971), *In Bluebeard's Castle*. London: Faber.

Tilly, Charles, ed. (1975), *The Formation of National States in Western Europe*. Princeton, NJ: Princeton University Press.

8

The European Communities and Eastern and Central Europe

Tibor Palánkai*

1. Reintegration into the World Economy

During the past few decades a new world economic system based on inter-dependence and integration has emerged. The process of internationaliza-tion and the growth of intensive economic cooperation contributed greatly to the increase of efficiency and welfare in the participating countries. The present high level of economic development in the industrial countries is, without exception, based on intensive international economic coopera-tion, enabling complex exploitation of the advantages of the international division of labor. High levels of development are inseparable from full and organic integration into the world economy. This thesis is mostly true, despite the fact that in the present world economy the interdependence is highly asymmetric, with substantial negative processes that work mainly to the detriment of the developing countries. Some regions and countries are at the losing end of the international division of labor and are pushed more and more into a peripheral position. The autarkic experiments in the past decades, however, have all failed, and the only developing coun-tries that have been able to catch up are those that entered into intensive international cooperation and are more or less successfully integrated in the global economy.

As a consequence of maintaining closed systems of bureaucratic planning and management, Central and Eastern European countries mostly deprived themselves of such opportunities. The present state of Eastern European

*Dr. Tibor Palánkai is Professor and Head of the Department of World Economy at the Budapest University of Economics.

economies, their lower efficiency and level of development, therefore, can basically be attributed to the lack of or improper integration into the world economy. In other words, the world economic isolation of the former CMEA countries is one of the basic reasons for their relative backwardness.

According to World Bank estimates, "over the last four decades, had the East European countries pursued economic policies similar to those of Western countries, their per-capita income would be one-third higher." (*The New York Times*, January 2, 1990) Therefore, world economic integration is of utmost importance for these countries, a goal which should be emphasized no less than domestic issues. Integration is not merely an option for Central and Eastern Europe (ideas about a "Third Road") but an absolute necessity.

Transformation strategies concentrating on marketization, privatization and democratization have to be implemented in the circumstances of serious economic crisis in Eastern and Central Europe. Most of the countries are heavily indebted and debt-servicing is possible only at the expense of decreasing investments and living standards for many years. These countries have mostly missed the technological revolution since the 1970s and their overall technological structure has become more and more outdated. The infrastructure and the service sectors have traditionally been neglected by the "planned" development policies, and the environment has been polluted beyond tolerable levels. Owing to several special factors (the collapse of CMEA trade, the effects of the Gulf War, internal political and ethnic instabilities, etc.) these countries are in deep recession. In addition, they have to cope now with a drop in production, rapidly growing unemployment, high inflation, and budgetary and external deficits.

Therefore, the Central and Eastern European countries now face the broad and complex tasks of transforming, consolidating and modernizing their economies and societies, undertakings which have to be dealt with simultaneously in an unprecedentedly short time. Any success is basically dependent on domestic economic and political reforms, but externally it will depend on whether it will be possible to integrate these countries rapidly into the world economy.

Close cooperation with highly developed regions is of special importance. Experience over the past few decades has more or less proved that less developed countries can achieve satisfactory development only if cooperating and interacting with more developed regions and partners. The policies of delinking have produced limited and highly questionable results, and the regional integration efforts of some less developed countries so far have not disproved the above assertions. Of course, there are no mechanisms which guarantee that integration with the developed countries brings about only benefits and that catching-up is automatically ensured. On the contrary, the global market mechanisms basically tend to increase gaps between more and less developed countries, and some vulnerable societies suffer great losses owing to world market developments. On the other hand, it is recognized that modern technologies, management and marketing techniques, capital resources and gains from intra-company cooperation can be obtained only in cooperation with developed regions.

Through regional integration the EC countries have established themselves as focal points in the world economy with high levels of development. The implementation of the single market program is likely to further increase the attractiveness of the region. The EC integration has widely exploited the advantages offered by close economic relations, particularly the "static" comparative advantages (cost differences) in the framework of a common market. Since the 1970s, however, the emphasis has shifted to dynamic comparative advantages (innovation and increasing efficiency), and, as a result of the technological revolution, the structural advantages (product innovation, technological sophistication) have gained in importance. Creating a single market is a complex response to that challenge: the EC can provide a model for eliminating or reducing "structural protectionism" (such as specific standards, technical or environmental prescriptions, etc.) that could be applied on a wider basis in world trade.

For the Central and Eastern European countries the development of close and complex relations with the EC is of strategic importance. The EC not only is the most attractive partner geographically, culturally and economically, but also serves as the gateway to the world economy. It is not by chance, therefore, that the Eastern and Central European countries are seeking association with the EC and most of them declared that they hope to be accepted in due course as full members of the Community. "The vacuum left by the collapse of the Soviet empire has had to be filled; and the EC alone can fill it." (*Financial Times*, December 2, 1991)

2. Helping the Reforms

Owing to emerging political changes, particularly in Hungary and Poland, the OECD countries (Group of 24) have committed themselves to facilitate the processes of transformation. At their meeting in July 1989 the leaders of the Group of Seven asked and authorized the Commission of the EC to coordinate a specific support program for Hungary and Poland.

This was an extremely important development in terms of political prestige and recognition of the special role the EC plays in the reconstruction of the Central and Eastern European economies.

The special action plan of the EC (PHARE – Poland and Hungary: Assisting Restructuring Economies) to help the two countries was launched in September of 1989. PHARE envisioned financial support to these two countries in various forms, such as food aid (to Poland only), join investments, and assistance in the fields of environmental protection and management training. The European Investment Bank has offered an ECU 1 billion credit which is guaranteed by the EC budget as well. Contingent upon IMF approval of an economic policy package, Hungary will receive a $1 billion bridging loan from the EC to deal with its structural balance of payment problems for five years. In fact, in order to ensure broad co-ordination of policy by the Group of 24 members, the conditions for financial support are that the Eastern and Central European countries must come to terms with and meet the requirements of both the IMF and the World Bank.

The assistance of individual countries of the Group of 24 is variable (the main contributors are Germany, Japan, the USA, Finland), and it includes financing certain projects, support for foreign investments, export credit guarantees, education and training, investment in protecting the environment and in the energy sector, and other matters as well.

The PHARE program offered several trade policy concessions to the two countries. On January 1, 1990, the EC eliminated all special quantitative restrictions, five years earlier than it had been designated by the Hungarian–EC trade and cooperation agreement signed in 1988. The quantitative restrictions remained in force only in the fields of voluntary export restraint (steel, textiles, mutton, etc.), but the quotas were also increased (by 13% and 23% for Hungary and Poland, respectively, for textiles in 1990). These measures affected 1,700 products, amounting to about 4 percent of Hungarian exports to the EC.

In addition, the Generalized System of Preferences (GSP) status was extended to these countries, and for a broad range of products they now enjoy free access or preferential treatment. The 1988 agreement, which applied the principle of MFN treatment by mutual consent, put Hungary on an equal basis with developed market economies such as the USA or Japan. Now this status has changed, and Hungary and Poland are categorized as developing countries. The tariffs on some Hungarian agricultural products (goose liver, onions, cherries, etc.) were also reduced.

In June 1991, the European Bank for Reconstruction and Development (EBRD), an organization designed to expedite the transformation and economic consolidation of Central and Eastern Europe, was established. Its initial capital is about ECU 10 billion, and the EBRD began its loan operations in 1991. The Bank's financial supporters originally included the Group of 24, six Central and Eastern European countries, the Soviet Union and some other countries (altogether 42 countries, including some developing countries). Later, the number of participating countries increased to 55. The primary objectives of the EBRD are financial revitalization and expansion of the private sector in these countries, support for the creation of joint ventures with the participation of Western capital, and contributions to infrastructural development.

3. Road to Association

The idea of connecting the Central and Eastern European countries more closely to the previously established European organizations (particularly the EC, but also EFTA) was already raised in the second half of the 1980s.

As a way of "returning to Europe," the possibility of full membership in the EC had been broadly discussed in some intellectual and political circles in most of the Eastern and Central European countries already in 1989. On the EC side, the idea of association was raised by several leading EC politicians (Helmut Kohl, Jacques Delors, Hans-Dietrich Genscher) in the autumn of 1989; and the most specific proposal was offered by the former British Prime Minister Margaret Thatcher, who in a statement in the House of Commons on November 14, 1989 proposed a "Turkish type" of association for interested Central and Eastern European countries.

Officially, the idea of offering association to these countries was raised in early 1990, but it was stressed that the implementation of the more pressing EC integration plans (the "deepening" processes, such as the establishment of a single market, monetary union and political integration) should receive absolute priority.

The official decision on the issue that opened the way for concrete and practical preparation was made at the Dublin summit meeting of EC leaders on April 29, 1990: "Discussions will start forthwith in the [EC] Council, on the basis of the [EC] Commission's communication, on Association Agreements with each of these countries of Central and Eastern Europe which include an institutional framework for political dialogue." (*Financial Times*, April 30, 1990)

In general, it was agreed that trade liberalization should be the centerpiece of any association of Central and Eastern Europe with the EC. The Community offered "European agreements" to these countries which recognized the differences in levels of development and the specific problems of the region. The association agreements with Czecho-Slovakia, Hungary and Poland that were signed on December 16, 1991 are based on asymmetric trade liberalization measures, and have to be progressively implemented during a transition period that lasts until the year 2000. The agreements establish a full free trade area between the affected regions, which is essential for the Central and Eastern European economies in order to exploit all of the market benefits and impulses for the reconstruction and modernization of their economies. The three countries also negotiated free trade agreements with EFTA countries and among themselves (CEFTA). (In January 1993 CSFR was divided into two countries.)

Originally the association was offered by the EC to all of the former socialist countries of the region. Meantime, in some countries serious social and economic conflicts emerged and the dual goals of transition – a market economy and real democracy – proved to be incompatible (Romania and Bulgaria). In Yugoslavia a bloody civil war broke out and the future of the country became uncertain for a long time. In light of these developments, the association offer to these countries was postponed. Romania and Bulgaria concluded similar, but somewhat more limited association agreements about a year later than the Three. Meantime, the waiting list for association has broadened, and the Baltic states appear to have good chances for early association. In view of the break-up of Yugoslavia, an association may be offered to some of the republics later, provided an acceptable peace is created.

Politically, Hungary has made it clear several times that the country strives for full EC membership, and this aspiration is broadly supported by all the major political parties. The new, democratically elected government stated on May 22, 1990 that Hungary "is committed to the idea of European integration" and it aims at gaining "membership in the European communities" in the next decade.

Over and beyond the concrete economic benefits of an association, EC membership is attractive for several other reasons, too. Hungary has strong traditional cultural relations with France, Italy and Germany. The EC is considered to be a fulfillment of traditional European political and moral values. There are major expectations of economic improvement and of the stabilization of the democratization processes once a country has joined the EC. Despite their difficulties, Greece, Spain and Portugal are considered as examples of success. There is a deep conviction, particularly among Hungarian intellectuals, that the country culturally and historically belongs to Europe, and a stable and prosperous Europe can be achieved only through unification. Similar aspirations for full membership have been spelled out in each of the other Central and Eastern European countries.

4. Costs and Benefits of EC Association

The benefits of association with the EC (which also apply to similar arrangements with EFTA) can be compared to those that have arisen in different forms of market integration (free trade areas, customs unions or common markets). They can be further extended by several additional measures.

As a result of the formerly closed character of the Eastern and Central European economies, both structurally and institutionally, large potential "static" gains (latent comparative advantages) can be anticipated. Although Hungary has so far implemented some one-sided import liberalization measures, the opening will become mutual through free trade association. A free trade association may enable the countries of Eastern and Central Europe to exploit such advantages on a large scale, making it possible for producers and consumers to use the cheapest import sources for both production inputs and final consumption. This could lead to "trade creation" in both directions (replacement of inefficient and expensive domestic production by cheaper imports). These "static" advantages and efficiency gains could be substantial. In the areas where Hungary has a comparative advantage, export possibilities can be opened, and a conscious exploitation of them (by proper marketing strategies, flexible adjustment to market changes) could ensure over time a satisfactory external balance for the country. Parallel free trade arrangements with other partners (the other associating countries, EFTA, and even the USA) would assure that the diversion of trade would be minimal.

By opening the formerly closed domestic markets, their structures can be broken up, and really competitive market conditions can be created. Such a development would be extremely important. Thus far the reforms oriented toward marketization have often failed to produce the anticipated benefits precisely because monopolistic market positions have not been eliminated and so profits have remained a function of market position rather than expressive of increasing efficiency. Market competition could lead to the cutting of monopolistic prices and costs, to eliminating shortages, to improving the quality of goods and increasing efficiency in general.

Market competition and direct company contacts with Western partners would promote technological progress and the transfer of modern technologies as well as structural change. The bureaucratic central planning and the monopolistic position of state-owned enterprises were accompanied by an unreasonably slow rate of technological development, a lack of interest in innovation, and the general structural rigidity of the economy. Revolutions in technology have made drastic cost reductions possible (for example, by computerized systems of organization, new management structures, organization of cooperating partners outside the company). They have also led to a radical transformation of services and infrastructure (new information techniques and communication systems). The Central and Eastern European countries have missed much of this development, and thus the gap between them and the Western countries has increased. The competitiveness of Central and Eastern Europe has further deteriorated, and the region has missed many market opportunities (which have been seized by the NICs, especially in Asia). This was accompanied by serious distortion of their development. These countries had become severely indebted by the 1980s. There is no doubt that renewed emphasis on technology is of utmost importance; technological and structural modernization could help to realize enormous benefits once the market is adjusted.

The so-called dynamic effects of market integration can be exploited through association, too. Large open markets can give scope for utilizing the economies of scale and reducing costs in different fields of production. Technological progress, productive cooperation, and specialization in supplying components and in certain services lead to dynamic comparative advantages. Extensive participation in transnational company relations can increase microeconomic efficiency and ensure better access to global markets. These advantages can be extended by eliminating all the barriers to trade and cooperation (as within the EC owing to the internal market).

The larger markets can attract joint ventures and private capital investments. In the framework of market integration, capital resources can be mobilized and allocated in a more efficient way (particularly in common markets). The trade and the flow of technology, and the related capital movements, are interconnected. With larger markets, national economies are better placed to overcome structural and institutional bottlenecks in capital supplies. In this respect, Hungary's association and participation in the 1992 measures would improve the opportunities and the competitiveness of Hungarian enterprises. "Above all, the combination of market access in

the EC, import liberalization and the improved and more predictable legislative framework should further stimulate the inflow of foreign investment,
on which the three countries must rely for new technology and management. They hope that the association agreements will enable them to take
full advantage of their two main advantages: a cheap and well-educated
workforce; and proximity to the heart of an EC market about to become
the largest in the world." (*Financial Times*, December 2, 1991) Companies
from EC countries as well as the USA or Japan could take advantage of the
skilled labor force and the low wage rates in Central and Eastern Europe to
build factories there and ship products to the West.

An association may also improve the macroeconomic performance of
the countries concerned in many respects. It is generally assumed that the
dynamic effects of market integration increase the growth rates. The process
of economic growth can be stabilized beyond the market impulses by proper
economic policies, and in some fields by the coordination of policies. The
structural change can help the nation better utilize its labor resources (thus
reducing unemployment). Monetary cooperation (some sort of connection
to the EMU) is, as the experience of some members and outsiders clearly
proves, indispensable for stabilizing exchange rates and paving the way for
the convertibility of national currency. It is, of course, necessary from the
beginning to control tendencies toward accelerating domestic inflation. The
association can improve the chances (through trade preferences and other
support mechanisms) of avoiding serious external imbalances which would
likely result from integration into the world economy.

It must be stressed that the Central and Eastern European countries
(including Hungary) are not yet at all prepared for integration into Western
Europe. The above advantages, therefore, are highly hypothetical and they
may be realized only after a long and conscious preparation that must
include tough adjustments. It should be clearly understood, as well, that
association also involves several dangers. We need to be fully aware of
them. These dangers could generate substantial costs, sometimes arising out
of a confusingly close relationship to benefits.

(1) Structural changes based on and induced by market integration could
lead to uncontrollable and undesirable economic and social consequences
and tensions. The rapid elimination of inefficient enterprises and subsequent
bankruptcies could result in relatively high unemployment, which could be
aggravated by institutional and infrastructural rigidities (such as immobility
of labor because of housing shortages, etc.). The process can be moderated
by the asymmetric and gradual liberalization measures of association, and
also by proper and comprehensive domestic employment and social policies.

(2) Structural changes based on market integration may be subordinated
to an undesirable extent to the short-term commercial interests of foreign
companies, which may even reproduce the structural distortions on a new
scale. The growing foreign company involvement may concentrate simply
on the region's cheaper labor, while the high-tech capacities are not introduced. Foreign concerns might mostly invest in fields vulnerable to the

business cycle, leaving the country in trouble during a recession. These investments may also be limited only to certain sectors, leading to growing structural dependence of the country on the world markets. Or they could strengthen existing monopolistic structures instead of creating competitive alternative patterns.

Association, therefore, must be accompanied by comprehensive national structural policies based on carefully constructed preferences and incentives that consider the interests of both the foreign companies and the country. Recent experiences prove that these types of structural policies are absolutely necessary in order to strike a balance between host country interests and those of the foreign companies. Structural policies are also needed to avoid regional distortions arising out of market integration.

(3) Servicing the accumulating debt would require a surplus on the balance of trade and payments over a long period of time. Experience over the past few decades suggests, however, that market integration often leads to deterioration of the balance of trade and payments, particularly in the case of a less developed country. In spite of broad liberalization measures since 1988, this danger so far has not been demonstrated to occur in every instance. On the contrary, owing to rapid export expansion, Hungary managed to bring down its debt service ratio (percentage of debt service in export earnings) from 75 to 29 percent between 1986 and 1991. Once association is implemented, however, the balance of payments problems may emerge in the future because of structural weaknesses and inherited rigidities of the economy.

(4) Market integration can also cause deterioration in the macroeconomic performance of the affected country (depending on the economic policy). This particularly refers to the macrobalances, and not only the external balance. The country may suffer serious terms of trade losses through liberalization, and the continuous external imbalances may force a progressive devaluation of the national currency, which could result in uncontrollable inflation. Inflation and unemployment may induce economic policy-makers to set a course that is counterproductive from the point of view of consolidation and structural change.

On the other hand, of course, the country may be compensated for these losses. The need for monetary cooperation beyond simple free trade association must also be stressed in this context. One of the main shortcomings of the association agreements signed with the three Central European countries is that the EC has failed to address their financial difficulties in any respect.

To sum up, the association arrangement is accompanied by dangers and social costs which are neither totally unavoidable nor unmanageable. Some costs must be simply accepted, but they may be counterbalanced by the overall benefits of association. Others (e.g. unemployment) can be treated by appropriate economic policy measures, and the negative consequences can be reduced to a tolerable level. It is, however, very important to stress that an association is not automatically beneficial, and comprehensive integration strategies and measures must be developed both at the EC and domestic policy levels.

5. EC Interests in Association with the East

Western European countries are less enthusiastic about association with Eastern Europe than the other way around. In the short run, Western interests are particularly weak and vague in many fields, and there are spheres where interests conflict.

First of all, the political interests of the EC in accepting the countries of Eastern and Central Europe even as associated countries are fairly contradictory. The reforms and revolutionary changes in Eastern and Central Europe were received enthusiastically by the West at the outset. It was a common hope that the division of the continent by hostility and confrontation could be replaced by cooperation and friendly relations, and that the tremendous costs and burdens of military confrontation could be saved. It was also broadly accepted that the Eastern and Central European countries, by transforming themselves into democratic societies, were entitled to be integrated into the European unification process as full partners.

At the same time it seems that the feeling of urgency about taking these countries into the democratic club of Western countries is not nearly as strong as it was in the case of the accession of Greece, Portugal, and Spain. While under the conditions of bloc confrontation in Europe the fairly balanced economic pros and cons on both sides were unambiguously overridden by political considerations in favor of letting these countries into the EC, the disappearance of the bloc division has seemed to make comparable initiatives concerning Central and Eastern Europe weaker.

The changes in Central and Eastern Europe have also renewed the discussions about the EC's priority of "deepening" or "enlargement." There were anxieties and fears that any form of closer relations (association or membership) with the East might endanger political integration and undermine the progress related to the single market and monetary union. The region is afflicted in this period by serious social, political, national and ethnic conflicts, and the EC is clearly reluctant to undertake any full commitment to the security and stability of these countries. The Maastricht Treaty and subsequent decisions clearly indicate that priority is to be given to early membership of EFTA countries in the EC, while the question of admitting countries from Central and Eastern Europe is being postponed.

However, it must be stressed that the goals of EC deepening and integration with Central and Eastern Europe are not necessarily contradictory and incompatible. Though the countries in the East are definitely behind with respect to marketization and privatization, most of them are roughly at the same level of development as the Mediterranean members. Portuguese and Greek membership has not wrecked the EC; why should it be supposed that, for example, Hungary's admission would do great damage? It must also be emphasized that these countries are no less supportive of European unification than are present EC members and they have no reason to obstruct the integration process.

The developments after the revolutionary changes, in fact, indicate that the Central and Eastern European countries will not hinder the process of European integration. On the contrary, the changes have given new impetus to accelerating the implementation of plans for monetary union and political integration in the EC. Community officials point out that the revolutionary changes in the East have highlighted the need and urgency to continue the process toward a single market, and toward monetary and political union as well. (*Business Week*, November 13, 1989, p. 43) The EC's role in world affairs has been greatly upgraded by East European events both with respect to the coordination of aid and recently in handling the Yugoslavian crisis. The latter may contribute to the formulation of a security policy and role in the Community, even if the efficiency in settling the conflict has proved to be highly questionable.

In economic terms, Central and Eastern Europe is still a marginal partner for the EC, and this situation will not change overnight. The trade of the former seven European CMEA countries (including the USSR) with the EC was about 3.3 percent of the EC's total trade in 1990, which meant exports of ECU 36.6 billion to the EC and imports of ECU 33 billion from the Community. The foreign trade of the seven countries, with 380 million population, roughly equaled in the same year that of Switzerland (ECU 34.3 billion export) with only a 6.5 million population. The trade with the three associated countries (Czecho-Slovakia, Hungary and Poland) was only ECU 11 billion on both the export and the import side, while all six countries (i.e. the above three plus Bulgaria, Romania, and Yugoslavia) of the region had total exports of ECU 21 billion and total imports of ECU 22 billion with the EC.

The six Central and Eastern European countries have about 130 million people, and their combined trade accounts for only roughly 4 percent of world trade, while the share of the twelve member countries of the EC is more than 33 percent. There are also asymmetries in the trading relations among different member countries. More than two-thirds of Hungary's EC trade takes place with Germany and Italy (52.4 and 17.7 percent of Hungary's EC exports in 1990, respectively). (*Foreign Trade, Eurostat*, April 1991) Taking into account the heavy indebtedness of these countries, the prospects of rapidly dynamizing this trade are rather bleak, particularly in terms of Western supplies. It must be stressed, however, that in the long run the above disproportions have to be considered potential assets rather than liabilities.

The structural weaknesses of the Central and Eastern European economies create limits and counter-interests in trade and cooperation. Their exports are composed mainly of such materials and goods in which the expansion of trade is limited by static demand, and also by inflexible export capacities. These sectors are particularly vulnerable to cyclical changes.

In the short run, Hungary's export potential is mostly concentrated in such fields as textiles, steel and chemicals, which are considered "sensitive" products, and thus are subject to protection in most countries. This output of "crisis industries" often faces fierce competition both from West European producers and from developing countries.

One of the stress points of any Eastern and Central European future membership is agriculture. Most of the countries of the region have agricultural surpluses (potentially the same could apply to Romania or Bulgaria, which may overcome present shortages in a relatively short time in the future) and many have comparative cost advantages. Therefore Central and Eastern Europe would be a serious threat to the CAP (Common Agricultural Policy) as both a competitor and a candidate for budgetary support.

In the middle of the 1960s, agricultural goods accounted for more than 60 percent of the Hungarian exports to EC countries. This share decreased to 30 percent by 1981, and it was 25.6 percent in 1990. In the middle of the 1970s still more than half of Hungarian agrarian exports consisted of meat and live animals, which share fell to only a little more than 15 percent by 1990. Because of substantial and influential farm interests in many EC countries this situation cannot be significantly altered: the agrarian and "crisis industry" lobbies of the less developed EC members will exert the greatest resistance not merely to a full membership, but even to the association of these countries. This was well demonstrated by the rigidity of France's position toward the three association candidates concerning beef and goose liver exports, which disclosed that the EC is reluctant to give even minor and marginal concessions to these countries in "sensitive" sectors. There are particularly strong sectoral counter-interests (textiles, furniture, glassware) and fears against granting such concessions in the less developed member countries.

Of course, the interests and views of EC countries and peoples are far from being unanimous on these issues. Some are in favor of the overall development of relations, and they see the integration of Central and Eastern European countries as a factor pushing the EC to undertake long overdue reforms and structural changes. "Hungarian agricultural products have to find ways to EC markets," according to Professor Victor Halberstadt of Leiden University, "and the East European developments will force the common market countries to reform their agricultural system more quickly than otherwise." (*Vilaggazdasag*, February 13, 1990) Despite wide-ranging reforms over the years, these countries were considered as "state-trading" countries until recently, and there are still fears in the West about possible unfair competition and hidden protectionism inherent in their system.

The disappointing experiences of the past with respect to debt, as well as continuing political uncertainty in Central and Eastern Europe, have made many in the West reluctant to give more extensive help. On the other hand, the President of the EC Commission, Jacques Delors, stressed in a television interview as early as October 1989 that the EC felt obliged to help Central and Eastern European countries, and had the resources to do so. "It is in our interest, because if we do not help them, the political reforms in Poland

and Hungary can easily fail, they can fall back into the cold night of totalitarianism with all of its consequences, including the danger of a conflict."
(*Magyar Nemzet*, October 24, 1989) In a speech at the economic gathering of the CSCE (Conference on Security and Cooperation in Europe) in Bonn in March 1990, the Italian Minister of Foreign Affairs Gianni de Michelis proposed that the EC allocate $15 billion a year in aid to Central and Eastern Europe, which would mean setting aside 0.25 percent of Western countries GNP for such help. He also argued that "this relationship does not depend simply on generosity and political solidarity, but on our self-interest." (*Financial Times*, March 24, 1990)

Although aid to Central and Eastern Europe is seen less and less as a simple financial burden or as a politically and economically uncertain venture, the resources needed are substantial and the EC could easily find itself financially committed beyond its current capacities. According to Delors, if the six new democracies of the East get the same help under the same criteria as the EC's own less developed regions, it would require an extra ECU 14 billion a year in new EC resources, plus an additional ECU 5 billion a year from the European Investment Bank. (*Financial Times*, January 18, 1990) Altogether, that would mean an amount of ECU 100–200 billion for the EC rechanneled to the Central and Eastern European countries over a period of five to ten years. The annual budget of the Community was less than ECU 50 billion in 1991. The costs of German unification were estimated at about DM 140 billion in 1991 and they may have reached another DM 200 billion in 1992, magnitudes of expenditure that have substantially exhausted European capacities to help the other new democracies.

If the EC is committed to helping Central and Eastern Europe then the necessity of financial and budgetary reform can hardly be neglected. The reforms are particularly urgent because under present arrangements there is a constant danger of budgetary overspending owing mainly to common agricultural policies. In fact, the EC faced budgetary constraints already in 1988; these have been eased somewhat because of an increase in agricultural world market prices and the improved export possibilities of those products, which formerly had accumulated in large stocks. This budgetary relief, however, proved to be short-lived and the constraints began reemerging again in 1991 expenditures. The decisions on EMU in Maastricht mean substantial additional budgetary burdens (structural and "cohesion" funds) for the Community and according to "Delors package II." The Eastern and Central European countries can expect to receive only modest financial support in the future.

Helping Central and Eastern Europe on a larger scale might also adversely affect certain regional interests, in connection with the proffer of trade policy concessions. Less developed EC nations such as Spain, Portugal and Greece are concerned that some of the economic aid they had expected to gain from the newly integrated Community may go instead to Central and Eastern Europe. (*The Washington Post*, February 24, 1990) There are also financial commitments to the less developed countries outside Europe, particularly arising out of the Lomé Conventions. There have been traditionally tough bargaining sessions between the EC and the African, Caribbean, and Pacific (ACP) countries over the volume of aid, but this time Central and Eastern Europe may be blamed for any aid reductions.

There are also still fears about possible misuse and inefficient utilization of the resources transferred to Central and Eastern Europe. A report by the secretariat of the United Nations Economic Commission for Europe concluded that an aid program to the Soviet Union, Central Europe, and the Balkans comparable to the Marshall Plan would cost about $16.7 billion a year over a four-year period. As reported in the *Financial Times* (April 18, 1990), however, the ECE secretariat doubts the capacity of the Eastern and Central European economies to absorb aid on this scale efficiently. Therefore, the study puts emphasis on technical instead of financial assistance, which would first help to create the necessary legal, financial and institutional frameworks (for example, a Central European Payments Union) to improve the infrastructure, and to develop requisite market skills and conditions.

Despite dramatic political changes and the efforts to enact economically attractive legislation, the countries of Central and Eastern Europe do not yet offer sufficiently encouraging and convincing conditions for investment and business opportunities to most Western companies. There is no need to stress that foreign private investments and joint ventures would be of utmost importance for the technological and structural transformation and modernization of these economies. According to estimates by the Hungarian government, a minimum of $1.5–$2 billion in capital is needed annually to create a viable investment environment, beyond financing the $3–$4 billion debt service obligations in 1990–92. So far, however, somewhat less than $4 billion had been invested cumulatively in Hungary up to the end of 1992. There is a danger that, owing to the Yugoslavian civil war, foreign capital will remain reluctant to invest in the country on a larger scale.

Although the progress of democratization in most of the Central and Eastern European countries has been leading to positive changes in the investment atmosphere, several restrictive legal, institutional and economic policy factors remain with us. The attractiveness of Central and Eastern Europe from an economic viewpoint is still limited because of some persistent difficulties and certain discouraging social and political developments (such as accelerating inflation, balance of payments and budgetary problems, reemerging ethnic and nationalist conflicts). It should be appreciated that, as a function of changes and improvements, investment interest on the part of some foreign companies is growing, but caution still remains. The Yugoslavian civil war and the uncertainties in other countries have definitely had an inhibiting effect on the process.

Conversely, there are some fears and reservations that Central and Eastern Europe might be "too successful" in its adjustment and "too attractive" for foreign capital, particularly in the long run. Some EC industries are afraid that the region may become a cheap supplier of goods and a major competitor in a variety of products (labor-intensive products based on cheap skilled labor, mass consumer durables and other items). In particular the less developed EC countries see a direct threat in the Eastern and Central European countries because the latter may attract large transnationals, thus diverting capital resources away from them.

As has already been mentioned, such fears of the less developed members are not totally unfounded. Spain, for example, has attracted $45 billion in investment since 1986 and now fears that some of the private investment previously directed toward the developing Mediterranean nations might soon be rechanneled to the Central and Eastern European countries, which offer dynamic domestic markets for some products and, through their association, access back to the West European markets.

6. Benefits for the West

It must be stressed, however, that association with Central and Eastern Europe could provide great benefits and extensive market opportunities to EC countries (and, of course, to EFTA too). For example, Central and Eastern Europe can offer broad markets for the West, and the huge West European market could soon be extended to include the "hungry" consumers of Central and Eastern Europe. As Frans Andriessen said, "Eastern Europe, with its 136 million inhabitants with a high level of education and great material needs, will become an important trading partner to our mutual benefits." (*The Washington Post*, February 24, 1990) It is now widely realized that these potential opportunities are substantial, and that depending on the marketization of the Eastern and Central European economies they can grow considerably.

In some fields the opportunities for Western firms to sell are immediate because of a large hidden effective demand coupled with acute supply shortages on the one hand, and accumulated inconvertible money incomes on the other. Owing to heavy indebtedness these countries, of course, need and want to export to the Western markets rather than to buy Western products. But the hidden demand has been very rapidly activated, and in broad fields, in fact, the shortages have been effectively eliminated.

For example, owing to liberalization measures on both sides, Hungary's imports from the EC grew by 27 percent in 1989, by 8 percent in 1990 and by a further 30 percent in 1991. Hungarian exports to the EC increased by 20 percent in 1989 and by 16 percent in 1990. The share of the EC in Hungarian imports and exports was about 25 percent in 1989, it jumped to 31–32 percent in 1990, and it was nearly 50 percent in 1991. (*Külkereskedelmi Statisztikai Evkönyv*, 1990) It may be assumed that the trade liberalization measures of association will further increase this share in the future.

The potential markets are really enormous in the long run. For example, the number of cars per 1,000 people is 145 in Hungary, while in the USA it is 572, in Western Germany 446, and in Japan 235. The ratios for telephones are 134 in Hungary, 650 in the USA, 641 in Western Germany and 535 in Japan; for television sets it is 275 in Hungary, 621 in the USA, 377 in Western Germany and 250 in Japan. (*Financial Times*, March 6, 1990) The Hungarian level of comparative consumption of durables, as listed above, is a little lower than those in Eastern Germany and the CSFR, and higher than in other Central and Eastern European countries. The consumption of durables in the region, in general, is about one-fourth to one-third of that in the highly industrialized countries, and the housing situation is even worse. According to a report from the Economist Intelligence Unit in London: "Eastern Europe's demand for cars will exceed supply for at least another decade, even if current price restrictions and the general shortage of goods come to an end ... Eastern Europe's production capacity could double to 4.8 million cars by 2000," still leaving substantial possibilities for Western sales. (*The Economist*, December 2, 1989)

The potential demand may grow even more rapidly if the accelerated replacement of many durables owing to poor quality, energy waste and environmental pollution beyond Western standards begins to take place. The aggregate impact could be even greater if the related service sectors and the enormous possibilities in the housing sphere are included.

The advantages of market integration can be utilized by the EC in terms of both "static" and "dynamic" gains, and the region may offer great opportunities for the exploitation of economies of scale. As a cheap supplier, Central and Eastern Europe may be considered a welcome partner as well as an undesired competitor. These countries, as already noted, have comparative advantages, particularly in their skilled and cheap labor force, and they could easily be transformed into high-quality manufacturing zones for Western companies.

The modernization of outdated industrial structures and technological reconstruction offer immense investment and business opportunities. The long-neglected service sector and infrastructure not only are bottlenecks, but they also offer opportunities for investment and business expansion. Western experiences have proved that investments in this sector can bring attractive returns for investors. According to a British team which visited the Soviet Union under the aegis of the government's know-how fund program in September 1991, the need for and the possibilities of help in services and distribution are enormous. "They discovered a country that was logistically crippled. The primitive state of transport, storage, and distribution had given rise to wastage of horrific proportions with almost 40 percent of all produce being squandered. There are clearly great possibilities for Western companies to help develop the distribution infrastructure in Eastern Europe. For those with sufficient vision, patience and determination, an enormous and unprecedented business opportunity awaits. (*Financial Times*, December 4, 1991) Of course, the picture is different in the other countries, but the great opportunities are there with even better prospects for earlier improvement.

It is not too far-fetched to suppose that in Central and Eastern Europe, as a result of structural modernization and market expansion, there are good prospects for rapid economic growth. The closing of the gap in productivity and consumption in various sectors of the economy (motorization, housing, infrastructure, services, environmental protection, etc.) could secure dynamism within the whole economy for many years. An EC Commission report suggests that, if a proposed free market reform package were implemented, then the Central and Eastern European region could move from the present zero or negative growth to an annual rate of development of 5–6 percent after 1992–93. (*Financial Times*, May 15, 1990) The measures of 1992, if coupled with an association with such a growth region, could mean powerful potential dynamizing effects for West European economies, unparalleled in any other region of the world, except perhaps Southeast and East Asia.

Many experts predict higher growth rates in the 1990s than in the 1980s for EC countries, partly because of an expected rapid expansion of trade with Central and Eastern Europe, and partly because of the positive effects of the single European market. "The goal of Europe 1992 is to promote a renaissance of the Continent crippled by so-called Eurosclerosis that Europe suffered a decade ago," according to a report in *US News and World Report*, and "the architects of 1992 hope that by dropping barriers that impede the growth of globally comparative industries,... by cooperating on research and development, accelerating the establishment of Pan-European companies and taking other expansionary steps ... Europe could catch up with the US and Japan in five to ten years." (*US News and World Report*, November 27, 1989, p. 43) Some foresee that even Central Europe may become a new subregional growth and economic power center on the European continent. "The analysis of development path of the West European regions may suggest such a conclusion, that the center of gravity of European economic power may shift from the North French–Benelux–West German–British quadrangle – favourably for Hungary – toward East, in the direction of South German, North Italian, Austrian and Swiss provinces." (Horvath, 1991, p. 107)

By 1992 it had become clear that the problems of transformation are more complex and the accompanying crisis is much deeper and longer than expected. Western Europe also went into recession, owing, to a great extent, to the changes in Eastern Europe (German unification) and to high European interest rates. If the strict Maastricht criteria for monetary union are met, then rapid economic growth can hardly be expected in the EC during the 1990s. One should not exclude, however, the possibility that the positive processes may mutually strengthen each other in the two parts of the European continent. If this happens, it may help to overcome the present crises. There are some serious doubts and reservations, but such an optimistic scenario is not totally out of the question, especially in the longer run.

7. Western Assistance and the Developing Countries

It is beyond the limits of this chapter to analyze all the global economic consequences that might result from the association of the Central and Eastern European countries with the EC. However, the EC's extensive commitments towards developing countries are crucial and thus inevitably need special attention.

There is broad agreement among experts that the consequences of the changes in Central and Eastern Europe for the developing countries will be far-reaching, but in respect of their actual character and direction opinions are deeply divided. There are growing fears among developing countries that, as a result of the suddenly increased interest of the West in Central and Eastern Europe, resources may be diverted, and many worry that the EC governments may eventually rechannel a part of the aid earmarked for developing countries in the South to Central and Eastern Europe. The disappearance of the East–West rivalry, which formerly played an important role in aid determination, now may reduce the motivation and interest in helping the developing countries. The East may be more attractive than the latter for Western private capital because of historical, geographical and emotional ties.

There are mixed feelings about the recent revision of Central and Eastern Europe's status concerning the GSP; many developing countries see this as being directly disadvantageous to their export competitiveness. For many years, the developing countries have resented World Bank loans to Central and Eastern Europe because, on the basis of per capita income calculations, they seemed to them unjustified. Furthermore, the East may now enjoy substantial competitive advantages in free trade agreements, and some of the newly industrialized countries may be particularly affected thereby, despite the official statement, released by the heads of the world's leading industrial countries at their 1990 Houston economic summit of the Group of Seven, that their help for developing nations would not be undermined by support given to reforms in Central and Eastern Europe.

Of course, there are some observers, in both West and East, who feel that, because of inadequate aid distribution to developing countries (only a fraction of all aid reaches those in need), there is no justification for a priority to help the "Third World," particularly if its high social and economic diversity is taken into account. No doubt, some of the newly industrialized economies in the South are even in better shape than the economies of the Central and Eastern European countries because they have large competitive export sectors, established market institutions, developed infrastructures, and socially strong and viable middle classes. At the same time, some of the Central and Eastern European countries, as well as the countries arising from the former Soviet Union (particularly some of its regions), claim, not totally without foundation, to have similar problems to those of the developing countries (such as, among others, hunger, severe poverty and resource underutilization).

It must, however, be strongly stressed that the solution of the problems of poor developing countries is of utmost importance. The priority of their support should be maintained and therefore any cutting of the aid to them must be avoided.

It is very important that both the lenders and the receivers of loans make it clear that reductions in aid will not happen in the future. The Central and Eastern European countries should be supported in their efforts to integrate themselves into the international economy, including, as appropriate, their adhesion to international institutions. This will benefit not only their own people but also the rest of the world. This support must not be allowed to detract from the high priority placed on international development and cooperation with developing countries. The integration of Central and Eastern Europe in the EC will strengthen its role as a dynamic trade partner, as a market outlet, and as a source of technology for developing countries. (General Assembly of the UN, 1990, Para. 35) As Barber Conable, the former president of the World Bank, pointed out: although the World Bank's global mandate "requires us to take an active role in Eastern Europe, our human and financial resources will not be reduced in continuing the fight against poverty wherever it exists." (*International Herald Tribune*, May 7, 1990)

It has also been pointed out that, although the elimination of East–West confrontation may reduce some forms of aid to developing countries, demilitarization and the reduced importance of ideology, even at times of less aid, may be more beneficial to them. In the long run, the reduction of the East–West military rivalry and arms race should release substantial resources for civilian use, and, though there are difficulties inherent in the conversion process, the potential capacities for helping developing countries could increase. There are indications of growing cooperation between East and West in assistance to developing countries, particularly through international institutions, which could increase both the volume and the efficiency of aid.

Most of these converted resources are aimed at the East, in both their character and structure, and are thus simply not transferable to meet the needs of developing countries, political considerations notwithstanding. This applies particularly to private investment, where direct business calculations and political circumstances generally play decisive roles.

The consolidation of the Central and Eastern European economies and the management of their debt problems actually serve the interests of the developing countries. The default or bankruptcy of any Central or Eastern European country could have broad and undesirable consequences for developing countries. This is true even without mention of the fact that some Central and Eastern European debt had originated in the transfer of resources to developing countries. A consolidated and prosperous Central and Eastern Europe will have more resources and capacities for helping developing countries; the region represents a major, potential addition to the world market, and these countries, if successful, will themselves become sources of capital and technology exports. It is in the overall interest of developing countries that Central and Eastern Europe develops and grows.

Some of the NICs have already recognized the tremendous business potential of the region, and they are ready to take part in the consolidation of the region both as private investors (taking into account the appeal of such access to the broad European markets) and as financial contributors (as participants in the EBRD). Though the worries indicated above should not be ignored, the consequences of changes in Central and Eastern Europe for the developing countries and the world economy, if properly handled, are on balance beneficial for all sectors of the world economy.

REFERENCES

General Assembly of the UN (1990), *Declaration on International Economic Cooperation, in Particular the Revitalization of Economic Growth and Development of Developing Countries.*
Horvath, Gyula (1991), "Az európai régiók gazdasági együttmüködése" (Economic cooperation of European regions). *Europa Forum.* Budapest, I, No. 1 (August).

9

Transfer of Technology: Some Lessons from the International Economy

*Charles Cooper**

1. Technology Policies or Price Policies, Role of the State or Market Forces behind NIC Success?

The appearance of the "new technologies" has coincided with a period of particularly rapid change in strategies of economic development, and with the emergence of the newly industrializing countries (NICs) as a significant force in the international economy. This is not a pure coincidence. The success of the NICs, or at least of some of them, has been associated importantly with the successful adoption of new technologies of various kinds – and in the case of South Korea, Brazil, and probably also Taiwan with an active role of the state in encouraging the development of local technological capability in the industrial sector.

This chapter focuses on technology policies related to export development. It draws attention to the existence of a substantial school of thought for whom success in international industrial markets is to be ascribed as much or more to technology policies as to relative price policies of the traditional kind: in short "getting prices right" is not enough. Most successful exporting countries pay attention to creating the conditions for the realization of comparative advantage in the classical form, but they also concern themselves with more dynamic matters, especially technological change and "learning" processes, which cannot always be left to the market. How far these oppositions are relevant to present debates on liberalization in Eastern Europe is

*Dr. Charles Cooper is Director of the United Nations University Institute for New Technologies, UNU/INTECH, in Maastricht, Netherlands. He wishes to thank Ms. Branka Urem of UNU/INTECH for her contribution to the ideas in the paper.

hard to judge, but if the "technology" school of economists are correct in their analysis of the reasons for NIC success in export development, there surely are some points in common.

This chapter starts by sketching the main characteristics of technology policies under conditions of import substitution – or more generally of closed economy. These are then contrasted with the role ascribed to technology in countries seeking to build up industrial exports. In the last section some conclusions are drawn which relate to Eastern European conditions.

2. The Usual Concerns about Technology Transfer in the Context of Industrialization Strategy

The development economics literature on transfer of technology from the industrialized countries to the Third World has been concerned very largely with countries which were following policies of import substituting indus-trialization or – in the cases of India and China – with other variants of closed-economy industrialization. The focus of this literature was (and is) on contractual systems whereby firms from the technologically advanced industrialized countries made technological knowledge available to firms in the developing countries (which, in some cases, were multinational enter-prise subsidiaries). It made sense for economists to regard these contractual transactions as being the means whereby the seller's monopolistic advan-tages, arising from unique ownership of an innovation, could be shared with the buying enterprise in return for substantial explicit and implicit pay-ments. Licensed technological innovations were looked upon in this frame-work as important elements in oligopolistic competition in the highly pro-tected markets encountered in developing countries. Policy makers were advised to examine three main problems associated with these technology transfers: the costs of transfer; the inappropriateness of the technology being transferred; and the need to develop local technological capabilities.

The costs of technology transfers were seen as a problem mainly because of the so-called paradox of information, that is, that buyers of information cannot in the nature of the case know precisely what they are buying, and therefore, in a market where costs are determined by bargaining, may pay more than is required to get hold of the information (or technology). The problem of inappropriateness of technology was linked in many cases to maldistributions of income. It was asserted that most imported technology was required in response to upper-income consumers' demand for new and innovative products. The manufacture of these products required capital-intensive methods and, it was claimed, led to the employment of relatively few workers at relatively high wage rates. Imported technologies were therefore seen as one element in a process which strengthened tendencies towards a skew distribution of income. This line of argument was never universally accepted, since the strong assumption that technologies become progressively more capital-intensive, the higher the income levels of those who demand the products they are used to make, is contestable. For example, in modern industry simple wage goods may be made by highly capital-intensive methods.

The third area of concern about the import of technology was that its ready availability could lead to a substitution for the local development of technological capabilities rather than to a complementary relationship. This concern has theoretical as well as pragmatic foundations: it has long been argued that the prevalence of externalities in technological learning processes means that unaided market forces will produce less investment in local technological capabilities than is socially desirable.

With the shift in industrialization strategies towards export development, the focus of technology policy has shifted, at least in a number of the more successful exporting countries. The circumstances of export competitiveness require enterprises to pay attention both to the acquisition of innovative processes and product technologies in order to hold their positions in foreign markets, as well as to continuing productivity growth. This point is discussed in greater detail below. For the moment we note that this has led enterprises and governments to focus much more sharply on technology learning processes than before. This tendency is the more marked for the fact that acquisition of foreign technology (for example by way of licenses) is often more difficult for firms which operate in export markets than for those in closed import-substituting economies. The reason is simply that technology suppliers are more likely to fear future competition from such export-oriented enterprises and therefore to be more reluctant to grant licenses than in the case of closed economies (where distorted price structures make export competition from licensees highly unlikely). Hence there is likely to be a greater priority attached to the development of local technological capability than in the past, and notably less concern about the monopolistic costs associated with technology imports. Finally, the shift to export orientation probably also accentuates the need for speedy agreements with foreign licensors. Particularly in more innovative sectors, international competitiveness depends importantly on not being too far behind the technological frontier in the industrialized countries. The need for speed will work against the burdensome technology register and monitoring systems which were set up in many countries during the import-substituting period.

3. Implications of Technologically Stagnant and Dynamic Patterns of Export Development

The implications of the open economy for technology policies can be illustrated with the help of a little formal analysis. In the following, "technology" is reflected in an admittedly restrictive way by the productivity of labor (or rather, in its inverse, the labor input per unit of physical output). In order to keep things simple, we assume that workers spend all of their money wage on basic "wage goods." The analysis is partial: it is assumed that there are two sectors in the economy, one producing the export goods and the other producing the wage goods on which workers spend their income. There is no import of wage goods, nor are there any input–output relationships between the two sectors. The central concern in the following is to determine conditions for real wage increases, since that arguably is a crucial consideration in export-oriented economies.

Let

ω_ε = money wage in the export sector,
α_ε = labor input per unit physical output,
β_ε = producer's markup,
Δ_ε = cost of material input per unit value of output.

Then the price of exports (P_ε) in local currency is given by:

$$P_\varepsilon = (1 + \beta_\varepsilon) \cdot (\alpha_\varepsilon \cdot \omega_\varepsilon + \Delta_\varepsilon) \tag{1}$$

The subscripts ε refer to the export sector.

Equation (1) leads directly to the following relationship between the rate of change of output prices, money wages and labor productivity:

$$\frac{\dot{P}_\varepsilon}{P_\varepsilon} = \frac{\dot{\beta}_\varepsilon}{1 + \beta_\varepsilon} + A \cdot \left[\frac{\dot{\alpha}_\varepsilon}{\alpha_\varepsilon} + \frac{\dot{\omega}_\varepsilon}{\omega_\varepsilon} \right] + D \cdot \left[\frac{\dot{\Delta}_\varepsilon}{\Delta} \right], \tag{2}$$

where

$$A = \frac{\alpha_\varepsilon \cdot \omega_\varepsilon}{\alpha_\varepsilon \cdot \omega_\varepsilon + \Delta_\varepsilon}$$

and

$$D = \frac{\Delta_\varepsilon}{\alpha_\varepsilon \cdot \omega_\varepsilon + \Delta_\varepsilon}.$$

A and D measure the proportions of labor costs and material costs respectively in prime costs.

Equation (2) makes clear that in a fixed exchange rate system money wage increases will damage competitiveness unless producers can be constrained to accept a lower markup on costs, or technological advance reduces labor costs per unit of output. To show the effect of such money wage increases on the real wage, we need to examine the wage goods sector.

Using similar definitions to those for the export sector, the price of wage goods output can be written as:

$$P_\delta = (1 + \beta_\delta) \cdot (\alpha_\delta \cdot \omega_\delta + \Delta_\delta) \tag{3}$$

where the subscripts δ refer to the wage goods sector.

Then the real wage in the export sector is given by the following:

$$\bar{\omega}_\varepsilon = \frac{\omega_\varepsilon}{P_\delta} = \frac{\omega_\varepsilon}{(1 + \beta_\delta) \cdot (\alpha_\delta \cdot \omega_\delta + \Delta_\delta)} \qquad (4)$$

Plainly the implications for the real wage of a rise in export sector money wages depend on how money wages in the wage goods sector respond. If the rise in money wages in the export sector is passed on fully to the wage goods sector, real wages in both sectors will rise, though the rise will be smaller, the smaller the proportion of materials costs in prime costs.[1]

This framework makes it possible to distinguish two main types of industrial export-promoting policy. The *first* type is associated with the system of export zones, which are effectively screened from the rest of the economy. The export zone system is usually associated with so-called traditional industries (food, beverages, textiles and clothing, leather goods, etc.) and with the continued use of older technologies in those sectors. In recent years, however, even the traditional sectors in the developed market economies have been subject to new forms of technical change. As a result, in order to sustain their competitiveness in the absence of technical advance, there has to be a fall in wages, often to very low levels. This type of export promotion therefore depends on low money wages – and hence real wages – in the export sector and on the ability to **reduce** wages there in response to technological change in international markets. In turn, this can only be accomplished by preventing unionization of the workforce and incorporating politically weak and vulnerable groups into the production process. This type of export industry has been especially associated with the employment of women, and particularly younger women, who while they remain in the parental home can be employed at very low (marginal) real wages. In the long run, this type of policy is sustainable only if real wages in higher-income competitor countries rise fast enough, compared with labor productivity, to cushion the need for further reductions in the local export sector's real wages. In general this does not seem to happen and long-run prospects for technologically stagnant export production are generally unpromising. In principle, it should be possible to improve real wages by securing rapid technological change in the production of wage goods (as equation (4) suggests), but in general in countries where exports are based on low real wages the institutional ability to increase the efficiency of production of wage goods is rather weak.

The *second* type of export promotion is centered on achieving an adequate rate of technological change and labor productivity growth to permit export expansion to be consistent with rising real wages. And, as a consideration of the above analysis suggests, this is accomplished not only by technological change in the export sector itself but also by reducing the costs of production and the prices of wage goods. Successful export development with rising real wages depends critically on a successful technology policy which encompasses both these objectives. Equation (2) shows in a rather simple-minded way what is at stake. It shows that if the relative prices of exports are falling on international markets, rising real wages depend *inter alia* on a rate of technological change, as reflected in $\acute{\alpha}_\varepsilon/\alpha_\varepsilon$, great enough to offset the rate of increase of money wages without endangering profit margins. The drive for technological change in the export sector is not only essential to permit rising money (and real) wages without endangering export prices. It is also essential if markups in export production and hence profits and ultimately capitalist "animal spirits" and investment are to be maintained. In the end the money wage rise will be translated into a rise in real wages provided that prices of wage goods do not rise too much.

These dynamic considerations are just as important as and arguably more important in sustaining export-oriented industrialization than any process of liberalization to "get prices right" in the short and medium term. The recent patterns in successful export-oriented industrializing countries show how they have maintained the competitiveness of production whilst achieving the dual objectives of sustaining often vigorous growth of real wages along with a nearly constant factor share, and hence profits over a long period of time.

Figure 1 shows the indices of export volume for South Korea and Hong Kong (the old "NICs") and Malaysia (a putative new "NIC"). The exceptional growth in South Korean exports stands out. Manufacturing exports from Korea grew by a factor of approximately 35 over the period 1969–87. Hong Kong, which has probably achieved less diversification in the product structure of its exports, has been less impressive. In recent years, notably in the eighties, Malaysian manufacturing exports have grown remarkably rapidly; between 1969 and 1987, export volume expanded by a factor of 10.

Figure 2 shows how South Korea's manufactured export growth has been associated with a high rate of increase in real wages accompanied by an equivalent rate of productivity growth.[2]

The result has been sustained competitiveness along with nearly constant factor shares in value-added. The period around 1980 when there was substantial labor unrest in South Korea is an exception, since the wages share rose slightly – as a result of sharp increases in money wages – but the factor share ratio was soon re-established as profits were "rebuilt." Malaysia has followed a similar path (see fig. 3). Real wages have been rising fast since the mid seventies, with virtually constant factor shares and sustained exports. In recent years, Hong Kong's experience has been less favorable (see fig. 4), since wage rises have been achieved at the cost of quite large increases in labor's share of value-added, which undoubtedly squeezed profits.

Technological factors underlie these growth patterns in two main ways: first, through increasing the efficiency of production by the incorporation of new processes; and, second, by incorporating new products for which export demand is comparatively high. The sustained success of South Korea is to be accounted for, to an important extent, by a fairly continuous process of change in product composition of exports towards products for which income elasticity of demand in industrial countries is high.

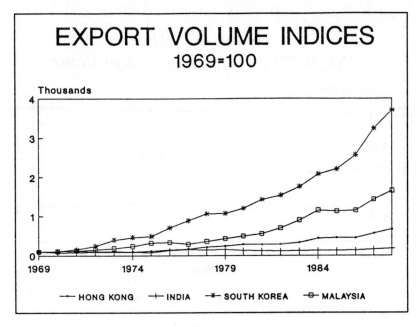

Figure 1

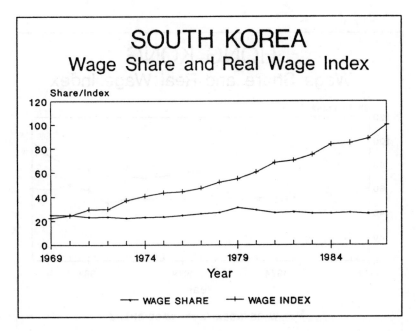

Figure 2

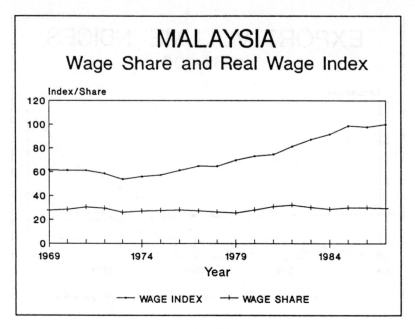

Figure 3

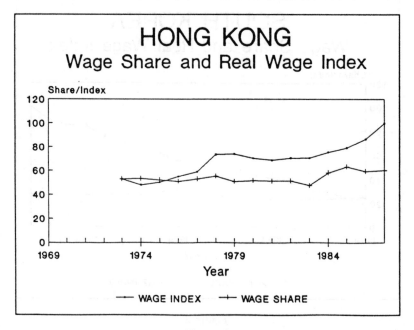

Figure 4

A number of points can be made about these patterns of export development.

First, the trade theory underlying liberalization policies does not have much to say about the differences between technologically "stagnant" export development which depends on a falling real wage and the technologically dynamic patterns described above. Liberalization of trade on conventional terms is primarily concerned with the establishment of a regime of relative prices which will lead to static efficiency in the allocation of resources. In principle at least, efficient allocation of resources from this short-term point of view could be consistent with either technologically stagnant or technologically dynamic development. Yet from the standpoint of economic development and accumulation, long-term technological dynamism is arguably a more important concern than short-term efficiency. If we want to know what policies will produce technological advance as well as short-term efficiency, we have to look beyond traditional trade theories.

Second, mainstream economic theory does not have much to offer in general about the causes of technological change. Most theorizing[3] has been concerned more with the measurement of the effects of technological change than with its economic causes. On the other hand, in recent years an "economics of innovation" has been developed – in a somewhat heretical, Schumpeterian tradition. This offers economic explanations of technological change and, in Schumpeterian style, proposes that the competitive process as such is not about equilibrium levels of costs and profits, but about a continuum of disequilibria as firms vie with one another in searching for and adopting innovative technologies. In this view, the directions of innovation depend on a set of factors which include: the state of immediately relevant technological knowledge; the institutional set-up within which firms operate (e.g. the existence of relevant basic research perhaps in universities, or the organization of R&D activities in the economy); and most importantly the accumulated technological knowledge within firms. The emphasis on accumulated expertise is especially important. It implies the existence of learning economies or dynamic economies of scale, which are irreversible and which constitute important barriers to entry. The challenge to enterprises outside the industry, and seeking to enter, is to get established on a relevant technological learning path so as to be able to compete.

Third, it is clear that learning processes in enterprises require appropriate management, organization and investment within firms and that in some particularly successful countries – South Korea, for instance – government agencies have played a significant role in inducing the learning process. This is done mainly by various kinds of "infant industry" protection. In short, state intervention has been important for the achievement of technological change.

Fourth, and finally, research on innovation processes has shown that there are important differences between sectors in the extent to which firms generate and use innovations. Some sectors are essentially "user" sectors in that the firms in them do not generate innovations but apply the innovations

Table 1

	Hong Kong		S. Korea		Malaysia	
	Wage	Share	Wage	Share	Wage	Share
1969			28	25	61	28
1970			30	25	61	28
1971			31	23	61	30
1972			32	24	59	29
1973	53	53	38	23	54	26
1974	48	53	39	23	56	27
1975	50	53	41	24	57	27
1976	55	51	46	25	61	28
1977	59	53	54	26	65	27
1978	74	56	65	27	65	26
1979	74	51	72	31	70	26
1980	70	52	69	29	73	28
1981	69	51	68	27	75	31
1982	71	51	71	27	81	32
1983	71	48	75	26	87	30
1984	76	58	82	26	92	29
1985	79	63	86	27	99	30
1986	87	60	89	26	98	30
1987	100	60	100	27	100	29

produced in other sectors. Examples of this kind of sector are textiles, clothing and footwear, and wood products. Innovations used in these sectors are customarily incorporated in the plant and equipment they purchase from firms in the capital goods sector. In other user sectors, firms may receive innovations incorporated in the material inputs to production, e.g. in plastics molding and extrusion. "Producer" sectors for innovations are often capital goods sectors as the above implies. In addition, and of increasing importance within modern industrial structures, there are "science-based" sectors, like chemicals, or parts of electronics, or biotechnology sectors, where firms tend to use innovations which they themselves produce.

4. Relevant Lessons and Eastern European Specificities

The relevance of this discussion for Eastern European industry is fairly obvious. Economic reform and liberalization evidently imply that most Eastern European economies will open up to international trade. To differing extents, the success of the liberalization process is likely to depend on the quite rapid development of industrial exports. An important question therefore concerns the terms on which this export development is to take place: in particular, whether it is to be technologically dynamic and associated with socially desirable outcomes like a rising real wage, or, alternatively, whether it is to be technologically stagnant with all the social problems which that would imply.[4] In this section we give a brief account of some of the main problems which may be expected.

Before discussing the problems which will have to be overcome, it is worth noting that many Eastern European countries have an important advantage in relation to setting up technologically dynamic industries. This arises because they have a substantial supply of technologically skilled persons in the industrial sector, and a considerable and well-established scientific community. However, some qualification is needed. It seems clear that the existence of these skilled and highly educated people has not resulted in much technological dynamism in the past, and the reasons for this will need to be understood. Also, there are risks that if the transition to a market economy is particularly arduous a proportion of technically skilled people and of the scientific person power may well emigrate. Nevertheless, despite the caveats there is at least a favorable starting point in this respect.

From other viewpoints, conditions may be less favorable. Some of the matters which will require attention are discussed below.

The *first* problem is that under prior economic regimes, despite some important imports of technology from the West, productivity growth within the closed economic systems was slow. The reasons for this will have to be understood. They probably reflect two main difficulties. In the first place, probably because of a virtual absence of competitive threat, the incentives to organize the technological learning processes which lead to innovative competition have been weak. In the second place, the organization of science and technology in relation to the production system seems to have been inappropriate. It appears that in most Eastern European economies industrial research is done outside the enterprises in state-run research institutes. This pattern is unlikely to achieve comparable results in innovation to those achieved in a more open economy.

A *second* problem is that the capital stock in most Eastern European industries appears to be very old on the average. The reasons for this are not entirely clear, but they may well be associated with distortions arising from the emphasis on quantitative targets in central planning. It is conceivable that risk-averse enterprise managers faced with more severe sanctions if they fail to fulfill quantitative targets than if they are unprofitable will opt to retain an old plant and equipment so as to have as much capacity as possible available should the need for it arise. The obsolescence of the capital stock has two important consequences. The first is that in the transition to a market economy many enterprises will fail to meet the test of profitability in the face of international competition and industrial unemployment is likely to be high.[5] The second consequence is that the technological learning processes are likely to have been slowed down compared with those in competitor firms in the West – at least to the extent that the accumulation of technological capability is influenced by the kind of plant and equipment which firms have in their capital stock.

A *third* problem for enterprises in Eastern Europe is that competitive success will ultimately depend upon their capacity to overcome the barriers to new entrants posed by long-established learning processes and differentiation of innovative capabilities in Western competitor firms. This will not be easy by any means. It will require, firstly, that governments develop capability for effective "infant industry" subsidization during learning periods (which can be long). Then, secondly, it will require an ability to select industries for support. It may occur, for example, that it will be easier to start with sectors which are "user" sectors, in the sense that their innovations are mainly originated by firms supplying them with materials inputs and capital goods. These supplier firms will often be foreign.

A *fourth* problem is that market forces alone will not be sufficient to ensure the effective accumulation of technological capabilities in enterprises. This, at least, seems to be the lesson which the history of the technologically successful NICs appears to teach. State intervention of a selective kind will be necessary for success in industrial exports. There is a risk that the present enthusiasm for a switch to a market economy will lead to this requirement being overlooked.

Appendix

1. *Prices, wages, profits and profitability*

Let

ω = the money wage,

α = labor input per unit output,

β = producer's markup, and

Δ = value of material inputs needed per unit value of output.

Then the price of output is given by:

$$P = (1 + \beta) \cdot (\alpha \cdot \omega + \Delta). \tag{1.1}$$

It then follows that proportional rates of change are related as follows:

$$\frac{\dot{P}}{P} = \frac{\dot{\beta}}{1+\beta} + A \cdot \left[\frac{\dot{\alpha}}{\alpha} + \frac{\dot{\omega}}{\omega} \right] + D \cdot \left[\frac{\dot{\Delta}}{\Delta} \right] \tag{1.2}$$

where:

$$A = \frac{\alpha \cdot \omega}{\alpha \cdot \omega + \Delta}$$

$$D = \frac{\Delta}{\alpha \cdot \omega + \Delta}$$

The rate of price increase depends on changes in the producer's markup, the relationship between growth of money wages and growth of labor productivity, and the rate at which the value of material inputs per unit value of output changes.

Two helpful simplifications follow:

(a) if $\dot{\Delta} = 0$ then,

$$\frac{\dot{P}}{P} = \frac{\dot{\beta}}{1+\beta} + A \cdot \left[\frac{\dot{\alpha}}{\alpha} + \frac{\dot{\omega}}{\omega}\right] \tag{1.2a}$$

(b) if, in addition $\Delta \ll \alpha \cdot \omega$, then

$$\frac{\dot{P}}{P} = \frac{\dot{\beta}}{1+\beta} + \frac{\dot{\alpha}}{\alpha} + \frac{\dot{\omega}}{\omega}. \tag{1.2b}$$

2. Conditions for changes in factor shares in value-added

The following conditions are required in further analysis. Define

$$\sigma_\omega = \text{wage's share in value-added, and}$$

$$\sigma_p = \text{profit's share in value-added}$$

$$\sigma_\omega = \frac{\beta(\alpha \cdot \omega + \Delta)}{V_y} \tag{2.1}$$

and

$$\sigma_\omega = \frac{\alpha \cdot \omega}{V_y} \tag{2.2}$$

where

$$V_y = \text{value-added per unit output,}$$

With these we may define the factor share ratio $(r_{p,\sigma})$, as

$$r_{p,\sigma} = \frac{\sigma_p}{\sigma_\omega} = \beta + \frac{\Delta \cdot \beta}{\alpha} \cdot \omega \tag{2.3}$$

which by differentiation with respect to time gives the condition for shares to be constant or for the wage share to rise as

$$\frac{\dot{\beta}}{\beta} \cdot \left(\frac{\alpha \cdot \omega}{\Delta} + 1\right) - \left(\frac{\dot{\omega}}{\omega} - \frac{\dot{\pi}}{\pi}\right) \leq -\frac{\dot{\Delta}}{\Delta}, \tag{2.4}$$

where

$$\pi = \text{output per worker} = \frac{1}{\alpha}.$$

This is easy to interpret for the case where $\dot{\Delta} = 0$ (that is, where technical change does not change the value of material input per unit of output). In this case:

- if money wages increase at the same rate as productivity, factor shares remain constant if the producer's markup is unchanged, or, alternatively, the share of wages will increase only in the event that the markup rate is reduced, i.e. $\dot{\beta} \leq 0$.
- if money wages increase faster than productivity, wage share will increase unless there is a sufficient offsetting in producer's markup. Since such an increase in combination with the rising money wage would imply increasing prices for final output, it may be excluded if there is international competition – and especially if final output prices are effectively determined in foreign markets and are falling.

Outcomes are a bit more complex if there is technical change which reduces unit values of materials required in production. In this case, the right-hand side of the condition in (2.4) will be positive, and:

- if money wages rise at the same rate as productivity, wage share could increase even if the markup increases, as long as the increase is not too great. Essentially, wages and profits are in contest for the advantages of the growth in value-added per unit output resulting from the reduction in materials costs:
- the conclusion holds *a fortiori* if money wages increase faster than productivity.

3. *Value-added per worker and output per worker*

It will be helpful to be clear about this relationship in the discussion of empirical materials in the text.

Define

$$V_1 = \text{value-added per worker.}$$

Clearly,

$$V_1 = \frac{V_y}{\alpha} \tag{3.1}$$

and,

$$\frac{\dot{V}_1}{V_1} = \frac{\dot{V}_y}{V_y} - \frac{\dot{\alpha}}{\alpha} = \frac{\dot{V}_y}{V_y} - \frac{\dot{\pi}}{\pi}. \tag{3.2}$$

It follows from this that $\dfrac{\dot{V}_1}{V_1} = \dfrac{\dot{\pi}}{\pi}$, if $\dfrac{\dot{V}_y}{V_y} = 0$. In other words, under this condition the proportionate rates of change of the two measures of the productivity of labor are identical. However, there is no reason in general to believe that the condition will hold, and for our purposes the inequality condition,

$$\frac{\dot{V}_1}{V_1} \leq \frac{\dot{\pi}}{\pi}, \quad \text{if} \quad \frac{\dot{V}_y}{V_y} \leq 0,$$

is of greater interest.[6]

To see this first, note that

$$V_y = 1 - \frac{\Delta}{P}, \tag{3.3}$$

so that

$$\dot{V}_y \leq 0, \quad \text{if} \quad \frac{\dot{P}}{P} \leq \frac{\dot{\Delta}}{\Delta}$$

gives the conditions for the rate of growth of value-added to be less than the rate of growth of labor productivity. Using (1.2), this gives the condition as:

$$\frac{\dot{\beta}}{1+\beta} + A \cdot \left[\frac{\dot{\alpha}}{\alpha} + \frac{\dot{\omega}}{\omega}\right] \leq (1-D) \cdot \frac{\dot{\Delta}}{\Delta} \tag{3.4}$$

Now from (1.2), the general condition for price to be falling is:

$$\frac{\dot{\beta}}{1+\beta} + A \cdot \left[\frac{\dot{\alpha}}{\alpha} + \frac{\dot{\omega}}{\omega}\right] \leq -D \cdot \frac{\dot{\Delta}}{\Delta}. \tag{3.4a}$$

Consider the case where technological change leads to a fall in materials inputs per unit of output $\dot{\Delta} \leq 0$, and the right-hand side of (3.4a) is always positive whilst that of (3.4) is always negative. In this case, falling prices will only be identified with rates of value-added growth less than rates of productivity growth, if the price fall is strong enough.

Notes

1. If $\omega_\varepsilon = \omega_\delta$ then (4) becomes

$$\frac{\omega_\varepsilon}{P_\delta} = \frac{1}{1+\beta_\delta} \cdot \frac{1}{\left[\alpha_\delta + \frac{\Delta_\delta}{\omega_\delta}\right]}$$

and, plainly, the real wage will increase with a rise in the money wage; the rate of increase will depend on the magnitude of unit materials costs, Δ.

2. The productivity measure in Figures 2–4 and Table 1 is value-added per worker, which is a different concept from the measure of physical output per worker used in the analytical discussion above. Using the notation of (2) above, it is straightforwardly possible to show that the proportionate rate of growth of value-added per worker will be less than or equal to the rate of growth of labor productivity according to:

$$\frac{\dot{\beta}_\varepsilon}{1+\beta_\varepsilon} + A \cdot \left[\frac{\dot{\alpha}_e}{\alpha_\varepsilon} + \frac{\dot{\omega}_e}{\omega_\varepsilon}\right] \leq (1-D) \cdot \frac{\dot{\Delta}_e}{\Delta_\varepsilon}$$

So if there are no materials' savings due to technological change and if the producer's markup does not change, the rate of growth of labor productivity and rate of growth of value-added will be equal in the case where wage's share does not change, i.e. where

$$\frac{\dot{\alpha}_\varepsilon}{\alpha_\varepsilon} = \frac{\dot{\omega}_e}{\omega_\varepsilon}.$$

Evidently more complicated outcomes are possible, but, since factor shares are more or less stable in the cases considered below, the approximation involved in using value-added per worker to measure labor productivity does not produce any significant distortions.

3. With the possible exception of the Kennedy–von Weiszaker–Samuelson analysis of the "innovation possibility frontier."
4. Evidently, the socioeconomic impacts of technological change depend not only on the behavior of the real wage, but also on the effect on employment. This broader problem is not discussed further here.
5. It is worth noting that the financial collapse of enterprises for this reason, i.e. for the reason that economically arbitrary outcomes (like the failure to replace obsolescent capital stock) of central planning result in bankruptcies when the economy is opened to the external market, may have very little to do with real comparative advantages. Eastern European economists, concerned with the problems of transition, frequently remark on the fact that enterprises will be bankrupted even in lines of production where, on grounds of endowments, one might expect a comparative advantage. Even in these sectors, enterprise efficiency is sub-optimal, because of the legacy of the past.
6. Formally, one should include the inequalities running in either condition. However, it is only the "less than" case that is of real interest.

10

Science and Technology in Central and Eastern Europe

*Vladislav Kotchetkov**

1. Recent Changes in National Science and Technology Policies in the Advanced Countries

The climacteric changes in the political and economic spheres which countries of Central and Eastern Europe have been experiencing during the past several years gave rise to hopes of radical and rapid improvements in the well-being of the peoples in those countries. They also provoked enthusiastic comments in the media, along the following lines: strong winds of change and freedom are sweeping across the old continent with each nation prepared to work hard throughout the remaining decade of this century before taking that great leap into the third millennium!

Let us ignore this journalistic exaltation and analyze only the impact that those political and economic changes are having on science and technology in Central and Eastern Europe. Generally speaking, the time for those changes has not been optimal and, thus, has been less than favorable to the latter (if only there existed a favorable time for revolutions however "tender" they may be).

The growing competition in international technology markets has led to profound changes in the national science and technology policies of the industrially advanced countries. In fact, these S&T policies were altered by innovation policies. According to J. J. Salomon, this was the most important change in traditional science and technology policy which occurred during

---

*Dr. Vladislav Kotchetkov is the Chief of the Science Section in UNESCO. The opinions expressed by him here are not necessarily those of UNESCO and do not commit the Organization in any manner.

the past two decades. This, in its turn, provoked profound changes in the criteria and instruments involved in such policy. While the "classical" S&T policy was mainly concerned with issues related to scientific training, higher education and R&D, modern innovation policies deal with a much wider range of issues and subjects, being concerned with everything from industry through the banking system, and extending to such additional domains as vocational training, S&T literacy and managerial and entrepreneurial awareness. (Salomon, 1991)

The upsurge of new technologies (electronics, computers, composite materials, biotechnologies) has only speeded up the emergence of a new technological system or "techno-economic paradigm" which requires an increasing coherence among its multiple elements. Having been forced by economic competition, the advanced countries adjusted or deeply transformed their science and technology policies. In these circumstances the countries of Central and Eastern Europe face an extraordinarily difficult task: to reshape their obsolete and out-dated S&T systems. To make such sweeping changes will require a solid strategy based on a profound analysis of the existing situation in the R&D field since, as is recognized, R&D efforts constitute the strategic prerequisite for long-term economic growth.

2. Science and Technology in Eastern and Central Europe

Despite the common reappraisal of values in the newly established democracies of Central and Eastern Europe and criticism of the totalitarian period of their prior development we should not overlook that, for various reasons (such as national prestige, ideological competition, military confrontation), a considerable stream of resources, both financial and human, were deployed by these states in their science and systems of higher education. (See Table 1) This created an impressive S&T potential. In the late seventies and the early

Table 1 Number of R&D Personnel in Eastern Europe (1989)

Country	Scientists and engineers	Technicians
Bulgaria	50,585*	11,662*
Czechoslovakia	65,475	42,876
Hungary	20,431	14,113
Poland	32,500	54,000**
Romania	59,670	42,931
Yugoslavia	34,770	18,780
USSR	1,694,400	–

Source: "R&D Resources in the Former USSR (FSU) and Central and Eastern European Countries." UNESCO Statistical Paper prepared for the International Conference on Effective Use of Global Technical Resources, Stresa, 22–25 June 1992.
 *1987
**1985

Table 2 Number of Specialists Engaged in R&D in the USSR and USA (thousands of people)

Year	1981	1986	1989
USSR	1,434.2	1,599.4	1,654.4
USA	1,258.7	1,725.5	2,026.9

Source: "R&D in the USSR." Data Book, 1990.

Table 3 R&D Expenditures of Eastern European Countries (millions of US$)

Year	1980	1985	1989
Bulgaria	479.7	716.4	–
Czechoslovakia	1,460.5	1,633.1	1,468.4
Hungary	560.0	414.6	497.9
Poland	845.7	569.7	852.5
Romania	–	–	1,238.2
USSR	21,300*	28,600*	32,000*

Source: "Study on the Human and Financial Resources for R&D Activities in the East European Countries," UNESCO Working Paper (unpublished).
*Millions of USSR roubles

eighties, the former socialist countries of Europe employed well over half of the world population of scientists and engineers engaged in R&D.

If, however, one analyzes the comparative data in dynamics, it will be found that, for example, the superiority of the USSR over USA in absolute numbers of specialists engaged in R&D that existed at the end of 1980 was replaced by parity by the mid-80s. Furthermore, in 1989 the rate of increase in the number of those specialists was by 1.2 times higher in the USA than in the USSR. (See Table 2)

The situation with R&D personnel was even worse in other Central and Eastern European countries. In Poland, for example, employment in the R&D sector diminished by 33 percent in the period from 1975 to 1985. The absolute number of scientists and engineers engaged in R&D was also shrinking in Hungary during the period 1984–1989. In one recent year alone, 12 percent of all Hungarian scientists and specialists went abroad to work. From 20,000 members of the old East German Academy of Sciences, only 10,000 will be integrated in the future research system that is now being constructed. (*Scientist*, August 9, 1991, p. 619)

Table 3 shows R&D expenditures in those countries.

The comparative analysis of expenditures shows that the share of R&D spending in the state budget of the USSR was in the 3.4–4.5 percent range during 1970–1989 while in the USA this figure was around 7.9 percent of the total federal budget and it was planned to increase this share to 8.6 percent in 1991.

Table 4 Number of Nobel Prizes Awarded to Soviet Scientists

Time period	Number of Nobel prizes	Percentage of total Nobel prizes
1946–1960	4	11
1961–1975	3	7
1976–1985	1	2.5

Source: Pry & Vasko (1990).

In several countries of Central and Eastern Europe the cost of military-oriented R&D makes up a considerable part of the total science expenditures. The exact figures for military R&D in Czechoslovakia or Poland are not available but the Soviet data are now available. In 1989 15.3 billion roubles were spent for these purposes in the USSR, while in the USA $37.5 billion, or 71 percent and 62 percent, respectively, of the state allocations for science. (*Scientist*, August 9, 1991) Correspondingly, civil R&D expenditures were insufficient. Until recently, the USSR has been spending four to five times less than the Americans on civilian R&D.

Aside from the funding problem there is the matter of research equipment The latest survey carried out in the USSR demonstrated that the majority of Soviet research institutions accumulated a large amount of physically and conceptually obsolete equipment; 20.8 percent of this equipment is more than 10 years old, including one fourth of it which is older than 20 years. According to the same survey, the overall demand for scientific instruments in the USSR was satisfied in only 20–25 percent of cases. (Workshop, 1991)

The combination of these above-mentioned and other factors has led to the steady decline in the efficiency of scientific work in Central and Eastern European countries. This can be illustrated by the number of Nobel Prizes awarded to Soviet scientists from 1946 to 1985 and their percentage of the total number of Nobel Prizes. (See Table 4)

3. Characteristics of the S&T Systems in Eastern and Central Europe

In order to facilitate such analysis, we will identify common features of Central and Eastern European science and technology systems which exerted adverse effects on the development of science and technology in those countries and did not allow them, after all, to keep their proper place among the most advanced nations.

While proposing such generalizations, we also recognize that big differences existed among the various countries of Central and Eastern Europe with respect to their levels of scientific and technological development.

The first and foremost common characteristic was serious democratic deficits, excessive involvement of the state in all aspects of scientific life, and strong politicization of science, which extended to the displacement of science by ideology. The "prestige" considerations for science and technology projects were often more important than the requirements of the economy. To generalize, science in these countries was separated from the economy and society.

Another important feature that stemmed from the centrally planned type of economic activity and the rigid administrative and financial control was the organization of R&D. The R&D system of the Eastern and Central European countries was directly determined by the existing economic system. It reflected the organization of the economy in strictly sectoral terms and exhibited the "branchdom" syndrome. As a socio-economic phenomenon the "branchdom" syndrome means the stratification of the economy into rather isolated sectors operating in a monopoly mode and being managed and controlled by the highest party/government authorities. This sectoral approach prevailed also in R&D organizational structures throughout the region.

Basic research in Central and Eastern Europe was a responsibility of the Academies of Sciences created after the Soviet model. Each academy was organized as a kind of Ministry of Science, ruled over by the Presidium and reporting to a plenary meeting of academicians. The organizational principles, decision-making process, financing and resource allocation procedures were similar to those used in industrial ministries. However, an important difference compared with industry was that the same people (academicians) who occupied the posts in the major governing body (Presidium) were often at the same time the directors of research institutions. Therefore, the whole power (financial, organizational and executive) of the science establishment was concentrated in the hands of a relatively small group of academicians. This led to a situation in which science, being a specific sphere of social activity, turned increasingly into a closed system of its own – with all the attendant negative consequences that flow from monopolistic structures: promotion of group interests, stagnation of personal talent and poor management. This situation was typical of the Soviet Academy of Sciences and of the Academies in the various republics, but I believe that similar patterns were discernible, as well, in the academic societies in the countries of Eastern and Central Europe. (Workshop, 1991)

Applied or technological research was performed by the sectoral research institutions, which usually were under ministerial control. These institutions were well-staffed (500–1,000 employees in the Eastern and Central European countries and 2,000–4,000 in the USSR). The major part of their finances came from the state budget through corresponding ministries. Having a monopoly in each of their sectors of the economy, these institutions were interested neither in gaining a larger market share where they were the only suppliers nor in profit maximization. In order to maintain the technological level of their products, in particular in the field of military-related industries, these R&D establishments however, received funds, human resources and modern equipment at the expense of civil or non-prestigious industries. This led to a deep polarization between the prestigious and non-prestigious sciences – another common feature of Eastern and Central European science.

Another important feature of the R&D systems in the former socialist countries was the existence of strong inter-sectoral and inter-organizational barriers. Basic and applied sciences were separated from each other by the organizational autarky of the ministries and the Academies of Science. The coordinating role of the central bodies – State Committees for S&T which worked under the control of the Central Committees of the ruling parties – was strong on paper but rather weak and poor in reality. The organizational barriers between industries, universities and the academies and the artificially high level of restrictions and secrecy in their work split the scientific community into different groups. The economic mechanism of the diffusion of innovations did not achieve good results under these conditions. The introduction of innovations, the distribution of financial and human resources, and the availability of equipment were all determined by priorities set by the central authorities.

The only exclusion from this inept process was military-oriented R&D and related industries, the so-called military–industrial complex (MIC). This military productive sector of the USSR concentrated the most talented scientists, the best equipment, and the most skilled engineers and qualified workers, and received about three-quarters of total state budget's allocations for R&D in 1980. The Soviet MIC had its own educational institutions which maintained a considerably higher level than the average university institutions, had its own communication and construction systems, and many other advantages. Various economic and non-economic measures were relied upon to provide stable reproduction of skilled personnel: competition, higher wages, direct allocation of social benefits. Contrary to the practice in civilian industries, those ministries and enterprises belonging to the MIC were interested in innovations. There existed competition inside the MIC between various firms to get government orders for R&D.

The next distinguishing feature of the science and technology system in the former socialist countries was the overwhelming centralization of all types of financing. The state budget was the major source of financing for all types of R&D institutions. The contract system of financing played an insignificant role.

The structure of scientific personnel in the majority of Central and Eastern European countries did not satisfy the requirements of technological change. Contrary to the world-wide trends, the share of specialists in mathematics, computer sciences and physics decreased during 1976–1986 in the USSR. In the USA during the same period the number of scientists in the fields of mathematics and computer sciences increased 2.7 and 4.7 times, respectively. The age structure of the R&D staff was also worsening in the USSR, as R&D personnel was getting older. The proportion of persons of less than 40 years of age among the US PhD.s in 1985 was higher than among the Soviet scientists. This disparity was a result of 4.1 percent decrease in the number of postgraduate students in the USSR during the period 1970–88, while in the USA this number increased by 16.9 percent between 1980 and 1988. (Workshop 1991)

The most important gap of all was in the field of information services. According to some estimates there existed more than 3,000 public data- and knowledge-bases in the USA, while in the former USSR one can identify hardly more than about ten of such data-bases.

The library of Harvard University is known to receive 106,000 periodicals, while the best Soviet library on natural sciences which served up to 250 research academic institutions received only 4,000 periodicals in 1990. (Workshop, 1991) A similar situation continued in all Eastern and Central European countries, and it has deteriorated since that time.

All of the above-mentioned characteristics explain, to some extent, why the mechanisms designed to promote technological change in the centrally planned economies did not work. The technological changes that did occur were mainly of an imitative character. The innovations introduced in industries, including even those in the MIC, generally attempted to replicate those produced by the so-called "potential enemy," but substantially lagging behind the "enemy," though there were some exceptions.

4. Reforms and Recent Changes

Attempts to overcome this legacy of centralized R&D and the privileged status of the MIC were made by all Central and Eastern European countries even before the collapse of socialism. In Hungary, for example, the economic reforms of 1968 supposedly abolished the institutional influence of central planning and market mechanisms were introduced in the economy. As a result new conditions were created for R&D institutions. The national Science Policy of 1969 stated that scientific activity should serve the economy by contributing to its efficiency. New financing mechanisms were introduced. The amount of central subsidies for research institutes was frozen at the existing level and a system of contracts with foreign companies was introduced.

However, the reforms failed to evolve as originally expected. The enterprises and firms operating in the "shortage economy" were not interested in gaining a better foothold in the market, since everything produced could be sold since demand could never be satisfied. The sellers did not have to fight for buyers by improving the quality of products, by reducing prices and by introducing new products. According to studies, the proportion of new products in the state-owned sector during 1981–86 was very low, approximately only 1.5 percent yearly, with some 90 percent of all products unchanged over the course of many years. It would take about 67 years to achieve complete replacement of products, while the same cycle in the electronic industry of OECD countries was 6–10 years if calculated on the data for the same period. (Balash, 1991) Even two decades after the economic reform, Hungarian R&D institutions and enterprises were not yet operating in a genuinely competitive environment. These conditions are aggravated by frequent changes in the system of economic regulations and by problems arising from a budget deficit and a shortage of hard currency.

Similar reform attempts were made by other countries of Eastern and Central Europe, but they have unfortunately failed. The recent political changes in these countries have paved the way for a radical dismantling of the overcentralized system of economies, as well as for corresponding changes in R&D management systems.

Poland, for example, has made a radical and rapid move towards establishing a market economy since January 1990. Short- and long-term economic programs aimed at stabilizing and transforming the Polish economic system have been adopted. Important changes were also introduced in the R&D sector, such as the following ones: abolition of fiscal incentives for R&D, abolition of the central R&D Fund, introduction of a direct system of financing from the state budget under the authority of a Scientific Research Committee, reduction of the share of state funds in financing R&D, liquidation of big national R&D programs, while retaining several strategic governmental programs and a number of small research projects. Competition and a peer-review system for project selection were also introduced. (Jasinski, 1991)

In Bulgaria, where the financing of R&D from the state budget was scaled down by 50 percent in real terms in 1990, the Governmental Decree of March 1991 has introduced strict policy measures. These include: reduction of the research staff by 10 percent, introduction of self-financing for research units, and structural and thematic changes in R&D programs. As a result, the Bulgarian Academy of Sciences cut its staff by 1,300 researchers and closed two laboratories. (Simeonova, 1991)

The management mechanisms of Romanian science have also been reorganized since 1990. The former National Council for Science and Technology was abolished and the future of the Romanian Academy of Sciences has been debated. A Consultative Board for R&D was created for deciding major issues of S&T policy, including the allocation of funds. The Special Fund for R&D created by levying a tax of 1 percent on the profits of state economic units is far below the maintenance cost of the existing research units. Some of these units are on the verge of being dissolved. (ICSPS–UNESCO–Institute of Theory and History of Science, 1990)

The long-standing Yugoslav self-management experiment has also failed. In 1986 the Federal Assembly of Yugoslavia accepted a resolution on the strategy for technological development. It called for at least 2.5 percent of GNP to be earmarked for R&D by the year 2000. By 1990 the target was to reach 1.5 percent of GNP.

The system of self-managed communities responsible for science and technology has been replaced by ministries of science. Statistics indicate that, while in the late 60s Yugoslavia was, in terms of economic development, in the same group as Austria, Hungary and Spain, it is now at the bottom of the list of European countries. (ICSPS–UNESCO–Institute of Theory and History of Science, 1990)

"Perestroika" in the USSR began from an attempt to overcome the steadily increasing technological gap. According to some assessments, the technological gap in major industries between the USSR and developed countries increased from 10–15 years in the mid-50s to 20–30 years in the mid-80s. It certainly has been increasing in the high-technology sector. This was true despite the fact that the number of research institutions increased in the USSR by more than a thousand (from 4,196 to 5,307) over the period between 1960 and 1972. (Workshop, 1991)

Since 1987, radical steps have been initiated towards the transformation of the science management system. The central control over R&D institutions was considerably relaxed. Scientists and engineers have been given the right to set up research groups and to form their own associations, unions and R&D cooperatives. A series of legislative acts providing the legal foundation for entrepreneurship in the USSR have been adopted. This generated new sectors in R&D, the cooperative and private ones, which had not existed before. By October 1, 1990, 12,200 science-technological cooperatives were established with 284,100 employees. In addition, there were 750 centers of R&D activity for youth and 1,274 joint ventures of Soviet and foreign partner-firms. Thus, the total number of small innovation firms in the entrepreneurial sector of the USSR was around 13,000 by the end of 1990. Their sales amounted to 0.4 percent of GNP (about 4 billion rubles) in 1990. (Demchenko, 1991)

While this semi-private sector of R&D flourished, the academic and industrial sectors of R&D were experiencing a very hard time. The collapse of the state budget in combination with some badly grounded legislative measures produced a heavy blow to the R&D sector. In the first quarter of 1991 the state budget revenues were 70 percent smaller than foreseen.

In a system with highly centralized financing of R&D, as the Soviet system was, the above-mentioned budget deficit could not but result in a sharp decrease in R&D financing. Military R&D was the major victim since the cutbacks in military expenditure were effected mainly at the expense of R&D in this sector. In fact, expenditures on R&D in the MIC decreased by 33 percent in real terms in the period from 1989 to 1990. In 1991 many research institutions in the MIC did not have enough money to pay the wages of their research staff at a sufficient level. (Workshop, 1991) To prevent mass bankruptcy of industrial research institutions, the central government decided to provide each industry with special non-budget funds for R&D financing.

Unemployment in the field of science became a reality in the Central and Eastern European countries. In the former GDR every second scientist risks losing his or her job. The "brain-drain" process is gaining strength in all Eastern and Central European countries, while the influx of young researchers into this field has been considerably reduced.

Generally speaking, Eastern and Central European science is a unique cultural system with its inherent mode of thinking and specific approaches to the solution of scientific problems. This system was shaped as a product of a centrally planned economy combined with a specific ideology. Both are now in ruins and calls for the safeguarding of this cultural system are coming from the intellectuals of these countries. The role of the international scientific community in this cultural rescue should not be underestimated. (Kotchetkov, 1991)

5. International Assistance to Transform the S&T Systems

What could the international scientific community and its international organizations do to assist the Central and Eastern European countries in transforming their science and technology systems with the least possible losses in terms of human resources, time, and money? I would propose the following directions of effort for the purposes of reform:

(1) R&D in Central and Eastern Europe is in deep crisis. World experience shows that the only way out of the crisis is through a mastering of the innovation stream. However, the sharp decrease in resources available for innovations will not permit these countries to obtain a quick remedy for the situation. Currently an anti-innovation economic and social climate is dominant. Time is needed to introduce economically sound management in the R&D system. This should be done on the basis of studying the most important factors which influence the development of modern scientific and technological systems, the interplay of those factors, and especially the role of the state versus the market. The subject of such theoretical understanding should be the farreaching changes in the nature of science and technology policy. Encouraging the shift of science policy towards innovation policy is the most important change that should be studied by scientists and policy-makers of the Central and Eastern European countries. New methods and instruments are available to encourage such a shift, including social assessments of science and technology; public adjustment of clashes of interest among the producers and users of innovations and political reconciliation of the distinct interests of scientists, engineers, businessmen and the general public should be promoted and realized. In other words, science and technology should restore the broken links that held the economy and society together.

It is no secret that, owing to imposed unjustified restrictions and short-sighted governmental attitudes, scientists of the Central and Eastern European countries were not able to participate in the intellectual debates on the above-mentioned subjects related to changes in contemporary science and technology policies. Correspondingly, national science and technology policies were often based on ideological postulates rather than sound theoretical analysis.

In order to assist those countries in improving their national science and technology policies, UNESCO, in cooperation with a well-known NGO, the International Council of Science Policy Studies, has recently started a project on "Transformation of Science Management Systems of Eastern and Central European Countries during Their Transition to Market-Oriented Economies." The scientists participating in the project will analyze the major problems and formulate concrete recommendations addressed to the policy-makers of those countries.

The International Institute of Applied Systems Analysis (IIASA) has recently launched a project on "R&D Management in the USSR in Transition to Market Economy." The UNESCO Regional Office for Science and Technology for Europe (ROSTE) has initiated a project on the "brain drain" in Europe.

(2) The transformation of the existing systems depends on initiatives by people. The most important explanation for failure is the lack of professionals duly prepared to perform this task. The ignorance of scientists and engineers in business and management areas is the major obstacle in the way of developing the entrepreneurial spirit in the R&D sector.

Long domination of the authoritarian command-administrative system led to the formation of specific economic cultures (I would rather say "economic anti-cultures") in Central and Eastern European countries.

The task of developing a genuine and dynamic economic culture, by means of training, exchange of specialists, organizing courses in marketing and staff management, and organizing visits of Eastern and Central European specialists to study and to have experience in foreign firms, companies, banks and business schools, is a task of primary urgency. Personnel training has to become an inseparable element of each technological project and program to be carried out in Central and Eastern Europe with the assistance of the Western countries or international organizations.

The Commission of the European Communities, in close cooperation with UNESCO, might play an organizing role in such massive training of specialists from Central and Eastern Europe.

(3) Higher education in many Eastern and Central European countries needs to be substantially reorganized. The development of close ties between universities and industries is a pronounced trend in the new technology systems of industrialized countries. University departments not only carry out research activities in basic sciences but are also undertaking research for firms on a much larger scale. Many new firms have been proliferating in high-tech sectors and these firms are often set up by researchers working at universities. A recent survey in France, for example, listed 145 firms, launched mainly in 1984–87, which had been developed directly out of the activities of university laboratories. (ICSPS–UNESCO–Institute of Theory and History of Science, 1990) UNESCO and other intergovernmental organizations should encourage drastic reorganization in the higher education sector along these lines.

(4) The ongoing international efforts to convert the military–industrial complex to much needed civilian purposes require attention on the part

of policy-makers. We expect increasing pressure from politicians, scientific communities and the public at large for non-military industries. A rational conversion of the military sector should also be regarded as an efficient way of making sure that existing scientific and technological potential is not being lost.

This potential should be better used for the foundation of science and technology intensive R&D in non-military sectors of the economy. The priorities that were accorded the military industrial complex during the period of the Cold War create special opportunities to concentrate big resources to facilitate technological breakthroughs in civil areas. Joint efforts to achieve conversion could serve as an important focus for pan-European cooperation. In 1995, 45.8 percent of the R&D resources of the military complex of the former USSR are supposed to be redirected toward the implementation of civil-oriented R&D (against 29.6 percent in 1989). This shift should create promising opportunities for international multilateral and bilateral cooperation.

(5) The problem of the "brain drain" requires special attention on the part of the international community. A better utilization of scientific resources through the government support systems of international cooperation, as distinct from individual emigration and employment, is one of the possible contributions to the solution of the "brain-drain" problem in Europe.

Concluding my paper, I wish to emphasize the following:

The policy-makers in the Central and Eastern European countries should rely neither on the market nor on foreign investors to shape policy as to which of their industries will prosper and which will fail. After the euphoria about political and economic emancipation is over, a long-term strategy of scientific and technological development of these countries as a basis for transition from centrally planned to market-driven economic systems needs to be adopted. (Katz, 1991) The formulation of this strategy requires combining national efforts with experience and assistance from the outside world.

REFERENCES

Balash, K. (1991), "Lessons from an Economy with Limited Market Functions." A paper for the UNESCO–ICSPS workshop. Budapest, 24–27 June.

Demchenko, D. (1991), "Small Innovation Enterprises in the USSR." A paper for the UNESCO–ICSPS workshop. Budapest, 24–27 June.

ICSPS–UNESCO–Institute of Theory and History of Science (1990), "Science and Social Priorities – Perspectives of Science Policy for the 1990s." Proceedings of the conference. Prague, 5–7 June.

Jasinski, A. (1991), "Recent Changes in the Polish R&D System during the Transition to a Market Economy." A paper for the UNESCO–ICSPS workshop. Budapest, 24–27 June.

Katz, S. (1991), "East Europe Should Learn from Asia." *Financial Times*, April 24.

Kotchetkov, V. (1991), "The Tasks of Science in the Development towards a Peaceful World." A paper for the National Peace Congress. Münster, Germany, 1–3 February.

Pry, R. & Vasko, T. (1990), "Societal Status of Scientists and Engineers in Eastern Europe: Historical Background." A paper for the Second International Symposium of the Engineering Academy of Japan. Kobe, 29–30 September.

Salomon, J. J. (1991), "Changing Perspectives of Science Policy Insight into Innovation Process." *Journal of Scientific and Industrial Research*. Vol. 50, New Delhi, February, pp. 90–101.

Simeonova, K. (1991), "Changing Science Policy in Bulgaria." A paper for the UNESCO–ICSPS workshop. Budapest, 24–27 June.

Workshop (1991), "Research and Development Management in Transition to Market Economies." Proceedings of the Workshop. Moscow, 13–16 July.

11

Democratization of Eastern and Central Europe and the Relations between North and South

*Lal Jayawardena**

1. The Transition to a Market Economy

This paper is concerned essentially with the impact of the ongoing economic reforms in Eastern and Central Europe and the Soviet Union on the position and prospects for development of Third World countries. The process of political democratization is an essential precondition for successful economic reform since the transition from a command economy to a market-oriented system must have wider popular support, in view of the accompanying hardships involved. Here, it is assumed that democratization is sufficiently developed to give adequate support to the necessary economic reforms.

While all the countries of Eastern and Central Europe have now committed themselves to some type of market-oriented economic reform, they vary greatly in the rate at which they are moving towards a market economy, as well as in the sequence and timing of the policies adopted to achieve this objective. These differences are particularly evident in a comparison of developments in the former German Democratic Republic, Poland and Yugoslavia – which have been subject to the "shock treatment" of sudden and comprehensive liberalization of both domestic and foreign trade – and in Czechoslovakia and Hungary, where the reform process has been spread over a period of years. The former Soviet Union, as well as Bulgaria and Romania, are in a separate category since, though the "command system" has broken down, effective market-oriented institutions are not yet in place.

*Dr. Lal Jayawardena is Economic Adviser to H.E. The President of Sri Lanka and Deputy Chairman, National Development Council.

Table 1 Output and Investment in Central and Eastern Europe and the Soviet Union: 1981–91

	Annual growth rates (%)				
	1981–85 (average)	1986–88 (average)	1989	1990	1991[a] (1st qtr.)
Eastern and Central Europe					
Industrial output	2.7	3.3	0.2	−17.5	−13.0
Agricultural output	1.1	0.3	.	−3.5	.
Gross investment	−0.7	3.4	−1.5	−13.3	.
Soviet Union					
Industrial output	3.6	4.0	1.9	−1.2	−5.0
Agricultural output	1.1	2.1	0.8	−2.3	.
Gross investment	3.5	6.7	4.7	−4.3	−16.0

Sources: UN Economic Commission for Europe (1991b), Table 2.2, and (1991c), Table 3.
a. Compared with first quarter 1990.

The pace of reform, and the length of the transition to a reasonably efficient market system, must therefore be expected to vary considerably among the former CMEA countries. Moreover, it seems certain that the transition will take a substantially longer time and that the dislocations suffered will be substantially greater than had generally been anticipated even two years ago. In 1990 the economic situation worsened sharply in all the Eastern and Central European countries, with particularly large declines in industrial output – by 20 percent or more, compared with 1989 – in the former GDR, Poland and Romania. For Eastern and Central Europe as a whole, excluding the Soviet Union, the contraction in industrial output in 1990 is estimated at 17.5 percent, while a further sharp decline was recorded for the first quarter of 1991 (Table 1). In the former Soviet Union industrial production fell by 5 percent in the first quarter of 1991, with widespread shortages being reported at the consumer level.

The economic dislocation also affected the agricultural sector, while gross investment in both Eastern and Central Europe and the Soviet Union was cut back substantially. Much of the difficulties in Eastern and Central Europe arose from the collapse of the CMEA trading system and, more particularly, from the sharp contraction in Soviet demand for their exports, while their terms of trade substantially deteriorated. In the Soviet Union, major factors at work were the disintegration of the former federal structure, and the breakdown of the old "command system" while a new market-oriented institutional framework was not yet in place, accompanied by sharp falls in output and exports of energy and raw materials, and consequently in export revenue, resulting in large cuts in essential imports.

The magnitude of the economic dislocation in the former Soviet Union is extremely large while, as mentioned, progress in establishing a new market-oriented framework has so far been slow and largely ineffective. Even though the economic reform process is expected to gain momentum, following the failure of the August 1991 coup attempt the transitional period seems certain to be prolonged – at least to the latter part of the 1990s. Though some of the transitional economies of Eastern and Central Europe may well become fully integrated into the international economic system before then, it would seem prudent to assume that the early and middle years of the 1990s will be, to a large extent, ones of transitional difficulties in the former CMEA area, accompanied by significant unemployment, restricted levels of imports and slow growth – if any – in output of goods and services.

Once the transitional period is over, and the former CMEA countries are fully integrated with the international economy, perhaps towards the end of the 1990s, these countries should be able once again to achieve sustained domestic growth and expanding foreign trade, including trade with developing countries. However, the relatively gloomy outlook for the short and medium term is likely to have adverse repercussions on the export earnings and inflows of financial resources of Third World countries.

2. Trade Effects on Developing Countries

The impact of the economic reform process in Eastern and Central Europe on the exports of developing countries will be both direct, as regards Eastern and Central European countries as markets, and indirect, as regards consequential changes in Western markets.

Western markets are by far the most important outlets for developing country exports,[1] so that the indirect effects of economic reforms in Eastern and Central Europe may well outweigh the direct effects in Eastern and Central Europe itself. There are several indirect mechanisms which could affect the outcome. First, the extension of trade preferences, or the lifting of discriminatory import restrictions, by Western countries on their imports from Eastern Europe would involve an erosion of the preferential trade margins currently enjoyed by developing countries under the UNCTAD Generalized System of Preferences (GSP), and under the current Lomé Convention between the European Community and the associated African, Caribbean and Pacific (ACP) countries.

With the recognition by the European Community of the political independence of the three former Soviet Baltic states, consideration is now likely to be given to the negotiation of Association Agreements of these states with the Community. Agreements of this type between the Community and North African countries, for example, provide for preferential entry of goods from these countries into the Community market. Similarly, trade preferences are likely to be negotiated for the Baltic states, and probably for other Eastern and Central European countries also. In any case, Western countries have already considerably relaxed their discriminatory quantitative restrictions against imports from some Central and Eastern

European countries, though it must be noted that import quotas for these countries were not always fully taken up because of supply difficulties.

With closer trading links between Central and Eastern Europe and Western countries, Eastern exports of a range of foods and of labor-intensive manufactures – the two areas in which these countries have some comparative advantage – can be expected to expand, and to displace, at least to some degree, competitive exports, from developing countries. Moreover, these two product groups are also those in which the Southern European countries – Portugal, Spain and (southern) Italy – have major export interests, particularly in the Community market, and political pressure from these countries may well be exerted to limit their own loss of market share, consequent upon a reduction in barriers to imports from Eastern Europe, by seeking some offset in the form of a reduction in competitive imports from developing countries. In any event, it seems likely that some significant trade diversion in these two product groups will occur at the expense of developing country suppliers.

The process of trade diversion appears already to have begun in 1990, when those Central and Eastern European countries most advanced in the transition to market economies – Poland, Hungary and, to a lesser extent, Czechoslovakia – achieved a substantial expansion in exports to Western markets, in total a rise of over 25 percent compared with 1989, a major part of the increase being in food and manufactured consumer goods. (UN Economic Commission for Europe, 1991b, Table 3.3.6, and Appendix Table C.9) This contrasts sharply with the large contraction in 1990 in trade among the former CMEA countries, and the decline in exports to developing countries. (See Table 2) The impact of European trade diversion – which is likely to be accentuated by the inauguration of the Single Market at the end of 1992 – will, however, be attenuated to the extent that the degree of protection enjoyed by domestic producers in Europe is reduced as a result of the Uruguay Round negotiations. During the 1960s and 1970s the trade diversion effects arising from the continuing process of integration among the economies of Western Europe were to some extent offset by successive rounds of trade liberalization (though there were many exceptions as regards commodity exports from developing countries). Developing country exports, particularly of agricultural products and of labor-intensive manufactures, would seem essential to prevent a major loss of market share by developing countries during the 1990s.

Second, it seems unlikely that the Eastern and Central European transition will adversely affect the exports of capital- or skill-intensive manufactures from the Newly Industrializing Countries (NICs) of East Asia to Western markets. The NICs are now extremely competitive in world markets for a wide range of "high-tech" manufactures, such as electronic apparatus, computers, automobiles, etc., in which Eastern and Central European industry is notoriously backward. Even in labor-intensive manufactures, the market shares of the NICs are unlikely to be seriously threatened.

Third, a small number of developing countries have for many years been

Table 2 Foreign Trade of Eastern and Central Europe and the Soviet Union: 1988 to First Quarter of 1991

Annual change (%)

	Eastern and Central Europe				Soviet Union			
	1988	1989	1990	1991ᵃ (1st qtr.)	1988	1989	1990	1991ᵃ (1st qtr.)
Exports to:								
Former CMEA[b]	5.0	−1.4	−5.9	−25.5	−3.0	−1.5	−16.8	−13.2
Developed market economies[c]	10.7	6.5	11.6	14.8	7.8	7.8	12.3	−8.0
Developing countries[c]	1.8	−12.5	−14.3	−6.7	2.2	2.0	−9.5	−40.8
Total[c]	7.5	−3.5	−9.2	−10.7	2.7	−1.3	−4.8	−15.3
(volume)	(3.7)	(−2.1)	(−10.0)	—	(4.8)	—	(−12.9)	—
Imports from:								
Former CMEA[b]	−1.4	−2.3	−8.7	27.4	3.0	3.0	−1.7	−36.4
Developed market economies[c]	10.9	4.8	24.2	17.2	22.6	21.1	5.6	−47.7
Developing countries[c]	0.5	5.5	—	1.0	17.4	26.0	3.8	−47.2
Total[c]	3.0	−2.7	−1.7	0.4	11.6	6.9	5.6	−44.7
(volume)	(3.3)	(0.9)	(−0.5)	—	(4.0)	(9.3)	(−1.8)	—

Sources: UN Economic Commission for Europe (1991b), Tables 2.2.1 and (1991c), Tables 3 and 7.
Note: The 1991 figures are subject to serious statistical collection and definitional problems and must be treated with caution (see UN Economic Commission for Europe 1991c, pp. 9–10).
a. Compared with first quarter 1990. For both periods, the figures exclude the former German Democratic Republic from "Eastern Europe" and "Former CMEA".
b. In terms of transferable roubles.
c. In terms of US dollars.

heavily dependent on the Eastern and Central European markets for the bulk of their export earnings. Under various bilateral trade and cooperation agreements, some developing countries enjoyed stable prices for their exports well above world market levels (Cuba's sugar exports to the Soviet Union being the most important example). These countries now face severe financial difficulties as a result of the foreign trade crisis of the Eastern and Central European countries reflecting, *inter alia*, the change to trading at world prices as from the beginning of 1991, and the severe dislocations in the former Soviet economy.

Apart, however, from the relatively few developing countries which were CMEA members, the NICs, the majority of developing countries, stand to suffer loss of market share as a result of the economic integration of Eastern and Central Europe with Western markets. Market share loss could be attenuated, possibly to a substantial extent, by a large reduction – or phasing out – of import barriers of Western countries which obstruct exports from developing countries. Equally, a significant rise in the GDP growth rate in Western markets, particularly in the European Community, would offset, to a greater of lesser extent, a loss of market share by developing countries. But, at the present time, neither of these offsets would seem highly likely to occur.

In addition to the indirect effects of trade diversion, there are likely to be adverse terms of trade effects also, especially for the minerals and metals exported by developing countries. The former Soviet Union was itself the world's leading producer of many important minerals (iron ore, lead, nickel, manganese and potash), while changes in its exports of many others (copper, zinc, gold, diamonds and platinum group metals) can influence the world market substantially. During recent years, the combination of an acute shortage of convertible currency and falling industrial production has provided a powerful incentive for increasing Soviet exports of these minerals and metals to Western markets.

Soviet nickel exports to Western markets accounted for about 15 percent of Western supply. Central and Eastern Europe together with the Soviet Union, supplied between 1 and 3 percent of Western consumption of copper and aluminum, enough to have a significant effect on prices if supplies become plentiful. Soviet exports of both aluminum and copper rose substantially in 1990 and a further rise was anticipated for 1991. For both lead and zinc, the Soviet Union became a net exporter in 1990, having previously been a net importer.

This general rise in Soviet supplies is already adding to existing depressive forces on world minerals and metals markets. It has been estimated that the additional Soviet supplies will result in an average fall of 20 percent in the prices of metals traded on the London Metal Exchange in 1991, taking them close to their historic low points reached in 1986. (*Financial Times*, London, 11 September 1991) Price falls of this magnitude will involve serious foreign exchange losses for developing countries dependent on these minerals and metals for their export income.

Turning now to the direct effects of the economic reforms on developing country exports, it seems clear that the main initial impact so far of the reforms on imports into Central and Eastern Europe (other than the former Soviet Union) have been (i) a sharp rise in the cost of imports from the former Soviet Union from the beginning of 1991 as a result of the change to trade at world prices, and (ii) a substantial rise in imports from Western countries – mainly those in Western Europe – beginning in 1990 and continuing in 1991. Imports from developing countries into Eastern and Central Europe, however, were stagnant while those into the Soviet Union were sharply reduced in the early months of 1991. (See Table 2) The contraction in Soviet imports in 1991, which affected all sources of supply, reflected that country's acute shortage of convertible currency, as well as the underlying dislocation of the domestic economy.

The experience so far thus indicates a marked switch in the sources of imports into the reforming economies of Eastern and Central Europe in favor of Western suppliers. Within the total trade flows, however, there may be some commodities such as tropical fruits (e.g. bananas), coffee and cocoa, consumption of which has been severely repressed for decades in Eastern and Central Europe and the Soviet Union, and developing countries exporting such commodities could gain with the liberalization of the foreign trade regimes in Eastern and Central Europe.

The continuing severe shortage of convertible currency, both in Eastern Europe and the former Soviet Union and in the majority of developing countries, remains a major limiting factor, however, in efforts to expand East–South trade. Consideration needs to be given to possible innovatory financial arrangements or mechanisms which would minimize the adverse effects of the convertible currency shortage on this flow of trade. One mechanism which has been in use by many developing countries, so far confined to their trade with market-economy countries, has been countertrade (even though this has disadvantages similar to pure barter trade), and an extension of countertrade deals would be one way of avoiding the limitation to trade resulting from the scarcity of convertible currencies. Another possibility might arise if the various countries of Eastern and Central Europe entered into a "common payments union" for clearance of trade imbalances, which could at a later date be extended to those developing countries with which they have substantial trade flows.

A further suggestion was made (Müller, 1991) that the European Bank for Reconstruction and Development should "take over" commercial bank claims on developing countries (presumably by purchasing them on the secondary market). The Bank could then use these claims as credits to Eastern and Central European governments, thus providing the latter with an incentive to increase their purchases from developing countries. However, such schemes, even if successful, are unlikely by themselves to achieve a substantial and sustained growth in East–South trade. Of more fundamental importance in the transitional period would be greatly expanded flows of financial resources both to Eastern and Central Europe and to developing countries.

3. Financial Flows and Implications of Official Development Assistance (ODA)

Though Western governments have stated that aid to Eastern and Central Europe will not be at the expense of aid to developing countries,[2] many Third World representatives have expressed concern at the possibility of "aid diversion" in favor of Eastern and Central Europe. This concern reflects primarily the fact that "aid fatigue" on the part of the main donor countries (DAC–ODA for developing countries has stagnated at about 0.35 percent of GNP for several years) has coincided with the strongly expressed desire of Western governments to launch large new aid programs for Eastern and Central Europe. Moreover, as a consequence of the end of the Cold War, the strategic value of many developing countries to the West has been sharply reduced, and this is likely to reinforce the "aid fatigue" syndrome.

International financial commitments in support of economic reform in Eastern and Central Europe have risen substantially since 1989, when such financial support was focused on Hungary and Poland. By early 1991, total commitments for the area (excluding the former GDR) amounted to some US$24 billion, to be disbursed over several years. This includes US$8 billion agreed or under negotiation with the IMF, about US$6 billion in bilateral and nearly US$4 billion in facilities established by the Group of 24 Western countries. (UN Economic Commission for Europe, 1991b, Table 3.3.13) It is too early to document annual flows under the various programs covered, but if, for example, disbursements were spread over three years, the annual financial transfer (US$8 billion) would represent over 15 percent of the DAC–ODA total of US$48 billion.

The likelihood of aid diversion will also depend heavily on financial disbursements by Western governments to the former Soviet Union. At the Rome summit of European Community leaders in December 1990, a program of 1.15 billion ECU (approx. US$1.3 billion) of aid for the Soviet Union was approved.[3] However, a much larger financial support from the West will be required to support reconstruction and reform in the three Baltic states (which are now seeking up to US$3 billion from the West) (*Financial Times*, 29 August 1991) and to support accelerated economic reform in the rest of the former Soviet Union.

By early 1991, total bilateral credit commitments to the former Soviet Union amounted to some US$22 billion, including bilateral soft loans for restructuring and emergency relief, and trade credits. (UN Economic Commission for Europe, 1991b, Table 3.3.16) Most of this was used in 1991 and 1992 to settle outstanding debts and to finance essential imports. The medium-term outlook will depend on whether a credible reconstruction and reform plan can be devised in view of the uncertainties regarding the division of political power in the country, and the degree of social consensus on the proposed reforms. The earlier "Grand Bargain," proposed in the Yavlinsky Plan of June 1991, envisaged Western aid of US$20–35 billion a year, and, while such amounts seem unlikely to materialize in the near future, a reform program of even half that size could, together with aid to Eastern and Central Europe, represent a significant threat to the overall Western aid commitment to developing countries.

There is also the possibility of diversion of food aid from the European Community to Eastern and Central Europe (Poland being the largest recipient of such food aid in 1989–90), while Eastern and Central Europe is also likely to be a competitor for scarce technical, financial and management skills vital to institutional reform. (Overseas Development Institute, 1991)

Apart from aid diversion from Western countries, the economic dislocation and foreign exchange crisis confronting Eastern and Central European countries and the former Soviet Union has inevitably resulted in the collapse of their own aid flows to developing countries. These were never large (in relation to aid flows from the West), some US$4–5 billion a year, most of which came from the Soviet Union, and were heavily concentrated in relatively few countries (particularly Cuba, Mongolia and Vietnam). The latter now have to adjust to the cessation of this aid, as well as to the loss of trade and related preferences, mentioned earlier.

Given present levels of aid commitments, the risk of aid diversion from Western countries cannot be discounted. However, there may be a change of aid scenario in favor of the developing countries, if the needs for new aid commitments are recognized and sufficient political will could be mobilized to bring this about. The magnitudes involved under this scenario are set out in Table 3. The Preparatory Committee for the United Nations Conference on Environment and Development has endorsed this as a concept of partnership in additionality, which would be based on a developing country's clear articulation of policies and strategies and a program of action for their implementation. Resource transfers could take place in the framework of an agreement between donors and recipients based on development contracts enabling countries to implement long-term programs for sustained development.

To summarize, the net capital inflows required for sustainable development in developing countries need to rise during the 1990s from US$60 billion to US$140 billion, a substantial portion of which, by helping slow down population growth, serves the goals of both socially necessary growth and environmental protection. To place these figures in a policy context, it is necessary to relate them to the 1990 total of Official Development Assistance (ODA), which was about US$55 billion. The additional net capital inflow requirement of US$60 billion for 1990 thus would have implied roughly a doubling of official aid flows. For Japan, to take one important example, whose ODA stands at around US$9 billion or 0.32 percent of GNP, a doubling would imply very nearly reaching the accepted UN target

Table 3 Additional Demand for, and Supply of, Foreign Savings in Developing Countries and Eastern and Central Europe: 1990–2000 (US$ billions)

	Early 1990s	1995	2000
Demand for foreign savings			
Developing countries			
– Socially necessary growth	40	50	60
– Environmental protection	20	65	80
Total for sustainable development	60	115	140
Eastern and Central Europe and the former Soviet Union (borrowings in support of economic reform)	60	50	25
Total demand	120	165	165
Supply of foreign savings			
Increase in ODA of DAC countries[a]			
from 0.35 to 0.7 percent of GNP	55[b]	60	70
from 0.7 to 1.0 percent of GNP	—	50	60
Surpluses released by reducing US deficit, etc.	65	55	35
Total supply	120	165	165

Source: Jayawardena (1991), Table 7, p. 16.
a. Assuming a 3.5 percent average annual growth rate in real GNP from 1990 to 2000.
b. Relates to 1992–94 average.

of 0.7 percent of GNP. Japan's tax rates have already been increased to provide an additional US$9 billion to help pay for the costs of the Gulf War, and Dr. Saburo Okita, the Chairman of the WIDER Board and a former Foreign Minister of Japan, has urged that Japan should subsequently "institutionalize this increase" in order to divert the increment in revenue to development assistance. (Okita, 1991) A political decision by Japan along these lines, namely to reach the 0.7 percent ODA target in 1992/3, would constitute a very positive response to the South Commission's call for "doubling the volume of transfers of concessional resources to developing countries by 1995" (South Commission, 1990, p. 269) and would set a powerful example to other donors. The need to go even beyond this and increase the 0.7 percent target to 1 percent in the specific case of Japan has also been argued by Dr. Okita. Indeed, this increase to 1 percent has been recommended as the revised target appropriate in the 1990s for *all* developed countries in the Report on the Stockholm Initiative presented recently to the Secretary-General of the United Nations by Willy Brandt. (Brandt, 1991) The WIDER estimates of net capital flows needed for sustainable development during the 1990s, presented in Table 3, suggest the need to achieve the 1 percent target sooner rather than later.

In addition to the net capital requirements of developing countries, allowance must also be made for the foreign exchange support that is likely to be needed to sustain the reform process in Eastern Europe and the former Soviet Union. Recent research in WIDER by Professor Jeffrey Sachs and Dr. David Lipton (Jayawardena, 1991) suggested that, for Eastern and Central Europe *excluding* the former Soviet Union, total additional foreign exchange requirements would amount to some US$30 billion a year over the years 1991 and 1992. A similar magnitude is anticipated for the former Soviet Union over the coming five years so that the annual foreign exchange cost of supporting the economic reform process in the former Council for Mutual Economic Assistance (CMEA) area can be estimated at US$60 billion for the early 1990s. For the second half of the 1990s, however, the need for similar external assistance should diminish appreciably as the economies of Eastern and Central Europe become more efficient and closely integrated with the international economy.

As summarized in Table 3, the various considerations discussed above indicate an additional capital requirement for socially necessary growth and environmental protection in developing countries, plus the cost of supporting economic reform in Eastern and Central Europe, of some US$120 billion a year in the early 1990s rising to some US$165 billion in the second half of the decade. Some reduction in these levels of foreign savings requirements could be envisaged, to the extent that many countries – both in the developing world and in Eastern and Central Europe – which have had relatively high military expenditures in recent years are able to reduce their imports of military and related equipment and materials. Imports of major weapons by developing countries in the closing years of the 1980s totaled some US$20 billion a year, about 40 percent of which went to the Middle East countries. (SIPRI, 1989, Table 6A.2) International efforts to achieve a stable peace in that region, and to encourage the ending of civil wars elsewhere, should enable developing countries to reduce their imports of military equipment significantly, at least by mid-decade. For example, a report by an Expert Group on Africa's Commodity Problems appointed by the Secretary-General of the United Nations recommended *inter alia* that African governments "move quickly to reduce military expenditures from the current average of 10 percent of government expenditure to a maximum of 5 percent." (United Nations, 1990, p. 72) Reduced levels of military spending in developing countries would both make it easier for them to meet targets for sustainable development and enhance their moral claim to transfers of foreign savings. How far reduced military expenditures will be translated into a reduced demand for foreign savings in comparison with the picture presented in Table 3 remains problematic.

Turning now to the potential supply of additional foreign savings, it would seem that the additional capital requirements could be met essentially by a combination of two measures, viz. a significant rise in the current level of Official Development Assistance (ODA) from OECD countries and, given the ending of the Cold War, a phasing out of the US commitment to NATO, which cost half the US defense budget of US$300 billion, or some US$150 billion a year. This second measure would allow Japan and other surplus countries to switch to the developing countries an equivalent amount of savings hitherto absorbed in financing the twin deficits of the United States (in its budget and balance of payments), which amounted to US$150 billion each in the late 1980s. (Blanchard, 1989) The growth slowdown followed by recession in the United States in the early 1990s has been a major factor in the recent reduction of the US external deficit, and also a reduction in the external surpluses of Japan and several other countries. However, the slack in the economies of the latter countries, which represents in effect the counterpart to the fall in their surpluses, indicates that there exists industrial potential to restore the previous level of surplus given the adoption of appropriately expansionist domestic policies. To make this potential effective, however, the developing countries for their part would need to implement effective domestic policy reforms so as to attract the potential savings of the surplus countries.

Table 3 indicates possible combinations of higher ODA levels and surplus switching, both of which depend on relevant policy decisions by the OECD countries. Clearly, the non-attainment of the long-standing aid objective of 0.7 percent of GNP by mid-decade would make all the more important the implementation at an early date of policies directed to switching the surpluses of Japan and other countries towards developing countries. In that event, mechanisms will have to be found for tapping these surpluses, which are mostly in private markets. This can be done under the guarantee of interested countries, and might possibly involve new institution building along the lines of the European Bank for Reconstruction and Development (EBRD). Alternatively, resources could be raised by a tax on environmentally damaging activity, e.g. carbon emissions.

What Table 3 also suggests is that there may well be a division of labor, as it were, between the developing countries on the one hand, and Central and Eastern Europe and the former Soviet Union on the other, as regards the apportionment of the additional supply of foreign savings. The proposed increments to ODA would suffice, by and large, to look after the requirements of the developing countries, leaving Eastern Europe and the former Soviet Union to tap the surpluses released by US adjustment and available in private capital markets on more nearly market-related terms. What this amounts to is that the peace dividend from the ending of the Cold War could accrue in part as resource transfers to Eastern Europe and the former Soviet Union on market-related terms, while the balance could accrue as ODA to the developing countries on concessional terms.

Private Capital Flows

The economic reforms in Eastern and Central Europe and the former Soviet Union include legislation designed to encourage foreign direct investment, particularly through joint ventures. At the end of 1989 about 3,000 such joint ventures had been approved, while by a year later the number had risen to over 13,000. By end-March 1991 there had been a further increase to about 19,000 (UN Economic Commission for Europe, 1991d), at which date the total foreign capital committed could be estimated at about US$10 billion, though only a relatively few had actually commenced operations. There remain major obstacles to expanding the inflow of private investment capital, reflecting the inadequacy of existing legal systems in protecting the interests of foreign investors, weak economic infrastructure and shortages of intermediate inputs. In view of the vast size of global foreign direct investment flows, the relatively marginal flows to Eastern Europe are unlikely to involve any significant diversion of private investment funds away from developing countries.

There has, in any case, been a shift in the distribution of global direct investment flows away from developing countries over the past decade. Developing countries took an average of 25 percent of the global total in the first half of the 1980s, their share falling to 18–19 percent in the second half, the average for 1988 and 1989 being even lower at 17 percent. (United Nations, 1991) This decline reflected, in part, the difficulties of debt-burdened countries in attracting foreign private investment but, in part also, a large expansion in cross-border investment by TNCs within the industrialized areas, particularly the influence of the build-up to the Single Market in the European Community in stimulating the inflow of private capital into Community countries.

Of considerably more importance than the above as a possible influence on investment diversion are the very large sums being invested in the former GDR by private firms in West Germany. As this country has been a major source of private investment flows to developing countries, German economic unity could have the incidental result of reducing private flows to the Third World.

Interest Rates

The costs of German unity, in terms of public sector transfer payments from West Germany to the GDR budget, have been much larger than originally anticipated as a result of the rapid deterioration in the economic situation in the Eastern part of the country. For 1990, the public sector deficit was estimated at about DM72 billion (2.7 percent of German GDP), and was forecast to rise to about DM120 billion (4 percent of GDP) in 1991. (UN Economic Commission for Europe, 1991a, p. 105) The higher government deficit will tend to raise interest rates and, as already mentioned, reduce German investment abroad, while attracting foreign investment to Germany. Moreover, the sharp rise in demand in East Germany for West German products will tend to reduce German net exports of goods and services, and thus reduce that country's net capital outflow.

Though at this stage it is not possible to quantify with any precision the impact of German reunification on world interest rates, it would seem highly likely that the result could be a substantial addition for the highly indebted developing countries in the cost of servicing their foreign debt.

Debt Service and Debt Overhang

In spite of the increase in the inflow of financial resources from Western governments and the international financial agencies, the gross debt of all the countries of Eastern and Central Europe has continued to rise, from US$81 billion in 1989 to US$90 billion in 1990, while for the Soviet Union the rise was from US$59 to US$63 billion. (UN Economic Commission for Europe, 1991b, Table 3.3.12) The Polish government has for some time been seeking forgiveness of 80 percent of its foreign debt, and in January 1991 it was reported that the G-7 industrial countries had approved the writing-off of one-third of Poland's official debt – the same reduction as for the poorest African countries under the Toronto Accord – to be conditional upon the successful conclusion of an agreement between Poland and the IMF. (Ibid., p. 107)

The special treatment of Poland, in terms of debt rescheduling and post-ponement of interest payments, as well as debt forgiveness, raises once again the question as to whether priority should also now be given to reducing the debt service burden of heavily indebted countries in addition to those covered by the Toronto Accord.

4. An Overall View

The above discussion has indicated that the economic difficulties of the transition to market-oriented systems in Eastern and Central Europe and the former Soviet Union may well involve a number of adverse effects for developing countries: a trade-diversion effect resulting from a substantial reduction in trade barriers against imports from Eastern Europe into Western markets; a terms of trade effect resulting from increased Soviet exports of many important minerals and metals to Western markets; and an aid-diversion effect resulting from a sharp expansion in aid flows to the former CMEA area.

These likely effects imply the need for policy changes designed to reduce or offset them. In the trade field, if the Uruguay Round negotiations were to result in a substantial reduction in trade barriers, including income sup-port for agriculture in developed countries, this could minimize any loss in market share resulting from increased competition from Eastern and Central European suppliers. New mechanisms may also be required to underpin an expansion in East–South trade in the transitional period in which a severe shortage of convertible currency remains a major limiting factor. There is room here for some new international initiative to finance a substantial expansion in the volume of East–South trade.

The potential aid-diversion effect could also be reduced, or even eliminated, given the necessary political will on the part of Western governments, for example by increasing the resources available to the various international financial institutions by appropriate amounts, so as to ensure that concessional flows to developing countries are maintained or preferably increased.

Finally, the demise of the Cold War opens new opportunities for policy change to support both the transition to market economies in Eastern Europe and the development process in the Third World. This applies particularly to the conversion of the "military–industrial complex" to civilian purposes, and to the creation of new institutional mechanisms to ensure that an agreed proportion of the resources released from the reduction in military expenditure is earmarked for development purposes. This now appears all the more urgent in view of the probable adverse trade and aid effects on developing countries of the integration of the reforming countries of Eastern Europe into the Western economic system.

The terms of trade loss for developing countries exporting minerals and metals cannot easily be offset, though an expansion in aid flows to these countries should become an urgent issue for international policy. A prolonged period of depressed prices for minerals and metals might also stimulate the main producing countries to give serious consideration to supply management arrangements designed to achieve more remunerative prices while steps are taken to diversify their economies.

Notes

1. In 1989, Eastern and Central Europe took only 4 percent of developing countries' exports (excluding exports from OPEC countries).
2. Declaration of DAC member governments at their meeting in late 1989.
3. The program includes food aid, credit guarantees for exports of agricultural products and technical assistance.

REFERENCES

Blanchard, Olivier, et al. (1989), *Global Imbalances: WIDER World Economy Group 1989 Report*. Helsinki.

Brandt, Willy, et al. (1991), *Common Responsibility in the 1990s: The Stockholm Initiative on Global Security and Governance*. Stockholm.

Jayawardena, Lal (1991), "The Macroeconomics of Sustainable Development." In P. Dasgupta & K. G. Mäler (eds.), *The Environment and Emerging Development Issues. WIDER Studies in Development Economics*. Oxford: Clarendon Press.

Müller, A. P. (1991), "The Credit-worthiness and International Payments Ability of Sovereign States." *Intereconomics*. March/April.

Okita, Saburo (1991), "Japan: Better to Spend These Billions on Aid than on Arms." *International Herald Tribune*, 17 April.

Overseas Development Institute (1991), *Eastern Europe and the Developing Countries*. Briefing Paper. London, June.

SIPRI (1989), *Yearbook 1989, World Armaments and Disarmament*. Oxford: Oxford University Press.

South Commission (1990), *The Challenge to the South*. Oxford: Oxford University Press.

UN Economic Commission for Europe (1991a), *Economic Bulletin for Europe*. Vol. 42/90. New York, United Nations.

UN Economic Commission for Europe (1991b), *Economic Survey of Europe in 1990–1991*.

UN Economic Commission for Europe (1991c), *The ECE Economies in mid-1991*. Geneva.

UN Economic Commission for Europe (1991d), *East–West Joint Ventures News*. Geneva. No. 8, July.

United Nations (1990), *Africa's Commodity Problems: Towards a Solution*. New York.

United Nations (1991), *The Triad in Foreign Direct Investment*. Report of the Secretary-General to the UN Commission on Transnational Corporations. 18 March (EC/10/1991/2).

12

Europe: Hope with Many Uncertainties

*Carlos Blanco**

1. Ambiguities in Europe's Role in History

The relationship between Europe and Latin America has been marked by ambiguity. Sometimes Latin America hardly seems to exist as a far and slightly picturesque place interesting only for tourists and lovers of exotic adventures or for intellectuals who see in this continent the scenery of potential revolutions that are no longer possible in Europe. Sometimes, particularly during official visits of Latin American presidents to European capitals, Latin America is considered as a place full of possible investment and economic agreements owing to the potential of its natural wealth, which is unfortunately not well managed by a leadership too much influenced by the United States.

This ambiguity has produced variations of nearness and continuous estrangement, the latter resembling the policy of "benign neglect," once proposed by Nixon as the best policy towards Latin America, and the former accenting the enormous diplomatic and commercial activity of trade sponsoring, investments and cooperation between Europe and the region. Indeed, in the margin of the changing official rhetoric, the great European enterprises have hardly any chance or opportunity left to participate actively in regional trade and investments given the American omnipresence in Latin America. Holland, Sweden, England, Spain, France, Germany, Switzerland and Portugal sell and trade weapons and invest in technology, machines and goods within fundamental sectors like defense, transportation, communications, car insurance, construction plants, tools,

*Dr. Carlos Blanco is Minister for the Reform of the State of Venezuela.

oil, wine, watches, precision instruments, pharmaceuticals, medical equipment, home appliances, electronics, etc.

Countries like Italy and Spain have devoted extensive resources to scientific and technological cooperation to tighten relationships with some countries considered fundamental in the region, and to stimulate Spanish and Italian exports. Nevertheless, many of these hopes have not materialized, sometimes due to the lack of interest of European entrepreneurs, sometimes due to the lack of specific projects in Latin American countries.

For other people, Latin America is simply another part of the Third World, full of massive poverty, disease, political instability, social inequality, violence, corruption, lack of skills, severe violations of human rights, incapacity for environmental protection, a zone overwhelmed by drug traffic, with countries always on the brink of a coup d'état, dominated by incompetent military and civilian elites, which are corrupt and insensitive to the problems of their peoples. In that vision, Latin America is a second version of Sub-Saharan Africa, which is dispensable for the world economy, but which also merits some attention from humanitarian and human rights defending organizations, some help from European countries, some attention from anthropologists interested in races that are becoming extinct, some studies of flora, fauna and tropical diseases, some archeological work by specialists fascinated by the traces of the great Incan, Maya, and Aztec cultures.

In the important European media, the coups d'état and the revolutionary movements received some attention, particularly as seen through the eyes of Sartre or Debray, when Sartre and Debray used to be concerned about such matters. In that period, they were fascinated by Fidel Castro and Che Guevara. In the Europe of "the new philosophers," Postmodernism and Deconstructionism, not even revolutions seem to be particularly interesting.

The European ambivalence towards Latin America corresponds to the Latin American ambiguity with respect to Europe, despite the durability of their relationship. Since the very origin of the Latin American states, Europe was the first paradigmatical model, the inspiration and even the supporting material for the construction of different national projects. The "Bill of Rights" that English barons had obtained from "Jean Sans Terre" preceded the Declaration of the Rights of Man and Citizen, the heritage of the French Revolution. The Rationality of Descartes, the Freedom of Rousseau, the Separation of Powers of Montesquieu, the Steam Machine of Watt, the Positive Science of Auguste Comte, the Encyclopedia of Diderot and d'Alembert – the lights of Paris and the City Light were all products of the imagination of our precursors and liberators. The English weapons, the support of masonic lodges, the presence of all the O'Learys, O'Higgins, Browns and Smiths, together with the new ideas of liberty put forth by French Girondists and the struggles of popular armies on our plains, pampas and mountains, converged in the great fight against Despotism, Absolutism, Inquisition and Colonialism of the Spanish Bourbons.

And then, during the 19th century and at the beginning of the 20th, when each country had to face the challenge of creating a nation-state,

Europe was again the source of models and inspiration. The armies of Prussian style, naval fleets of British style, legal codes copied from the Italian ones, constitutions of Swiss and French style, public architecture that was successively neo-Baroque, neo-Gothic or neo-Rococo, according to the taste of our illustrious despots, often dressed up as French or German field marshals; locomotives, public lighting, music from the municipal open-air band, military goose step, ballet, opera, theater, medicine, university studies organized according to the scheme of Comte, tonics and cod liver oil, the latest fashions in Paris, all came to Latin America from Europe. Europe was the source of inexhaustible innovation, modernity and progress. In politics we were first Conservatives and Liberals, and later Social Democrats, Social Christians or Socialists. Our elitist parties became parties of the masses under the influence of Leninist Socialist ideas, institutions, ideologies, and political programs, and economic policies were copied from European archetypes. We were Romanticists, Modernists, or Neoclassical as measured and assessed by European literary circles. We cultivated Impressionism, Expressionism, Realism, Neoclassicism, Cubism and "Abstract" art, and all the avant-gardism with delay of some years, but always in response to European currents.

And together with the ideas and projects of progress and modernity that Europe offered, some of our ideologists proposed ensuring the successful import of things European by encouraging immigrants from Europe to populate the wide expanses of the Americas. The blood of enterprising, disciplined European workers was called upon genetically to enrich our peoples marked by Indian, Black and Spanish crossbreeding. It was hoped that Europeans would bring with them technology, science, and knowledge accumulated after centuries of progress and civilization. The railway tracks, the canals that would unite our navigable rivers, the chimneys of our industries, the public buildings of our cities, our theaters, academies, athenaeums and universities would flourish as a result of the presence of cultivated European immigrants. And our fields and savannahs, almost uninhabited, would yield abundant fruits under the plow of the industrious European peasants.

And when some of the more progressive intellectuals from our continent started to raise doubts about the validity and legitimacy of the European positivist project, another European import, Marxism–Leninism, took over the leading place in our ideological debate. The most timid adherents devoted themselves to criticism of the Frankfurt school, discussion of Logical Positivism by way of the Vienna Circle and the Popperites (followers of Karl Popper), and the inadequacy of what was called "American sociology." And when the crisis of Marxism took place in Europe and the "Stalinist deviations" of the personality cult were attacked by European intellectuals, and the long fight that started with Khrushchev and the Hungarian revolution flourished in the Prague Spring, it reached Italy in the form of Eurocommunism and the "Historic Compromise" of Berringer, and then the "French May" exploited the movement that forbids to forbid and that was going to take the sky by assault. In that time Latin America obediently went along with these European intellectual currents. We read the Dialectics of Concrete, we abandoned Konstantinov's manuals to discover Garaudy with his Leninist-Christian dialogue, Althusser, Poulantzas and his revealing Martha Harnecker; we recovered Gramsci, we had our local version of "revolutions" (or more modestly called university restorations) where students and professors were going to substitute themselves for the proletariat that had become bourgeois and serve as an avant-garde of the revolution. The most advanced leaders destroyed the bureaucratic leaderships of the communist parties. Not even the Second World War, or the Third or the Fourth would have the answers. Marcuse, Gramsci and the young people (preferably if they were university students) were the bases of the unnamed Fifth International, a Socialism with "a human face", even though provisionally crushed by the Soviet tanks and tear gas from the bourgeois police and just armed with paving stones, molotov cocktails, and bold ideas of liberty. These revolutionaries were called upon to change the world. The Red Brigades, the green movements, the white doves of antinuclear pacifists were replacing the old blue, white and red three-colored flag that had in its time represented what the Europe of liberty, equality and fraternity had to offer the world.

But the same Europe that produced the poetry of Yeats, Keats, Byron, Heine, Goethe and Rimbaud, that composed the music of Beethoven, Wagner and Tchaikovsky, that deeply moved audiences with the operas of Verdi and Puccini and made them happy with Rossini, light opera, Strauss and Spanish operetta; this Europe that taught new ways of seeing the world through Raphael and da Vinci, Michelangelo, Rembrandt and Rubens, El Greco, Velasquez and Goya, Monet and the Impressionists, Braque and the Cubists, Picasso and Miro, Mondrian and Chagall; this Europe that proclaimed the death of God and the Kingdom of Reason, the same Europe that produced revolutions in human knowledge by way of Marx, Darwin, Freud, Einstein and Bohr, as it had earlier done with Descartes, Spinoza, Kant and Hegel, and was to do again later with Sartre, Heidegger and Buber, the Europe of Reason, Art, Science, Technology, Culture and Humanism; this Europe that declared the supremacy of its civilization over the Earth has also produced along with all the cultural greatness all the forms of barbarism, such as slavery, colonialism, racism and xenophobia, fascism, Nazism, Auschwitz and Gulag, two world wars, the Jewish holocaust, the extermination of Gypsies, the mass murders of Polish and Russian people, the semi-slavery imposed on Hungarians, Romanians and Czechs, the exacerbation of ethnic hatred between Serbians and Croatians, Ukrainians and Russians, the recolonization of Lithuanians, Latvians and Estonians; this same Europe gave birth to Hitler, Mussolini and Stalin, brought about Red Terror, White Terror, concentration camps, hard labor, death and extermination camps, produced the guillotine and gas chambers, bayonet, tank and trench, as well as air bombardment of civilians, chemical weapons and dynamite, creating the space for Falangist youth, Fascios, Hitler youth,

Communist Pioneers, Iron guards, Hlinka guards, Black Hand militants, Ustashi, contemporary totalitarianism and Ultramontanism. It was Europe that set up the Iron Curtain and the Berlin Wall. All these negative energies were part of the legacy of the European civilization. The same culture that produced Humanism and Romanticism, Science and Progress, Rationality, freedom, aspirations and social justice, modernity and progress also generated barbarism.

After the failure of Nazism and communism and the "crisis of ideologies" and utopias, the same Europe that proclaimed the death of God and the success of Reason arrived at the end of the century with the announcement of the death of Reason, now embracing "Postmodernism" in order to emphasize the failure of modernity, the emptiness of ideas of "progress," the inability of science to produce any truth which was not merely conventional, and therefore "arbitrary." The principle of uncertainty or indetermination of Heisenberg, the Second Theorem of Gödel, the Conventionalism of Kuhn, the Irrationalism of Feyerabend, the supremacy of hazard in the birth of universe and life according to Monod, Arbitrariness of language according to Saussure, the legacy of Sartre's Existentialism, the ecological mess caused by Industrialization, Consumerism, Pragmatism, Materialism, and Hedonism of post-war culture, along with failure of the 19th-century's social utopias. All this, along with the barbarism produced by Gulag and Auschwitz, was merged to discredit the unattained project of modernity. Hazard, Rationality, the empire of science and technology, the search for universal laws of knowledge and laws of history, the claims of transcendental purposes for human species in the universe, the pretensions of morality based on humanism and reason were the critical focus of the new European avant-garde. They were condemned as naked kings. It was alleged that Humanism and Science had produced only wars, destruction, totalitarianism, threats of nuclear holocaust, the destruction of nature, ecological degradation, genocide against peoples and cultures, and colonialism and slavery of peoples and spirits.

Despite all this, Europe has not become culturally exhausted. Its intellectual vanguards remain active and influential. Meanwhile intellectuality delights in scaring away good bourgeois with its devastating criticism. Post-war bourgeois Liberalism had created societies with greater social security, greater life expectancy, higher levels of consumption and income, better material ease and economic prosperity, better opportunities of study and personal progress, greater productivity than any other known by the old continent in all its previous history and among the most successful ever known by mankind. Under the nuclear umbrella of NATO, encouraged by the initial support of the Marshall Plan, threatened by the dilemmas of Cold War, Western Europe developed the European Community within an environment of democracy, human rights, and moderate policies never seen before. And before the catastrophe of Eastern Europe, Western Europe reached the end of the 20th century playing again the dynamic role it had played since the end of the 19th century. The collapse of communism, the fall of the Berlin Wall, the reunification of Germany, the dismantling of the

Warsaw Pact, perestroika and glasnost, all found Western Europe ready to abandon its own unification and embark upon the eventual construction of a Europe able to rescue Eastern Europe and ready to incorporate it into that "big European house," stretching from the Atlantic to the Urals, the Europe once dreamed about by visionaries, the theme of many utopias generated over the centuries on the old continent riven by continuous war and hatreds.

With these great historical happenings Europe becomes again the place of high hopes, huge problems, important lessons, backwardness, success and failures relevant for Latin America. Europe appears as a possible partner to support the restructuring of the international order, to offer the best opportunity for non-industrialized countries, providing an alternative to American hegemony, or, by contrast, an ethnocentric and preoccupied fortress, closed by way of protectionism and self-complacency.

Whether Europe chooses the self-closing or the protagonist responsibilities of a new power within a new world order is a dilemma whose resolution will not only affect Europeans but also influence other peoples, including those in Latin America.

2. The Big Hope

From war debris, after the fight against the ghosts of Nazism and fascism and resisting the double external and internal pressure of what was perceived as Soviet expansionism and the threat of communist parties, Western Europe has built democratic political systems that, even if supported by popular vote, represented the preferences, ideologies, fears, and projects of elites. Europe behind the "iron curtain" depended on American dollars, American weapons and troops, American technology, and American good will (this dependence reached its emotional climax when Kennedy declared during a celebrated visit to the Berlin Wall, "Ich bin ein Berliner"). Gaullism and the French "force de frappe" challenged American hegemony as represented by NATO, but real autonomy for Europe was achieved when the Rome Treaty, establishing the European Economic Community, began to bear fruit, starting with the Iron and Coal Community. This first common market encouraged the growth of the European Community that today competes for first place in the world economy.

But in the political domain there were obvious limitations on Europe's independence. Could the Italian Communist Party, the biggest in the West, become part of the government of a country that was a member of NATO? Such was precisely what the "historical compromise" called "Eurocommunism" proposed. Was Willy Brandt's Ostpolitik compatible with German commitments to the Atlantic Alliance? Were the claims of independence made by de Gaulle a real threat to the bipolar order?

Even if European countries were protected by nuclear weapons that could be used only on the basis of Washington's decision and the continent was full of NATO bases under the United States' command, European societies advanced towards democratization. Further, economic prosperity in Europe led to the development of a strong civil society. Pacifists and ecological movements, initially marginal, increased in influence, and were able to make their concerns and programs an integral part of the political European debate, inducing the British Labour Party and the German Social Democratic Party to adopt many of their positions. Student movements reformed French education and a series of political changes arose from the fall of Salazar, Franco, and the dictatorship of the Greek colonels. These developments caused the incorporation of Portugal, Spain, and Greece into the European Community and democratic life.

The Polish revolution of Solidarity, the overthrow and shooting of Ceauçescu in Romania, Havel's ascent in Czechoslovakia, together with the fall of Honecker and the reunification of Germany, Gorbachev's perestroika, and the triumph of Yeltsin produced great changes in Europe. Profound shifts in Hungary, Bulgaria, and even the isolated Albania, the general collapse of communist regimes, all these events produced in Eastern Europe an uncontainable wave of democratic movements, a spontaneous eruption of groups rooted in civil society that had been absent or excluded from the public life before.

In this climate of new freedoms there emerged not only progressive and democratic movements, but also heirs of the old chauvinism, integrism, ethnic and religious fundamentalisms, old and new fascisms, racisms, xenophobia, antisemitism, old hates and opiums, which World War II had defeated only provisionally and that communism with its slogan of "creating a new man" had left untouched and even revitalized despite decades of authoritarian and totalitarian control.

The English revolution ended with the Restoration, the French Revolution was destroyed by the imperial dictatorship of Napoleon, the government of Kerensky ended with Lenin and later with Stalin, the popular Italian movement ended with fascism, the Weimar republic was terminated by Nazism, the Spanish republic was destroyed by Franco, the fourth French republic led to the authoritarian Republicanism of the fifth and its "Imperial Presidency."

Thus Europe is not only the new center of the big hope because it is able to reestablish democracy and freedom after two hundred years of the great revolution that changed the world, but also the focus of a great fear. The general will of the sovereign people, the magnificent European invention that underpinned the legitimacy of the absolutist monarchies of despotism and that later legitimized universal democracy as the sole system of governance, nevertheless produced dictatorships even more tyrannical and sanguinary, on the basis of popular support that was present in the past and could reemerge again.

3. Big Problems

Not withstanding that Europe is engaged with concerns about peace, cooperation, integration and democracy, it is also a continent deeply affected by big problems produced by nationalism, ethnic conflicts, internal inequalities, and, in some cases, by violence. Traditional French fears are revived by the reunification of Germany. British resistance to European integration, which recognizes community as embodied in the bureaucracy of Brussels, is manifested by opposition to monetary unification and to any suggestion of political integration. Scottish, Basque and Corsican nationalisms seem robust. Claims of statehood by Lithuanians, Latvians, Estonians, Armenians, Georgians, Slovenians and Croatians reveal the vitality of nationalism in Europe.

Ethnicity arising from different national European identities based on genetics and language rather than on the changing borders of the nation-states makes the inhabitants of Silesia, Pomerania, and East Prussia keep being "Germans" although they have Polish nationality. Because of ethnicity, Romanians discriminate against Hungarians who live in their territory, Bulgarians discriminate against Turkish residents within their borders, Armenians discriminate against Azeris and vice versa, Spaniards discriminate against "Sudacas," the French discriminate against Algerian and Moroccan *pieds noirs*, Germans discriminate against Spanish, Turkish, and Arab immigrants and more recently, as well, against Polish immigrants. The Swiss discriminate against all foreigners to the extent that they organize plebiscites that mandate their expulsion; Poles discriminate against Jewish people (although fewer than 2,000 Jews now live in Poland). Moldavians and Latvians discriminate against Russians, Serbians and Croatians discriminate against Albanians in Kosovo, the British discriminate against Asians and the peoples of the Caribbean who were once subjects of the British Crown and qualify as citizens of the Commonwealth and who enjoy a legal right to live in Britain. Virtually all Europeans discriminate against the Gypsies who have survived the extermination policies of the Nazis.

Reinforcing ethnic nationalism and racial discrimination are patterns of economic inequality, uneven access to education, health services and social security, employment with lower salaries and social prestige, and cultural discrimination that ranges from attempts to forbid Moslem girls from entering French schools to efforts to force the change of family names belonging to members of the Turkish minority and the prohibition of the Russian language in Lithuania or Hungarian in Romania.

And then there is violence: the national religious violence of the IRA in Belfast, nationalist operations by Basque ETA, the ideological and terrorist violence of the Red Army Faction in Germany and the Red Brigades in Italy, the fascist violence of neo-Nazi groups, skinheads in Germany and France, ethnic violence between Armenians and Azeris, the anti-cessionary violence of former Soviet forces in Lithuania or of the Yugoslav army in Slovenia and Croatia. There is also the potential violence of expelling 100,000 foreigners from France, persons who are not considered political refugees any longer. There is the potential violence arising in reaction to insurmountable barriers erected to prevent the entry of the supposed millions of immigrants who might abandon the Soviet Union and Eastern Europe for the West, and who now are not searching for freedom but escaping from the undesirable economic and political consequences of their new liberty: unemployment, inflation, and ethnic and political violence.

4. Big Lessons

Despite these tensions, hatreds and violences, Europe has been able to offer exemplary lessons on how to create an ambitious common project regardless of differences and antagonisms. The adventure of European economic integration constitutes the most successful project of this sort in history, one that creates a common multinational economic space. It constitutes an exemplary paradigm of an ability to face the challenges of reconstructing and developing countries that a few years before and for a long time had been fighting one another on cruel battlefields. Germany and France had fought three wars since the birth of the German state in the 1870s. Italy had successively been an enemy of and allied to Germany in the passage of only 20 years. And even with the present memory of the last war and its terrible consequences of nationalist animosities and mutual mistrust these countries could start, together with the Grand Duchy of Luxemburg, a cooperative experience that turned out to be the seed for several "economic miracles." Likewise from this start the European powers created a dynamic economic community that today includes another six countries and which has become today the point of attraction for the rest of the continent. The Europe of the Six, which later became the Europe of the Ten and even later the Europe of the Twelve, is inevitably called upon to become in the near future the Europe of All. An economic unity which was confined at first to two essential products – coal and steel – finally became a common market, a total economic community that fixed as its deadline the 31st of December 1992 for the elimination of the last barriers of any kind to the free circulation of goods, services, information, capital and people. And all this has taken place despite cultural, linguistic, national, political, and ideological differences and in the face of unequal development that has always separated European states and which still separates them.

For Latin America, which is united by a common colonial past, by language and culture, and by a political vocation of integration and special cooperation that has been iterated a thousand times, the example of the European success is stimulating and debilitating at the same time. It is stimulating because it reveals how far and how fast it is possible to attain the highest levels of integration and to transcend thereby any difference or antagonism when a genuine political will is present, even if this will is not equally shared by all partners. It is debilitating because, in contrast, Latin America, which seemed to have everything necessary to reach integration with minimum obstacles, has not even been able to institute a fully functioning free trade zone, and even less a real common market. We have developed behind each others' backs, we have always been oriented towards

extraregional suppliers and markets, with minimum commercial relationships among ourselves. It is easier and more economical for Latin American
countries to communicate by mail or telephone with Miami or New York
than with any other Latin American capital. Flights are more frequent,
maritime routes are more regular, movements of people are more numerous, trade is more active between Caracas and Miami than between Buenos
Aires and Caracas or between Lima and Managua. Each Latin American
country is more integrated with the United States than with any other Latin
American nation, except for some border zones, where despite governmental restrictions on traffic, trade, and immigration, an integrative dynamic has
operated.

There have been several and frequent formal attempts at integration
but they have been full of exceptions, exclusions, restrictions and non-
compliance even in relation to concessions in recently agreed upon steps
toward integration after years of struggling, haggling and discussions that
are equivalent to the non-existence of integration. With the oft-repeated
argument of "not yet being prepared" to accept the competence of neighbors, all attempts at real integration have been postponed indefinitely, and
even abandoned. While Europe was integrating at full speed and against all
risks, and was even incorporating countries with very unequal levels of
development such as Greece, Spain and Portugal, the Latin American
countries stressed their perpetual differences or, ironically, their structural
coincidences that made their economies competitive rather than complementary. Differences of currencies, salaries and rates of inflation, arbitrary
protectionisms achieved through political influence more than by way of
relative competitive advantages, absurd definitions about the "strategic"
importance of almost any productive activity that wanted privileged protection (from cars to chocolates, from tubes to shirts or glass frames) – these
are the alleged obstacles to integration in Latin America.

The European lesson is very difficult for Latin America to adopt: "We are
not Swiss," said an important political leader of Venezuela. But there is an
implicit lesson that seems universally applicable: no nation-state, no national
economy has by itself the capacity to maintain a process of real self-sustained
growth, supported only by its domestic market under the contemporary
technological conditions, given the behavior of transnational corporative
giants. Not even societies with such a wide demographic base as China,
India, the Soviet Union or the United States can plan their growth only
"internally," even if at prior moments of their history this could have been
possible or even desirable.

All the European experience of the last two centuries shows a frenetic
search for external resources, raw materials and markets for their products,
having recourse to armed confrontation to achieve control over these
sources and markets. The regional community project in Europe is a tran-
sitory alternative to imperial and colonial wars that stopped being feasible
for European nations in the new political circumstances that derived from
the last great war. The military supremacy of the United States and the

Soviet Union, the collapse of colonialism, and the need for reconstruction of economies devastated by war obliged Europeans to set forth a different horizon. Their "outside," the "outside" of each European country, got reduced. The lesson of the community was to unite the limited national economies of Europe and to make them become only one economy, only one space of production and trade. Today, after the period of bipolarity and Cold War has passed, Europe has emerged as one of the three economic powers of the world that is able to compete on a global scale with the United States and Japan. And this time there is little (or only a marginal) danger that this economic competition will lead towards armed confrontation.

In order to make this potential project an effective reality of a "trilateral" world, it will be necessary to extend the economic unity which has already been achieved into political domains. This process is going to be much more difficult since the convergence of political positions on matters of security and defense that existed during the Cold War has disappeared. As yet, Europe has not found a unified outlook with respect to world affairs that is not directly responsive to security threats posed against the region as a whole. Except to allege that the American presence is still necessary on the continent without specifying why, there is no evident common European position at this point. The European role is not very clear in a world where threats to peace and security do not seem to be localized in the East of Europe any longer but now appear in other regions of the world which are very distant from the field of NATO concerns. The war in the Persian Gulf during 1991 revealed that Europe is not ready yet to adopt its own military and political role. Instead, each country in Europe assumed a position that primarily reflected its particular relationship with the United States and the Middle East countries confronted by war.

The United States argued on behalf of European involvement beyond what was strictly necessary to handle the security challenge. This claim is not very prudent in the case of Germany. Earlier a triumphant United States after the Second World War had imposed severe restrictions on Germany's role. Nevertheless it seemed that some American elites were dissatisfied now that Europe in spite of its economic power was refusing to play its alleged part in a unified military and political approach on behalf of the West. At the same time, there was some American concern that a politically united Europe with an autonomous and coordinated military policy would emerge as a rival to the political and military hegemony of the United States, which nowadays does not have any rival for global leadership.

On the other hand, European citizens born after the war but who know the history of this century seem not to be well-disposed to giving up the economic advantages that were achieved while under the American nuclear umbrella. A more active and belligerent role for the European countries outside of the European scope would divert resources at the expense of the quality of life and levels of consumption and well-being that had been attained after decades of effort and work – risking death to reestablish the power of prospect for European consumerists, hedonists who were satisfied, pleased and nationalist, but otherwise localist, in their political identities. For these Europeans the attitude during the Gulf War was this: if Americans want to play the role of policemen, let them go to the desert.

But the European abstention from playing a global military role does not imply that they avoided the coordination and unification of some political positions, but these shared views do not represent anything similar to economic integration in terms of current international importance. The common position with respect to the Arab–Israeli conflict and the decision to establish conditions governing any special relationship of Israel with the Common Market relating to the Middle East Peace Conference, as well as the earlier veto to the entrance of Spain, Greece, and Portugal until democratic regimes were established in these countries, are examples of the kind of European coordination that has been reached on subjects of common policy in external affairs.

Other political institutions of the community like the European Parliament, though constituted by popular election, still have very little influence in the political life of the different countries. This does not apply to the European Community Court, which settles conflicts directly related to economic engagements and whose decisions are binding, or to the European Court of Human Rights to which not only the states have access but also individuals with grievances against their own governments.

European institutions that go beyond the old concepts of sovereignty and interfere in what have been considered "internal affairs" have had an extraordinary political impact on Latin America where governments have taken refuge in "non-intervention" to shield themselves from challenges to policies and practices that violate the rights of their own citizens. The civic lesson of making the respect for human rights an affair of international responsibility of European states instead of treating it as an internal affair on the basis of national sovereignty and security will take a long time to be learned in Latin America. Dictatorships like those that existed in Chile, Argentina, Nicaragua, Guatemala and El Salvador should have been excluded from regional activities, as was proposed recently by Venezuela in the OAS, an approach similar to what the European Council imposed for years on Franco, Salazar and the Greek Colonels. The Contadora and the Group of the Three have been the only Latin American experiences of effectively coordinating foreign policies beyond what is merely declarative. Venezuela has been actively engaged in both of these diplomatic innovations.

5. Big Backward Movements

Together with large hopes, fears, problems and lessons, to the eyes of Latin America Europe seems to experience big backward movements. In the economic field, regardless of the advantages gained by regional integration, or because of them, there is a protectionism that is of a more and more severe nature with respect to the outside world, and, to some extent, even with respect to its own partners. The agricultural policy of the different countries of the community not only obliges European consumers to pay higher prices for their food than the prices that should be paid if due account is taken of the abundant agricultural production, it also puts the GATT framework under great pressure, restricting opportunities of access to European markets by the Third World. The impact of European protectionism on exports of meat from countries such as Argentina or of fruits from Chile has been very large. But even some of the members of the European community with less industrial development and a bigger agricultural sector, such as Spain, have engendered boycotts and import exclusions as a result of lobbying efforts by French farmers. The frequent surplus of dairy products in Europe that do not reach markets owing to protectionist policies produces envy and resentment in other latitudes that are crushed by chronic hunger. Such poor countries do not have the means to pay for, transport and deliver products that could represent the difference between living or dying for thousands of people of the Third World, while for Europe these policies only yield differences in prices for the prosperous, well-fed, spoiled, and protected farmers.

The American–European confrontation with respect to protectionism and agricultural subsidies during the Uruguay Round of GATT seems only a symptom of a more radical attempt by Europe to oppose more open international trade. This accords with the liberalism that Europe itself had evolved during decades in its relationships with the rest of the world. Of course, Europeans just reproduce the client care that the United States gives to its own rural electors, taking into account that European agricultural producers represent a more numerous and more important political force than does its American equivalent. On the other hand and paradoxically, the same productivity produces a surplus that tends to depress prices resulting from a surplus of supply without any place in the market. Such a situation could likely cause the abandonment of agricultural activity for more income-producing activities, thereby generating a future scarcity. That is why there is not a country with significant agricultural production that does not subsidize agriculture, thereby erecting just as important obstacles to others as those that would arise from high tariff and other restrictive practices.

Similar protectionist trends are developing in industrial and manufacturing fields partially as a response to the challenge represented by Japan and the United States in the European market itself. But this dynamic discourages the expectations of many Latin American countries, especially for those countries which are not included in the Lomé Conventions. Existing trade barriers almost eliminate any hope that Europe could become an alternative market for the eventual export of Latin American manufactured goods. This restricts industrialization horizons in Latin America to the most elementary goods and primary processing roles, with lesser aggregated value than could be obtained from the sale of products associated with final consumption. Areas of manufacturing production in which, owing to available raw materials, cheap energy, and less expensive manual labor, it might be possible to compete favorably, do not make the development effort if European markets of greater consumption capacity, along with the Japanese and American ones, are perceived to be inaccessible fortresses that limit their imports to raw materials and goods at the primary processing stage.

Further, the new Integrism has a smaller scope but a far bigger potential today. The violence that results is not limited to the movement led by Bishop Lefebvre and associated with opposition to the liturgical changes agreed by the Second Vatican Council. But the intermingling of national and religious identity reminds us of a long history in Europe, a history that includes such terrible massacres as that of the French Huguenots on Saint Bartholomew's Eve, and a cruel religious war during the Reformation. These memories are brought back to life today by some long and intense European conflicts. The seemingly never-ending struggle in Belfast between Catholics and Protestants, the confrontations between Christian Armenians and Moslem Azerbaijanis, the encounters between Catholics, Protestants and Orthodox adherents in the Baltic countries, between Catholic Slovenians and Orthodox Serbs are almost a rebirth of the ancient past. Two hundred years of separation of Church and State had eliminated the tradition according to which citizens had to convert to the religion of their kings or risk the penalty of being considered a traitor. And even if we are not moving close to a return to the Integrism imposed by absolutist monarchies in Europe, some people on the continent, as well as the majority of the population in the Middle East, have never separated their national identity from their religious faith. In Poland, Solidarity made use of this merged consciousness as a weapon against their communist rulers and the Soviets. In the new democratic Poland the role that the Church intends to play in electoral policy and even in the shaping of civil legislation evokes a spirit of a new fundamentalism, parallel to the one growing rapidly in the Islamic world or to the American Christian fundamentalism which has promoted a political program that leads to constitutional reforms that tend to impose the religious opinions of these particular groups on the society as a whole. The nasty, at times violent, debate about abortion is suggestive of the dangers here.

In a world of uncertainties aggravated by the failure of the political utopias of the previous century, religion can again provide certainties, and seems able to fill the emptiness produced by ideological crisis. The positive reevaluation of the role of religion psychologically and culturally has a definite value. However, it can be politically explosive if it is used for providing a justification for xenophobia, intolerance, and persecution of unbelievers. These menaces have emerged in the revolution of Ayatollahs in Iran and in the apparent inability of Islam to solve the problems that modernity has presented to it without relying on violence, in violence in Belfast, and in the potential danger of explosions among the millions of Moslems present in the Soviet Union if the Islamic fundamentalism that has spread throughout the Arabian world encourages a new chauvinist pan-Slavic role for the

Orthodox Russian Church. This possibility is still incipient but explicit in the Pamiat (Tradition) movement in Russia and in the political activism of the Catholic Church in Poland. These remain local phenomena and have not yet been generalized in all Europe.

Two hundred years after the French Revolution and more than seventy years after the Russian Revolution, the persistence and reappearance of confrontations and antagonisms for religious reasons as in Ireland, the Caucasus and the Balkans seem to erase with one stroke of the pen centuries of secularism and the separation of political and religious affairs, retransforming beliefs long considered by most citizens to be a private affair into burning public questions that are to be debated and resolved by means of politics that is at the service of faith. Religiosity and nationalism, the two strongest ideas of Western history are, when united in one single cause, a serious and dangerous source of terrible violence among peoples. The reappearance of this phenomenon in the form of a new Integrism in Europe naturally revives old fears and adds to them new scares.

6. Big Changes

The accelerated changes that we have witnessed in Europe during recent years seem to be the expression of giant transformations of social life. Within the transnational spaces in which individuals, groups and organizations of a country make close contact with their counterparts in other countries for the sake of pursuing various economic, ideological, and cultural interests without intervention by the state, there seems to emerge a return to tribalism and localism. Loyalties to transnational causes such as ecology, human rights and nuclear disarmament cohabit with tribal identifications that set apart and even are opposed to the ancient pretension of the "nation" state as the ultimate depository of loyalty by the citizenry. The national identity is no longer associated with the state and returns to a more primary ethno-linguistic group, to the original tribe no matter its locus in relation to state boundaries.

The states themselves develop political institutions to face common problems that cannot be solved by reliance on "traditional" ways or through national political activities. Parties, social institutions, political activity, and national speeches are undergoing enormous transformations that point at the same time in global, transnational, multinational and local directions. The pragmatic offer of European political parties can no longer be reduced to answers to national problems. This offer must include clear definitions of the party position with respect to integration, with respect to proposals intending to accelerate the process of the creation of a monetary union, with respect to a policy of European defense or more ambitious coordination of policy vis-à-vis third parties. The political debate is likely to include opinions arising out of the ideological tradition of the parties or may focus on supporting or rejecting proposals coming from the European bureaucracy in Brussels.

A government such as that of Margaret Thatcher, which won three con-
secutive general elections and maintained its power for a longer period
than any other British government was able to do after the Second World
War, was finally challenged by trends inside its own party relating to disagreements about the rhythm and extent of European integration. Leadership by the Labour Party has become again a believable option once it
abandoned advocacy of unilateral nuclear disarmament, a position that had
earlier separated Labour opposition from the electorate mainstream. The
opinion of European political organizations about the role that the United
States should now play in European defense in the light of the dissolution
of the Warsaw Pact and the collapse of the Soviet Union has become as
important as the position taken about the role of the state in the management of trains. After the failure of communism, social democrats and
Christian democrats consider that they represent the wave of the future, but
being conscious of the current skepticism concerning political ideologies
and utopias they articulate their ideas about the future by taking positions
with respect to very concrete aspects of local and transnational policy, like
tax policy, monetary unity, agricultural subsidies, treatment of immigrants,
social security that accompanies workers beyond borders, or the language
that should be used in teaching minorities. The ideological identity of a
political organization no longer enables us to predict its particular position
with respect to electors' concerns.

Air quality, the danger of accidents in nuclear energy plants, pollution of
rivers and forests, the production and sale of armaments to governments
that violate human rights, control of exchange rates, financing and support
of changes in the Eastern and Central European economies, support to the
new Russia, the challenge that the Americans and the Japanese present to
the European economies, the consequences of German reunification and
the dissolution of the Warsaw Pact, the European responsibilities in situations like those of Kampuchea, South Africa and the Middle East, aid for
developing countries, the dilemma caused by tension between territorial
integrity and self-determination for the peoples of former Yugoslavia or the
former USSR, are among the concrete issues on which the political parties
formulate their positions.

The fact of merely enumerating topics about which contemporary parties
and governments must define their positions and agendas erases what in the
past were clear lines of political and ideological identity.

7. Success and Failure

A double movement of forces advances simultaneously: the centripetal
forces that organize big spaces supported by global economies, and the
centrifugal forces of ethnicity and nationalism that tend toward the dismemberment of state unities, revalidating local, idiosyncratic and partic-
ularistic aspects of civic life. It seems that as the economic space tends to

homogenize humanity, creating consumers of identical goods, services and ideas generated by an omnipresent and equalizing technology, this same identical person acts to save his personal soul from anonymity and disappearance by affirming that which is distinctively his or her own specific, idiosyncratic, heterogeneous qualities that establish difference by way of cultural identity, language, race, religion.

In the European case this double movement towards unification and dismemberment seems to be correlated with "success" and "failure" in the different parts of the continent. The failure of the Soviet project put into motion disintegrating, secessionist and disaggregating trends in Eastern Europe. The rebellion by the members of CMEA and the Warsaw Pact, followed by the declarations of independence from the Soviet federation by the Baltic countries, Armenia and Georgia, decisively weakened and dismantled the arduous construction of unification and control that the USSR had built inside and outside of its territory over the course of its several decades of existence.

The economic success of Western Europe that emerged from the debris of a world war has made Europe one of the most active places of material and technological development in history, thereby encouraging the unifying and integrating trends that in turn reinforce the success of the community project. The achievements of those centripetal trends seem also to make Western Europe a powerful magnet that attracts to its core the pieces arising from the dismemberment of the Eastern bloc, accelerating its process of disaggregation. Hungary, Poland, Czechoslovakia, Slovenia and Croatia, each seem to see their future as being associated in some way with becoming an integral part of the European Community. Germany is the only partial exception to this trend as its future is already somewhat realized, although painfully, by unification.

We seem to be attending the dawn of another Middle Ages when the attempt was made to create a single Christian community from the debris of the Roman Empire, resulting in the Holy Roman Germanic Empire, yet ending in the fragmentation of feudalism. In this new Middle Age, post modernism tries to render incompetent the pretensions of science while ethnic linguistic chauvinism seems to be destroying several multinational states; fundamentalism and religious integrism have arisen from the debris of the Enlightenment. The end of Taylorism and Fordism was accelerated by the cybernetic revolution, a transition from the age of Ford to the age of Wiener that marks the revindication of segmented markets, including from the particular to the specific in the form of impersonal mass consumption to serve a global market.

8. Crisis of the Nation-State

The nation-state, the great European invention for the organization of collective life, the locus of the ultimate loyalty of peoples, organizer of economic space, institutionalizer of order in that space, "sovereign" in relation to people and other states, guarantor of material well-being and physical security of people under its jurisdiction, guardian of property – the state so conceived as the maximum expression of a "human" civilization seems to be in crisis.

The complexity exceeds the capacity of the state to manage it. The problems are too big or too small to be tackled by the nation-state. The coercive aggregation of territories and populations that started with England, France and Spain and ended with Italy and Germany facilitated the construction of a political economic space in which the limits of effective authority would mark the limits of the "national identity." But this successful centuries-old attempt has started to collapse. And for those that have not yet been able to integrate and nationalize their inhabitants it is now too late. The nation-state seems to be unable not only to solve the basic material problems of well-being, security, prosperity and development of its inhabitants but also to meet widely shared human needs for ideological and spiritual identity. Basque and Scottish peoples after centuries still affirm their specificity and difference with respect to Spain and Great Britain, and more specifically with respect to their Castilian and English colonizers. Croatians never accepted the Yugoslavian project. The various Baltic peoples reject federation under Russian rule. The integration of nation-states by authoritarian aggregation appears increasingly as a simple act of colonialism that is coming under attack virtually everywhere.

In place of a Europe of states there exists the possibility of a Europe of peoples based on the principle of voluntary choice and union based on the sovereignty of people and not the will of the state. This process is, in turn, supported by the capacity of a suprastate composed of economic and political institutions to solve the problems that have exceeded the nation-state's capacity. Housing, health, education, physical and social security, employment, food, sports, recreation, political freedom, access to culture: such basic needs of humanity can no longer be reliably provided by state/nation institutions. New local and global ways of organizing collective life are becoming at the same time possible and necessary. And if this is so, it implies new loyalties, new values, a new morality, as well as new policies and institutional arrangements.

9. Monocentralism or International Pluralism

The disappearance of the Warsaw Pact has ended the Cold War and the bipolar order that dominated international life during more than four decades. The absolute military superiority of the United States has induced some to say that the new structure is a "unipolar" or monocentralist system. Others believe that not even the American technological capacity is able to impose itself from a single center upon a hierarchical and stable international system – perhaps because American hegemony does not have a sufficiently sound economic base for sustaining the project, or maybe because hegemonies as they have been understood during the last two hundred years are themselves coming to an end, or maybe because economic technology seems to be more important today than military technology as the foundation of international political superiority. What is true is that power appears increasingly fragmented and in any case it is concentrated in the big economic spaces, one of which is Europe.

Fundamental changes in the international system have been produced and accelerated by the changes that led to the collapse of the Soviet Union and to a crisis of identity for the organizations created to face the problems of the Cold War and bipolarity. NATO, which was born as a part of the deterrent designed to prevent Soviet expansion and which is centered upon the defense of Europe against a possible Soviet attack, needs to redefine its function if it is to remain vital. If at the beginning the Three Musketeers were based on the identification of an enemy and a common threat, what happens to the alliance when the enemy and the threat disappear?

The United States has just announced that the Eastern and Central European countries, the former allies of the USSR in the Warsaw Pact, are no longer nuclear targets of NATO war plans. The threat of destruction assumed by the doctrine of massive retaliation is now reduced only to the territory of the former Soviet Union. Poland, Hungary, Romania, Bulgaria and Czechoslovakia and, of course, Eastern Germany, now reunified and thus part of NATO, are no longer viewed as security threats to Europe.

In its turn the former Soviet Army seemed destined for a while to become a police force or force of public order, oriented to prevent the secession of unsatisfied members of the new Commonwealth of Independent States with which Moscow tried in vain to save the Union from the centrifugal forces that were announcing its eventual dismemberment, or it might have become a conservative force to serve the bureaucracy of the official Communist Party, whose privileges were already threatened by the processes initiated by perestroika which inevitably jeopardized the hegemonic monopoly of power that the party-state had enjoyed for more than seventy years. Some observers believed that the Soviet military leadership, threatened with unemployment, were a potential threat to stage a coup d'état which would try to revoke the democratizing and liberating processes of glasnost and perestroika and would return the USSR to its international military role, thereby causing a renewal of the Cold War.

This scenario does not any longer seem very plausible. Even the use of force could not now reestablish the USSR and bring it back to the political military position it had in the past. The contest for legitimacy of Marxism–Leninism, the failure of central planning, and the intrinsic weakness shown by the economic apparatus of the Soviet state would hardly allow the country to be ruled at this stage by an alliance of military and conservative communists that had retaken a position of ideological and political leadership such as the one which existed also in many parts of the Third World, including Latin America. Whoever governs the country, the so-called Soviet model has ceased to be a believable one. It is no longer able to capture the imagination and engage the loyalty of elites in the rest of the world who are still searching for a formula for overcoming underdevelopment.

10. Latin America's Expectations

The system of the former USSR is not a model any more, but the European Community certainly seems now to be the most influential model for Latin America. For Latin American countries, Europe seems to provide an alternative option to total absorption by American economic hegemony. That is why the Latin American countries are concerned about the consolidation of the European Economic Community and the possibility that this consolidation would close off access for our trade to European markets. A protectionist and closed Europe would represent a hard blow against our hopes of fostering non-traditional exports and of diversifying our exports and markets. To promote these goals we need an accelerated search for ways of association and articulation, bilaterally and collectively, among our countries and in relation to the European ones. The agreements between the Community and the Andean Pact are part of this attempt to ensure that the European common market does not become a closed and stagnant market in relation to Latin American trade.

Apart from the trade aspect, Europe is seen also as a possible technological alternative as it allows an open transfer of technologies. The long series of bilateral agreements on technical cooperation between countries of the European Community and Latin American countries provide access to European technology and know-how as a means to diversify our economy and lessen our dependence.

At the same time, advance toward democracy in the Eastern and Central European countries and fundamental changes in the economic policy of the countries that are abandoning the model of central planning for an economy in which the market plays a more important role in the allocation of resources may serve as an important lesson for the Latin American countries that are determined to institute similar democratizing and liberating processes.

More political freedom together with more economic freedom seems to be a common trend in Europe and Latin America. Nevertheless, the hastened changes in Eastern and Central Europe and the expectations that those countries will receive major technological, economic and financial support from Western Europe as well as the reconversion of the Eastern and Central European economies have caused some concern in Latin American circles. The large scale of demand for financing resources that the reconversion of economies from socialism to capitalism requires suggests that the assistance capacities, efforts and interests of Western Europe will be diverted towards Eastern and Central Europe. Meeting the demands of Eastern and Central European countries will leave less room for political attention and less availability of scarce financing resources for other parts of the world, including Latin America.

The hope of attracting European investment, loans, credits, technology and commercial demand to Latin America seems to be threatened by the evident priorities of Europe itself from the perspective of the Community countries. If European leaders fashion a global political and economic vision of Europe's role in the contemporary world after the end of the Cold War, they should be able to include Latin America and the rest of the Third World in their outlook too. But if their vision is a closed Europe, then the project to build a "common European house" will have little interest in playing a global role.

The way Europeans solve this dilemma will obviously be a central concern of Latin American countries during the next several years. Maybe the resolution of the dilemma depends not only on how Europe sees its own role in the world but also on how it perceives Latin America: whether as a potential market for European exports; or as a possible place for European investment; or as a possible supplier of natural resources, energy and tropical products; or as a region of little interest because any of these functions could be carried out by Africa or Asia, continents which have had closer relationships in recent history by way of the Commonwealth and Communauté and where a destructive rivalry with American economic, political and cultural ambitions is far less likely.

The obvious preference of Latin America is that Europe sees us as an area of multiple associations, essential for balanced global development, essential to avoid crystallization of a new hegemonic world order or a world system of relatively stagnant domains in which the United States, Europe and Japan become poles of new hermetic and separated blocs, each locked behind protectionist barriers, thereby eliminating opportunities that the technology of production and communication offers for the construction of a real global economy on a planetary scale.

11. Thinking about the Future

The decisions that the European leadership makes with respect to its own future will affect not only the future of Europeans but also the future of millions of people in Latin America. Not only will the thinking of the ruling classes be relevant but also that of intellectuals will be influential in shaping a vision of the role that Europe hopes to play during the years to come and thus the conception that will guide Europe's relationships with the rest of the world.

In 1992, Europe returned to the preface of 1492 in which the adventure of world expansion started, a process that has laid down the bases of a planetary civilization.

The political, economic and technological conditions offer Europeans an option that few civilizations have had in the past. Europe can resume its rise after several decades in which the center of world affairs had apparently moved toward the United States and the Soviet Union in an irreversible way, leaving Europe in a secondary role, remembering its past glories but having passed its principal moment.

The defeat of Nazi fascism, the end of colonialism, bipolarity, the relative technological backwardness of Europe compared with the United States and Japan, and the memory of two world wars were among the factors that seemed to bring down the European curtain. Everything then pointed to an old, closed, decadent Europe without the energy or vigor to compete against the new rising cultures, resigned to its role as the wise retired "grandfather" who could warn others about the lessons of the past but who had few things to say about future prospects. Europe could be a place for historical tourism, full of ruins of an old magnificence. Now, however, the double process of consolidating the economic potential of the Community and the dismantling of the socialist bloc has given Europe a new historical chance. The opportunity of a "second debut" as a catalyzing center of big international changes exists as does the challenge of playing a central role again in world history.

"Endogamy" could become the lethal illness of what might otherwise be a rising civilization. If Europe easily succumbs to the temptation of self-contemplation and introspection, if it accepts as inevitable the compartmentalized scheme of a tripolar world of stagnant blocs, if it allows that complacency, hedonism and indifference to define the limits of its interest in world affairs, then it will lose this historical opportunity of playing again the leading role that it had established for itself five hundred years ago and that had seemed forever finished in 1945.

Because of this, 1992 may be the date either of self-closure and reconstruction of Europe as a "fortress," or of a new Europe becoming a dynamic focus in restructuring the world order.

For Latin America the resolution of that dilemma is critical. Its own future depends in great measure on whether Europe will be an accessible partner for trade and cooperation disposed to invest, to trade, to exchange ideas and knowledge, to transfer technology and to open its doors to flows of goods and people.

But whatever the strategic decision that rules the future of Europe, it does not seem very possible for Latin America to allow Europe to ignore it and resign itself to a scheme of stagnant compartments. As heirs of the same European tradition in each stage of their modern and contemporary history, the Latin American countries are also heirs of the unfinished project of the Enlightenment and modernity.

If at the time the arrival of Europeans in America served to rethink and redefine European utopias by infinitely widening the possibilities of imagining life in freedom, today Latin America has made its own destiny the unfinished program of European Enlightenment: a world with more freedom and democracy is the guarantor of a world with more progress, prosperity and justice. Latin America is the testimony that the historical project of the European civilization can be finished. And if Europe tries to abandon this grander vision of its possibilities, then it is likely that there will be many in Latin America who will be there to remind it and to stake a claim on Europe's future.

13

The Agenda of European Politics in the 1990s

*Mihály Simai**

1. The End of an Era and the New Beginnings

The second millennium which is approaching its end has been a Europe-centered epoch. It started with the era of European Recovery, which had its beginnings in 955, when Emperor Otto defeated the Magyars in a fierce battle near Augsburg. Over the next centuries Europe built up its own distinctive culture, based on an efficient combination of political, military, economic, technological and scientific power. It transformed itself and, additionally, had a major impact on the development of all other continents and their peoples. Sometimes, it completely destroyed their traditional cultures, broke their resistance and replaced the native cultures with a version of the European one. (In fact Europe itself has been a heterogeneous region from both cultural and political points of view.) There were cases when Europeans learned from non-European cultures, incorporated ideas and practices from them and used them to increase their own power and influence. There was, in this respect, a certain mutuality in influence and adaptation. European power in the global system reached its peak in the early part of the 20th century when ten empires were rooted in the continent and nine of them had possessions in other parts of the world. Europe has also had many dark decades during the past thousand years. Long and devastating wars have been waged on its soil. European politics "produced" some of the worst political regimes in human history. The decline of the power of

*Dr. Mihály Simai is Professor in the Institute for World Economics, Hungarian Academy of Sciences, Budapest.

Europe in the world during the 20th century reached its bottom in the early years of the Cold War.

Although the Cold War was a global confrontation, it started in Europe, arising out of the continent's split following World War II. Europe was the main "theater" of the Cold War; it witnessed both the pulling down and the lifting of the iron curtain. To use Kissinger's words, the glorious sunset of the Cold War was the Gulf War, and yet the collapse of the Cold War structure has been, of course, a longer and more complex historical process. For most contemporary observers it has become increasingly evident that the global costs of the Cold War were enormous and that the East was on the losing side. The Soviet Union and its allies could not bear the loss of resources caused by the arms race, which became an increasing drain on their already weak and inefficient economies. Even on the basis of the Leninist concept of peaceful competition between two systems, as formulated in the early 1920s, which posited the rate of increase and comparative level of social productivity of labor to be the factors that determined who would be the winners and the losers in the long run, the outcome of the contest was, in fact, predictable as the Western world was well ahead in the new scientific and technological era and could adjust its economies and societies to the constantly changing requirements of the Cold War far more flexibly than the rigid, dictatorial regimes of the East. The economic and technological processes resulted in an increasing gap in almost all important economic and social indicators, which began to widen at a faster rate in the 1970s. The people of the Central and Eastern European countries and of the former Soviet Union revolted also from time to time and in different forms against the dictatorial regimes imposed upon their societies. The spread of ideas about freedom, democracy, human rights, and national self-determination had been undermining the one-party system and its political structure. No serious contemporary analyst dared predict, however, the concrete events, or their sequence, of how the collapse would eventually occur. Because of the balance of mutual deterrence and an increasing rationality relating to an awareness of general human interests, some experts expected a major historical compromise to be struck between the two superpowers. Other, more pessimistic, experts continued to anticipate a major conflict erupting at some point. The military forces on both sides of the Cold War operated on the basis of this latter presumption.

Oddly enough, the post-World War II years represented the longest peaceful period in the history of Europe, with only two relatively minor conflicts: the quashing in 1956 of the Hungarian revolution by Soviet military forces, and the brief war over Cyprus in 1974 between two NATO allies, Turkey and Greece.

The end of the Cold War should also be connected with the disintegration of the Soviet empire and the collapse of Central and Eastern European communist political structures, which by the end of the 1980s had become increasingly heterogeneous. The differences between the various communist regimes and the progressively diverging interests of these countries undermined even that cohesion which had been created by Soviet dominance and by the common interests of the ruling elites. However, the dissolution of the Warsaw Pact and CMEA and the withdrawal of Soviet troops from Eastern Europe have not been a typical Cold War strategic gain for the USA or NATO, for no other reason than that the main enemy ceased to exist as a continental global power, leaving behind somewhat of a Pandora's box for the West. The resulting situation has inaugurated a new geopolitical era in global affairs and, particularly, in Europe. The outcome of the changes and forces at play in the early part of the 1990s is highly uncertain, and many different possible scenarios can, in fact, be extrapolated.

There are a couple of important question marks about the political future of Europe in the new era. There are, first of all, important *security issues*.

Europe during the Cold War period had a classical bipolar security system. The continent has been divided into two military blocs and those neutral countries which were outside of them held the view that the two blocs in fact neutralized each other in war – waging options and capacities. The two blocs represented such a high level of risk to each other as to make military options unattractive scenarios. The two blocs imposed a high level of bloc discipline on their members and were able to control the intensity of conflicts between them.

This relatively simple and efficient structure does not exist any longer. The *character of the security threat* has also changed. Similarly to the United States, the countries in the Western part of Europe no longer have any concrete "strategic enemy" and none seems likely to emerge on the horizon of global politics for some time. Where are the new security dangers? In a way, they may be "written on the wall," as the reemergence of the past chaotic patterns of interstate relations or as a process in which Europe may move "back to the future." (Mearsheimer, 1990)

Could those patterns result in increasing antagonism and potential violence in specific circumstances? Could the spread of nationalism once again become a factor to undermine a new global order, thus comprising a source of global instability analogous to earlier periods of European history?[1] Is it at all relevant to think in terms of traditional power politics and apply the balance of power concept in an era of European integration and global politics? There are no easy answers to these questions.

In Western Europe, the era of "traditional" nationalism is over. In the period of European history when nation-states were formed, nationalism was associated with individual liberties and independence, expressing the interests and values of the victorious bourgeoisie and, basically, all other social groups liberated by the changes. National interests were defined more in a "systemic" way against the old regime. Even in that era much blood was shed in Europe for rights officially to use the name of the nation, the language, the flag and citizenship, or other symbols of national identity and sovereignty. Later, when nationalism became more organic and exclusionary, national interests were increasingly defined by antagonistic relations with other nations. The expansionary, racist, militant, bellicose and totalitarian brands of nationalism of the first half of the 20th century, the primary example of these being Nazi Germany, represented the vanguard of the process of Europe's nationalization. Even though today there are forces in Germany and in other parts of Western Europe that invoke Nazi traditions, and there are dangers of nationalist revivals, especially as a force against immigrant laborers, these will probably remain a minority in European politics, provided Europe is able to sustain those forces which have been dominant during the past 30–40 years. Violent nationalism is not now on the political agenda of the countries in Western Europe.

A concrete and immediate threat to European security is rooted in the *political and strategic environment* which has emerged after the collapse of communism in Central and Eastern Europe and the disintegration of the Soviet Union. This may not result in a premeditated or "structural" East–West conflict (although accidental events of course cannot be completely excluded). Unsolved and reemerging ethnic and national issues have been, however, already resulting in serious violence in former Yugoslavia and in certain parts of the former Soviet Union. There could be further secessionism, territorial disputes and other types of violent conflicts. In the Eastern part of the continent therefore new security issues are emerging, resembling those that had been characteristic before the two world wars. For the West, the problems caused by such conflicts could become very important, extending well beyond their humanitarian implications and the dangers of a mass outflow of refugees. There are not only nuclear weapons in the East but also many nuclear power stations, the explosion of which could cause severe problems for the whole continent. There is also a danger of international terrorism connected with unresolved ethnic tensions. One cannot exclude, of course, additional types of problems, such as the direct or indirect involvement of one or another important Western country as a supporter or a partner in those conflicts, which in turn could result in political and strategic confrontation.

An important but highly uncertain aspect of the future of European security is connected with the potential impact of *conflicts located in other regions*, especially in the Middle East and North Africa, on Europe. Europe is not an active agent in other regions and continents any longer. It is more a "price-taker." Those conflicts, however, may influence access to vital fuel and raw material supplies. They may result in a great number of refugees. Some countries, like the United Kingdom as the center of the Commonwealth or France which has strong ties with its former colonies in Africa and retains strong overseas interests, may become directly involved in those conflicts. The participation of the European countries in the UN's global collective security structure has been and will continue to be an important linkage between European and global security, at least institutionally.

An additional, and probably the most important, security issue goes beyond the military problems: this is the *economic and environmental security of the continent*. Economic problems are especially crucial in the case of the Central and Eastern European countries, where a difficult transformation process from the socialist type of system to one or another form of modern capitalism will be going on at least throughout the 1990s. The dismantling of the legacy of the "centrally planned" system of the economy of the past and the building up of a future system in a way is a social process of "creative destruction" that creates grave economic and social problems. The issues of economic and environmental security are, of course, not confined to the Eastern part of the continent. The efficient management of those problems and risk factors would require a more intensive regional cooperation, but also a more active participation of the countries of the whole continent in global multilateral cooperation structures.

The future concrete agenda which will require the collective management of European security in the post-Cold War period will be to a great extent determined by the outcome of a few specific but interrelated socio-political and economic factors that are shaping the changes on the continent.

The most fundamental issues relate to how, at what speed and with what consequences the economic and political unification in Western Europe will develop in the future, and how far and in what forms it will extend to the East. The unification process is in fact a "redefinition" of Europe and its security problématique, inevitably with major long-term global consequences. Several other changes on the continent and beyond it are already shaping the 21st century and will, to a very great extent, be influenced by the intensity and the character of unification. Another major change, the outcome of which cannot be separated from the issue of Europe's political future, is the longer-term consequences of the disintegration of the Soviet Union. Here many questions arise: will the "Russian Empire" be restored in some way, will it assume a different form than as the Commonwealth of Independent States, or will it gradually disappear, leading to the dissolution of this very framework? If the "Empire" disappears as such, how soon will Russia alone be able to consolidate its economic, political and military power and again become a major force in continental politics, thereby ensuring itself a paramount role in European and global affairs.

The success or failure of the transition to a modern market system in the countries of Central and Eastern Europe (including the successor states of Yugoslavia) and of the stabilization of their domestic economic and political affairs will also have a direct bearing on the future security of the whole continent, including that of Western Europe.

A key issue will be Germany's role. The future changes in the domestic policies and international aspirations of the new unified German state will exert major influences on both European and global politics. Most of all the future impact of the new German state is, of course, interrelated with the wider European problématique – the political and economic framework of the continent within which Germany will have to exist. In this context, the domestic forces of Germany (in both economic and political terms) will be of decisive importance.

All of these issues taken together, or even considered individually, are of an extremely complex nature. They address the most important building, or possibly stumbling, blocks of any future "new order." Any one of them could become an important source of global and European peace, creating new opportunities for cooperation, or, on the contrary, of global and regional instability.

2. Character and Speed of the Integration Process

The future of the political unification process, its character and speed, will be determined in coming years by a set of complex factors: the changing interests of EC members, the issues to which they will have to react by unilateral or common policies, and the success of economic integration. The latter poses such operations as: what will the impact be of the single market, how fast will the steps towards a common currency be taken, what will be the influence of integration measures on domestic sociopolitical problems, and is integration perceived as facilitating the harmonization of national policies? All of these factors will play a crucial role in forming (or transforming) the attitude of the public and of the political leadership on the difficult issues of European unification. Indeed, the opportunities for political stability and economic prosperity are great, in many ways unprecedented, and are increasingly better understood by the different political groups.

Along with the opening of new opportunities, however, there are also new, key challenges to individual nations, which are becoming more evident; nations are thus being forced by the domestic and international environment to formulate and articulate more clearly their perceived national interests. In the late 20th century, the peoples and nations of the continent are much more interconnected by capital and commodity flows and by migrations than ever before. Increasingly strong mutual regional interests have been shaping the integration process, understood not only as the customary "common protectionist" policies enacted against Europe's chief competitors, but bearing upon a wide spectrum of issues ranging from regional security to science and technology. Europe will have to remain competitive in the changing global market; integration must be seen to serve this end. The European Community has been able to develop common policies in certain important areas which have proved helpful in expanding the volume of mutual trade and capital flows between EC members. It has used such instruments, among others, as price mechanisms and special funds to help balance their gains and losses. In agricultural policies, for example, it has constructed a harmonized structure of diverse interests. This process has been greatly supported by the positive responsiveness of the macro-policies of member states, but also by the common needs and actions of various regional micro-actors.

While at this stage there certainly are diverging views and interests in many areas between EC member countries (the problems in Yugoslavia having brought a few of them to the surface), there are at least no major power struggles that remind one of past centuries of change on the continent. Europe, if united, could become a formidable political actor and economic competitor in a world exhibiting major trends towards regionalization. A united Europe could also become a strong and important partner of other key economic regions that are evolving in the global system. The importance of the issues of global competition and cooperation and the increase of European competitiveness have not gone unrecognized over the last few decades. These developments have had a strong influence on international agreements in such major areas as trade relations, capital flows, and immigration. This influence, however, has yet to produce an effect on Europe's common economic policies, which do not exactly express the orientation of a Europe with liberal trading interests. The existing pattern of policies has resulted from compromise between protectionists and liberals.

Has the process of European integration, in which Germany has become the strongest pillar, reached the "point of no return"? Using the language of Hegel and Fukuyama: has the history of national fragmentation come to an end in Western Europe? Based on historical experiences the answer must be a qualified "no." Nevertheless, the qualification is very important to articulate. History does not present only one alternative. Regarding Europe, several plausible scenarios of future events can be depicted.

One of the scenarios with the greatest probability is the continuation of the integration process. This process serves, first of all, the basic interests of the European nations in many important areas of their economic lives. The establishment of the single market will probably further strengthen the process of integration. The unification of Germany has contributed to the efforts of some of its partners to take more concrete steps towards political integration in terms of a federation of European states, and establish new structures for creating a strong framework which could integrate a growing united Germany – like, for example, the symbolic Franco-German military corps. It should be noted that a few, more cynical, observers have posed a rather delicate question on alternatives. Will the united country be the Germany of Europe, or will the united continent be the Europe of Germany, or will there be a third alternative: an alliance of a future Germany with a future Russia, causing countries in the Western part of the continent to seek a continuous presence and assistance from the USA? The final answer to this question can be given only by the unpredictable games of history. At this stage, however, one can say that the content of the immediate answer will be greatly influenced by the outcome of those efforts which were initiated in the early 1990s in Maastricht.

The Maastricht Treaty may represent a turning point in European history by adopting the joint principle of widening and deepening, by opening a new agenda for future European integration (the establishment of the European Monetary Union, based on a common currency), and by declaring the goals about a future political union. At this stage, one cannot completely exclude another scenario, a "retreat" from the Maastricht commitments or even some other setback in the integration process. This alternative seems to have a low probability and is likely to be realized only in the event of a major economic or political catastrophe, which would either make joint solutions seem impossible or impose high, perhaps intolerable, political or economic burdens on one or another member. Also, if new aspirations of a future political elite in one country or another could not be satisfied within a European framework this could disrupt the integration scenario. Here the major source of problems is likely to be the middle powers and not the smaller ones. The changes within the Community and in Europe in general have different implications for them and the potential gains and losses may be distributed in such a way that their interests could be damaged by the deepening or widening of the Community.

The debate on the issues of political integration has ignited instances of deep disagreement between EC members over the process of developing a "United States of Europe." At this stage, the debate among member countries is not about movement toward, or away from, integration, but is rather focused on two models of European integration. There are and there will be important and influential political groups within the European states that are interested in maintaining sovereignty over political and economic affairs and make efforts to protect some of the main pillars of national sovereignty. These efforts go beyond the protection of national cultural identity in an economically and politically integrated continent. They reflect lasting differences within the member countries – in both their public and private sectors – between the two main conceptions of the integration process. One group wants to strengthen the central institutions and accelerate progress toward a unitary state of Europe as a final goal. The other group advocates increased European cooperation on a wide range of issues while maintaining decentralized structures for a system which is sufficiently flexible to accommodate differences between the relative economic strengths of the countries, and between their diverse domestic interests and practices, including the role of diverse democratic procedures in budgeting, taxation, social policies, and so on.

Members have clashed over such questions as the character of the political institutions, the relationship between national and regional political structures, and the nature of common military forces. The events in Central and Eastern Europe, interestingly enough, have provided the basis for some of the arguments against unification. One columnist has written that "the architects of Europe should learn from the collapse of the Soviet Union and Yugoslavia, two federations masquerading as countries. Their recent history has shown, that while nationalism can be suppressed for a time, it cannot be destroyed. Any attempt to impose a rigid central government system will be resented and cause a revolt." (*The European*, London, September 13–15, 1991, p. 8)

In all European countries there is, of course, a strong desire for a politically stable and united continent without frontiers. Regarding political unification, the events in Central and Eastern Europe and in the former Soviet Union have caused a degree of apprehension about nationalism and its potential dangers, and about the possibility of not being able to create reliable protection against the resurrection of old continental problems. The challenges for the Community will be manifold in the 1990s. One of them is connected with its external dynamics and the progress towards supranationality. The Community is in the process of transferring power from the nation-states to supranational structures by way of a series of treaties, rules and directives. This process is far from simple. The defenders of the nation-state, in fact, introduced important "safeguards" in the Maastricht Treaty. The first of these safeguards is that, in certain sensitive matters such as foreign policy, defense, policing and immigration control, the states will maintain the key authority. The second safeguard is the principle of subsidiarity, expressed in the formula that only if and insofar as the objectives of the proposed action cannot be adequately achieved by the member states can the proposed action be undertaken at the Community level given its scale and effects. (*The Economist*, July 4–10, 1992, p. 15)

Several conditions of the "single market" program remain to be fulfilled on the national level. Agreements on the creation of a single currency and a central bank will have to go through a ratification process in national legislatures, during which the UK's reluctance may cause some problems. Social policy will be another very difficult area, where detailed agreements have not yet been achieved. Another serious problem facing the EC will be the extension of its frontiers beyond those of its current 12 members. Austria and Sweden will probably be the next candidates for membership; Czechoslovakia, Hungary and Poland, along with some other countries, are queuing up in the wings. The Baltic states and other CIS countries, as well as other Central and Eastern European countries, are also interested in joining. This may not be too easy for the EC to accommodate, and in any case will certainly not take place during the 1990s. The future relationship with the former socialist countries in Europe is both an internal problem of the EC and a difficult regional and global issue. The debate about "who should be admitted and when" reflects not just temporary disagreements. The member countries of the EC are afraid of economic dilution and the political difficulties emerging from the greater diversity of interests.

The perspectives of the Central and Eastern European countries, which consider "Europeanization" as a panacea for many of their political and economic diseases, are very different. They would like to become integral parts of a European system that has proved to be more successful thus far than any other past experiment on the continent, not only in terms of economic progress that is badly needed in that region, but also in terms of those many complex political issues that involve bringing together such traditional enemies as the French and the German nations and making national frontiers increasingly obsolete. The original ideas of Jacques Delors about the European space, which would be a network of countries located in concentric circles like the moons of the sun, the managerial functioning of which would be performed by the Community, have become irrelevant in the environment of the Soviet Union's disintegration and the agreement reached with the

EFTA countries. Neither can there be a "European fortress" in the new era.

Any talk of future expansion raises critical issues concerning the specific interests, support, and opposition of some present members. Germany, for example, has been much more interested than some of its partners in the participation of the Central and Eastern European countries. Further expansion of the Community also raises some fundamental questions regarding the future, such as, first of all, about the optimal size of an economic or political union. The EC might over-extend itself from the viewpoint of operational efficiency. It will be increasingly difficult for it to manage its own enlargement and satisfy outside expectations without disrupting the delicate balance of interests and opportunities of its present members that is necessary to maintain its cohesive character. The responsibilities of the present members and of the bureaucracy in Brussels are much greater in the early 1990s than ever before because the future of the rest of Europe, indeed of the entire continent, will depend to a great extent on the success of the integration process in creating a new multicultural European entity. In the coming years, Europe and the Community will have to contend with increasing North American and Japanese competition as well, which will probably present the most important external challenge. An additional challenge and problem for Europe will be its relationship to the developing world and especially to its traditional client regions, which will not only be expecting more meaningful economic and technological support from Europe, but will be the source of mass migration of millions to various European countries. In order to cope with these migrations, Europe must have a well-functioning and expanding labor market and be able to sustain popular support for an increasingly multicultural society.

3. From the Union to the Commonwealth and Beyond

The transformation of the former second superpower, the Soviet Union, is still at a very early stage, and most of the 1990s will probably witness the vicissitudes and shocks of the transformation process. The strategic importance of the region in global politics and the military might of the former Soviet Union make the issue of transformation one of the central problems of global politics in the 1990s. The new structure, the Commonwealth of Independent States, while it could become an instrument for a re-fashioning of the Russian empire, could alternatively become an instrument enabling a group of democratizing nations to preserve those unifying elements that have recently proved useful and practical in organizational terms. If the latter should happen, then the CIS in time could become structured and function in a manner comparable to the European Community.

Whichever of these alternatives is realized, the character and functions of the CIS will finally be clarified and developed, although probably by way of long and difficult challenges in the midst of which the possibility of civil violence cannot be dismissed. Will the Commonwealth provide sufficient security to its members in international politics and in the global economy? Historically, Russia had always been a power of major significance in international affairs in centuries past, successful as it was in establishing the largest and most diverse continental empire in modern history. Will the Russian republic have the capacity to maintain a continuation of its imperial heritage despite the strain of transition? What kind of a superpower might Russia be in the new era? As all of the political arrangements concerning the Commonwealth, and the structure of its military forces and frontiers, are presently ambiguous and unstable, it will be some time before these questions can be answered.

What is, however, evident, according to the main scenarios, is that even under optimal domestic and external conditions it will take a long time to overcome the serious economic, political, ideological, moral, and economic crises that beset many of these Commonwealth states. For a long time constructive changes will be hampered by internal political power struggles, and ethnic or religious conflicts. Past dynamics of change in imperial Russia or later, in the Soviet Union, have never been smooth and surprise-free. The size of the country, the multiplicity of "built-in" problems and conflicts, and the deeply rooted bureaucratic inertia in resisting modernization efforts and reform have made change problematic. There are, however, a few areas where some of the basic determinants of the future attitude of Russia in global politics can begin to be discerned.

First, the geo-strategic position of Russia has radically changed. A belt of independent states, large enough to be more than just a traditional "buffer zone," has been established between Western Europe and Russia. This belt has pushed Russia geographically far away from Central Europe. Ukraine and Belarus want to join the Community in the long run. Their relations with the West will be more diverse as they will try to sustain the best possible relations with the USA and also with their traditional European partner, Germany. The eastern parts of Russia, in Asia, will increasingly link their destinies to the evolving major global concentration of economic power on the Pacific Rim and will likely be interested in establishing the closest possible ties with these Pacific and East Asian countries.

Second, Russia will have a strong interest in keeping together as much as possible those parts of the former Soviet Union where large Russian minorities are living. Russia will seek to protect the interests of these minorities, but at the same time will use them to sustain as much Russian influence as possible. (There are now about 25–30 million Russians living outside Russia in the territory of the different former Soviet republics.) Russia will sustain its efforts to keep the countries of the CIS together and, if possible, even expand its scope to some of the former members of the USSR.

Third, as a power that spans two continents, Russia will probably seek to influence the policies of the neighboring countries by establishing regional cooperation zones and other agreements in order to build friendship and economic ties.

Fourth, owing to the abandonment of the communist ideology and the concomitant messianic orientation toward global politics, Russia will probably pursue a pro-Western foreign policy, looking for structural cooperation with the main Western powers, and be less interested and involved in the developing world (except its immediate neighbors). Russia will almost certainly have much cooler relations with the remaining socialist countries.

Fifth, the main security concerns of Russia will be, first of all, to block within its frontiers any secessionist trends and to resolve outstanding territorial disputes with several former republics, as well as to contain potential expansionist endeavors of Islamic powers located in close proximity.

Sixth, following long traditions, Russia will maintain a relatively strong army for domestic purposes and also for prestige and regional security. This military capability will also be an important instrument in Russia's political relations with the former members of the Soviet Union.

Seventh, Russia will become actively involved in multilateral institutions in general but especially in Europe and in Asia.

Eighth, for many years to come, owing to the severity of domestic problems and limited resources, Russia will act mainly as a status-quo power supportive of overall global stability.

What remains an unanswered question at this time is the extent to which the establishment of independent nation-states replacing the Soviet Union will increase global and regional stability; indeed, the reverse might occur, with these entities becoming sources of international instability. This question cannot be answered in abstract terms by idealizing and advocating the process of change, or by considering it merely as a struggle for national self-determination against autocracy. The issue of self-determination is very complicated, especially in a region of mixed ethnic or religious populations, and does not necessarily correlate neatly with considerations of stability. In the republic of Ukraine, for example, there are important religious and ethnic differences between the western and eastern parts of the country. The diversity of the population is even greater in the case of several Asian republics. There are Russian minorities in all these republics, and in some instances their size is such as to comprise almost 50 percent of the citizenry. Given the radical views of the different separatist movements motivated by ethnic frictions and political rivalries, there is a great probability that various referenda and declarations of political independence will ensue, quite possibly leading to the establishment of additional independent states on the ruins of the Soviet empire. Such a process of continuing dissolution could be the beginning of a long era of political instability.

All of the important powers of the world are in the process of formulating their policies towards the new Commonwealth. The former chief adversary, the United States, has a strong interest in avoiding lasting instability and chaos in that region, and an equal interest in the stabilization of a loose political structure that will be strong enough to provide sufficient security for the peoples of Commonwealth. In this context, as has been already mentioned, the CIS could represent a countervailing force to the expansionist aspirations of other potential powers in Euro-Asia, while not having the power to jeopardize the security of these nations and regions. A key issue here involves the future of the former Soviet army and the control of the enormous nuclear arsenal, as well as the oversight of the military–industrial–science complex, which, however, given a shortage of financial resources, has automatically been shrinking, and is already now a mere shadow of its former might.

Relations with the new pluralistic structure arising from the ruins of the Soviet empire will be a very important issue for European countries. In the case of certain European countries, this relationship has so far been dissimilar in nature to their traditional ties with Russia. Previously, for example, France had regarded Russia primarily as a geopolitically important balancing force against Germany. Germany, on the other hand, regarded Russia as a major economic partner and is increasingly inclined to do so again. In the final years of this century, Germany will be the most important European power having strong political and economic interests in the future of the CIS. This is due in part to the fact that there are still Russian soldiers on German soil; Germany has made major financial commitments not only to provide them with services, but also to facilitate their departure and settlement at home. Germany also has strong economic interests in establishing special relations with the Commonwealth and possesses the capabilities needed to do so. The European Community as a whole will have to define its relations with the CIS and with the individual states within it. Some of the successor states are interested in separate association agreements with the EC, which would make the overall pattern of relationships substantially more complicated. Defining the relations with the countries of the CIS is, of course, in the security interests of the Western European countries, and hence will require further consideration. They do not need to consider these relations, at least for many years to come, as a serious military security issue, in the sense of posing a direct threat. However, the question is: will Europe be able to accommodate these CIS countries within the European regional framework, and, if so, in what form? CIS countries could become important markets for European goods and capital, and sources of raw materials and of scientific capabilities, and hence closer relations could strengthen Europe. There is, also, an indirect incentive for the European countries to help out the CIS, namely, a growing anxiety that mass emigration from the former Soviet Union is likely to occur if the CIS is not able to stabilize the economy of its member states relatively soon.

Relationships of the former Soviet Union with its erstwhile allies are even more complicated because of their geographic proximity and historical role as a security belt or buffer zone between Russia and the West. Further, these partners are still dependent, though to a diminishing extent, on Russian supplies of oil and natural gas and on the Russian market, which had previously purchased a bulk of their exports. Most of them have historically had some conflict with some of the now independent states of the CIS: the Ukraine, for instance, incorporates the former eastern part of Poland and

controls a region that historically had belonged to Hungary; territorial disputes could also arise between Romania and the Ukraine. These and other
problems indicate that, while the disintegration of the Soviet Union will
result in significant and favorable changes that open new opportunities, the
international community must be watchful of the problems and prepared to
address them; indeed, the geopolitical significance of the CIS will require
major adjustments in the strategic thinking of many countries in the world.

4. The Great Transformation: Will the Future Repeat the Past?

The Central and Eastern European region has also been identified as an
important source of uncertainties about the international system, especially
as it relates to Western Europe. At the same time, however, in many ways
there are new, and in this century perhaps unprecedented, opportunities for
the nations of the region to become a more organic part of the wider international economic and political system, and to accelerate their own modernization, thereby improving the living conditions of their peoples.

While this region is often considered homogeneous, it is in fact one of the
most heterogeneous areas of Europe from the point of view of comparative
levels of economic development, cultural tradition, and ethnic problems.
The six countries of the region have a combined population of about 120
million people. The region is burdened with at least 14 minority conflicts, six
of which are serious. In fact, several in former Yugoslavia have already
erupted in severe strife. The future of these countries will be determined
through the interplay of various international and domestic factors, forces
and problems. It is not merely their degree of success in democratizing or
in building a liberal market economy that will shape the direction of their
development. The rapid and often unexpected changes in these countries
are taking place under conditions of a deep economic crisis that was the
legacy of a rigid, inefficient system that could not adjust to the world
political economy and blocked all efforts that were made to achieve socio-
economic modernization.

The character and the outdated nature of their external economic relations were also responsible for the crisis. There is no prospect of rapid
improvement of economic performance or of a spectacular and immediate
reversal of the decline in standards of living. In any circumstances, even the
most successful among these countries will have to undergo a long and
painful internal process of social and political transformation. The direct
consequences of this process are in marked conflict with the more hopeful
expectations of the population, although perhaps to a lesser extent than in
the former USSR. The resulting discontent may become a source of lasting
socio-political instability, which could aggravate ethnic problems that have
already surfaced during the wave of changes of recent years. Furthermore,
the international consequences of instability in Central and Eastern Europe
may have adverse effects on investment and trade.

The political and ethnic frontiers established in this region after World War I, which were basically embodied in the Versailles peace treaties and restored following World War II, created new sources of latent conflict and tension in the system. During the past forty years the dominating regimes have not been able, and in fact have not even been ready, to ease and dissolve these potential dangers. Nobody could seriously expect the different nationalities or ethnic groups in the region to undergo a melting process, even under the communist regimes that emphasized loyalty to social classes rather than loyalty to nations. There were three important and interrelated causes of the problems for Central and Eastern European regimes other than the difficulties arising from this ideological approach of giving priority to class over nation. *First*, the Soviet Union basically followed a policy of promoting the establishment of autocratic economic regimes that were connected bilaterally with the Soviet economy and for about two decades have had very little experience in multilateral affairs. As a result, and quite ironically, new economic foundations of nationalism were established and strengthened during these years. *Second*, these dictatorial regimes limited the movement of people even between socialist countries for a long period, as rigid economic frontiers were coupled with even more rigid political frontiers. *Third*, there were much fewer (if any) formal guarantees for respecting national minority rights other than those declared with regard to human rights in general. Some countries in the region, e.g. Romania, followed a policy of forced assimilation of minorities. As a result of political changes and the collapse of Soviet hegemony in the region, not only did old ethnic problems rise to the surface, but a new element – separatism – appeared in the political life of some multi-national states, such as Yugoslavia and Czechoslovakia. These ethnic problems and the national minority issues have led to a civil war in Yugoslavia and demonstrate how they could be the sources of tension, conflict, and violence throughout the region.

The revival, or strengthening, of nationalism is an important risk factor in the new global system and may produce disintegration, fragmentation, and conflict in this region, as well as in the international system at large. According to a well-known expert on ethnic problems, there are currently more than 5,000 ethnic groups in the world, many of them with their own territorial base, that are potentially searching for national independence, and could cause trouble. (Stavenhagen, 1986)

In Western Europe difficult ethnic problems can be observed in the United Kingdom, France, Spain, and Belgium. There are also serious minority problems, connected, for example, with the presence of a large number of guest workers and refugees, in Germany and in many other countries, including Switzerland. (Switzerland, incidentally, is an excellent example of a democracy that functions without pulverizing or melting its different ethnic communities.) Nationalism and fragmentation are very important dangers and problems in many other parts of the world, such as, for example, India, China, the Sudan, and Ethiopia. The Middle East is yet another example of the problems of violence linked with ethnic and minority issues.

While it is true that such issues as separatism, autonomy, and self-determination that are connected with the resurgence of nationalism, minority aspirations, and ethnic conflicts in Central and Eastern Europe have recently been receiving greater global attention, it does not mean that they are to be seen only in light of recent changes. This class of issues has always been a leading concern of these states. Nationalism in this region of the world can become aggressive with great rapidity. If this occurs, it may result in international confrontations and dangerous conflicts, as developments in Bosnia suggest. Historically speaking, this is a serious consideration because Central and Eastern Europe is situated in the traditional buffer zone between great powers and has been generative of past conflicts that have played catalytic roles in precipitating both world wars in this century.

Another reason for giving keen international attention to this area has to do with the role this region played in the Holocaust. The mass murder of many minorities, especially Jews and Gypsies, has become part of the "historical memory" of the world with respect to this region. The hatred among certain nations in the region has also historical roots, with the great powers being able to capitalize on this factor in the past by helping certain nations establish their own states and oppress others. This could be repeated again in a range of particular circumstances that could again lead to great power confrontations.

Another factor makes the problems of nationalism even more complicated in the region than elsewhere. During the Cold War period, the struggle on behalf of "national identity and self-determination" of the people in this region not only was considered a legitimate goal in general, but also functioned as a political instrument in the pro-democracy struggle against Soviet domination. Not surprisingly such nationalist aspirations received strong support from many Western countries. Nationalism in a new era, in settings with weak democratic and liberal traditions, and in settings where social problems and economic difficulties are deep, building upon a historical heritage of hatred, forced assimilation, and oppression, could easily become explosive and result in widespread chauvinism and xenophobia. Such a dynamic could endanger the stability of the whole European continent, and is already foreshadowed by what has been happening in the former Yugoslavia.

These ethnic problems and minority issues could be aggravated by the evolving social problems in the region that are connected with the economic difficulties, rooted in the former system and arising from the traumas of transition. The changes in Central and Eastern Europe have been basically peaceful (with the exception of former Yugoslavia). The peoples and governments of the region have displayed their political maturity thus far. The process of transition to the Western-type market system, however, is still at a very early stage. The rejection of communism will have to be followed by the completion of difficult and painful tasks in order to stabilize democracy, consolidate the economy and achieve integration in the global market system.

The transformation process in Central and Eastern Europe has also confirmed the old experience of systemic changes, namely, that changing the political institutions is the easiest and the fastest part of the process. It is much more difficult to change values, popular perceptions and attitudes.

Among the political goals of the people and movements that fostered the transformation process in Central and Eastern Europe, democratization, pluralization, and reintegration into Europe were basic priorities. New democratic constitutions were adopted in most countries, and fundamental constitutional reforms were introduced in others. On the basis of the changes and reforms, new political institutions have been established, corresponding to the ideas of civil society and Western-type democracies. The first democratic elections since the late 1940s took place in each of the Central and Eastern European countries during 1990. The results of these elections were different and in most cases the new legitimate governments were formed by a fragile coalition or they had an unstable majority.

How strong and how safe is democracy in the region? Since the beginning of the changes this question has been raised time and time again, both within the region and outside, and for more than one reason. Firstly, there were no strong democratic traditions in the pre-World-War-II period in this part of the world. Secondly, the middle class, which is probably the most important social group on which an efficient parliamentary democracy is based in the West, is generally weak in Central and Eastern Europe. Thirdly, there is growing apathy and indifference among the broader masses, which is reflected, among other things, in the relatively low turnout for the elections. Fourthly, the socio-economic difficulties connected with the transition to the market system, such as rising inflation and growing unemployment, have been increasing popular discontent and paving the way for a rise of demagogic politics, the beginnings of which are already present in these countries. It is therefore not easy to give a realistic and balanced answer as to the relative safety of democracy in the region.

It is, of course, clear that today the social structures of these countries differ greatly from those of the pre-World-War-II period. They are no longer "traditional" peasant societies in which authoritarian rule could be easily imposed. They have a large professional group, a broad industrial working class, and other social groups, including a small but growing entrepreneurial middle class. Most of these groups had enough of the dictatorial regime during the past forty years. Any open or even a disguised political effort to introduce new dictatorial regimes would certainly be strongly opposed.

While there are political groups in the Central and Eastern European countries that would like to continue the pre-war system and, as a Polish historian, Jerzy Jelicki, put it, some of them may consider "what existed in between" – meaning the past decades – "enclosed in historical parentheses," the world and especially Europe are fundamentally different from the pre-World-War-II years. Today Germany is a strong democratic state in a democratic European system. European institutions operate as important safeguards of democracy. The return to Europe and the development of organized relations within the European Community will necessarily be based on democratic values and institutions that should reinforce democratic commitment on a domestic level.

Another process that would be extremely dangerous from the point of view of democracy is the revival of the old inter-war issues and political structures in new forms. The search for scapegoats, the wave of chauvinism and anti-Semitism, and the manipulation of Christian values for nationalist, populist demagogy would result in international isolation and national catastrophe for the countries of Central and Eastern Europe.

Democracy is, of course, a process which must be learned on the basis of national political experiences. It also has a strong international "demonstration effect," but this can play only a limited role since it cannot influence the interests and determine the attitudes of the masses. The shaping of democratic political culture in its different concrete manifestations has been the result of long processes of learning in the West. One of the important dimensions of backwardness in Central and Eastern Europe has been the limited, underdeveloped nature of its political culture. The period of the last forty years of dictatorial rule has not been the "best school" for these purposes. It would also be extremely important for the countries of the region, not only from the point of view of the future of European politics but also from that of the learning process, to become organic parts of a community of friendly, democratic and free nations in which fundamental democratic values determine the functioning of the system, including interstate relations. Economic stagnation or decline and economic deprivation cannot be a sound basis for the process of learning democracy and for promulgating new, democratic values. If the first massive experiences with democracy for the "silent majority" of the population are inflation, unemployment, increasing inequalities and a declining standard of living, the result will be fear, alienation, and distrust. For forty years, oppressive regimes, under the slogans of communism, tried to convince the people that they have to sacrifice their present welfare for the sake of a brighter future. This discredited utopia must not be replaced by vague new promises that contradict daily experience. Without concrete present results, popular disillusionment is certain to arise, and will threaten the stability and democratic character of the new institutions and governments.

In such circumstances, the success of the changes in Central and Eastern Europe depends not only on the wisdom of the new leadership and the degree of national consensus supporting the emerging system, but to a very great extent on external conditions. Will the region eventually become "Europeanized," with open, increasingly symbolic frontiers that allow the free flow of goods, capital, know-how, technology, and people? Or, instead, will this region face a "golden curtain" separating it from the West? The answer to these questions is fundamentally linked to the successful or failing management of risks in relation to Central and Eastern European countries over the course of the coming decades.

5. The Unified Germany: Old Concerns and New Realities

Another complex issue for the future of the European security structure involves the path that the unified Germany will follow. The German role has consequences for European and global affairs, especially from the point of view of comprehensive security considerations. The economic costs of German unification have been very high. In economic terms, the estimates of total costs vary with different German experts, ranging from 600 to 1,000 billion dollars (which figure includes the costs of modernization for the former Eastern Germany). All agree, however, that the costs will be much higher than had been originally anticipated and that the process will last much longer. There are and will be also human costs like unemployment (20 percent of the former East German labor force were jobless at the end of 1991) that correlate with and add fuel to the growing xenophobia in Germany. The potential benefits of unification, however, will outweigh these difficulties. Unification in and of itself has strengthened global security because it has defused the "German question" as a potentially explosive factor.

No serious student of European history has ever considered the division of Germany to be a final, perpetual verdict on the destiny of that nation. The question always was: when and how will unification take place, at what price, and paid for by whom? Would it entail a third world war or rather a regional conflict in Europe, sparked perhaps by a civil war? Would there be anything remaining of Germany after any such war? A few, more "optimistic" East German experts anticipated a peaceful confederation of a social democratic Germany and a democratized socialist GDR, which, in the first phase, would neutralize each polity, leaving the respective military forces in place, and empowering a special integration group to plan and negotiate succeeding phases, e.g. by standardizing infrastructure. The way unification actually took place was somewhat unexpected in that it has contributed to the improvement of the international strategic environment. It was a peaceful change, occurring with the consent of the great powers. The new unified Germany is an economically strong, politically stable democratic state, and is the most important power in Europe, having an increasing potential role in global politics and a leading role in world trade and finances. The role that Germany will play in European and global politics remains imprecise at this time.

The unification of Germany has raised some old and new concerns in Europe. While it has been generally recognized that neither the new Germany nor Europe or the world are politically configured in a way even remotely similar to past geopolitical structures and interrelationships which characterized the pre-World-War-I or pre-World-War-II decades, the sheer fact of Germany's historical responsibility for two world wars in this century has become a source of concern and uncertainty regarding any scenario of future political evolution. One of the main questions is whether, after the collapse of the Soviet empire and the diffusion of power in global politics, there will be any power to balance the increasing role of Germany in Europe, and, if not, what the consequences of this new power structure would be for European and global politics. These issues have become especially important for the two other dominant powers on the European continent, France and the United Kingdom. In France it has become especially difficult to forge a new international identity that would define its attitude vis-à-vis strategic problems and the future path of European integration amidst this new configuration of forces. France is primarily concerned with how to use its weight and influence most effectively in the new era for increasing stability and reducing the risks caused by the changes.[2]

For some French politicians and strategic thinkers, the strengthening and deepening of the integration process through firm Franco-German cooperation in all possible areas still seems to be the answer. Some others look at the issues from the point of view of the necessary role of the balancing powers and thus take into account the interaction of France, Germany, and Britain, and the role of the Atlantic framework. (Moisi, 1991)

Germany as united has already acquired, and will increasingly acquire, all of the qualifications of a major international power, indeed of a superpower. Germany's population is around 80 million; the labor force is highly qualified and well motivated; the share of the country in global output is close to 10 percent, the third largest in the world; and it is the largest trading nation, with 30 percent of global trade in manufacturing. Germany is playing a leading role with respect to new technologies. And, in keeping with its historical traditions, Germany possesses a large, well-trained and disciplined army. The unification of Germany and the changes in Europe will inevitably alter German political attitudes and demands. One legitimate demand, for example, is that the country's international position be normalized. This would mean, first of all, the departure of all foreign armies from German soil. While the international ambitions of any state, including Germany, will be influenced by domestic political, social, and economic factors and forces, all subject to the tides of change, the political options for a future Germany (or any other state in the system) will, of course, be determined by the international environment in which it has to live and act. From the point of view of Germany's future role, an economically integrated Europe with a federal political structure would be the most reliable framework for avoiding the repetition of historical dangers. In joint political institutions governed by binding rules it would be very difficult for any nation to pursue ambitious, dangerously individual political goals. The achievement of such a structure would depend very much on the political orientation of the now unified Germany. But will the German attitude toward Europe and toward the integration process in general undergo transformation in this period of consolidation? One potential risk factor present here should not be overlooked. In some segments of the German public a certain Euro-fatigue can be detected, especially in local politics. There is a certain "re-nationalization" mentality in the German population that has emerged as a byproduct of reunification. This does not yet signal a redefinition of the priority, longer-term political goals of Germany within its national framework. It does, however, suggest a new approach that locates national interests in the center, with Europe, and particularly European integration, being looked upon with cool eyes through lenses of benefit considerations, and, hence, with greater skepticism.

The agenda of European politics in the 1990s is full of difficult problems. No European and external power can overlook these challenges. Their successful management requires strong and efficient regional and global cooperation.

Notes

1. Here I use the concept of nationalism according to a broader understanding, not just as an effort to pursue national interests and subordinate everything else to them, but as an ideology, which is exclusionary, presuming superiority over other nations, which may become a motive force for policies to justify subordination, domination, and, in the final analysis, violence.
2. An American commentator stated: "France is finding especially painful to accept Germany's new profile. For 35 years France enjoyed political leadership of the community, thanks to its alliance with Germany's economic power." He quoted an unnamed German official according to whom: "The myth of French grandeur is disintegrating and this is creating a deep crisis of confidence in France." ("After the Cold War: At the East–West Crossroads." *The New York Times*, March 25, 1992, p. A 10)

REFERENCES

Mearsheimer, John J. (1990), "Back to the Future. Instability in Europe after the Cold War." *International Security*. Vol. 15, No. 1 (Summer), pp. 5–56.

Moisi, Dominique (1991), "The Place for France is in NATO." *International Herald Tribune*. November 7.

Stavenhagen, Rodolfo (1986), *Problems and Prospects of Multi-Ethnic States*. Tokyo: The United Nations University.

14

The New Dimensions of European Economies: Integration and Disintegration in the Post-1992, Post-communist Era

*Albert Bressand**

1. Interaction of Two Landslide Transformations with Different Scenarios of Integration or Disintegration

The conjunction of the European Community "1992" program, of radical political changes in Eastern and Central Europe and of the breaking apart of the former Soviet Union is not simply adding "new dimensions" to the European economies: a process of historic proportions is underway, in which economic, political and technological forces cannot be clearly separated. Changing patterns of economic integration are a first-order force shaping economic developments of all types, and yet the very notion of "economic integration" needs to be redefined in a radically different political and international context.

For better or for worse, the European continent is at the center of the first large-scale rethinking of international economic cooperation since the Marshall Plan, the creation of the Bretton Woods and UN organizations, and the post-war reconstruction effort. Major risks could take shape: a resurgence of nationalistic forces with their roots in the 1918 Versailles Treaty era could be the unfortunate successor to the falling apart of the post-World War II geopolitical framework. But the opportunity also exists to break new ground.

What is at stake is not simply trade and growth but the way European societies are organized and the type of relationships they can enter into among themselves as well as with the rest of the world. The definition of

*Dr. Albert Bressand is the Managing Director of PROMETHEE Transnational Networks, Paris.

national sovereignty – whether over natural and environmental resources or over the fine print of countless regulations – is part of the agenda, more explicitly than ever before.

Never a clear-cut one, the border between economics and politics is totally blurred, at least for the present decade: the task is not so much to integrate existing units as to create, re-create or transform local, national and regional entities as part of the European process.

On the Western side of the continent, the critical agenda for the European Community (EC) has clearly outgrown the economic issues addressed in the "1992" internal market perspective to encompass the monetary union and political union under discussion in the two Intergovernmental Conferences. The relations between national central banks and their national governments are already open to redefinition, and the search for a common foreign policy has major implications for national identities.

Meanwhile, on the Eastern side, success in a very complex – sometimes treacherous – transition toward market economics is the decisive, break-or-make test of political change in Central and Eastern Europe.

This conjunction in time of two landslide transformations could be a convergence or a stalemate, or a collision, of historic proportions:

(a) The "collision" scenarios are those in which each side of the continent would become an obstacle to the other side: economic protectionism and lack of appropriate support and initiatives on the part of the EC could deprive Eastern and Central Europe of the benefits of a truly free market environment. Political backlash and ethno-nationalism could be the unpalatable consequences. Vice versa, political tensions stemming from the fall of the Soviet empire could bluntly reveal the limits of the EC as a political actor.

(b) The "stalemate" scenarios are those in which democracy would coexist with technocracy, limiting the new horizons to managed trade, beefed-up quotas and emergency food aid.

(c) By contrast, the "creative convergence" scenario is one of cross-fertilization between economic integration and political audacity. The free movement of people, goods, services and information behind the "EC 1992" momentum would become a source of pan-European economic dynamism. Meanwhile, the spirit of political openness at work in post-communism, post-Cold War Central Europe and in the former Soviet Union would be the catalyst of rapid progress in the field of foreign policy, collective security and political integration for the whole of Europe.

It would be beyond this chapter to provide a fleshed-out description of these scenarios, especially in light of the amazing and often rapid changes of recent years. Merely attempting to lay a foundation for the type of rethinking now called for, the chapter will concentrate on the changing nature of economic integration. Speaking as a West European, I will emphasize the lessons from the EC experience in integration matters, as well as the limits of what the EC as such can do.

Outline

The first section briefly looks at the previous patterns of economic "globalization" as they had taken shape in the 1980s: in many ways, they have shaped the expectations and conditions in which the revival of economic integration in Europe has taken place.

The second and most detailed section focuses on the new concept of economic integration that has gradually taken shape around the "Europe 1992" process. Unfinished as this process is, it already represents a watershed in the type of corporate strategy and in the type of political and regulatory responses shaping economic globalization. Drawing on analyses developed by PROMETHEE, the type of integration associated with the 1992 program is better understood in terms of corporate networking and Europe-wide networks than in the traditional trade specialization paradigm. Similarly, we see the proposed European Monetary Union (EMU) as the quite ambiguous last stage of a broader process of regulatory convergence which tells little about how sovereignty will be allocated in the political and security field.

Because of the pace-setting nature of its integration policies as well, of course, as of its sheer economic magnet-power, it is clear that the EC finds itself at the center of a new European dynamic that could span – or fail to span – the Lisbon–Vladivostok land mass. The third section of this paper will therefore present a tentative map of integration and disintegration forces at work in Europe in terms of four clusters of countries. I propose to label these clusters the *Community*, the *proto-Community* (namely the remains of a "Europe of Seven" now known as the European Free Trade Association), the *para-Community* (namely Central Europe, the three Baltic countries and such new nations as Slovenia and Croatia that belong to the same political and cultural "community" as the EC but that still face major obstacles to achieving full economic integration) and the *anti-Community* presently emerging from the disintegration of the Soviet Union and Yugoslavia.

The term "anti-community" is not meant to suggest any hostility – on the contrary, mutual attraction has never been as strong – but, rather, the fact that this part of the continent is currently moving in opposite directions from the EC: disintegration rather than integration, multiple currencies rather than monetary union, national laws rather than regional directives, and so forth.

Readers easily turned off by neologisms are nevertheless invited to rejoice at the prospect that Europe is at last rediscovering its Greek roots ... In any case, the post-1992 perspective is so widely open that a modicum of linguistic trauma is the very least of what one should prepare for.

Lastly, the fourth section looks at the implications of further European integration on the EC model for transatlantic relations and for multilateral cooperation.

2. The 1980s, a Decade of Global Strategies and Regional Dialogues

The 1980s will be remembered as a strange time in terms of economic integration patterns. The term "globalization" became a buzzword, but the reality under it was geographically and politically fragmented:

- Geographically, the "global economy" of the 1980s was basically a trilateral one, with a strong group of newcomers from Southeast and East Asia elbowing their way into it. "Delinking," a concept put forward in the 1970s by radical developing countries' speakers, came into being as a boomerang: the debt crisis and the substitution of technology for natural resources and for cheap labor left Latin America, Africa and South Asia outside this new industrial revolution.
- The politics behind this "fragmented globalization" dynamics was of a regional and bilateral nature. True, the GATT Contracting Parties met in 1982, at American urging, for their first ministerial meeting since the completion of the Tokyo Round. But it took until 1986 to launch a new multilateral trade round at Punta del Este, and the possibility of bringing the Uruguay Round to a successful conclusion is still in doubt seven years later. By contrast, the EC has been able to make progress well beyond its own expectations with respect to its "internal market" objective. The USA, meanwhile, has been led to place high priority on the conclusion of bilateral "free trade agreements" first with Israel and, more importantly, with Canada. Global implications have begun to be discussed, rightly or wrongly, largely in terms of "Fortress Europe" or of "regional blocs."
- Last but not least, the decade closed with the outright dislocation of the one region where military, political and ideological links had made economic regionalism a compulsory gift from materialist heaven, namely Eastern Europe. The "Complex program" of the 1970s had been the last concerted effort by the Comecon countries to adapt to the changing nature of economic interactions. Throughout the 1980s, the "convertible rouble" failed to provide the tool for a genuine multilateral integration strategy. The substitution, in 1990, of the dollar for this non-convertible convertible and the wide spectrum of policies experimented with in the post-communist Europe – from Polish shock therapy to Czech and Slovak gradualism – triggered a collapse of trade among former partners that left this part of Europe as the orphan of economic integration.

3. The Unexpected Model: The European Community as a Post-interdependence Construct

Integration as a Bottom–up Process

The European Community's "internal market" program, which had been launched with the signing of the 1985 Single Act (a program referred to thereafter, in short, as "Europe 1992"), stands out therefore as the single most important source of innovation to be achieved during the 1980s regarding economic integration.

Yet, at first, the 1992 program was not an effort to break new ground with respect to economic integration but, rather, an effort to catch up with the USA and Japan by removing the numerous barriers that prevented the EC from benefitting fully from technological and economic change. Indeed, the 1984 Single Act and the set of 279 market opening measures lumped together in Lord Cockfield's White Book could be seen as mere restatements of the "common market" objective which had been set up in the 1957 Treaty of Rome and which was supposed to have been achieved in 1968.

In practice, however, this minimalist view of the "1992" process has been overcome by a set of converging pressures from the corporate world and from society at large:

- Large European corporations realized with increasing clarity that they needed to globalize in order to survive.
- Smaller corporations came to look at Europe as the arena in which to realize the degree of deregulation and the decrease in tax pressure that they felt they needed to remain competitive in an increasingly open world economy.
- Tired of standing behind lines of trucks at customs houses or of being denied some economic rewards available in the country next door, individuals also made rapid progress in the art of bypass and cross-border shopping.

Individuals and small and medium companies have become increasingly aware of the potential of tighter European integration in relaxing the grips of national authorities and the oligopolistic rents accruing to some of their favorite corporate champions. In France, mavericks such as the Leclerc distribution group and the UTA airline – a company now absorbed by Air France – have been systematically challenging restrictive national laws and state monopolies before the European Court, on subjects ranging from the pharmacists' monopoly over the sales of baby milk formulas to the allocation of air routes.

A major factor in this bottom–up process was the role played by the European Court of Justice, which is seldom mentioned yet is a key actor in the "Europe 1992" process. The possibility for corporations and individuals to take their grievances to a court standing – in some respects at least – above the national order opens the national regulatory process and national policies to challenges without an equivalent outside of Europe. In particular, the Court's 1979 "cassis de Dijon"[1] decision was a major blow to non-tariff barriers of all types while its December 4, 1986, insurance decision established that cross-border delivery for all services was legitimate under the Treaty of Rome. From airline cartels to utilities and government procurement, the story of "1992" is one of fortresses dismantled rather than of walls erected.

As individual actors turn to the European Court to enforce an increasing array of rights to interact across borders, policy makers have decreasing confidence in their capacity to enforce policies that would depart too much from those of the more open European countries. Hence the policies put in place tend to incorporate an ex-ante European perspective, quite apart from a formal ex-post negotiation process. A perfect example is the priority given by the French *socialist* government to the reduction of taxes on *capital* gains rather than on earned income.

The New Dynamics of Corporate Interconnection

An analysis of the corporate strategies and of the Europe-wide structural policies behind the "1992" momentum (see notably "1992: the Global Challenge," *Project PROMETHEE Perspectives*, No. 9, Paris, March 1989, and Bressand, 1990) brings to light a number of features going beyond trade specialization and macroeconomic interdependence. The new dynamics is centered on services, corporate cross-border networking and advanced public infrastructures with a strong information technology component. It can be further analyzed by identifying *networks* as the critical organization principle behind many of these new aspects of European integration.

Rather than simply seeking exports and economies of scale, European-based companies are now focusing on developing Europe-wide delivery systems, corporate alliances, production networks and electronic market places. Rather than just shipping goods across borders, they are seeking customized, in-depth interactions with clients, suppliers and partners, through an expanding gamut of networking strategies, many of which have a strong information and advanced communication content. In this sense, the physical elimination of customs houses is a misleadingly narrow symbol of the deeper and more complex ways in which corporate strategies are reshaping the new phase of economic integration. (For a discussion of the broader agenda of globalization lying beyond the now narrow post-war notion of free *trade*, see "Beyond Free Trade," *Project PROMETHEE Perspectives*, No. 8, Paris, January 1989.)

When Allianz, the leading German insurance company, seeks to develop its business in Spain, it does so neither through "exports" (that is, cross-border delivery) nor through traditional "foreign investment" in their insurance sector but through a networking arrangement with two Spanish *banks* interested in innovative and cost-effective use of their distribution networks and in which Allianz takes a significant yet far from dominant 5 percent equity stake. (See, for example, Bressand, Distler & Nicolaïdis, 1989.)

Looking at corporate strategies, we have shown in past work that *four types of networks* were now being mobilized by corporations:
• Two of them are data-networks: depending on whether they are internal to one corporation or shared among several, we refer to them as (a) *intracorporate* networks and (b) *transcorporate* networks. Computer Aided Design and Manufacturing (CAD-CAM) networks and Computer Inte-

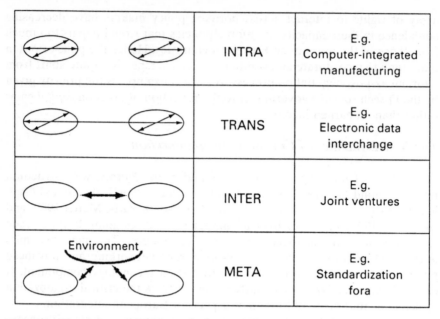

	INTRA	E.g. Computer-integrated manufacturing
	TRANS	E.g. Electronic data interchange
	INTER	E.g. Joint ventures
Environment	META	E.g. Standardization fora

Figure 1   The Networked Corporation as a Combination of Four Types of Networks (Source: PROMETHEE)

grated Manufacturing networks (CIM) are well-known examples of intracorporate networks. Meanwhile, Electronic Data Interchange (EDI) is the fastest-growing type of transcorporate network: linking manufacturers, suppliers and dealers, it makes possible new types of production integration.

• Two other types of networks are of a strategic nature: (c) *intercorporate* networks include strategic alliances and joint ventures of all types, while (d) *metacorporate* networks are intended to influence the corporate environment through lobbying, standard setting, and rulemaking. (See Figure 1)

Obviously, many obstacles may get in the way of this unprecedented development of cross-border corporate networking in Europe. But a number of policies in place, within the 1992 White Paper framework as well as outside of it, can be seen as facilitating or fostering these various types of corporate networking strategies:

• The July 1987 *Green Book on telecommunications* sets the stage for the development of Europe-wide intracorporate and transcorporate networks as well as of value-added networks in general. The 1990 Green Book on satellites, the still in the making Green Book on mobile telecommunications and the RACE program (seeking to foster Europe-wide broad band Integrated Services Digital Networks) will further accelerate the shift from national systems centered on public monopolies toward open network provisioning in which customized private networks can flourish.

- The European Commission is giving its blessing to the development of Europe-wide electronic networks (in PROMETHEE's terms *"networked markets"*) bringing together market participants in sectors such as travel services, the chemical industry, electronic banking services, etc. The competing Amadeus and Galileo computer reservation systems are now at the center of the strategic alliance process reshaping the European airlines industry and influencing its transatlantic linkups. (Bressand, 1989) Similarly, the green light given by the Commission to the European Payment Council's project will allow credit cards issued by all European banks to have access to all Automated Teller Machines (ATMs) throughout the Community.
- The European Commission launched in 1984 the *ESPRIT program* followed by a number of more specialized programs such as Brite and Science that facilitate cross-borders intercorporate networks (joint ventures, common projects, precompetitive R&D, etc.). At French urging, governments followed suit in July 1985 with the more flexible, closer to market, *EUREKA program*, in which the EFTA countries and even Canada are also involved. More than 3,000 companies or research organizations are now involved in about 470 active projects with a total value of 8.18 billion ECUs.
- Together with these cooperative programs, the creation of new standards-setting fora bringing together public and private actors, such as the European Telecommunications Standardization Institute (ETSI) in which PTTs, manufacturers and users come together to develop standards, reinforces the development of what we call European *"meta-networks."* European companies that did not talk to one another ten years ago are now routinely involved in setting Europe-wide standards in fields ranging from computer assisted driving to digital cellular phone and credit cards.
- In the meanwhile, the encouragement of cross-border, multi-lingual studies and research by students, teachers and scientists represents the counterpart for individuals of these corporate networking programs. The *Erasmus and Comet programs* are already having an important influence on higher education by promoting studies in several European countries and by opening breaches in the walls of well-entrenched national education fortresses.

These initiatives and de facto structural policies are a response to the obsolescence of the industrial policy model as it had been pursued by a number of European governments. While these limits had been reached a long time ago by the smaller European countries, the early 1980s marked the limits of the national consolidation process in the larger countries in sectors such as telecommunications, electronics, and automobiles. The national champion policy was becoming too costly and too ineffective for both governments and their champions: to take only one example among many, even the sizeable French PTT procurement program could no longer provide support and subsidies commensurate with the 1 billion dollar R&D effort called for by the new generation of public telephone switches.

A More-than-Economic Community: How Much EPU in EMU?

The turning point in the credibility and visibility of "Europe 1992" was undoubtedly the June 1988 Hanover European Summit when all governments – including the newly elected French socialist government – agreed to full liberalization of all capital movements by as soon as July 1990.[2] Free capital movement, something unheard of in a number of continental countries since the 1930s, represents a watershed for individuals and for small and medium firms that did not enjoy the same capacity as large corporations to move money across borders.

Moving toward monetary union, an objective that most observers had come to see as hard to contemplate in the turbulent context of the early 1980s, is now accepted as a natural implication of the progress already made. With what was then the stand-alone exception of the UK – which is hardly distracting the eleven continental countries from going ahead anyway – the transfer of sovereignty associated with a common currency not only was accepted as a goal but was, to some extent, implicitly considered as having already taken place.

A common monetary policy was seen as a common-sense need, however problematic it has become in the 1990s. In 1981 and 1982, France – and the hard-liners in the French Socialist Party who lost power on that occasion – learned the hard way the costs of following expansionary policies that went against the EC tide. Similarly, at their political polar opposite, Margaret Thatcher's England met with unsatisfactory results from adherence to monetary isolationism: inflation was the most obvious consequence of the fiercely independent monetary policies followed in the name of sterling's role as a petro-currency and of the lack of sufficient convergence among national economies.

Furthermore, the domestic implications of moving toward a German-style relationship between government and central bank are now welcome in countries like France where the central bank had too often been asked to bail out the Treasury from less than prudent fiscal policies: Europe is the perfect excuse to do good for oneself by correcting flawed but time-honored and cherished national practices.

Hence the ambiguity of the transfer of sovereignty associated with EMU. On the one hand, a national currency is a fundamental dimension of national sovereignty (witness the eagerness of separatist republics like the Ukraine to mint their own coins). On the other hand, a transfer of sovereignty is widely considered to have taken place anyway. Jacques Delors confessed in a September 6, 1991, interview that he was worried about the prospect of "economic policy being narrowly equated with fiscal and monetary policy." In his view, a genuine EMU should recognize "the leading role of politics, without which Europe would gradually restrict itself to being a free trade zone deprived of internal consistency – and therefore highly vulnerable – and deprived also of the social objectives that give its ultimate meaning to political action." (*Libération*, September 6, 1991, p. 23)

This fundamental ambiguity was to have been resolved, in one way or the other, at the Inter-Governmental Conference (IGC) on Political Union. At this stage, prospects on that side are rather sober as it seems that what will be labeled "political union" will be little more than coordination mechanisms involving little additional transfer of sovereignty ... The linear concept of an "internal market" leading to EMU, itself leading to EPU, can be misleading.

In any case, understanding the nature of the "1992" integration process and its implications for the next decade takes us beyond the black and white dichotomy between market interactions and the high politics of national sovereignty. The thrust of the 1992 program has to do with *regulations*, a grey zone of increasing importance for economic interactions between these two arenas.

Indeed, for all the talks about quotas and safeguards clauses, a "common market" had been in place since 1968. What made the creation of an "internal market" necessary was the growing importance of regulations pertaining to all types of interactions in an advanced, technology- and information-intensive economy. Removing customs houses was by far the easiest part of the 1992 program. Providing the legal and regulatory framework in which insurance companies, dentists, accountants, broadcast satellites, marketing agencies and millions of other Europeans could move around was the far deeper challenge.

In this respect, *the "1992 model" is one of overlapping sovereignties and mutual recognition rather than a supranational construct.* It is in this sense that it holds possible lessons for the broader pan-European integration that has been so controversial.

In addition to the traditional top–down intergovernmental process and to the bottom–up process based on individual legal action that we have briefly described above, the "1992" dynamics is also noticeable for the importance of *lateral influence.*

An important lesson for European integration in the 1990s is the role played by the critical decision of the twelve European Community countries to break away from previous, and increasingly futile, efforts to harmonize regulations and technical norms in favor of a much speedier process based on a limited number of core principles and on *mutual recognition.*

Mutual recognition means that national authorities will now accept that other European governments can grant rights to their own national firms as well as to third-country firms, based on their own regulatory criteria rather than on those of the host country. In particular, under the "second banking directive," banks, financial services providers and many other corporations will be able to carry on a number of activities on a European scale under their *home country regulations.* (Schwartz, 1988) There is a limit to this "lateral" opening in the sense that some core principles must be followed. But the legitimacy of lateral norms is confirmed in the 1979 "Cassis de Dijon" European Court of Justice landmark decision: standards and norms considered acceptable in one of the EC countries will have to be accepted in all others.

In many ways, "mutual recognition" reinforces the relevance and the impact of the corporate cross-border networking strategies that we see as the true foundation of the "1992" momentum.

As remarked by Michel Albert (1988) – chairman and chief executive officer of the AGF insurance group – mutual recognition as will be practiced in Europe has no equivalent in the world and goes beyond the federalist vision derived from the US experience. As he likes to stress, Europeans have accepted direct interaction and competition among national regulations and tax structures without creating, at least at this stage, the political institutions with which a transfer of sovereignty of that order had always been associated.

4. Fragmentation plus Integration: The "Four Clusters" European Galaxy

In the aftermath of the failed putsch in Moscow in August 1991 and of the landslide of declarations of independence that swept over the Soviet empire, the EC experience has come to be referred to as a major beacon for the European continent as a whole. The French Minister of Finance, among others, repeatedly alluded to the EC experience during his visit to Moscow in early September 1991 in an effort to convince the former republics to keep a single currency and to preserve an open trading system among themselves. More prosaically, the EC has found itself in the position of acting as a catalyst for the resumption of food trade among former Comecon countries after the move from the "convertible" rouble to the dollar in Eastern and Central Europe.

The reality, however, is not one of an extension of the EC model to the whole continent but, rather, a tension between an integration dynamics which, indeed, is centered on the EC and a disintegration dynamics in which the search for freer relationships with the Russian Republic is the critical variable (in a very different and more violent context, a similar trend is at work in Yugoslavia). This fundamental tension is the European expression of a global trend that John Lewis Gaddis, in his recent *Foreign Affairs* article, has identified as the successor to the Cold War bipolarity as the central organizing principles for international relations.

The PROMETHEE think-tank is engaged in an effort to map the various integration/disintegration scenarios that could follow from this fundamental tension. Obviously, our work is at a very early stage and I will only indicate in this section the four basic clusters of countries that we are using to draw this map and to identify the changing nature of integration in Europe. As indicated at the beginning of this chapter, it is not possible in an analysis of this type to separate economic integration from political and cultural integration.

Disintegrating Empires: The "Anti-community" Model?

In economic and political terms, the Soviet Union was once the most tightly integrated part of Europe. The central control of the Communist Party coupled with central planning, the command economy and public ownership of property had no equivalent anywhere in the world, at least on such a massive scale, for such a diverse group of nations and with such detailed implications in terms of everyday economic life.

After a long period during which the dysfunctions of this integrated system had become more and more apparent, the same region has very rapidly entered a state of economic chaos bordering on complete collapse. The failure of the August 1991 coup has however unlocked many new – and often conflicting – possibilities. A far-reaching reassessment and negotiation process is under way to redefine the type of integration to be maintained between the various economic and political units of this immense mosaic.

The patterns that are beginning to emerge from this massive restructuring process are clearly pointing in the opposite direction to integration. In this sense, the similarity that a number of observers have seen between the EC and what might emerge from the Soviet Union could be a fleeting illusion at a time when two cars moving in opposite directions briefly intersect.

Thus, our map of integration in Europe is organized around the complex mixture of convergence and divergence patterns stemming from the coexistence of the Community on one side and of a region which we refer to as the "anti-community" on the other. The use of the prefix "anti" is not meant to suggest antagonism but to indicate that the same organizing concept (the still imperfectly defined and open-ended "community" one) is being approached from two opposite directions and, possibly, with opposite implications for the future.

This "convergence through divergence" pattern can be illustrated by trends at work in the former Soviet empire (and, in a narrower and more violent context, in the former Serbian empire known as Yugoslavia). Most prominent among such trends are:
- the reactivation of national borders and customs posts between former Soviet republics, at a time when the EC is suppressing its own internal border posts;
- a move from one currency to at least half a dozen currencies, contrasting with the EC attempt to move from twelve currencies to one;
- a pre-eminence given to national rules and principles at a time when the EC is experimenting with the various forms of regulatory integration and overlaps described above.

Like the encounter between matter and anti-matter, this conjunction in time between the Community and anti-community dynamics will be a source of tremendous energy and transformation for the continent as a whole.

The Para-community

The relationship between the EC and former Comecon (CMEA) countries is very different in nature from the almost black and white contrast that can be drawn, at least at this moment in time, between the EC and the former Soviet Union.

Old links acquire renewed relevance. Ties of great historic importance – beginning with those rooted in the former Austro-Hungarian Empire – can still make their impact vividly felt. We refer to this group of countries as the para-community in the sense that they are very close to the EC countries politically and culturally but quite far apart, at the present stage, in economic terms. A good illustration of the resulting paradox can be found in the field of telecommunications where the same countries that use what Eva Ehrlich has labelled "quasi phones" (namely phones that can be used only at certain times after a long delay and with totally unpredictable results) have nevertheless leap-frogged into adopting basically the same regulatory structure that the EC was still in the process of putting in place.

The type of relationship that these countries establish with the EC will have a major impact on global European integration patterns. This is true in the sense not just of the development process in Central Europe and the Baltic region but also of the framework it will set for pan-Europe and of the ensuing implications for economic dynamism in Europe.

There is therefore something tragic in the contrast between the historic agenda that EC negotiators are faced with and the backburner on which they put the matter to rest until the twelve present members were done with their ongoing "internal" agenda. At heart, the EC strategy at this point is to defer action and to gain time.

History, however, does not always knock at the door when one is fully dressed up: the Community was, indeed, in the process of buttoning up the pajamas of the internal market and of choosing the dressing gown of monetary union. Standing in the corridor behind the door were the EFTA six, a group of closer neighbors in short sleeves that had come to Brussels in the hope of borrowing a larger business suit. Nevertheless, this is the historic moment when long-term relationships between the twelve and at least the three Central European countries must be defined. Here again, the subject at stake is not textile quotas, steel quotas, agriculture quotas, shipping quotas, trucking quotas and other West European lobbies' favorites. The real issue is Polish identity, Czech and Slovak identity, Hungarian identity and, like it or not, European identity.

In this respect, I want to be on record against the incredibly shortsighted policy followed by my own country, at this moment, with respect to association agreements with Central Europe. In the months and weeks following the dismantling of the "iron curtain," German reunification, an aborted coup in the Kremlin and the collapse of communism, a proposal to increase (if one can call it increase) by a puny 3 percent the ridiculously low quotas in place to keep Polish, Czechoslovak and Hungarian agriculture and textiles out of Europe is the last example of what South Africa once worshipped under the name of petty apartheid.

With respect to Central European countries, culture, history and inter-linked democratic processes should take precedence over considerations of a crowded internal agenda and risks of market disruption. Western Europe has much to learn from the many Vaclav Havels and Lech Walesas, known and unknown, who have given new expressions to fundamental European values.

In General de Gaulle's famous terms, *"l'intendance suivra"* (a comment on the relationship between politics and the nitty-gritty of economics). After all, this is exactly how the "internal" market is being built: the fact of having agreed on a shared long-term objective back in 1984 has suddenly made possible a myriad of detailed decisions, many of which had proven elusive for decades before and some of which (such as agreeing on a common indi-rect tax structure) were deemed quite out of reach.

The Baltic countries belong in the same group. Yet the time horizon for deeper integration cannot be totally similar to the one pertaining to Central Europe. First, independence as it materialized in early September 1991 still has to be put in place concretely. Difficult issues pertaining to prop-erty ownership, foreign debt and security agreements have to be addressed. Also, some time must be left for the full development of an internal politi-cal life which had been long suppressed for over forty years and which has been so long dominated by the single overarching objective of achieving independence.

The Proto-community: A Catalyst, or a Roadblock?

Obviously, relations between the Community and the para-community are made more complex by the choices the EC has to make regarding the group of Western European countries that has always been a key trading partner and that had gradually come to see closer integration within the EC as the only route still open. Once part of a "Europe of Seven" that was the first of many less than successful British responses to Franco-German initiatives, the European Free Trade Association (EFTA) is now a poorly integrated group of countries with no answer of their own to the political side of the integra-tion dilemmas. Yet EFTA is a very significant economic force on the Euro-pean continent.

5. Europe as Part of the Global Economy

Further integration – or disintegration – in Europe will be one of the major influences shaping the global economy in the late 1990s and early twenty-first century. Vice versa, the key players in this global arena will not stand idle while Europe defines and pursues its objectives. As has already been the case for the "1992" process, Americans are likely to ask for "a seat at the table" in any "common house" that Europe will undertake to build.

Already, a clear illustration of this open nature of the European arena was the reaction to President Mitterrand's proposal for a European Confederation. Also notable was the emphasis placed by President Havel, at the Prague conference, upon the need for the level of American involvement in any such scheme to be at least equal to the level of Soviet participation. Although subsequent events make such a literal formula inappropriate, the issue posed by Havel remains.

Thus, European economies in the 1990s can be discussed only as tightly interconnected to the global economy and notably to the advanced countries of North America and East Asia. In this respect, lessons can again be drawn from the "EC 1992" experience in assessing possible economic developments in Europe as a whole.

A Fortress or a Shockwave?

In the late 1980s and early 1990s, the international debate about the external implications of "Europe 1992" has been dominated by the "Fortress Europe" label. Interestingly, the term itself is quite ambiguous as it can suggest not just protectionism but also a strengthening of European competitiveness. More importantly the term does fail to capture the real nature of the "European challenge" that "1992" might indeed represent for non-Europeans.

The fortress Europe debate fails to capture the nature of the change most likely to be confronted after 1992 both in the EC and in Europe at large. It is probable that tensions will develop, indeed that they are already evident. But these tensions are not of the traditional protectionist or even "blocist" nature. Rather, they arise out of the stronger affirmation of a European "identity" that represents a challenge for other countries – most particularly for the United States – whether or not it is accompanied by freer trade.

Will the United States and the EC Divorce?

As illustrated by the difficulties of the transition toward a market economy in the former Soviet Union and even in the Central European countries, a market is not simply the absence of obstacles to trade. It has to rest on a complex foundation of rules, expectations and behavioral norms, a number of which call for close regulatory supervision. The debate ignited by the series of financial scandals of the summer of 1991 is a good reminder of the role played by such frameworks in the appropriate working of markets.

In this sense, the creation of the European "internal market" was not simply the removal of the 279 "barriers" listed in Lord Cockfield's White Paper of 1984 but also involved the proactive creation of new regulatory frameworks. In doing so, Western Europeans have been making choices, taking positions and more generally expressing an identity which was bound to be quite often at odds with the choices and expectations of the United States as well as of other countries.

Because of the central role that American values, practices and legal standards played in the post-war Western economy, America naturally feels challenged as a result of the sheer size of the European market as well as of the greater European assertiveness that quite inevitably accompanies successes on the road toward internal integration. Yet, the 1992 program was in many ways an acknowledgment – an explicit one in the UK, a tacit and sometimes reluctant one in some continental countries – of the effectiveness of the *deregulation approach* pioneered by the USA since the late 1970s.

The type of tensions that can develop from this type of competition and self-affirmation process has been well described by Harry Freeman, formerly Executive Vice President of American Express and now a forceful and insightful spokesman for a coalition of American companies with an interest in the current GATT negotiations:

We are truly at a watershed in US–EC relations. After a relative cohabitation in goals since World War II, our communities have entered into a period of separation, with the EC carving for itself a new identity. The US didn't; it should. The choices made in the coming months will determine the nature of our new relationship, the potential outcomes of which are far more significant than usual. (Freeman, 1991)

The Gulf War of 1991 as well as the persisting importance for Europe of the US security umbrella can only reinforce American unhappiness with what might be called, paraphrasing Jean-Jacques Servan-Schreiber, the "European challenge." Indeed, Harry Freeman is among those who remind Europeans that the USA will not forever devote about twice as much of its GNP (about 6 percent) to the common Western security effort without asking more explicitly for some compensatory counterpart in economic arenas, while the Uruguay Round multilateral trade negotiations provide an initial test of these expectations. The $55 billion that Japan, the Middle East and European allies were asked – not always softly – to contribute to the Gulf War effort is a striking illustration of the far more explicit links that may develop between economic and security relations, at least until the European continent can be regarded as a fully stabilized and secure part of the world.

The new dimensions of economic integration described in this chapter will see their course, their direction and their implications very much influenced by success or failure in the pursuit of this broader cooperative environment.

Conclusion: The "Sleeping Beauty" Has Awakened

Economic developments in Europe will depend to a massive extent on the future shape of European integration. Whether on the Western side or on the Eastern side of the continent, what integration entails is now subject to substantial revision. One should already remember the extent to which European Community politicians have been taken by surprise by the "1992" process that they had themselves put in motion. As for the events that have unfolded in the Soviet Union and in the region once known as Comecon, it is an understatement to say that they became real before becoming thinkable, in the sense, I mean, of the manner in which politicians and economic managers think.

Only a few years ago, an optimistic vision of pan-European integration was, at best, a dream of a "sleeping beauty." The "sleeping beauty" is now awake and there is no story we tell to imagine what will now happen to her. I have tried to suggest that the "1992" story is an invitation – of course a far more mundane and limited one – to make the best of the unthinkables come true. Seizing this invitation would be the most powerful engine for progress and prosperity in Europe.

Notes

1. The 1979 "Cassis de Dijon" ruling dealt with the case of a small German importer of liqueur de Cassis produced in Dijon (France). Could imports be prohibited because of an alcohol content which was too low to qualify under German law as a liquor and too high to qualify as wine, hence bewildering the German consumer? The Court answered that free access to the territory of any other member state implied that national norms could not be used to discriminate against an import. This ruling was followed by a number of others related to the import/export of meat, wheat and pasta within the Community. *Cassis de Dijon* has remained the judicial reference point for the enforcement of mutual recognition.
2. December 1992 in the case of Portugal, Greece and Spain.

REFERENCES

Albert, Michel (1988), *Crise, Crack, Boom.* Paris: Le Seuil.

Bressand, Albert (1989), "Computer Reservation Systems, Networks Shaping Markets." In Albert Bressand and Kalypso Nicolaïdis (eds.), *Strategic Trends in Services.* New York: Harper & Row, pp. 51–64.

Bressand, Albert (1990), "Beyond Interdependence: 1992 as a global challenge." *International Affairs.* Vol. 66, No. 1, January.

Bressand, Albert, Distler, Catherine & Nicolaïdis, Kalypso (1989), "Networks at the Heart of the Service Economy." In Albert Bressand and Kalypso Nicolaïdis (eds.), *Strategic Trends in Services.* New York: Harper & Row.

Freeman, Harry (1991), "Implications of the United States and the EC Divorce." Lecture delivered at the Mid-Atlantic Club of New York City, Arden House Conference, April 6.

Schwartz, Marc (1988), "L'Europe Financière." *PROMETHEE Report No. 47.* Paris, February.

15

The Future of EC Institutions: Reform Process in the 1980s

Gianni Bonvicini*

1. Institutions and the Community: Reform in the 1980s

At certain times, debate on institutions, both national and multilateral, becomes ineluctable. Institutions are not simply an architectural exercise; they establish the character of their surroundings and represent therefore the point of arrival or the point of departure of a given historical and political circumstance.

Institutions are not neutral with respect to the environment in which they operate; on the contrary, they tend to shape it with their procedures, laws and operating ability. At the same time, the environment determines the suitability of existing institutions and influences the form of new ones, set up to shape present and future circumstances. (Wessels, 1990)

At the beginning of the process of Community integration, the events and the resolution of the actors at that time determined the form and the limits of the EC institutions. Today, after almost forty years of activity, the common institutions and laws constitute an "acquis communautaire" which is subject to its own internal dynamics of reform and which conditions future plans. At the same time, the external environment, undergoing radical change, confronts the Community with new problems and demands and influences its role and future form. The past and the future converge in demanding a different institutional arrangement for the Community system.

Is this the logic that has led towards the European Council of Maastricht on the 9th and 10th of December 1991, during which the Twelve agreed

*Dr. Gianni Bonvicini is Director of the Istituto Affari Internazionali, Rome, and Editor of the Institute's English-language quarterly, *The International Spectator*.

upon new forms of integration both in the economic–monetary field (the Conference on Economic and Monetary Union – EMU) and in the so-called "high politics" sector (the Conference on Political Union – EPU) of foreign and security policies?

Maastricht in itself represents one step forward in a process of institutional reforming which had started up at the beginning of the eighties. It is not the final point, but it reaffirms the dynamic character of EC institutions. They must adapt themselves continuously to new internal and external factors. This time, among the endogenous elements we can put particular emphasis on the perceived need of completing the '92 free market with a stronger convergence among states in economic and monetary fields, on the willingness to deepen the Community before opening it to new members, and finally on a rather new element, a clearer social and popular perception of the importance of the existence of the Community. On the side of the external factors, as we will comment in the next pages, the most evident are the growing role of regionalism in global affairs, the progressive disengagement from Europe by the United States, the new concept of comprehensive security, the different qualitative meaning of any future enlargement of the Community, as part of a reinforced foreign and security policy of the Twelve, and, more generally, the new role that the concept of integration is bound to play for any future pan-European architecture.

The last ten years have seen a host of projects and plans for reform of the EC. This extraordinary and dynamic decade, institutionally speaking, was ushered in by the Genscher–Colombo Plan drawn up by the two foreign ministers in 1981. (Lay, 1983)

The felt need at that time was directed at completing the already operating monetary system (EMS) through better Community organization in the fields of foreign policy (European Political Cooperation – EPC) and, to some extent, security policy. Institutional procedures, similar to those of the Community, were to be extended to these two sectors – strictly intergovernmental at the time – to enhance Europe's global role and to link EPC more closely to the Community's external economic activities.

Thus, the plan sprang from a need for rationalization – more the result of the Europeanist attitudes of the two foreign ministers than of any objective international situation. Except for a worsening in East–West relations over the Euromissiles – a particularly embarrassing issue for the Europeans, but, in any case, nothing really new in the history of the Cold War – the world seemed static, without any real prospect of change.

But the Solemn Declaration concluding the Italo-German plan and issued in Stuttgart in June 1983 was a disappointment for all: the essential points of the plan, concerning more binding decision-making procedures within EPC, were shelved because of the opposition of France and other partners who wanted to maintain the EPC's intergovernmental character.

After the Solemn Declaration of Stuttgart, pressure for reform of the Treaty intensified in view of the imminent enlargement of the Community to include Spain and Portugal. All agreed that the errors of ignoring demands for deepening made in 1973 during the first enlargement of the EC, which brought in Great Britain, Ireland and Denmark, were not to be repeated.

On that earlier occasion, absolute priority was given to the political aspects of enlargement: opening up to the British was an attempt both to "counterbalance" the Paris–Bonn axis and to make up for the hostile and strongly anti-US attitudes of General de Gaulle who, as is well known, considered Britain a kind of Trojan horse for the Americans. The emphasis given to political considerations undercut the debate on deepening and focused attention on widening.

Indeed, some important institutional moves were made in the seventies, such as the launching of EPC (1970) and the establishment of the European Council (1974); but almost all these measures were strictly intergovernmental and, therefore, not augmenting the supranational character of the original European Community.

Furthermore, no actions were taken during the first enlargement to eliminate the main obstacle to the correct functioning of the Community's institutional mechanism, i.e. the voting procedures within the Council, which resulted from the famous Luxemburg compromise as proposed by de Gaulle in 1966. The abrogation of the system of qualified majority voting, determined by the prevalence of so-called "vital national interests," turned out to be such a fundamental mistake that it almost thwarted even those reforms apparently in keeping with the supranational spirit. This included the institution of own resources (1975), the European Parliament's control over them and, finally, the direct election of the Assembly in Strasbourg from 1979. These reforms all came into being with a handicap, as they were constrained by the preponderant intergovernmental mechanisms of the EC.

2. The Positive Outcome of the Single European Act

In this state of affairs, the European Parliament decided in 1984, at the initiative of Altiero Spinelli, to draw up the Draft Treaty establishing the European Union. (See European Parliament, 1984) This document posited some fundamental criteria for future debate: unity of the economic, foreign and security policy aspects of the integration process; the principle of subsidiarity as the basis for division of powers among Community institutions, member states and regions; re-introduction of a majority voting system; democratic legitimization of the system.

Less explicit, in my opinion, was the search for a "government" of the Political Union, the prerequisite for a qualitative jump towards more accentuated forms of supranationality.

As is agreed, the Draft Treaty was one of the most important elements, perhaps the most important one, taken into consideration when the European governments undertook partial reform of the Treaty of Rome and approved the Single European Act (SEA) at the end of 1985. (Meriano, 1987)

Despite initial perplexities, the SEA fulfilled some expectations and provided a number of fundamental and practical responses to concerns that had been growing about the proper functioning of the Community. It indicated some partial solutions for greater rationalization and effectiveness of the European integration process. Nothing exceptional, really: there was no need felt at the time to define European Political Union in any precise way; the urge was simply to bring some order into an arrangement that was tottering after long years of quibbling with Great Britain over budgetary matters.

There was, however, an awareness of having to correct to some fundamental flaws in view of the imminent enlargement to include two such problematic states as Spain and Portugal, especially in light of the difficulties experienced after the entry of Greece in 1981.[1]

Identification of the positive features of the SEA may be useful in view of future reforms.

The very name "Single Act" can be traced back to the need to bring together under one roof the various branches of European activity, from the EMS and the EPC to such bodies as the European Council, relegated for years to an institutional limbo. Thus, it embodied the principle of consistency in the integration process so often called for in past plans, such as that of Belgian Premier Tindemanns in 1976 and the 1981–83 Genscher–Colombo Plan, to mention only the better known.

This principle, which is still one of the cornerstones of the debate on the future of the "European Union," as defined in the Maastricht Treaty (above all when foreign and security policies are seen as part of the EC and not as standing on their own), was, however, incorporated into the SEA in a very elementary manner. In fact, Maastricht does no more than register the various activities of the Twelve; it does not "Communitarize" them, as it should have. This means that the decision-making procedures have not been changed, even though efforts have been made to bring them into a common framework. Consequently, the Community method will apply to all matters provided for by the Treaty of Rome and to those added by the completion of the internal market arrangements of 1992; the intergovernmental method will apply to all other matters, in particular EPC.

It is clear that the "Communitarization" of European Union policies, both old and new, remains an open question. An answer will have to be found in order to respond to those three basic principles underlying any acceptable pattern of reform for the Community: efficiency, effectiveness and legitimacy of the Community decision-making system, as well as of the resulting common policies.

In other words, the principle of consistency must be extended from the policies for which it is associated in Art. 30 of the SEA (in this case between foreign policy and foreign economic policy) to the field of institutional procedures, putting an end to the limits and the confusion that the alternate adoption of intergovernmental and Community methods continues to create. It is absurd and anomalous, for example, that a declaration condemning the behavior of a third country requires unanimity (in the EPC) while application of economic sanctions to the same country requires a qualified majority according to Art. 113 of the Treaty. (Wessels, 1990, p. 31)

Experience to date indicates that *institutional consistency* must become one of the cardinal principles behind the strengthening of Community institutions.

The real novelty of the SEA is the elimination of an old taboo: the return of the qualified majority voting procedure to the Community Council. Although limited, the rehabilitation of this old procedure has made the Community decision-making procedure more efficient; it has greatly speeded up the approval of directives on matters to which it is applied. Recent studies confirm that this innovation has brought new life and credibility to Community operations. (See the appendix.)

The central treaty provision from this point of view is Art. 110a, which deals with the harmonization of national provisions through approximation. It also extends the qualified majority vote to social policy, research and technology, the modification and suspension of customs duties, the free exercise of services, as well as other matters. Some important areas, such as fiscal provisions and the movement of persons, are nevertheless excluded – the very areas in which the decisions concerning 1992 lag the farthest behind.

Attempts have been made to get around these remaining obstacles and possible curbs on the application of the majority vote by clarifying the decision-making competencies of Community bodies: the competencies of the Council were specified through modification of the procedural regulations in 1987 and those of the Commission through rationalization of Committees and the conferral of greater executive powers.[2] The purpose of these reforms was to give the Commission a broader mediating role by reintroducing to some extent the majority consensus-building function that had been so effective in the initial period of the Community.

In parallel to the reintroduction of the majority vote, the objectives and the methods for the most rapid achievement of legislative harmonization were defined more precisely. Unlike in the past, the Commission was instructed to return to the practice of rather broad directives, leaving it up to individual member states to implement them in detail.

This strategy is in keeping with another fundamental principle: equivalence. If complete harmonization as set down in Art. 8a of the SEA is not achieved by 1992, the criterion of equivalent provisions may be applied according to Art. 100b, in the sense that the provisions judged equivalent by the Commission and the Council shall temporarily be considered valid in all member states and, thus, outside national boundaries.

This is perfectly in line with another of the founding principles of the Treaty of Rome, made famous by its application in some cases before the Court of Justice. The principle is known as mutual recognition. Through its consistent application, the harmonization process could be greatly accelerated and simplified. This principle can obviously not be applied automatically, but it nevertheless has great potential if backed by an increasingly active and authoritative role of the Court of Justice, the real federating element on the plane of the Community's law.

The last interesting feature of the 1986 SEA to have an effect of institutional deepening was the modification of the competencies of the European Parliament (EP). Although limited to the so-called "cooperation procedures" provided for in Art. 149, the results have been better than expected. In matters pertaining to the ten new relevant articles of the SEA, most of which are related to the internal market, the EP is now able to influence the legislative process by amending or rejecting the Council's so-called "common position" during a second reading. If the Council wishes to disregard the decision of the Parliament, supported by the Commission, a unanimous vote is required, and this is obviously difficult to attain. (Ronzitti, 1990)

It follows that a close alliance between Parliament and the Commission is now again a prerequisite for effectively influencing the orientation of the Council. An extension of cooperation procedures to all areas would give more legitimacy to the role of the EP and the Community decision-making procedure as a whole.

The powers granted to the EP in case of association or application for membership in the Community must also be considered (Art. 237 and 238 of the Treaty). The consent of the Parliament is essential in an area which will be of crucial importance for the Community and the rest of Europe in the coming years.

In conclusion, the experience gained from the debate leading up to the reform of the Treaty and, subsequently, in relation to the implementation of the SEA can provide important guidelines for the current phase of proposal and debate on further reform of the Treaty.

3. Returning to Lessons from the Past

Returning to some of the points made above, we would like to point out several of the "successful" elements that have contributed to bringing new life into the process of European integration, long stymied by stagnation and Euro-pessimism.

The first was the decision taken by European governments to link enlargement of the Community to its deepening. Ratification of the SEA took place at the same time as the entry into the Community of Spain and Portugal, thus avoiding a repetition of the error made in 1973, when widening was undertaken without regard to deepening, that is, a contemporaneous reform of decision-making structures.

In fact, the famous motto "completion, deepening and widening" was totally disregarded. The institutional changes undertaken were sporadic, sometimes contradictory and, in any case, not conducive to the efficient functioning of Community machinery. Indeed, the latter became increasingly cumbersome and complex with the addition of uncoordinated organs, competencies and policies.

As mentioned, the SEA was actually aimed at bringing some order and rationality into the chaos by putting an emphasis on a number of important principles (harmonization, consistency, equivalence, etc.) and mechanisms which had fallen into disuse (majority vote). And this coincided with the formal entry into the Community of the two Iberian countries.

Another element that contributed to the achievement of consensus in Luxemburg in 1985 was the "package deal" approach: rather than searching for agreement on a single policy or institutional change, discussion centered on a set of policies and institutional improvements.

The driving power behind this move was definitely the Commission, headed by its president, Jacques Delors. After a few years of debate on reforms, the Commission had identified consensus on completion of the internal market as the prerequisite for definitively strengthening the Community's economy and enhancing its international role. On this basis, it received the consent of the British government, long an advocate of the free market; the German government, aware of its opportunity to confirm its economic leadership; and the French government, eager to use the occasion to shock the French economy into coupling with the German one.

But in order to achieve this result – already agreed upon in the Treaty of Rome but never attained – by the 1992 deadline, institutional changes improving efficiency were required. In addition to approximately 280 directives on the completion of the internal market, the Commission suggested the introduction of some procedures intended to streamline decision-making; in particular, the majority vote on most of the matters was proposed. This mix of policies and procedures turned out to be a very dynamic combination and led to the swift implementation of most of those directives not requiring unanimity.

A third element, perhaps less apparent but no less important, is the fact that this reform sprang more from the "force" and perceptions of European society than from the good will of its political leaders. One important novelty in the debate on the validity of the SEA is the attention that the fateful 1992 deadline has aroused in the economic and business worlds and, more generally, in the citizens who have made efforts to assess what impact the date will have on various sectors of their economic and social lives.

Not even the launching of the European Monetary System in 1978 generated the same kind of expectations and consensus in European society. Basically, the real supporters of 1992 were people involved in business and banking, simple citizens, not politicians, who were, on the contrary, somewhat fearful of losing further terrain to European sovereignty.

This constituted a radical change with respect to the early fifties, when the economic world was reluctant to set out on the European adventure, while political leaders were full of enthusiasm and conviction. More generally, a clearer perception of the importance of the large free Community market is one of the most significant achievements of the EC's forty-year history. The economic success of the common market, the simplification of daily life through harmonization of Community laws, the overall improvement in standards of living and the stricter protection and safety standards (to give only a few examples) have contributed to forming the consensus needed to give a new surge of energy to Community integration, in spite of the precautions and second thoughts of governments. Thus, the Community, with its laws, its policies and its institutions, is taking root in European society.

4. Towards Further Reform of Community Institutions

The Fundamental Reasons

One of the most interesting consequences of the implementation of the SEA has been that institutional reform has not slowed down to await completion of the internal market. Although the SEA called for some verification, such as in the EPC after the first five years of functioning, a pause might have been expected after the breakthrough in 1985. Instead, under external and internal pressures, new institutional revision was undertaken with extraordinary rapidity.

The first incentive to proceed with reform after ratification of the SEA was the plan for Economic and Monetary Reform, stubbornly introduced by the President of the Commission, Delors. The Commission's reasoning was simple: it would be difficult to complete the single European market – void of all barriers – without flanking the already functioning monetary system with a more structured economic and monetary union, including a central European bank and a common reserve fund.

Ultimately, the implications of this proposal of the Commission went beyond simply setting up some mechanisms for monetary control and management, such as the central bank; they called for a real government of the European economy able to ensure compatibility between national and Community economic policies. In short, implementation and realization of the plan for Economic and Monetary Union required improvement of all Community institutional mechanisms. (See EC Commission, 1990)

While this has constituted an element of continuity in the debate on institutional reform after the SEA, other factors have favored a widening of the debate. In particular, the upheaval in Eastern Europe in 1989 turned attention to foreign and security policies as central factors in European union. Up to that time, European security had paradoxically been ensured by the East–West confrontation and the ensuing American leadership in the military field. Furthermore, the division of Germany had accentuated the need to link its Western half to the West and the Community. This was the basis of the equilibrium between Paris and Bonn and the foundation of the process of Community integration.

As these conditions have now changed, the bases for the construction of the future Community must also be changed accordingly. Fear of centrifugal tendencies in Germany, which is concentrating on its problems of national unification and intending later to assert its geostrategic leadership in central Europe, has spurred France to relaunch European Political Union in addition to the economic union already begun in response to Delors' proposal.

Thus the need for two intergovernmental conferences, rather than the one planned on economic union, arose to bridle Germany, with the consent of Chancellor Kohl, by common foreign and security policies which are seen as guarantees for maintaining stability in Western Europe.[3]

The dissolution of Eastern Europe as a bloc has complicated the future role of the Community: the rapid disappearance of all forms of cooperation among Eastern countries, both economic and military, has once again urgently raised the general question of the relationship between integration and nationalism.

Furthermore, with the increasing fragmentation of the East and the formal end of the Soviet Union itself and with the independence of states contiguous to the former empire, the Community will have to decide what guarantees of economic development and security it can offer, and, above all, whether and in what way it can act upon the growing instability caused by nationalistic phenomena in the East, while, at the same time, preventing such nationalism from affecting negatively the cohesiveness of the Community. Common European economic, foreign and defense policies must be adopted to provide an effective response to the needs of a disintegrating East.

Partially related to this dilemma is the serious problem of Community enlargement. (See The Six Institutes, 1991) It is no longer a matter of giving a gradual and acceptable answer to two or three smaller and economically weak states: applications have come from EFTA countries, from Mediterranean countries and from some Eastern countries. This could lead to a doubling of the number of Community members in only a few years.

Moreover, the countries applying for membership differ from one another and are moved by different reasons: the EFTA countries are basically motivated by economic considerations and reject any political or security commitments; the Eastern countries seek not only economic, but also political and security guarantees; beside economic factors, the Mediterranean countries are moved by questions of stability and coupling with Europe in an area of potential conflict.

In this light, enlargement takes on a different dimension and calls for the deepening of the policy of widening which has to date served simplistic and pragmatic ends. From now on enlargement will assume a strategic character, as it can no longer overlook general political and security (as well as military) considerations.

Reform of the Community must take these basic factors into account. While a few years ago the problem was how to ensure effective government of the European Community, today Community institutions are faced with decisions on how to enhance their roles to be able to address, at least partially, the emerging new needs.

What Institutions for the Future?

One premise must be set forth: under present conditions, deepening must have prevalence over any widening. Although priority was given to widening in the past, in particular in 1973, and widening and deepening were also undertaken together in 1985, in the nineties attention must be focused on deepening. This does not mean postponing the requests for enlargement *sine die*, but it does mean giving priority to internal institutional improvement. This philosophy has been partially applied in Maastricht. The heads of government of the EC have first agreed on the institutional reinforcement of the European Union and only in the Presidency conclusions have they declared a willingness to start the process of negotiations "as soon as the Community has terminated its negotiations on Own Resources and related issues in 1992," meaning that also budgetary questions, in addition to the institutional ones, must be solved beforehand. (See European Council, 1991, p. 3)

Thus the institutional question remains central. In recent months, many Community bodies, including the European Parliament, the Commission, the individual governments taking their turns at the EC Presidency, and specialized institutes and associations have developed a large number of proposals. In addition, personal representatives of the heads of government have been working on preparations for the European Council in Maastricht.

The outcome of all this activism has been as usual throughout the history of the Community reform process, namely a rather unorganic compromise. From the very beginning it was hard to believe that the meeting in Maastricht could have resolved all questions; the process of institutional reform will continue for the indefinite future. It is important, though, that it maintain the dynamism demanded by the exceptional circumstances today and, above all, that it be guided by a common strategy to be established in the present setting and not improvised on each occasion.

The institutions required for the future will have to meet the criteria set down in accordance with the guidelines of the European Council: efficiency, effectiveness and legitimacy.

Moreover, since Community institutions, more than any other multilateral institutions, represent the most significant product of the transition from the old form of conflictual state to a new form of cooperative state, it is clear that the principle of subsidiarity, if possible in the most advanced meaning of the term, must be applied: the Community must be assigned all tasks whose scope and effects go beyond national boundaries. This approach has a decentralizing or federative effect, unlike the efficiency-oriented approach, which attributes those tasks to the Community which it can best carry out and consequently leads to centralization. (Committee for Institutional Affairs, 1990) Under this point of view Maastricht has struck a compromise: both concepts of subsidiarity have been included in Art. 3b, when it refers to "reason of the scale or effects of proposed action." (Draft Treaty on Political Union, 1991, p. 4)

In addition to fulfilling these criteria, which now enjoy broad consensus, Community institutions will have to possess the characteristics needed to respond credibly to present and future commitments. That is, they must be capable of playing an influential role in various internal and external fields.

It has already been pointed out that internal dynamics are also pressing for institutional adaptations. The stability of the internal market and monetary accords could be jeopardized if these measures are not accompanied by other steps towards economic union. And in the future the stability of that union could also require some effective social policy measures.

It is doubtful whether the future cohesion of the union can be maintained with the present budget and the limited redistributive policies adopted to date. In a more advanced stage of economic union a common fiscal policy and a much larger budget are likely to be required to permit the adequate discharge of the function of allocating resources. Such a development was already requested by Spain in relation to the Maastricht European Council and monetary stabilization. If these are to be the objectives of the EMU, then Community legislation will inevitably have progressively to limit the room for maneuver and the autonomous decision-making power of member states.

As a result, the Community will become increasingly responsible to its citizens. The President of the Commission, Jacques Delors, has repeatedly stated that almost 80 percent of economic and social legislation will be passed by the EC. This raises two main problems: the first concerns the governing capacity of the EC, with the extension of the qualified majority voting procedure to all social and economic legislation to streamline the decision-making procedure; the second concerns the democratic deficit, that is, the low level of legitimacy of the present Community decision-making process. Thus, the powers of control and co-legislation of the European Parliament must also be increased.

However, the strengthening of the economic and social roles of the EC does not only have internal implications: it is obvious that the establishment of an area of economic and monetary stability and autonomy will have external consequences both globally (the Group of Seven, GATT, etc.) and regionally.

Above all, the development of policies promoting economic cooperation and association with areas neighboring to the East and to the South would lay the foundation for and encourage the growth of a foreign policy supporting the ever-increasing economic activity of the Community.

Coordinated and uniform responses must become normal routine, not sporadic events. The concept of consistency must no longer refer only to policies; it is also required upstream at the decision-making level. The Communitarization of the EPC means, firstly, application of qualified majority voting procedures not only to "joint action," as agreed in Maastricht, but to the whole range of issues governed by the political decision, secondly, definition of an executive role going beyond the present precarious troika system, and lastly, associated with the EP, extending to the field of foreign policy the competencies that the EP is presently taking over in the economic field. All of these complex and controversial matters must be included among the aims of future institutional reforms.

Finally, the Community cannot get around defining its position in the security field. Undoubtedly, the current geostrategic situation has created a security void at the edges of the Community.

The irreversible demise of bipolarism in the field of defense and the evident American withdrawal from Europe demand new responsibilities of the EC and a redefinition of that concept of "civilian power" which it built up under the United States' protective wing. How can Europe escape occupying itself with local crises in Eastern Europe or the Mediterranean? It would be absurd not to keep a close check on questions pertaining to nuclear, chemical, and biological weapons proliferation, not to respond to the needs for stability and security emerging in Eastern European countries.

What must be avoided at all costs is the renationalization of the defense policies of EC countries in solving these problems. That would pave the way for the irreversible destabilization of all of Europe. Thus, a consistent response from the Community is needed here as well. The answer given in Maastricht to this need has been rather weak, not going far beyond a declaration that is supportive of coordinating attitudes and policies. (Draft Treaty, 1991, pp. 14–17)

The problem is not only one of adopting policies, but above all one of establishing binding competencies and procedures in the field of security and defense. It is clear that the EPC's currently limited role in the field of security is inadequate. Security policy is an important and specific aspect of Community activity; as such, it must be brought on a par with other Community policies and cannot be kept as a sub-product of the EPC.

The principle of consistency with other Community policies must be respected here, too, but what is really of central importance is consistency among institutions. Security policy can be assigned to the WEU in the future, as long as it is handled according to rules comparable to those in force in the Community and with effective functional and procedural links to the EC. An EC security policy dissociated from the foreign and economic policies of the EC could become an element of instability within and outside of the Community.

This once again brings us to the questions of a governing body, appropriate voting procedures and parliamentary controls, questions that obviously cannot be left up to the present WEU Assembly and must be answered by a democratically legitimized Parliament.

Deepening First

These prerequisites for the reform and partial renovation of European institutions are valid even for a Community limited to twelve members: they respond to the internal and external requirements of the 1990s. The prospect of enlargement merely underlines the urgency and the importance of these prerequisites, which are aimed at maintaining a high and efficient level of EC integration.

It is evident that enlargement to include Eastern European countries would definitely raise the pressure for redistribution policies and, as a consequence, for budget increases; in the same way, requests for security guarantees would inevitably lead to greater EC responsibility and competencies in this field. The same reasoning holds true for enlargement to other countries, such as those of EFTA or the Mediterranean.

In the present geostrategic situation, the Community needs to give absolute priority to political and institutional deepening. This must be seen not as an egoistical closure to pressing requests for membership, but as a *sine qua non* for the EC's continued presence as a credible element of stability in Europe and a pole for broader aggregation in the future.

More precisely, the Community must strengthen the basic qualities that have contributed to its success throughout the years: a stable and peaceful system; an area in which member states have found the instruments and policies with which to solve their problems of economic well-being and collective security; a system of cooperation that has allowed for a painless transition from conflictual to cooperative state.

From a strictly institutional point of view, the priorities to be set, in the aftermath of the partially successful European Council of Maastricht, follow from the logic of our reasoning. The central question remains the identification of a form of effective and unitary government of all present and future activities. The extension of the majority vote in the Council is one of the main instruments, but not the only one. One body (the Council, for the foreseeable future) must handle all matters and must gradually adopt Community procedures in all sectors (communitarization of common activities and mechanisms).

The Commission must have complete executive powers in all matters dealt with by the Council and must maintain its right of initiative and extend it to all Community competencies.

The European Council should essentially deal with the application of the principle of subsidiarity, deciding which matters to include in the Union; it should not, however, be given governmental tasks in the strict sense of the word.

Finally, the powers of the European Parliament must be strengthened to facilitate policies of cooperation and, later, of co-legislation. This expansion of role is a direct consequence of and response to the acquisition of new competencies by the Community and follows from the adoption of effective forms of governance, starting with the qualified majority voting procedure in the Council.

Any number of practical formulas of constitutional engineering are possible: the important thing is that they respond to the criteria advocated here and satisfy the basic requirements of a rapid strengthening of Community integration.

As recent history has demonstrated, the Community is the only real nucleus of stability in a changing Europe and a changing world. (Aliboni, et al., 1991) To dissipate this asset would be likely to throw all of Europe into chaos. The Maastricht European Council has succeeded in reinforcing the perspective of a European Union capable of answering the challenge of the future. Now the task will be that of maintaining the correct route and following the strategy specified above.

Appendix

Time Elapsed between the Transmission to the Council of a Directive and Its Adoption before and after the Coming into Force of the Single European Act

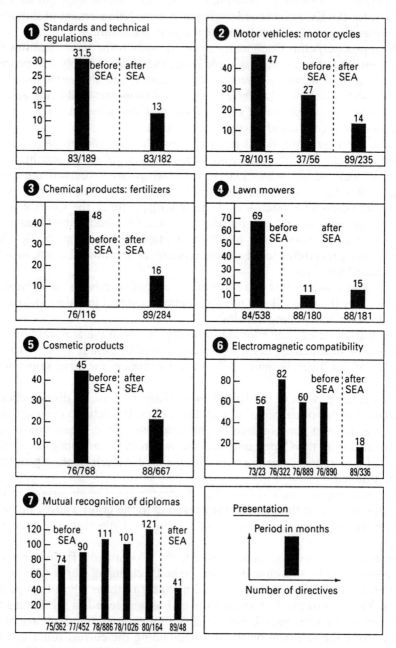

Source: Ehlermann (1990), p. 67.

Notes

1. Greece requested (and obtained) the opportunity of renegotiating the economic terms during the period of transition and maintained an anomalous attitude on the most crucial issues treated in the EC context.
2. I refer here to the so-called comitology clause which was implemented by a Council Decision of July 13, 1987.
3. The starting point for the Conference on Political Union was the letter sent by Mitterand and Kohl to their colleagues in April, 1990.

REFERENCES

Aliboni, R., Bonvicini, G., Merlini, C. & Silvestri, S. (1991), "Three Scenarios for the Future of Europe." *The International Spectator*. Vol. XXVI, No. 1 (January–March), pp. 4–27.

Committee for Institutional Affairs (1990), "The Principle of Subsidiarity." Working Paper No. 83354, Rapporteur V. Giscard d'Estaing, European Parliament, Strasbourg, 5/4/1990.

Draft Treaty on Political Union (1991), Doc. SN 252/1/91 Rev 1, Maastricht.

EC Commission (1990), "Economic and Monetary Union." Sec (90) 1659, def., Brussels (21 August).

Ehlermann, Claus Dieter (1990), "Commission Lacks Power in 1992 Process." *European Affairs*. No. 1.

European Council (1991), "Presidency Conclusions." SN 271/1/91, Maastricht (11 December).

European Parliament (1984), *Draft Treaty Establishing the European Union*. Luxemburg (February).

Lay, F. (1983), *L'iniziativa Italo-tedesca per il rilancio dell'Unione Europea*. Padua: Cedam.

Meriano, C. E. (1987), "The Single European Act. Past, Present, Future." *The International Spectator*. Vol. XXII, No. 2 (April–June), pp. 89–99.

Ronzitti, N. (1990), "The Internal Market, Italian Law and the Public Administration." *The International Spectator*. Vol. XXV, No. 1 (January–March), pp. 3–17.

The Six Institutes (1991), *The Community and the Emerging European Democracies*. A Joint Policy Report. London: Chatham House.

Wessels, W. (1990), "Basic Considerations for the Institutional Debate." Paper written for the June 1990 Annual Conference of the College of Europe on "The Institutions of the European Community after the Single European Act: The new procedures and the capacity to act." Wessels, "The Institutional Debate – Revisited, Introductory Remarks," Paper, *College of Europe*. Belgium: Bruges.

DATE DUE

DEMCO, INC. 38-2931